Between Basti Dwellers and Bureaucrats

Related Titles of Interest

ABDULLAH, T. & ZEIDENSTEIN, S.
Village Women of Bangladesh

BAPAT, M.
Shelter for the Poor: The Case of Poona

BARNETT, A. *et al.*
Rural Energy & the Third World

EPSTEIN, T. S. & WATTS, R. A.
The Endless Day

FORBES, D.
Petty Commodity Production & Underdevelopment

GANESAN, S.
Growth of Housing & Construction Sectors: Key to Employment Creation

GULATI, L.
Profiles in Female Poverty

HAZLEWOOD, A. & LIVINGSTONE, I.
Irrigation Economics in Poor Countries

JENNINGS, A. & WEISS, T. G.
The Challenge of Development in the Eighties

MADELEY, J.
Human Rights Begin with Breakfast

MILES, I. & IRVINE, J.
The Poverty of Progress

MKANGI, G. C.
The Social Cost of Small Families & Land Reform

VAN NIEUWENHUIJZE, C. A. O.
Development Begins at Home

STREETEN, P. & JOLLY, R.
Recent Issues in World Development

TAYLOR, J. L. & WILLIAMS, T.
Urban Planning Practice in Developing Countries

Journals of Interest

Habitat International
World Development

Between Basti Dwellers and Bureaucrats

Lessons in squatter settlement upgrading in Karachi

Edited by

J. W. Schoorl
J. J. van der Linden
K. S. Yap

PERGAMON PRESS

OXFORD · NEW YORK · TORONTO · SYDNEY · PARIS · FRANKFURT

U.K.	Pergamon Press Ltd., Headington Hill Hall, Oxford OX3 0BW, England
U.S.A.	Pergamon Press Inc., Maxwell House, Fairview Park, Elmsford, New York 10523, U.S.A.
CANADA	Pergamon Press Canada Ltd., Suite 104, 150 Consumers Road, Willowdale, Ontario M2J 1P9, Canada
AUSTRALIA	Pergamon Press (Aust.) Pty. Ltd., P.O. Box 544, Potts Point, N.S.W. 2011, Australia
FRANCE	Pergamon Press SARL, 24 rue des Ecoles, 75240 Paris, Cedex 05, France
FEDERAL REPUBLIC OF GERMANY	Pergamon Press GmbH, Hammerweg 6, D-6242 Kronberg-Taunus, Federal Republic of Germany

First edition 1983

Library of Congress Cataloging in Publication Data

Main entry under title:
Between basti dwellers and bureaucrats.
Bibliography: p. 295
1. Squatter settlements—Pakistan—Karachi.
2. Slums—Pakistan—Karachi.
3. Housing policy—Pakistan—Karachi.
I. Schoorl, Johan Willem, 1927- II. Linden, J. J. van der. III. Yap, K. S.
HD7361.5.K37B47 1983 363.5'09549'183 83-6307

British Library Cataloguing in Publication Data

Between basti dwellers and bureaucrats.
1. Squatter—Karachi (Pakistan)
I. Schoorl, J.W. II. Linden, J.J. van der
III. Yap, K.S.
307'.336 HV140.5.K/

ISBN 0-08-027971-6 (Hardcover)
ISBN 0-08-030229-7 (Flexicover)

In order to make this volume available as economically and as rapidly as possible the authors' typescripts have been reproduced in their original forms. This method unfortunately has its typographical limitations but it is hoped that they in no way distract the reader.

Printed in Great Britain by A. Wheaton & Co. Ltd., Exeter

Preface

Large-scale and rapid urbanization is a relatively recent phenomenon in Thirld World countries which involves numerous and often unexpected problems. In tackling these problems one is therefore faced with two important constraints. On the one hand, knowledge and experience of the process of urbanization is limited and this results in strongly-contrasting views being expressed on how to go about solving these problems and even on how to define them. Often, the theoretical discussion on Third World urbanization seems to develop separately from the day-to-day reality which administrators and policy-makers in Third World cities have to face, while practical approaches are applied without any references to the theoretical insights gained. On the other hand, the speed of urbanization and the rapid increase of concomitant problems is such that solutions are ever more sorely needed.

A confrontation of the still incomplete theoretical views and the pressing practical problems is urgently required, but opportunities for this confrontation are as yet limited.

It is within these two perspectives that the present book was compiled. Insights and experiences gained in Karachi over a twelve-year period devoted to research, as well as at attempts to develop and implement an approach to solve the housing problems of Karachi's low-income population need reporting, analysing and evaluating. In view of what was said earlier, the insights expressed and experiences gained have their limitations and it is no wonder that different authors express different views, even when discussing the same phenomena. Thus, this book cannot be more than an attempt to present some tentative answers to the pressing problems of low-income housing in Karachi. It should be viewed as a contribution to the much-needed discussion on how to deal with housing problems in Karachi and other Third World cities.

We acknowledge with gratitude the valuable help provided by many colleagues in the preparation of this book both in Pakistan and the Netherlands. Mr J. ter Haar of the Geography Department of Amsterdam Free University prepared the map "The bastis of Karachi" and prepared some of the drawings. Ms M. P. Beagley corrected the English text of the articles and Ms M. P. Kreuze and her colleagues of the Faculty of Social Sciences, Free University, typed the manuscript. Last but not least, we gratefully acknowledge the subsidy of the Directorate General of International Cooperation, Ministry of Foreign Affairs, Netherlands Government, which made publication of this book possible.

The Editors

Contents

Introduction

1. GENERAL

In 1979 the Amsterdam Free University's (AFU) participation in the execution of a slum improvement project in Karachi came to an end. Although there may be a possibility of further involvement at a later stage, at least for the time being, this twelve-year period has been terminated. During this period, the Free University, and especially the Department of Development Sociology, has been involved, in some way or other, in Karachi's housing and its related problems.

At this moment, it is useful to review and evaluate AFU's activities in Karachi and this is the reason for composing the present book. The goal of "review and evaluation" is threefold:

- During the past 12 years substantial knowledge and understanding of the problems of low-income housing in Karachi has been gained. This knowledge has been recorded regularly in reports which formed the basis of activities in each following stage. Again at this moment, it is appropriate to record knowledge and insights gained.
- Closely related with the previous point is the fact that in each stage new problems and questions arise. Precisely because AFU's withdrawal from Karachi was caused by immense problems in the execution of a slum improvement project, as will be apparent from the relevant chapters, it is imperative to mention these problems and to analyse them, as far as possible.
- Finally, the question arises about the place of a University involving itself in the practice of tackling development problems. This question pre-eminently requires careful evaluation.

2. HISTORY

In the history of AFU's activities in Karachi, clearly defined phases can be distinguished. Here, we shall briefly describe these phases.

2.1. The Azam Basti Research, 1967-1969

A Dutch midwife who, on behalf of a church aid organization worked in Azam Basti, one of the squatter settlements of Karachi, proposed that aid in this settlement should comprise of more than the mere medical aspects. In order to find out what kind of aid would be required and how this aid was to be given, AFU sent two researchers to investigate conditions in Azam Basti and to advise on how more comprehensive development aid could be given in this area. In their recommendations,[1*] there is strong emphasis on the need for local and federal authorities' involvement in developing Azam Basti. The legalization of the settlement, the bringing about of facilities and the regulation of further developments cannot possibly be handled by private organizations, although these could be helpful in the process through financial and/or personnel inputs. Besides this point, the recommendations stress that the level of facilities should be relatively low, in order to make a project in one settlement replicable in other areas of Karachi.

In view of the emphasis, in the Azam Basti Report, on the government's role, it is of the utmost importance that the report attracted the attention of the National Planning Commission of the Pakistan Government. The Planning Commission showed much appreciation for the report, because it gave a good insight into the circumstances of a community which was viewed as problematic, but about which very little was known at the government level. The Planning Commission would welcome more in-depth studies of this kind, on which to base its policies.

2.2. Joint Research Project IV (JRP-IV), 1970-1975

In 1970, the Governments of Pakistan and The Netherlands entered into an agreement by which a joint research project was undertaken for a period of 5 years. Execution of the project was entrusted to the Karachi University and AFU. The Plan of Operations stipulates the following aims for the project:

1. Operational policy-oriented research.
2. Training of participants.
3. Institution building.

Regarding the first aim the Plan of Operations further explains that research should result in recommendations for policy and execution and that "pilot experiments" are to be undertaken and evaluated as an integral part of the research. In the course of the project, a large amount of research was carried out. Both problem-oriented studies and in-depth studies in several slum areas have resulted in a number of recommendations for policy and execution.

A continuous problem has been how to reach authorities at different levels, when working in a university. On the one hand, there was a danger of a too academic approach on the part of the project; on the other hand, the authorities were in no way bound to even consider the recommendations. However, in the course of the project, contacts with authorities became ever more intensive; the working programme for the last project year was framed completely at the instigation of two local government institutions. In this connection, it is also worth noting that during the last project year a civil engineer took part in the Dutch team. When he translated the project's recommendations into technical detail, the reproach that the recommendations were not

---

*Superscript numbers refer to References at end of article.

sufficiently practical, was refuted.

Yet, during JRP-IV's 5 years, a pilot project never came off the ground. The reasons that local authorities put forward - a too theoretical approach, wrong choice of areas - became less and less worthy of belief when studies and areas were selected at the request of these authorities and recommendations included detailed technical aspects. Therefore, by the end of the project, the inescapable conclusion was that continuation of JRP-IV would be of little use - at least for the slum dwellers. The "local bodies" appeared to be an insurmountable barrier for a university, especially when the often professed backing by the Central Government defaulted at critical moments.

However, during the final stages of JRP-IV, and shortly afterwards, circumstances warranted hope for a change. The Administrator of KMC (Karachi Metropolitan Corporation) who earlier had already shown interest in cooperation with JRP-IV, wanted to formulate and execute a policy for slum improvement that resembled JRP-IV's recommendations in many respects. Besides, this time the Administrator was being backed by the World Bank which had indicated its interest in financing a large scale slum improvement project along these lines.

2.3. Interim Period, 1975-1977

By the time the Dutch JRP-IV team left Karachi, two experts were stationed within KMC by the United Nations Development Programme. Their task was to formulate the new policy and to simultaneously undertake the first steps in the execution.

Within KMC, a separate department was created that was charged with slum improvement, and KMC requested AFU to provide some advisors for this department to assist it in its activities. The World Bank indicated that it would appreciate advisory assistance from AFU's side in the case of World Bank's financing KMC's project.

2.4. Dutch Advisory Mission (DAM) in Karachi Slum Improvement Implementation Unit, 1977-1979

From the very beginning, AFU's aim has been to see the recommendations, which had resulted from different studies, implemented - albeit on an experimental basis only. In this respect, the DAM phase was an important step in the right direction, compared with previous phases. Namely, in the bilateral agreement on this project, it was stated that "the aim of the project is to improve the slums of the Karachi Metropolitan Area." This formula does not only indicate that "slum improvement" had been opted for as a policy (as against a previous policy of "slum clearance", relocation and/or rehousing), but it is also clear that this time the main focus was on execution. DAM's location within KMC was also a logical choice: most slum areas of Karachi are within KMC's jurisdiction and KMC's different departments together would be able to execute all of the various parts of a slum improvement programme.

Cornerstone for the project is a KMC policy document "An Improvement Policy of Substandard Urban Areas".[2] Three main principles, spelled out in this policy, are:
- residents' participation, both in planning and execution,
- the inseparability of improvement and legalization,
- the principle of self-financing.

Thus, this project started under the favourable conditions of a very intense preparation and agreement on the main principles of the execution. However, again in this phase, taking the step from planning to execution turned out to be impossible. This can be explained, partly, by relatively accidental facts. There was, for instance, the highly inopportune pronouncement by a politician, who, during an election campaign, promised that the land of a slum area to be regularized would be leased against payment of a ridiculously low Rs 4,- per square yard. This promise destroyed the principle of self-financing, and, as a consequence, the replicability of this kind of project. Even execution of the project to which this politician had referred, was made impossible. Also, there was a change in KMC's power structure, which meant a major part of the support for the project was lost.

This and similar facts were reasons why the World Bank finally gave up the idea of financing KMC's slum improvement programme. By the time this decision was taken, the Dutch team was already in Karachi. Besides the "relatively accidental facts", no doubt, more structural causes for the failure of the project can be indicated. Probably some of the "accidental facts" can also be better understood as - not so accidental - results of more structural causes.

Although initially it had been anticipated that DAM's two-year period would be extended by another 3 years, insufficient prospects that execution would be possible within a reasonable period were sufficient reason to discontinue DAM's advisory services to KMC.

2.5. History - Some Concluding Remarks

During the 12 years of AFU's engagement in Karachi, different developments have taken place. There has been a change of cooperating institutions: first, AFU worked with a private organization, later with the government. Within the cooperation with the Pakistan Government, again a shift can be noted from Federal Government plus university to a local executing institution.

Parallel with these changes is the development of the focus of activities: first the aim to give recommendations for the improvement of one slum area; later, the research included more general policy matters as well. During the last phase the emphasis was on translating what was written in the policy which had been accepted as a principle, into execution activities.

To some extent, these changes can be viewed as a natural course: in the first phase an insight was gained into the socio-economic conditions of a community at the micro level of one squatter settlement. In a next phase, some macro data were also collected and analysed, so that a base for policy formulation could be laid. In the last phase the execution of this policy was attempted.

3. AIM OF THE BOOK

Such as we have briefly described above, a number of developments can be distinguished in the history of AFU's activities in Karachi. One of the developments runs roughly parallel with the cycle of scientific research: after collection, classification and interpretation of data, the formulation of policy proposals followed. In a next phase these policy proposals were translated into execution activities. These activities - or the lack of these activities - are the subject of the final phase: the evaluation. The evaluation in its turn produces the questions which require further research. With this research, the next cycle starts.

In this book, articles have been assembled which reflect the developments of AFU's activities in Karachi. In view of the cyclic development described above, it is logical that there is a certain emphasis on the evaluation that is clearly required at this stage. However, this evaluation is only possible, when main points from the previous stages have been made sufficiently clear. Therefore, research, policy formulation and execution will receive due attention.

The structure of the book is reflected in the shape of introductory articles to each part of the book. After each introductory article, other articles follow in which general points from the introductions are elaborated or illustrated.

The first part is on Karachi in general. The next one concerns the squatter settlements of Karachi. The third part is devoted to policies for the squatter settlements. Part four is on the translation of policy into action, whilst the fifth part deals with the problems in execution. A separate article reviews the questions that arise regarding the place of a university which is actively involved in coping with development problems. In this connection, finally, also one article has been included which deals with technical and methodological problems encountered during research in Karachi's squatter settlements, and the attempted solutions to these problems.

REFERENCES

1. J. H. De Goede and T. J. Segaar, *Report Azam Basti*, Amsterdam, 1969.
2. KMC, *An improvement policy for Substandard Urban Areas*, Karachi, 1977.

Part I

Karachi

J. J. van der Linden

1. INTRODUCTION

A main emphasis in this book is on the living conditions of the urban poor in Karachi and on attempts to cope with the problems of low-income housing.

In this part of the book, a sketch of the context is given. Meyerink's article describes Karachi's historical development and its reflections on the spatial organization of the city. In his article, several details and illustrations of the socio-economic conditions of Karachi's population are presented. Hashmi's article describes the government machinery that is to deal with all the problems with which the rapidly growing metropolis is faced.

In this introduction, only a brief description of the dimensions of Karachi's housing problem will be presented. For this, firstly, a rough indication of Karachi's dominant position in Pakistan is given, followed by a sketch of its population growth. Finally, an inventory of the housing problem proper follows.

2. THE PLACE OF KARACHI IN PAKISTAN

Karachi is the largest city and the main industrial and commercial city of Pakistan; it is the nation's only major port.

Karachi's dominance is evident from the following figures. The Metropolitan Area supports 6% of Pakistan's total population and 22% of its urban population. It contributes approximately 15% of gross domestic product. It generates about 42% of value added and 35% of employment in large scale manufacturing. It accounts for approximately 50% of bank deposits and 72% of capital issued. It generates, according to one estimate, roughly 25% of all Federal revenues.[1]

3. THE GROWTH OF KARACHI

Pakistan is presently going through a period of rapid population growth and urbanization. From 1951 to 1971, the population growth was calculated in the order of 2.7 to 2.9% per year, and it may be as high as 3.3% now.[2] In the same period, the percentage of the urban population increased from 17% of the total population to 28%.[3] According to UN Urban-Rural projections, this figure will rise to 41.2% by the year 2000.[4]

In these processes, Karachi takes a prominent place: in 1971, Karachi housed 5.8% of the total population and 20.6% of the total urban population of Pakistan.[5] Its population may be estimated at around 6,000,000 by 1980. The population growth of Karachi was extremely high during the period 1941-1951, namely around 10% per year, which growth can be mainly attributed to an estimated 600,000 refugees who came from India during or shortly after Partition. Karachi's population growth is now estimated at around 5%, and it is anticipated that this will remain so at least until 1985.[6] Roughly half of this growth can be attributed to migration, the other half representing the natural growth.

Besides the important refugee element mentioned above, large numbers of migrants from all over Pakistan are represented in Karachi. Amongst these, migrants from Punjab and North West Frontier Province take a prominent place. Migration from the two other provinces, Baluchistan and especially from Sind, is much more limited.[7]

4. HOUSING IN KARACHI

A majority of Karachi's population is poor: in 1973-1974, it was estimated that some 80% belonged to the "low-income groups", i.e. those having a monthly household income below Rs 500.--.[8] Forecasts indicate a shift in the income distribution after 1974, but even so, the low-income groups would still comprise some 65% of the Karachi urban population by 1985.[8]

These low-income groups in fact have no access to the official housing market: "The low-income groups are denied access to housing credit, cannot obtain plots in locations of their need and are subjected to a resettlement and harassment when they live in unauthorized areas."[9]

Several government attempts to provide decent housing for the urban poor have either completely failed or met with only very limited success.[10] As a result, large parts of the low-income population have been forced somehow or other to deal with their housing problems all by themselves, i.e. informally and often illegally.[11] Presently, some 2,000,000 inhabitants of Karachi live in thus formed informal settlements, covering an area of over 10,000 acres.

There is a wide gap between traditional approaches to the low-income housing problem on the one hand and the way in which the poor cater for their housing needs on the other hand. This gap can - for instance - be illustrated by a comparison of the average cost of three different types of "semi-pakka" self constructed houses[12,13] with the price of the cheapest official "low-cost" house type, which is more than twice as high.[14] Another illustration of this gap is a proposal, by which "The erection of fresh jhuggis[15] will be dealt with as a serious criminal offense, punishable by at least one year rigorous imprisonment."[16]

It should be noted that when this proposal was made, the number of new illegally constructed houses in Karachi was at least 10,000 yearly. Clearly, more realistic, alternative approaches were, and still are, required.

Fortunately, the need for a different approach to the low-income housing problem is also being felt within the Pakistan Government at different levels. For example, the Chief, Physical Planning and Housing, Planning and Development Division, Government of Pakistan, proposed the following policies "to be considered for adoption in the next few years:

> ...all the existing houses in slums and katchi abadis (substandard urban areas), irrespective of the quality should be preserved. Slum areas and katchi abadis not occupying land required for public purposes, should be regularized to give ownership to residents and to pave the way for the environmental improvement."[17]

Evidently, such proposals imply the baselines for a completely new and unorthodox way of dealing with low-income housing problems.

In subsequent parts of this book, the development of such an approach and efforts to apply it, will be described.

REFERENCES

1. Master Plan Department KDA, Karachi Development Plan 1974-1985, Karachi, 1974, p. 14.
2. *Ibid.*, p. 1.
3. T. J. Segaar, *Karachi en de basti*, Amsterdam, 1975, p. 21.
4. G. Beier, A. Churchill, M. Cohen and B. Renaud, The task ahead for the cities of the developing countries, *World Development*, 1976, IV-5, p. 369.
5. T. J. Segaar, *op. cit.*, p. 24.
6. *Ibid.*, p. 30.
7. S. H. Hashmi, *The slums of Karachi, a conspectus*, Karachi, 1973, p. 28.
8. Master Plan Department, *op. cit.*, p, 51.
9. *Ibid.*, p. 196.
10. See also Part III of this book.
11. See also Part II of this book.
12. Semi-pakka houses are houses of which the walls are made of concrete blocks and the roofs of asbestos cement or corrugated iron sheets. Different types within this category reflect differences in quality, e.g. plastered or unplastered walls and floors.
13. J. van der Harst, *Cost of residing of low-income groups*, Karachi, 1974, p. 114.
14. T. J. Segaar, *op. cit.*, p. 46.
15. Jhuggi - hut.
16. A. Ali, *et al.*, *Operation rehasp*, Karachi, 1969.
17. Asad Ali Shah, *Housing in Pakistan*, Islamabad, 1977, p. 8.

Karachi's Growth in Historical Perspective

H. Meyerink

1. THE COLONIAL PERIOD

When the British had conquered what is now India, they expanded their territory towards the West. In 1843 the province of Sind was conquered and in the following years British India assumed its definite borders. Thus, different, more or less independent feudal states with ethnically different populations were subjugated under one rule. As was the case in other areas, this part of India too was modified by the British in such a way that it could optimally serve the metropolis' interests.

Amongst other things, this implied that:
- The power of some of the feudal rulers was enhanced with British support. In this way, peace and order could be maintained with relatively little military interference.
- From now on, taxes were raised in money, so that the tax payer had to produce for a market. Many, especially small farmers encountered financial problems and lost their land, i.e. their means of production, to moneylenders and big landlords. There was an increase in the number of landless labourers and a concentration of landed property in fewer hands.
- By producing for a market, the farmers became dependent on a demand that was fixed by English export firms. This is one of the causes of monocultures springing up. Very often, products were cultivated that served as raw material for British industries.
- Although the construction of large irrigation works in geographically favourable regions enhanced production, it also increased regional disparity.
- Railways were laid to facilitate quick movement of troops and transport of agrarian products. Finished products of English industry were marketed to distant places via this distribution network.
- In accordance with British colonial model, an educational system was created, in which the young local elite were trained for functions in the administration.

As a consequence of some of the above-mentioned developments, the organization of space also changed. In the precolonial period, an infrastructural network had come about which was directed towards inland towns and connections between these towns. During the colonial period this network was increasingly directed towards the coasts.

Lahore, which in the Moghul period had been the most important city of the North West retained its military and administrative functions, but economic activities shifted to cities like Bombay and Karachi.

1.1. Karachi

Before the coming of the British, Karachi was only a fishing and commercial port of subordinate importance.

In 1843, the British established their administrative centre for the province of Sind in Karachi. Its military importance was great, as it was the port closest to the metropolis. Commerce and related activities also grew but were hampered in their development by the dominating position of Bombay.

Only after 1953, when Karachi was no more subordinated to Bombay, could it develop as a commercial centre in its own right. The development of Karachi from a fishing port to an economic and administrative centre implied the growth of a number of activities, for which much labour was required, such as in the administration, commerce, banking, services, building industry and crafts.

In 1843, Karachi had about 14,000 inhabitants; after 50 years their number had increased to 90,000 and in 1947, at independence, to 400,000.

Naturally, the socio-economic development and the increase of the population had spatial consequences. The old centre retained its function for local traders and small craftsmen. To the west, in the delta of Lyari river, the residential area "Lyari" came into being, in which labourers and other low-status personnel resided under miserable circumstances.

East of the old centre, the British rulers developed a completely new part of the city according to English tradition. Around the seaport, they created a spacious administrative centre with large buildings in neo-classic style. Some 4-5 kilometres inland, the Cantonment area was laid out. A wide road, Bunder Road, connected the two centres of domination: the Cantonment and the administrative centre. Along this road, towards the port, the offices of commercial firms were located, while the residential quarters of the British were laid out at the other end of Bunder Road: ranging from bungalows with large gardens and servants' quarters, for the officers, to two- or three-storeyed houses for the lower ranks amongst the white. From amongst the local population, only the notables, big land owners and commercialists lived in the clean part of the city. Here of course, there were also schools, hospitals, churches, shopping areas and plenty of parks. In this way, the dominating position of the rulers was reflected in the spatial structure of the city in which separation was a main element.

2. DEVELOPMENT AFTER 1947

In 1947, British India attained political independence and was divided into two states: India and Pakistan. The first years after independence were characterized by confused conditions. Mass migration from India to Pakistan and vice versa took place and many had to try and build a new existence in a new country. Because of the disappearance of many of the top functionaries, Pakistan was confronted with numerous problems in policy and administration.

There was a high turnover of governments. The economy of Pakistan was completely dependent upon agriculture, which in its turn was geared to foreign, and especially British, markets. There was hardly any industry. In 1958, General Ayub Khan seized power in Pakistan. Under his regime, a development started that determines the economic situation of Pakistan to a high degree, even today.

2.1. Industrialization

The policy aimed at rapid economic growth through industrialization. The financial position of the rising capitalists did not enable them to quickly establish an industrial apparatus under free market conditions. The idea behind the policy was that industrialists should be allowed to make high profits which they would re-invest in new industries. The rapid economic growth so achieved would, in the long run, benefit the whole population. Massive government support took shape in the following measures:
- high import duties on foreign products,
- overvaluation of the rupee,
- special import licences for industrialists to purchase machinery and raw materials abroad cheaply,
- a system of bonuses on export products.

Foreign exchange needed for industrialization was mainly obtained from export of agricultural products and through foreign loans, especially from the U.S.A. This policy has not achieved its goals, but instead has resulted in a number of negative effects which still are characteristic of the socio-economic situation in which Pakistan finds itself. As such characteristics, I mention:
- Dependence on foreign nations. To realize the ambitious government plans, enormous debts were incurred. Clearing of these debts is an increasingly great problem to Pakistan. In 1960, 3.6% of the export was used for paying off debts; in the mid-sixties, the percentage was around 10 and in 1970 it was almost 20.[1] Because of this financial dependence, main creditors, especially the United States, also gained influence in politics. This influence diminished somewhat under Bhutto's regime (1971-1977).
- Subsidies on the import of machinery stimulated the creation of relatively capital-intensive industries. As a result, employment generation effects were not very substantial.
- Under the government protective measures, much investment was made in industries that cannot compete internationally.
- One of the most serious consequences of the government policy was that it resulted in concentration of economic power: forty-three families owned 53% of the shares in non-financial firms, 91.6% of the shares in private banks, and 75.6% of the shares in insurance companies.[2]
- The aim of inducing the industrial elite to reinvest by allowing them huge profits was not attained. Much of the profits made was spent on consumption of luxury goods, such as cars, bungalows, etc. At the same time, labour was underpaid, so that the gap between rich and poor widened steadily.

The exploitation of labourers, partly a result of the abundance of labour, can be mainly understood from the developments in agriculture.

2.2. Agriculture

In agriculture too, a number of important changes occurred during Ayub Khan's regime. Amongst these changes, the "Green Revolution" started in the sixties, takes a first place. As was already mentioned above, the production and export of agrarian products formed the basis of the economy. Logically, the government stimulated the introduction of new varieties of rice and wheat that yield high if sufficiently irrigated and fertilized. The "Green Revolution" also entailed a sharp increase in the number of tubewells. According to Gotsch and Falcon, "these 25,000 tubewells represented an initial investment on the order of Rs 250 million, a sum thought impossible in West Pakistan's traditional agriculture."[3] The result was an increase in agricultural output, which in Pakistan had been virtually stagnant in the 12 years after independence. The annual compound rate of growth rose from slightly over 1% in the earlier period to 5% in the sixties.[4]

However, this development has also entailed such negative by-effects, that in a number of respects, the "Green Revolution" must be considered a failure. Only large farmers could profit from government support and from the introduction of better seeds and fertilizers, which required high investments. Small farmers could not afford these. The application of fertilizer gives optimal results when the crops are sufficiently irrigated. As in some regions irrigation is not possible, regional differences were increased.

Besides, the introduction of tubewells was possible on large farms only. Government loans were only available to large farms, because these alone could provide sufficient guarantees. The position of the small farmers deteriorated continuously. Many were forced to sell their land to pay off their debts. The number of landless labourers increased. At the same time, the government also stimulated the use of tractors by exempting them from import duties. As a result, many agricultural labourers lost their jobs. The increase in agricultural job opportunities lagged far behind the population growth. Another development negative to the agriculture, was that the big landowners consumed or reinvested part of their profits in the city. Keith Griffin concludes that in the year 1964-1965 Rs 3600 million (i.e. 15% of the gross output) was transferred from the countryside to the urban centres.[5]

As a result of population growth, the transfer of capital from countryside to city, the deteriorating position of the small peasants, the pressure on land, the increase of the number of landless labourers and mechanization, the percentage of the total labour force employed in agriculture decreased from 70 in 1947 to 48 in 1974.[6] At the same time, the urban population steadily increased. Because the city is the core of economic development, it is there the chances of finding employment are best. Therefore, many people from rural areas migrated to the cities.

Table 1. Increase of Urban Population in Pakistan[7]

Year	Total population (x1,000,000)	Urban (x1,000,000)	Population (%)	Increase urban population (%)
1901	16.58	1.62	9.8	-
1911	19.38	1.69	8.7	4.3
1921	21.11	2.06	9.8	21.8
1931	23.54	2.77	11.8	34.5
1941	28.29	4.02	14.2	45.
1951	33.78	6.02	17.8	49.9
1961	42.88	9.65	22.5	60.4
1972	64.89	17.04	26.3	76.6

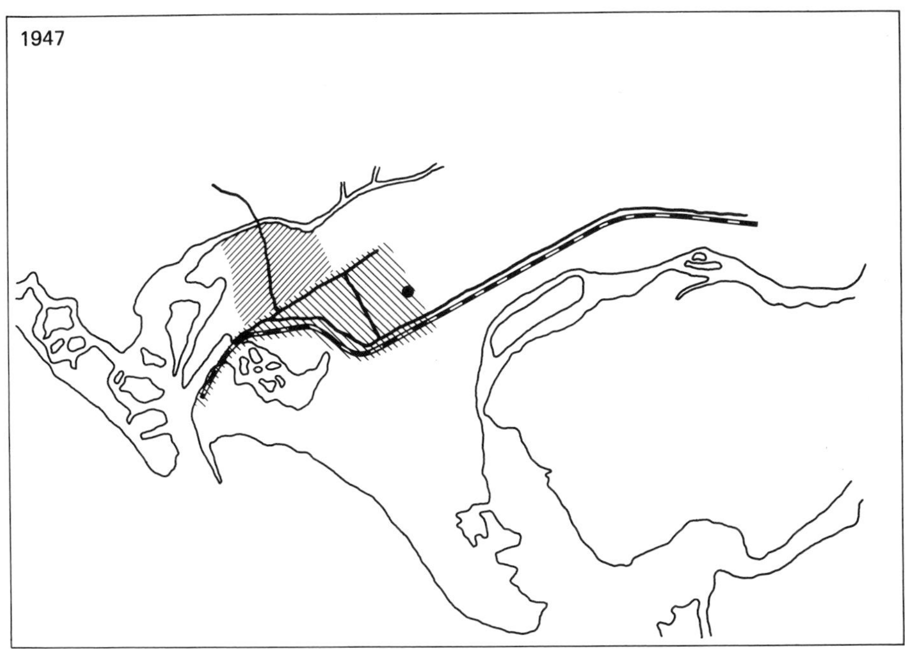

Fig. 1.

3. KARACHI AFTER 1947

In the preceding part, I have already indicated that during the colonial period Karachi grew from a fishing port into the administrative and economic centre of this part of the British colony. Consequently, the communication network in this part of the colony was directed to Karachi. In 1947, Karachi became the capital of the newly-created state of Pakistan. Logically, Karachi became the centre from which industrial development was initiated. For, it was the only port and the focal point of commercial firms, banks and government institutions. Moreover, plans for a large industrial area had been made already before independence and some infrastructure had already been brought into this planned area (mainly water and electricity). Understandably following Partition many refugees from India settled in Karachi. Also many of those who could no longer survive in agriculture tried to find employment in Karachi.

As a result, the composition of Karachi's population is very heterogeneous. The original inhabitants of the region, Sindis, now constitute a minority, with Pathans, Punjabis, Muhajirs and Baluchis, together constituting more than 90% of the city's population.

Table 2. Population Increase in Karachi[8]

Year	Population (x1,000,000)
1941	0.43
1951	1.14
1961	2.14
1970	3.23
1971	3.50
1972	3.50
1974	4.16
1975	4.22
1978	5.36

3.1. Employment

The industrial and commercial development of Karachi gave rise to large scale capital-intensive industries, banks and commercial firms. However, this sector provides employment to a small percentage of the population only.

Table 3. Karachi Metropolitan Area: Non-agricultural Output and Employment, 1974[9]

Item	Output (')	Share of output (%)	Employment (x1000)	Share of employment (%)
Manufacturing & Mining				
(a) large scale	234	32.4	202	16.2
(b) small scale	29	4.0	150	12.0
Construction	78	10.8	72	5.7
Public Utilities	14	1.9	16	1.3
Trade: Wholesale	115	15.9	24	1.9
Retail			190	15.2
Banking & Insurance	45	6.3	20	1.6
Ownership of Dwellings	25	3.4		
Transportation	89	12.3	126	10.1
Services	93	13.0	450	36.0
Total	722	100	1250	100

(') In Rs karors 1969/1970 constant factor costs (1 karor = 10 millions).

As can be easily observed from this table, sectors with a large output contribute relatively little in terms of employment. This is especially true of large scale industry, banking and insurance. Unfortunately, we have no figures on employment in Karachi for different years so as to compare the development of employment in different sectors. However, figures on the urban modern sector in Pakistan for 1964 and 1970 give fair indications of the trend.

Table 4. Employment in Pakistan 1964 and 1970[10]

Sector	Number employed 1964	Number employed 1970	% of total labour force	
			1964	1970
Mining & Quarrying	20,143	24,123	0.5	0.5
Manufacturing	377,401	454,080	12.0	11.5
Construction	73,757	71,089		
Public Utilities	37,227	58,566	1.0	1.3
Commerce	22,501	39,603	0.6	0.9
Transport & Communication	67,792	87,978	1.8	1.9
Services	356,893	494,973	9.5	10.8
Total	955,714	1230,402	25.4	26.7

From this table we can see that over a period of 6 years the increase of employment in the urban modern sector was no more than 1.3%. During the same period, the average yearly population growth in urban areas was 4.5% and the growth of the labour force 3.4%. We may safely conclude that the loss of job opportunity in agriculture was only partly compensated for by the modern industrial sector. As a result, an increasingly large part of the population had to try to find employment in the other sectors. Many people work in small shops and workshops. Others can be considered as belonging to the labour reserve army. Often, they are self employed as hawkers or coolies.[11]

The presence of this large structural labour reserve army - i.e. the abundant availability of labour - enables the employers to keep wages low. A labourer can be very easily replaced by another labourer, e.g. in case of illness. Labour Unions have little chance to interfere in this situation. Even the wages of those working in the large scale sector are so low that they hardly enable the worker to maintain his family. Saving is an impossibility. The developments in industry in the city have not resulted in achievement of the goal "prosperity for everybody". On the contrary, socio-economic differences have increased, and in view of the development of employment in the different sectors, the existence of a structural reserve labour force has become evident.

In the next section I will show how these differences are reflected spatially, by reviewing growth and structure of the city of Karachi.

4. SPATIAL GROWTH AND STRUCTURE OF KARACHI AFTER 1947

4.1. The First Years

By the end of the colonial period, Karachi was already the focal point of economic life in this part of the colony. Here was the location of banks and commercial firms, from here contacts with the homeland were maintained and from here, the whole area to the north was dominated. We have already seen how, in 1947, the city was divided into a British and an indigenous part, and how, again, within the British part, there was a separation between home and work and the military encampments.

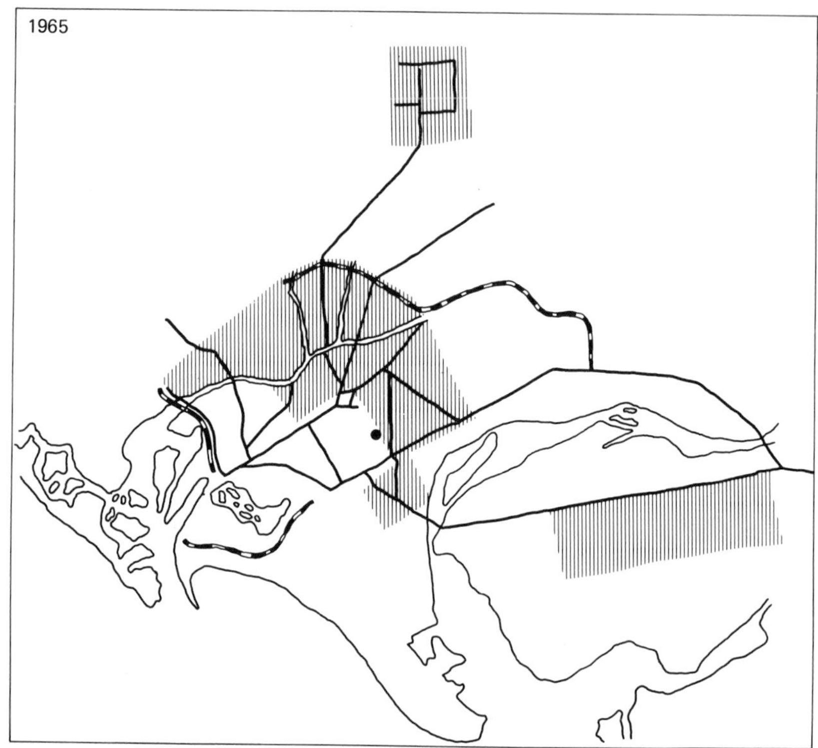

Fig. 2.

To the approximately 600,000 refugees who came to Karachi during the first years after independence, the working and living conditions were miserable. There was shortage of everything. The newly-arrived refugees had to try to find shelter themselves, somehow or other. The rich amongst them could sometimes buy a house or get one allotted. The less fortunate had to build for themselves in open spaces in or close to the centre. Most huts were constructed of scrap material and reed. As a result of the ruler's departure, the communal services hardly functioned. Only after a few years the first residential extensions were planned, plots demarcated and the infrastructure was brought in. In these new residential areas, the future inhabitants had to construct - or arrange construction of - their houses themselves. These extensions came about through pressure from middle and higher classes who had formed building societies. Of course, the extensions laid out as a belt around the existing city, were accessible only to these groups. The majority of the population, having no or very lowly-paid jobs, had no option but to squat on any open space close to the centre.

4.2. Living Close to Work

Because of its potential, Karachi was the obvious place to start large-scale industrial development, such as was envisaged during the regime of Ayub Khan. Sind Industrial Trading Estate (SITE), the industrial area, which had been planned already in the colonial days, was now laid out, port facilities were improved and facilities were offered to large investors. The administrative and commercial centre of the colonial period was extended further. In the vicinity of the centres of economic life, many very small enterprises came about, such as workshops for repairs, teashops, etc. Here also the labourers gathered who offered cheap services, such as coolies, etc.

Because of the abundance of (unskilled) labour, labourers have to constantly compete with each other, not only in the small enterprises mentioned above, but also in the large-scale industrial sector. They earn low wages, have long working days, their labour situation is insecure and the working conditions are bad. In order to be able to compete on the labour market, they have to minimize costs of shelter, transport, etc. As a result, large low-income settlements came into existence around the highly-developed capitalistic centres. Shershah Colony is a very obvious example.

4.3. The Struggle for Space

The uncontrolled growth of these popular neighbourhoods increasingly hampered the efficient functioning of the large-scale production process. In the centre of the city, streets became increasingly narrower, as more and more people had to live there and more and more shops and workshops were set up. As a result, these areas became practically inaccessible to traffic. Offices could not be built because open places were occupied illegally. Besides, to the rulers, the slums in the centre of Karachi were an eyesore. Karachi was the centre of development and it had to reflect the progress made in Pakistan.

Therefore, during Ayub Khan's regime, an ambitious plan was launched to create two new townships - Korangi and North Karachi - at 10 miles from the city's centre, in order to relocate 600,000 slum dwellers. The existing slums could then be demolished and the land could subsequently be used for the construction of offices, main roads, etc. A firm of foreign experts, Doxiadis Ass., was engaged and high loans were obtained for the execution of the plan. This plan envisaged both the provision of houses plus services and the creation of employment. A number of central slums were bulldozed and the inhabitants were shifted. Half way through the execution, however, the programme had to be discontinued, because it was already clear that it did not achieve its aims. Particularly the lagging behind of employment generation was a major cause. The majority of the population of the new townships had to go on working in or close by the city's centre. Long travel times and high costs weakened the position of labourers shifted to the new townships. Many sold their houses and tried to find again a place close to the centres of job opportunities.

4.4. Popular Settlements and Expulsion

At the same time densification in the residential areas of the centre took place as a result of population growth and migration. But other, more powerful groups also compete successfully for space in the centre: representatives of banks, commercial firms, hotels, project developers, construction companies and speculators. In their efforts to acquire land, they are mostly aided by the municipal institutions. When legal arrangements for the acquisition of land are insufficient, other ways are also used. At this level, corruption and the intermingling of interests is tremendous. With all these developments taking place, there is an enormous rise in land prices.

The consequences for the popular settlements near the centre are very serious. On the one hand, the demand for living space in these areas, by low-income groups rises, on the other hand, expansion of large-scale activities into these areas takes place. As a result, also here, prices of land and rents rise sharply, many families are forced to double up and houses and plots are split. On the outskirts of the settlements, houses are being bought up by speculators, construction companies, etc., who build four- and five-storeyed blocks. This development is especially obvious in Lyari, close to Lea Market.

To the low-income groups, living in or near the centre becomes increasingly difficult. Only areas which have no or little value for powerful groups remain within the reach of the poor. In the centre, these are the dangerous and left-over areas, such as riverbeds and strips alongside the railway tracks. The other alternative to the poor is living far away from the city's centre, where land values are almost nil. But even there, low-income groups cannot dwell legally. This land is in the hands of local or provincial authorities which do not sell it to the low-income people. So, even in these desert areas, where there are no facilities, there is always a chance that inhabitants will be evicted from their houses. One result of this insecurity is that the inhabitants have to pay for protection.

Of course, the difficulty of large portions of the population to house themselves gives rise to resentment. Sometimes, the competition for land leads to rioting, e.g. when a slum is demolished to make space for the construction of an office. But this happens in incidental cases only. The process of expulsion mostly takes place much more gradually, and government institutions contribute their bit to maintain law and order amongst the population. Formulated in this way, it might seem as though there were a well-defined plan, a kind of conspiracy between government and economically powerful groups in society. In reality, also many situations exist where there are divergent interests between, and even within these groups.

However, despite these differences, again and again it is the low-income people who get the worst of it. In Jacob Lines, for instance, the government had plans to demolish the popular settlements and resettle the inhabitants in flats. Much propaganda was made to convince the residents that they would benefit by the execution of these plans. The first flats have been built, but are much too expensive for the original population of the area.

Another project destined to house low-income groups is the "Metroville". This "Site-and-Services" project has existed for 5 years. From the approximately 4000 plots, only seven had been built upon 1979. Problems of allocation of the plots and substantial speculation have also made this project inaccessible to low-income groups. The only real effect is that the government can use the existence of a "Site-and-Services" project as an alibi when confronted with frustration or resentment on the part of the poor.

Also improvement of existing popular settlements results in an accelerated buying-out and expulsion of the inhabitants, especially in central areas. Through application of the norms for the width of streets, these areas are opened up for traffic and consequently become more attractive to commerce and industry. Besides, the occupier of the land now gets a legal title. From then on, transactions become legal and the free market mechanism of offer and demand can function "better" in a situation of scarcity, for the previously limited illegal market is now open to everybody. Obviously, this especially benefits the financially better-off sections of the population.

4.5. Residential Areas of the Middle and Higher-income Groups

The municipal authorities plan and develop residential areas almost exclusively for middle and higher-income groups. This fact is caused by a complex of factors. The large-scale "modern sector" exerts pressure on the government institutions to create the conditions for housing their skilled labour at the lowest price possible, in order to keep the component for housing cost in the workers' wages at a minimum. Members or organizations of the middle class can often pressurize government agencies directly, as the planning and executing staffs themselves belong to this class. This does not only apply to planning and execution of plans for developing of residential areas, but also to interventions in the building sector to reduce building costs.

The shortage of developed land for this group is largely artificial as it is caused by much speculation in land. The majority of developed plots in middle class residential areas are lying vacant for years; but new plans are continually being framed.

Allotment of the plots to persons or organizations is a very lucrative business. All kinds of relations exist between the staffs of the planning institutions and the private sector of brokers and speculators. Roughly the same applies to the residential areas of the higher-income groups. Here, individual networks and influence play a very important role, as the upper class is related to the level where policy decisions are being taken.

5. SNAPSHOT OF KARACHI, 1978

When looking at the spatial structure of the city of Karachi in 1978, some points require attention:

- there is a strong spatial segregation of residential areas of different income groups,
- there is a strong concentration of large-scale industrial and commercial firms: the industrial areas Landhi and SITE, Central Business District, Port and Airport,
- there is a network of wide roads between these centres of large-scale enterprise,
- also, road connections between these centres and the residential areas of middle and higher-income groups are well developed,
- the low-income residential areas are located in the centre or on the periphery of the city.

This situation can only be understood when viewed as the spatial expression of the above-mentioned processes.

6. DIFFERENCES IN HOUSING

I have indicated how socio-economic differences are reflected in the spatial structure at the city level. Not much has been said about the factual differences in housing circumstances of the different groups. These will now be described with the help of four examples which allow a comparison.

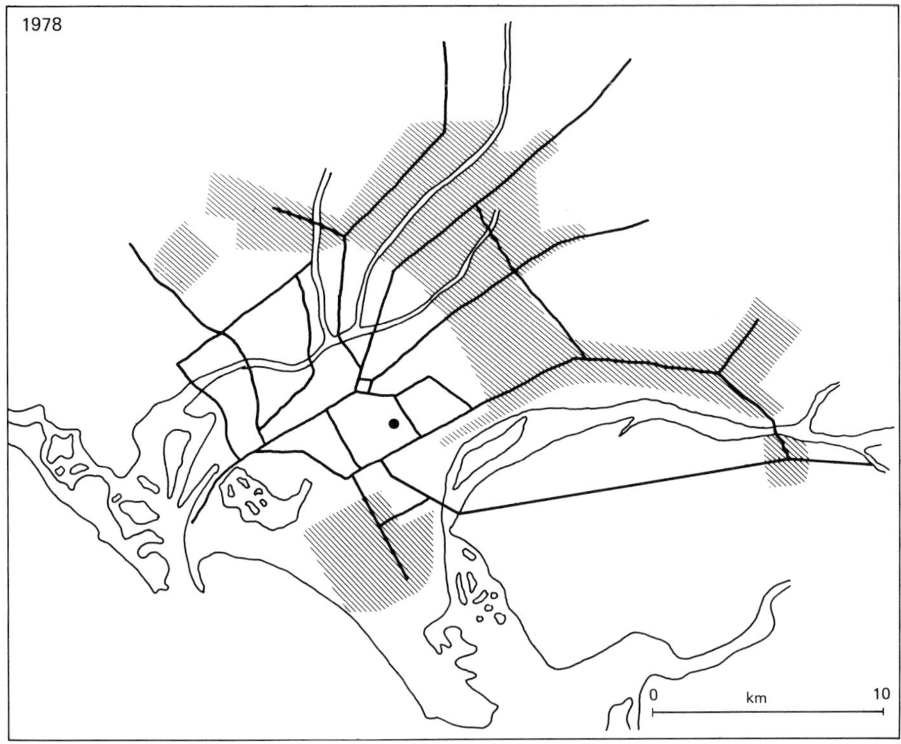

Fig. 3.

To illustrate how the high-income group is housed, Defence Officers Cooperative Housing Society has been chosen as an example; for the middle-income group, Nazimabad serves this purpose. As examples of the residential areas of the low-income groups, two areas were selected, one in the centre, Lyari, and one on the periphery, Orangi. From all these areas, only small parts were subjected to detailed elaboration. For Defence Housing Society, this is Phase I, for Nazimabad, this is Block 5C, for Lyari, it is Miran Naka and for Orangi: Mohammed Nagar.

6.1. Defence Housing Society - Example of the Residence of the Rich

Defence Officers Cooperative Housing Society was constituted in 1952 as an independent organization with the aim of (re-)housing military officers during the chaotic period shortly after Partition. The Society is empowered to the whole organization and plan development in the area under its jurisdiction.

Land was bought against the very low price of Rs 1.50 per square yard from the Cantonment Board which owns large stretches of urban land in Karachi. A townplanner of the Society drew a plan which was executed by small private contractors. The developed plots were allotted to the officers who had subscribed (against a fee of Rs 2000.--) by ballot. After payment of the development costs, these officers got a lease to their allotted plots. Afte

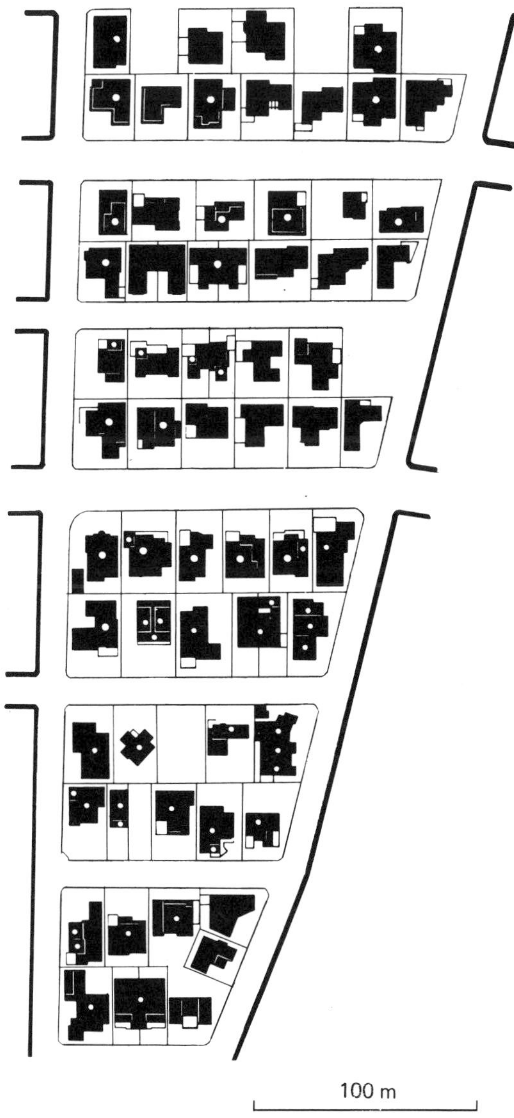

Defence Housing Society

Fig. 4.

Fig. 5.

execution of the plan, the land was again handed over to the Cantonment Board which is charged with the maintenance.

This development method appears to be quite successful. In 1956, the first phase of 275 acres was developed. At this moment, the plans of the Society regard 6100 acres. Also apartment buildings are now being built by the Society. It is no wonder that many officers apply for allocation of a plot: in the free market, these plots fetch twentyfold! Indirectly, this is a substantial subsidy to the military top ranks.

Here, I will deal with the oldest part of the Society area, because practically all the plots have been built upon. Houses in later developed parts are even more luxurious: at present, the "Spanish Villa" is very popular here.

Phase I, some data

Total area	6.5 hectares
Number of plots	67, out of which 6 have been split into two and 5.5 are vacant
Number of dwellings	67
Density	10 houses per hectare
Public area	2 hectares
Private area	4.5 hectares
Average plot area	700 m^2
Total built upon area	1.9 hectares
Average built upon area per plot	285 m^2
Average garden area per plot	415 m^2
Dwelling area (including storeys)	2.5 hectares
Average dwelling area per house	380 m^2

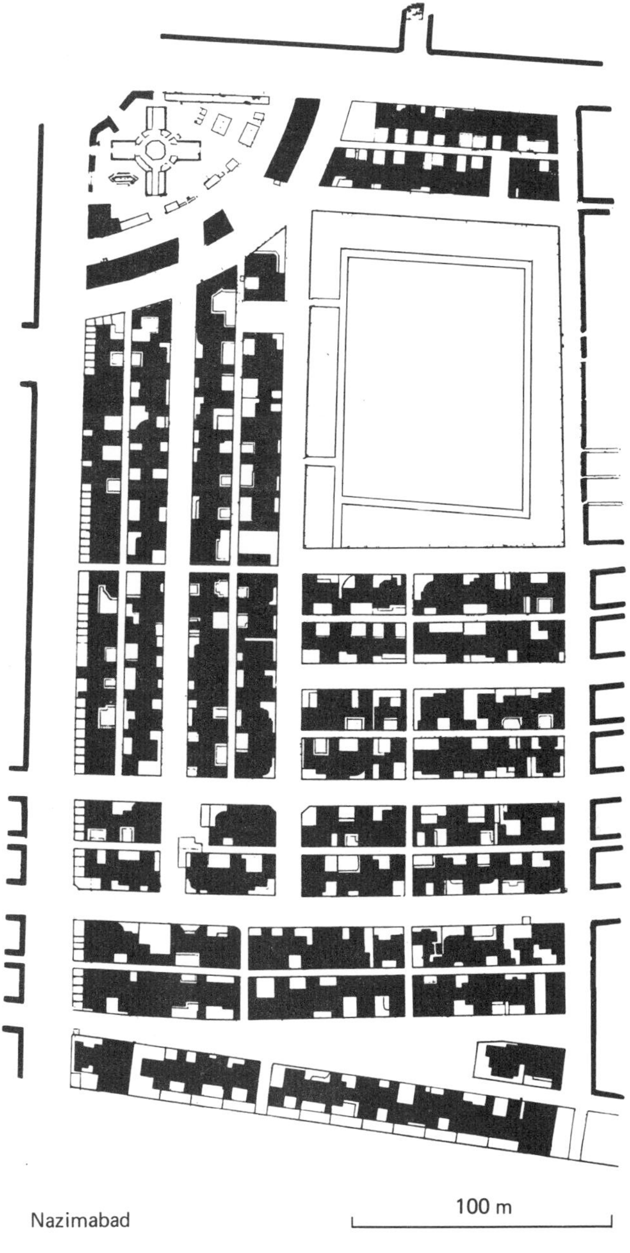

Fig. 6.

Fig. 7.

The houses have been designed by architects, and built by small but professional contractors. In the building process, use is made of light machinery, such as a concrete mixer. Yet, the process is very labour intensive.

In the area, there are no shops, cinemas, schools or medical facilities. For these facilities, the inhabitants have to go to the city's centre. This does, however, not pose much of a problem, as most of the residents own two cars and a four-lane road gives connection to the heart of the city within five minutes.

Of course, all the houses have connections to the sewerage system, and to the distribution networks of gas and electricity. Water comes only for two hours per day, but all the houses are equipped with an underground storage tank from where the water is pumped to a tank on the roof. By this system, water supply is secured throughout the day. As a result, lawns are beautifully green and the cars all well washed. In Defence Housing Society as a whole, the daily water consumption amounts to 80 million litres per day - i.e. 10% of the total supply in Karachi, although the population of the society is 0.5% of Karachi's total population. Payments for water supply amount to Rs 50.-- per month per plot.[12]

It appeared that, in 1977, 90% of the residents and 70% of the owners are not in the army. 60% of the houses were let. The rent for a four-roomed house amounts to approximately Rs 3000.-- per month. The market value of such a house was about Rs 600,000.--. Large parts of Defence Housing Society are not yet built upon, because the owners wait for further rises in price.

6.2. Nazimabad - Example of a Middle-income Residential Area

Nazimabad was developed by the Karachi Development Authority (KDA) in 1956. It is part of a belt of middle-income residential areas developed around the city. The distance to the city is approximately 6 kilometres. KDA acquired the land from the Province and did the planning for the area. The execution of the plans is handled by private contractors engaged by KDA. After payment of the development costs, private persons can get a lease to a plot.

At its inception, Nazimabad was just a piece of "developed desert", a very dusty area without properly functioning services. Public transport especially posed many problems. By now, the situation is completely different. There are plenty of bus- and minibus connections to practically all parts of the city. There are sufficient shopping facilities, there are institutions of primary and higher education, there is a large hospital and many private medical institutions. The conditions of housing and dwelling environment will again be reviewed with the help of a small unit: Block 5C.

Block 5C, some data

Total area	8.2 hectares	
Number of plots	197 (including three open plots, excluding a KMC-market)	
Density	24 dwellings per hectare. This implies 40 families per hectare, as of more than 50% of the houses the storey is let	
Public area	playground	1.4 hectare
	streets	3 hectares
	KMC market	0.3 hectare
	total	4.7 hectares
Private area	3.5 hectares	
Average plot area	175 m^2	
Total built upon area	3.1 hectares	
Average built upon area per plot	155 m^2	
Average area patio	20 m^2	
Dwelling area (including storeys)	± 5 hectares	
% Houses with second storey	± 60%	
Average dwelling area per house	260 m^2	

As can be observed from the map to some extent, the building blocks form closed units in which the houses are joined although different in shape, height and colour. Most houses have been built stage wise. Especially during the past 10 years, many owners built a storey on their houses for the sake of letting it or to house a relative in it. Because of the shortage on the housing market, renters can be easily found. Moreover, houses in Nazimabad fetch high rents because of its location and the quality of its services. In 1977, the monthly rent of a storey was around Rs 500.--. In 1979, this amount had doubled.

The houses have been built by small contractors, who use mainly simple tools in the building process.

The houses are connected to the sewerage system, and the distribution networks of water, gas and electricity. Gas and electricity are paid for according to consumption; for water, a yearly fee is due. Here again, the houses have an underground storage tank for water which is pumped to a roof tank, from where it is distributed to the various parts of the house. So,

Fig. 8.

Fig. 9.

water is available in the house throughout the day. Streets are daily kept clean by KMC-sweepers, who show a tendency to skip the backlanes.

6.3. Lyari, Miran Naka. An Example of a Low-income Residential Area in the City's Centre

Lyari is one of the old popular settlements of Karachi, situated in the delta of Lyari river. With its 600,000 inhabitants, it is also one of the largest popular settlements. Even in the precolonial days, this marshy area was already inhabited. There were, for instance, caravan serais (the route to Baluchistan and Afghanistan passed through Lyari) and milksellers lived here with their cattle. During the colonial period, the population increased as a result of the growth of economic activities in the city. Labourers built their houses on open spaces. The British hardly interfered and did no planning for the area. To them, only the main road through the city and the octroi post at the river were important. Interference on the part of the colonial rulers started only after British scientists had discovered that there was a relation between the housing environment in such areas and epidemics. For epidemics affected the city as a whole, including the British part. The Karachi Municipal Corporation was instituted to cope with this unhealthy situation.

During the first years after Partition, many refugees settled in Lyari. The area became increasingly inhabited, and until this day, the process of densification is going on continuously. Through the enormous growth of the city, Lyari has meanwhile become part of its centre. Regarding job opportunities, its location is excellent, for it is near by the Central Business District and the old centre, the industrial area SITE and the sea port. It is a very good location for labourers, and especially for those having no fixed jobs. To the production apparatus also, the location is favourable. In the previous sections, we have already described how industrialists, commercialists and speculators buy pieces of land in these areas. The dwellings of the erstwhile residents are then pulled down and replaced by four- or five-storeyed tenement buildings, mostly with a shop or workshop on the ground floor.

Previously, under Ayub Khan's regime, attempts were made to clear the whole area all at once. This, however, turned out to be impossible as there was much resistance from the residents and other interested groups. Yet, through the high and rising land values, the process of buying out and expelling the original inhabitants keeps on taking momentum. This process is further accelerated by a municipal programme of slum improvement. Advocates of this approach argue sometimes that the effects of expulsion are not all negative as the expelled residents do receive substantial amounts of money for their plots and houses, so that they share in the benefits of improvement.

Some notes are, however, due in this respect. Firstly, the residents have to live some place after shifting. To them, the only way of preserving some of the money gained is to go and live far away from the centre, i.e. far away from employment and public facilities as, for example, schools. In the second place, the really large profits are made by those who can make substantial investments in the land, e.g. by building tenements. These profits amount to a multiple of what the expelled residents could possibly gain. So, the contrast between rich and poor increases and there is no question of some income distributional effects. In the third place, the original inhabitants often have to spend the money received on not directly productive uses, such as their daughter's wedding, payment of debts, etc. Often also luxury items of consumption are being purchased. No doubt, some individuals may profit somewhat by selling their houses, but the position in society of the low-income groups as a whole deteriorates. By the expulsion process, the area as such improves and becomes a better sight, but this does not bring the solution of the housing problem any closer, on the contrary.

To give an impression of what the housing conditions in Lyari are like, I will now elaborate somewhat on one small part of it, Miran Naka. It is located relatively far from the city's centre, so that it still is the residence of the low-income groups.

Miran Naka, some data

Total area under review	6.9 hectares
Number of plots	670 (including a fire station, mosques and a playground)
Density	98 plots per hectare (when excluding fire station, mosques and playground: 110 plots per hectare)
Public area	1.2 hectare
Private area	5.7 hectares
Average plot area	85 m^2

The average area per dwelling, however, is substantially smaller than 85 m^2, as many of the large plots are used for keeping cattle or as "godowns" (i.e. storage). Many houses are on plots not larger than 20 m^2. Most of the inhabitants have built houses of cement blocks, but the quality is very poor. During rains and floods, the blocks are heavily affected. Only close to the main road, some houses are of a fair quality.

In the colonial period, Miran Naka was a so-called octroi post at the crossing of Lyari river and the road to Lasbela. The settlement that came about around this place was somewhat away from the city of Karachi. Here, cattle keepers and milk sellers from Lasbela lived. Milk was sold in the city every day. After Partition, the population of Miran Naka increased, and it soon became part of the city which grew in all directions.

According to a JRP-IV report,[13] the inhabitants belong to the lowest income groups. A large majority of the labour force here is employed in blue-collar jobs, often under insecure conditions. Most of them (80%) reach their place of work on foot.

The favourable location of the area as regards employment opportunities explains the concentration of many labourers in Miran Naka. This, of course, has its consequences on the living conditions. High densities and narrow lanes are amongst such consequences. Over the years, after much pressurizing by the inhabitants, the municipal authorities have introduced a number of facilities in Miran Naka, such as public standposts, public latrines, electricity and garbage dumps. However, construction and maintenance of these services are poor. Also, they are insufficient to cater for the needs of the dense population, which results in overburdening the facilities present. All this causes a very unhealthy situation. Around the public standposts, there are pools of stagnant water and mud. The collection of garbage does not function well, so that much garbage lies about in the streets. One of the public latrines has meanwhile been demolished as it caused too much inconvenience of dirt and stench to those living nearby.

Fig. 10.

Fig. 11.

6.4. Orangi, Mohammed Nagar, an Example of a Low-income Settlement in the City's Periphery

Orangi is one of the largest residential areas where the low-income groups can still find housing. It is a desert area at the north-western edge of Karachi, some 15 kilometres from its centre. According to 1977 estimates, the population was about 500,000. Orangi consists of a legal and an illegal part. The legal part was developed by KDA and the inhabitants have proper tenure documents. KDA started developing urban land here in 1967 by demarcating plots and bringing in some infrastructure, such as water, roads and electricity. KDA bought the land from the provincial authorities at Rs 7.-- per square yard. After development, the price comes to around Rs 40.--. The price of plots is subsidized however, and those who get a plot allocated, officially pay Rs 14.-- per square yard. They have to construct their houses themselves or through a contractor.

Again in this project, the combination of an enormous shortage in housing and the small scale on which a solution was sought, caused much speculation. Only those having good contacts with the executing agency can secure the allocation of a plot, often against some extra payments. Therefore, the real price is often much higher than the official Rs 14.-- per square yard. In the legal part of Orangi, some 100,000 people live. The fact that around this legal area, some 400,000 people live illegally, shows to what extent urban planning fails in catering for the housing needs.

I have elaborated on one small area in the illegal part of Orangi, to show how land- and housing markets function for the majority of the low-income group.

Mohammed Nagar, some data

Total area under review	4.4 hectares
Number of plots	230
Density	52 houses per hectare (by deducting one very large open plot, this figure comes to 62 houses per hectare)
Public area	1.3 hectare
Private area	3.1 hectares
Average plot area	135 m^2 (when excluding the large plot: 115 m^2)
Average built upon area per plot	24 m^2
Average area garden/patio	91 m^2

Mohammed Nagar is a clear example of an illegal subdivision.[14] Plot-sizes and the street pattern neatly coincide with those of the nearby areas which KDA developed. Also main roads in Mohammed Nagar connect to main roads in the legal part. Of course, the road network has hardly any relation with actual use, as there are no cars in the area, except for a few minibuses that keep to the main roads.

The first inhabitants, in 1971, paid Rs 25.-- for a plot. After 6 years, the price had risen to approximately Rs 2000.--, By now, most of the plots have been sold, except for one very large plot (visible on the map, left below). Mostly, the inhabitants build their houses themselves. During the first years, often this is only a reed hut, but after saving some money, many inhabitants manage to build a house of concrete blocks with an asbestos sheet roof. Often loans are taken for this purpose, especially from the blockmaker in the area. For the construction, also the services of a mason are often hired.

In the beginning, water was brought into the area by a tank wagon. Very little water was being used (some 1 gallon per person per day). Now, there are thirteen public standposts in Mohammed Nagar. These have been paid for and installed by the residents themselves. Obtaining permission from KDA to connect their supply line to a main took no less than 5 years. There are no medical or educational facilities in Mohammed Nagar, and hardly any in Orangi. For these, people have to go to Nazimabad. Consequently, most children do not go to school; expenses on transport and education itself are too high.

REFERENCES

1. K. Griffin and A. R. Khan, A note on the degree of dependence on foreign assistance. K. Griffin and A. R. Khan (eds.), *Growth and inequality in Pakistan*, London, 1972, p. 190.
2. L. J. White, *Industrial concentration and economic power in Pakistan*, Princeton, 1974, pp. 58-59, 76-78 and 95.
3. C. H. Gotsch and W. P. Falcon, *Agricultural development in Pakistan, lessons from the second plan period*, Cambridge, 1966, p. 12.
4. S. R. Bose, East-west contrast in Pakistan's agricultural development. In K. Griffin and A. R. Khan, *op. cit.*
5. K. Griffin, Financing development plans in Pakistan. In K. Griffin and A. R. Khan, *op. cit.*, p. 44.
6. E. Frank, *Illegale wijken in Karachi, een onderzoek naar de mogelijkheden van de doe-het-zelf benadering*, Rotterdam, 1978.

7. Government of Pakistan, *Census of Pakistan 1961*, Vol. I, Karachi. Government of Pakistan, Provisional figures released for the 1972 census.
8. N. Hussain, *Problems of urban growth in Pakistan and a two-pronged remedy*, The Hague, 1974.
9. Master Plan Department KDA, *Karachi Development Plan 1974-1985*, Karachi, 1974, pp. 88-89.
10. M. Mujahid, Migration and earning differentials in Pakistan. *Review of World Economics*, Vol. III, 1975.
11. See H. Meyerink and R. Vekemans, Class structure in a basti. Elsewhere in this book.
12. Interdisciplinaire Studiegroep Planologie, *Huivesting in Karachi, situatie en strategie*, Delft, 1977, p. 74.
13. R. A . Chughtai, T. E. L. Van Pinxteren, H. Kiestra and M. H. Weijs, *Miran Naka*, Karachi, 1975, pp. 22-25.
14. See J. J. van der Linden, *The bastis of Karachi*, the functioning of an informal housing system. Elsewhere in this book.

How Karachi is Governed*

S. H. Hashmi

1. HISTORICAL BACKGROUND

Karachi had its first municipal government as early as 1852. A decade later the Karachi municipality levied a house tax on property owners; thus it became a pioneer in the introduction of direct taxation in the Indo-Pakistan Sub-continent. The municipality continued to progress and undertake an increasing number of functions; its revenue also rose steadily.

When Pakistan became an independent state in 1947 the Municipal Council was a wholly-elected body; this was, however, replaced in 1959 by one part elected, the other part nominated in accordance with the provisions of the Municipal Administration Ordinance of that year (enforced until 1971). The elected component comprised the chairmen of the city's union committees;[1] the nominated component represented women, "special interests" groups and bureaucrats. The elected mayor gave place to an appointed chairman, who was a government official.[2] The advantages of an arrangement of this nature were envisaged as improved communication between the people and the bureaucracy.[3] However, this benefit was negated by the system's "built-in" dual governmental control mechanism. Control was exercised not only through the bureaucrat-chairman but also through a "controlling authority" - the Deputy Commissioner of Karachi - empowered to veto municipal corporation decisons.[4]

The elected representative-bureaucrat combination also suffered from some other not insignificant shortcomings. Rather than serve as the mouthpiece of his constituents, the elected Basic Democrat often found it expedient to be in the good books of the bureaucrat. Another flaw lay in the chairing of the municipal committee by a government official who was prone to transfer within such a short period of time that his contribution to municipal government was likely to be negligible.

*Some sections of this paper have appeared in the author's "Karachi Metropolis: Challenges of a Growing Population and the Government Response" in *Journal of Administration Overseas*, Vol.xiv, No.3, July 1975, London.

2. MULTIPLICITY OF MUNICIPAL AGENCIES

At local level Karachi, like other cities of Pakistan, is faced with the problem of a multitude of agencies, all performing municipal and related functions. Thus between 1958 and 1971, almost 400 local bodies, responsible in some measure for municipal functions, were in existence in the Karachi Metropolis.[5] At present, the following agencies exist:

(i) Municipal Authority
Karachi Metropolitan Corporation

(ii) Cantonment Boards
Karachi Cantonment Board
Drigh Road Cantonment Board
Malir Cantonment Board
Manora Cantonment Board

(iii) Ad-hoc Authorities
Karachi Development Authority
Karachi Port Trust
Sind Industrial Trading Estate
Landi Industrial Trading Estate
Cooperative Housing Societies

(iv) Local Council
District Council

(v) Local Offices and Offices of Provincial and Central Government partly responsible for performing Municipal functions
Pakistan Public Works Department
(responsible for providing some municipal services to areas where central government has provided housing to its employees)
Sind Highway Department
(responsible for the maintenance of roads in certain areas of the city)
Military Estates Service
(responsible for cantonments)
Civil Aviation Authority
(responsible for maintenance of airport and adjoining areas)

2.1. Karachi Metropolitan Corporation

The Karachi Metropolitan Corporation constitutes the principal local government body of the Karachi metropolis. It is charged with the responsibility of maintaining and extending services like public health, sewerage and drainage, retail water distribution, fire protection, recreation and road building (see Table 2). Its role expanded into the field of education in 1973. Following the nationalization of primary schools that year, the KMC has been assigned the responsibility of managing most of these schools. In the field of public health also, it has expanded its activities: it has recently moved into the area of curative health as well.

The sources of revenue for KMC have included property tax, octroi (an indirect tax, of the sales tax type, levied on goods entering the city of Karachi for consumption), water, conservancy and fire rates and a number of licences and fees (see Table 1). In 1972-73 the collection of the entire property tax was transferred to the Excise and Taxation Department of the Provincial (Sind) Government. Prior to this the KMC collected its share of the property tax amounting to half of the total. Another modification that

Table 1. Karachi Metropolitan Corporation - Current Receipts 1979-1980

Serial no.	Particulars	Rs in millions	Percentage
1	Octroi	253.21	56
2	General Tax (Property Tax)	51.26	11
3	Water Tax	46.83	10
4	Rent (Land & Building Shops & Market)	28.43	6
5	Conservancy Rate	26.55	6
6	Grant for Primary School	10.20	2
7	Fire Tax	8.03	2
8	Share of Betterment Tax	5.00	1
9	Advertisements Tax	4.45	1
10	Show Tax	0.88	-
11	Vehicle Tax	0.04	-
12	Miscellaneous Receipts	20.77	5
	Total	455.65	100

Source: Karachi Metropolitan Corporation, *Facts in Figures*, Vol.V, 1979-1980, p.25.

Table 2. Karachi Metropolitan Corporation - Service-wise Expenditure 1979-1980)

Serial no.	Service	Rs in millions	Percentage
1	Public Health	89.61	23
2	Water Supply Service	89.61	23
3	Communications	45.60	12
4	Education	44.12	11
5	Medical Service	32.34	8
6	Drainage & Sewerage	22.97	6
7	Recreational Service	13.82	4
8	Fire-fighting Service	4.28	1
9	Social Service	4.26	1
10	Municipal Secretariat Revenue Collecting Dept. Debt. Servicing Charges	46.22	11
	Total	392.83	100

Source: Karachi Metropolitan Corporation, *Facts in Figures*, Vol.V, 1979-1980, p.27.

was made in the revenue-sharing formula according to which the KMC was allocated only 38% of the total property tax collected in the city of Karachi.[6] Also, in the same year, the motor vehicle tax, revenues of which had traditionally accrued to the KMC, was taken over by the Provincial Government and no revenues from this tax were allocated to the KMC[7] till 1979.

The recently enforced Sind Local Government Ordinance has given a new impetus to KMC as a local body, all of whose members are directly elected by the people on the basis of universal, adult suffrage with an elected mayor as the head of the executive, who is not controlled or directed by a bureaucrat, as was the case throughout most of Karachi's recent history (as well as that of other Pakistani cities).
(For a list of KMC officers, see the organization chart.)

Karachi Metropolitan Corporation - Organization Chart

Administrator

Financial Advisor	Chief Officer	Chief Engineer
	Deputy Chief Officer	Superintending Engineer SE I
Coordinator, Planning, Evaluation & Monitoring Wing	Health Officer	
	Chief Medical Officer	SE II
	Director, Land and Estate	SE Mechanical
Chief Assessor & Collector	Legal Adviser	
	Deputy Taxation Officer	Planning Coordinator, Lyari
Stores Purchase Officer	Director, Education	
Senior Accounts Officer	Director, Parks	Planning Coordinator, North Karachi
	Information Officer	
Management Accountant	Chief Fire Officer	Planning Coordinator, Landhi Korangi
	Labour Welfare Officer	Director, Engineering Design
Project Officer, Data Processing Centre	Manager, Printing Press	
	Manager, Sports Complex	
	Superintendent, Zoo	
Auditor	Superintendent, Food Laboratory	
	Aquarist	
	City Librarian	

Source: Karachi Metropolitan Corporation, *Facts in Figures*, Vol.V, 1979-1980.

2.2. Karachi Development Authority

The most powerful rival to the Karachi Metropolitan Corporation is the Karachi Development Authority (KDA). This organization was created in 1957 as a successor to Karachi Improvement Trust. Its objectives were (a) providing control, direction and encouragement to the development of housing projects which were desperately needed because of the tremendous increase in population of the metropolis, and (b) assuming responsibility for overall planning in the metropolitan area. Later, responsibility for the city water supply was a function partly entrusted to KDA. The arrangement was that the KDA would supply water in bulk to the KMC, by far the largest consumer, and also to the Trading Estates, the Housing Societies and other agencies performing municipal functions. These bodies would assume responsibility for retail distribution within the areas under their respective jurisdiction. Under this arrangement, however, the KMC finds itself in the role of a loss-making retailer since it is unable to collect sufficient dues from the consuming public to reimburse KDA to whom it is thus in perpetual and increasing debt.

2.3. Cantonment Boards

The Cantonment Boards form another disparate piece in the variegated local administration structure. When created by the British, a cantonment board was a self-administered military station in the vicinity of a large city. With the burgeoning of urban areas many cantonments were physically absorbed into the city itself, as was the case with Karachi. However, the cantonment areas continue to lie outside the jurisdiction of the Metropolitan Corporation and each has an independent administrative system headed by the station commander. Since the Ministry of Defence is the "controlling authority" for cantonments, this system embodies the presence of the central government on the local scene.

2.4. Other Agencies

Other authorities situated within the physical limits of Karachi, many of which do not avail themselves of the services of the Metropolitan Corporation, are Cooperative Housing Societies which mushroomed since Partition. Karachi presently has more than 150. Many of these societies perform some municipal functions such as construction and maintenance of roads, and the provision of water supply, sewerage and drainage. Whereas in the past the contribution made by these societies in meeting the acute housing shortage was valuable, they have proved inept in the role of municipal service agencies on account of their lack of means and trained personnel.

Besides the host of purely local authorities with municipal responsibilities functioning within Karachi, there are also a not insignificant number of quasi-local bodies, the local establishments of provincial and central governmental departments. It is curious that governments at supra-local levels, aware of the limited resources and heavy responsibilities of Karachi's local government, has endeavoured to come to its aid, not by strengthening the Metropolitan Corporation, but by undertaking to provide functions, itself thereby adding a further element of complexity to the existing tangle.

The administrative patchwork of authorities assigned local functions without clearly-demarcated jurisdiction not only creates bottlenecks in the rendering of municipal services, but is also problematic for other concerns engaged in providing utilities. The Karachi Gas Corporation, for instance, faces the situation of having to obtain approval from nineteen different authorities for plans detailing new gas mains for the city. Maps must thus be made and remade until assent is forthcoming from all these bodies.[8]

3. PROVINCIAL GOVERNMENT'S CONTROL ON KARACHI'S LOCAL GOVERNMENT

The Provincial Government is provided with formidable powers over the Karachi Metropolitan Corporation. According to the Sind Local Government Ordinance of 1979 the "Government shall exercise general supervision and control over the (Corporation) to ensure that... (its) activities conform to the purposes and provisions of this ordinance" and the "Government may make any order it deems necessary to bring" the activities of the Corporation "in such conformity."[9]

Further, if in the opinion of the Provincial Government any act of the Corporation is not in conformity with "the law", the former can suspend that act and compel the Corporation to take such action which the government may deem fit.[10]

In addition, the working of the Corporation has to be inspected at least once a year by an Inspecting Officer appointed by the Provincial Government.[11] If, as a result of the Inspecting Officer's enquiry, the Government is satisfied that the Corporation is not able to run a particular department efficiently, it may suspend the authority of the Corporation over that department for a specified period of time and may itself take over the management of that department.[12]

Similarly, if the provincial government is of the opinion that the Corporation has persistently failed in discharging its duties or meeting its financial obligations, the former may declare the Corporation to be superseded for a period not exceeding six months. During this period of supersession, the Mayor and members of the Corporation would cease to hold their offices. The functions of the Corporation would be performed by an authority appointed by the Government and all funds and property of the Corporation would be vested in the Government which would have the power to expand them.[13]

The Provincial Government also has certain financial powers: it may direct the Corporation to levy, increase, reduce, suspend or abolish any tax, rate, toll or fee, which the Corporation is competent to levy under the ordinance. If the Corporation does not comply with the direction of the Government, the latter itself may make necessary arrangements to give effect to the direction. Similarly the Government has the right to "modify" the budget approved by the Corporation.[14]

These are impressive powers which are provided to the provincial government in the Ordinance but it is too early to predict the extent to which they would be exercised by the government and thus hinder the development of local government in Karachi.

4. CONCLUSION

Notwithstanding the considerable powers entrusted to the provincial government, the Sind Local Government Ordinance of 1979 must be regarded as a progressive and positive legislation, particularly in its restoration of fully representative local government. However, there remain other important matters which lie outside the provisions of the ordinance. The Cantonment Boards, Ad-hoc authorities, Central and Provincial Agencies dealing with local affairs all continue to function even after the enforcement of the new law.

It is apparent that the Federal and Provincial Governments must give their urgent attention to the question of administrative reform aimed at avoiding all unnecessary duplication of municipal functions and powers. A desirable and necessary step for the rationalization and increased efficiency of municipal government is the abolition of authorities such as Cantonment Boards and the KDA. Similarly, municipal functions must be transferred from such federal and provincial agencies as the Public Works Department and the Highways Department to the municipal authorities. Not all such changes, can however, be expected to materialize in the near future. The simplest of the needed major changes appears to be a merger of Karachi Development Authority with the Karachi Metropolitan Corporation. The questions relating to the abolition of Cantonment Boards and the transfer of municipal functions from the federal and provincial governments to municipal authorities, are matters of general policy and must necessarily be decided on an All-Pakistan basis. However the problem of KDA's future can be tackled without delay. The KDA symbolizes the bureaucratization of local government; since bureaucratic power was at its zenith during the Ayub Khan and Yahya Khan regimes (1958-1971), KDA thrived at the expense of the then partly representative institution, the Karachi Municipal Corporation. It is the policy of the present government to curtail bureaucratic power and to increase the power of local government bodies directly elected by the people. It could, therefore, be expected that the KDA will either be accorded a subordinate independent status or that it will be merged with the Karachi Metropolitan Corporation. The latter would be a step in the right direction, since overall planning and certain other municipal functions, presently performed by KDA as a separate and autonomous entity, would then be discharged by a municipal body, which would be in a position to have an overall view of the problems of the metropolis and which would also be accountable to the people.

As mentioned earlier the abolition of Cantonment Boards may not be an easy matter. The cantonments are directly under the Federal Ministry of Defence and it is doubtful if this Ministry would surrender its "empire" very readily. Moreover, cantonment boards are scattered all over Pakistan and if they are abolished in Karachi the Ministry of Defence would doubtless be confronted with demands for their abolition elsewhere.

Similarly, such well-entrenched and powerful federal and provincial government agencies such as the Public Works Department and the Highway Department would put up strong resistance against the transfer of some of their functions to local authorities.

It is apparent that local government in Karachi as in other parts of Pakistan, after its severe mauling for more than two decades will need to acquire much new muscle to fight for its due rights and powers.

REFERENCES

1. The Union Committee was the lowest rung in a pyramidal hierarchy of Councils introduced as a system of local government under the Basic Democracies Scheme, in force in Pakistan between 1959 and 1971.
2. For further details about the structure and functions of municipal government in Pakistan see G. N. Jones, Municipal Administration in Pakistan: Elements Contributing Towards a Modernisation Complex, *NIPA JOURNAL*, Karachi, VI, No. 4, December, 1967, pp. 190-199.
3. Former President Ayub Khan gave the reasons for adoption of this system as follows: "The association (of Basic Democrats) with the officials had produced two wholesome results: in the first instance, it was acting as a check on the working of the government and secondly, and more important, it was providing the Basic Democrats with an opportunity not only to understand how government functions but also to supervise and guide its functions". *Friends Not Masters*, London, Oxford University Press, 1967, p. 228.
4. Government of Pakistan, *The Municipal Administration Ordinance*, 1960, Karachi, Government of Pakistan Press, 1960.
5. Karachi Local Authorities Reorganisation Committee, *Final Report*, Karachi, 1968, pp. 3-4.
6. A. P. Hafiz, *Is the Local Tax Base Adequate? A Case Study of the Karachi Metropolitan Corporation*, Karachi, University of Karachi, 1978 (mimeo.).
7. *Ibid.*
8. T. R. Sharique, "Natural Gas Supply for Karachi", in *Problems of Urbanization in Pakistan*, eds. S. H. Hashmi and G. N. Jones, Karachi, National Institute of Public Administration, 1967, p. 228.
9. Government of Sind, *The Sind Local Government Ordinance 1979*, Karachi, 1979, Article 53(1) and (2).
10. *Ibid.*, Article 53(3).
11. *Ibid.*, Article 55.
12. *Ibid.*, Article 57.
13. *Ibid.*, Article 58.
14. *Ibid.*, Article 72.

Part II

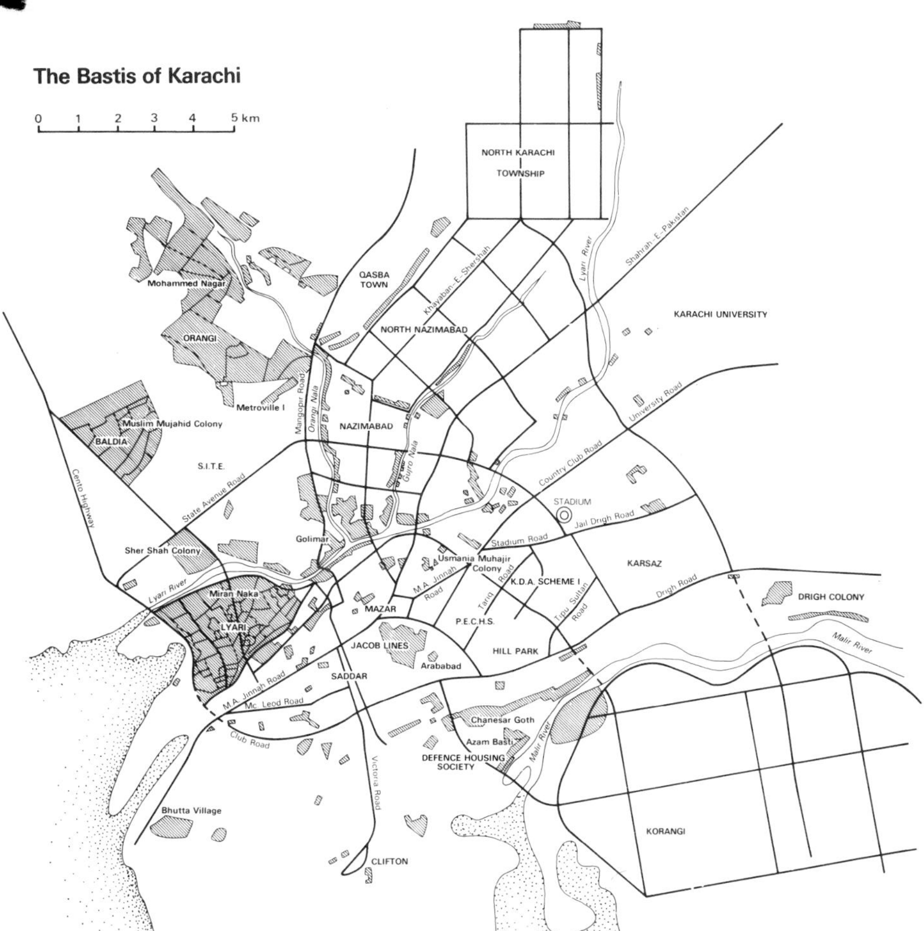
The Bastis of Karachi
0 1 2 3 4 5 km
NORTH KARACHI TOWNSHIP
QASBA TOWN
Khayaban-E-Shershah
Shahrah-E-Pakistan
Lyari River
Mohammed Nagar
ORANGI
NORTH NAZIMABAD
KARACHI UNIVERSITY
Metroville I
Muslim Mujahid Colony
BALDIA
Mangopir Road
Orangi Nala
NAZIMABAD
University Road
Gujro Nala
Country Club Road
S.I.T.E.
Cento Highway
State Avenue Road
STADIUM
Jail Drigh Road
Golimar
Stadium Road
Sher Shah Colony
Usmania Muhajir Colony
KARSAZ
Lyari River
M.A. Jinnah Road
K.D.A. SCHEME I
Miran Naka
Drigh Road
DRIGH COLONY
MAZAR
Tariq Road
Tipu Sultan Road
LYARI
P.E.C.H.S.
JACOB LINES
HILL PARK
Malir River
Arababad
SADDAR
M.A. Jinnah Road
Mc. Leod Road
Chanesar Goth
Club Road
Azam Basti
Malir River
DEFENCE HOUSING SOCIETY
Victoria Road
Bhutta Village
KORANGI
CLIFTON

Fig. 12.

The Bastis of Karachi; the Functioning of an Informal Housing System

J. J. van der Linden

1. INTRODUCTION

Besides countless "mini slums",[1] there are, in Karachi, between 250 and 300 "bastis".[2] By the term "basti" we mean all kinds of spontaneous settlements, i.e. those settlements that came about without official government planning. Used in this sense, the concept of basti comprises all kinds of squatter settlements and passively urbanized villages. Together these bastis cover an area of an estimated 12,000 acres and house between 1,500,000 and 2,000,000 people.[3]

From the map "bastis of Karachi" it can easily be seen that bastis are located all over the city, although some areas of concentration can also be distinguished. Such concentrations include a triangle-shaped area "Lyari" in the city's centre, which consists of many passively urbanized villages and some of the relatively old squatments; other obvious concentrations are Baldia and Orangi Town, both in the north-western part of Karachi, and both consisting almost completely of squatments.

Almost everywhere in the world squatter settlements tend to be located in areas of second choice, e.g. in riverbeds, and at the periphery of the cities. In the case of Karachi, indeed, one of the concentration areas is alongside watercourses.

Bastis on the periphery were also created in great numbers over the past 30 years. However, as the city grew rapidly, many of the formerly peripheral bastis find themselves right in the city by now, and new bastis tend to be located even farther away from the city's centre.

Living conditions in bastis vary greatly. Over the years, some of the bastis have become very decent places with fairly good houses and having a quite reasonable level of facilities like water-supply, sewerage, garbage collection, storm-water drainage, electricity, etc.

In other bastis, practically all these services are absent and sometimes the housing stock consists of mere reed huts, or of double storeyed shacks made of wooden planks and tin sheets.

In order to find the causes of these differences, and to detect which conditions and mechanisms enhance the quality of a basti's housing condition, an inventory of the Karachi bastis was made which tried to frame a typology and to show some of the dynamics causing changes in the housing conditions.

2. THE TOOLS FOR DESCRIBING THE BASTIS OF KARACHI: LEGAL STATUS, PHYSICAL DEVELOPMENT AND AGE

For the Latin-American situation, Turner has developed a typology of squatter settlements by using levels of physical development and degrees of security of tenure as criteria.[4] We have tried to do the same in Karachi, but we introduced a third variable: the age. Because, if a correlation between security of tenure and physical development can be demonstrated - such as Turner did - the dynamics of the process may still be obscured. If bastis have a low security level and a correspondingly poor physical development, this may have very different meanings in the cause of young and relatively old bastis. The difference is comparable to that between a one-year-old baby and a twenty-year-old man, neither of whom can walk. What, in the first case, is a healthy situation, full of potential and promise, is, in the second case, a reason to be concerned, although the possibility of healing is not by definition excluded.

Thus, when introducing the age of bastis as a third variable, we can reveal much about the dynamics of their development: we can distinguish between groups of bastis that develop more or less rapidly and those which stagnate in their development.

Here, it is not the place to go into much detail about the construction of the typology. We will mention a few main characteristics only.[5]

2.1. Legal Status

Officially, only two possibilities can exist regarding the legal status: legal or illegal. Therefore, it is difficult to judge the "legality" of illegal settlement. In Karachi, however - as elsewhere - the basti dwellers judge the level of security of tenure by the services and facilities that the government provides to an area. Namely, they see the provision of these services and facilities as a sign that the government recognizes the existence of a settlement, and that clearly, the government is not planning to bulldoze it shortly.

Moreover, the different services and facilities, when used as a touchstone to measure the level of security, have different weights. Water - for instance - may be provided by the authorities on compassionate grounds, although these authorities consider the settlement as only very temporary. The provision of sewers on the other hand implies a certain intended permanency, and as such carries more weight as an indicator of the level of security. Besides, the different "hope-providing items" appear in a fixed order of sequence, so that we can consider the appearance of each next item as marking a next level of security of tenure.

Of the many items indicative of the level of security ("hope-providing items") we retained the four which we thought to be the most meaningful ones, viz. the provision of water, the provision of electricity, the raising of taxes and the provision of a sewerage system. Thus, five levels of security of tenure can be established, represented by settlements where respectively 0, 1, 2, 3 or 4 of these items are present.

2.2. Physical Development

We measured the physical development of bastis in terms of the condition of the houses. Again, it was difficult to attach weights to different types of houses. Karachi houses people of very different ethnic backgrounds and this is reflected in the materials which people use to build their houses. When asked about their preference for different kinds of building materials, however, representatives of different ethnic groups reacted very much alike. Thus, the ranking of different building materials by the basti dwellers gave us a key to a typology of houses.

We have distinguished seven house types, which we can roughly describe as follows:

I: very temporary: only reed matting or pieces of tin have been used.
II: temporary: partly, more durable materials (mud, stones, wood) are used for walls; or a roof of a somewhat superior nature covers the house which otherwise has been built the way described under I.
III: prolonged temporary: walls are made of mud, stones or wood; or a combination of concrete blocks and the materials mentioned under I.
IV: semi-permanent: all walls are made of unplastered concrete blocks; the roof is made of material superior to reed matting or tin (e.g. corrugated iron or asbestos sheets), but no reinforced concrete.
V: provisional permanent: as under IV, but with at least one wall plastered with cement.
VI: permanent: the house has a reinforced concrete roof.
S: stagnating temporary: double-storeyed houses of the materials described under I and II.

Samples were taken from each autonomous settlement. From these samples, for each basti the distribution of the different house types can be known and shown as a profile in a bar diagram.

From the profiles, an index was calculated, which meant the settlements could be ranked according to the physical development of the houses.[6] It should be noted that this index is no more than a tool to arrange the settlements in a certain sequence. The index should not be mistaken as an independent standard, nor should the index "0" be considered as a kind of borderline between "up to standard" and "sub-standard".

2.3. Legal Status and Physical Development Combined

In the following table, the level of physical development and the degree of security of tenure have been combined. The figures presented are strongly suggestive of a correlation between both variables: no bastis fill the cells; in the upper left and lower right corners of the table and there is an outspoken clustering on and around a diagonal. Thus, we may repeat the conclusion from world-wide experience, also confirmed by van der Harst's studies in Karachi:[8] whenever people have a reasonable security of tenure, they show themselves able to solve their housing problem, albeit within the limits of their economic potential.

We will, however, leave this table for what it is, because, as stated earlier - it is only after the introduction of the third variable, the age, that we can see the dynamics of the development process. We will deal with this variable in the following paragraphs when describing different categories of bastis.

Table 1. Numbers of Autonomous Settlements in Karachi, According to Security of Tenure and Index of the House Conditions[7]

Index house-conditions	Number of hope-providing items				
	0	1	2	3	4
+270 to +54	-	-	1	7	42
+53 to +9	1	6	12	10	21
+8 to -45	-	19	16	9	6
-46 to -99	7	30	8	2	3
-100 to -242	16	27	5	2	-

3. SQUATTER SETTLEMENTS

We have introduced the age of the bastis as a third variable in order to be able to see beyond the mere relationship between security and physical development, such as shown in Table 1. In fact, for a majority of the bastis, the combination of the level of security of tenure and the index of the house conditions (between certain limits) correlates with a certain age group. Thus, a pattern of development can be established, by which both the bastis' level of security and level of physical development increase with age.

If, however, relatively old bastis are characterized by low levels of security and physical development, evidently, the development process does not take place, although the correlation between security and physical development may be clear. Therefore, we set some arbitrarily chosen age limits so as to distinguish between developing bastis and bastis which stagnate in their development.

3.1. Developing Bastis

Almost 70% of the post-Partition settlements show a steady development. According to the process of development, however, two broad type-groups of developing bastis can be distinguished.

3.1.1. Developing bastis with smooth development

The most common development pattern of bastis is illustrated in Fig. 13, showing the profiles of the house conditions of bastis with respectively 0, 1, 2, 3 and 4 "hope-providing items" present.

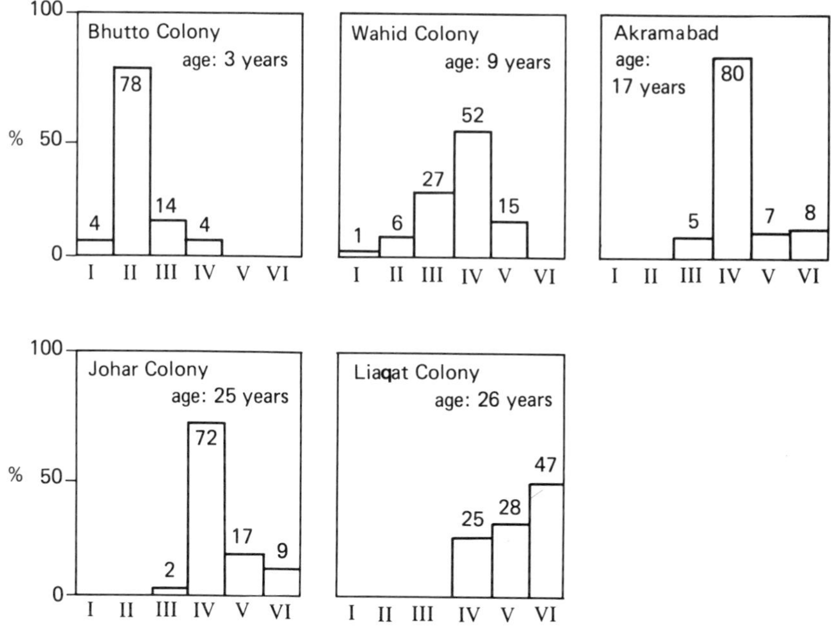

Fig. 13. House Conditions in Five Selected Bastis with Smooth Development.

When following the histories of individual bastis, we found that indeed bastis do approximately pass through the stages of our above illustration.[9] In the last stages, the fear of being forcibly shifted has disappeared. Houses of type VI, for which a large investment is needed (reinforced concrete roof!), appear.

The high priority which squatters attach to the condition of their houses is well reflected in the fact that each change in the security level is followed by action on the part of the residents.

Bastis of this type mostly come about without much organization. Often, their inception is marked only by a smaller cluster of families just settling on a vacant piece of land, without payment and without much planning. Plots may be of unequal sizes and streets sometimes twisting and narrow. However, very soon, the dwellers organize themselves strongly in order to resist government's attempts to evict them, to improve their settlement and to request certain facilities from the government.

Normally, the residents are more than willing to pay for such facilities, as these - besides serving their intended function - also enhance the security level of the basti. An interesting case in this connection concerns a group of squatters who managed to illegally force their tax-payments on the government, the receipts of which were supposed to provide a legal pretence to their claims to the land.

More often than not, improvements in bastis in terms of facilities and security of tenure are obtained without there being even a semblance of a policy for the particular settlement on the government's side. In the absence of such a policy, improvements achieved are based on favours granted rather than on the recognition of rights. In line with this, the improvements come about through the actions of individuals rather than institutions.

When short-term, *ad hoc* action is required (e.g. the retreat of the demolition squad, an unofficial permission to connect an illegal water tap), bribes are often used. For the sake of longer-term goals (e.g. the official extension of certain facilities to the basti), the personal interference of influential persons (either in the administration or amongst the politicians) is often used.

In later stages of the life of the basti, when the fear for eviction is lifted, the voluntary organizations often collapse. Sometimes they revive when discussions start about leasing the land. By that time, we find the inhabitants and their organizations no longer offering all kinds of cooperation with the government, but rather opposing it to get the rates reduced.

3.1.2. Developing bastis with partial initial development

A different process can be observed in a rather large number of bastis located at the periphery of the city. This type of settlement rests on illegal subdivision of government land.

Main characteristics of the system of illegal subdivision are:
- protection against eviction is guaranteed by leaders, who - in their turn - obtain protection from politicians and/or key-persons in the administration. Although settlers do not get any documentary proof of their unofficial tenure rights, *de facto*, their security of tenure is high,
- the lay-out of this type of basti has been planned through the leaders. Often, guidelines for the planning are given unofficially by the administration. Usually, the leaders also organize the provision of some basic facilities like water supply and transport,
- settlers have to buy their plots with money. Often, the first settlers pay a nominal price only, depending upon the location of the basti. By the time the basti gets inhabited, prices of plots rise, particularly of the potentially commercial plots which the leaders have reserved along prospective main roads.

These colonies attract many people from other bastis, who have established themselves in the city and can afford to live at greater distances from their jobs than most of the fresh migrants. The attraction of these bastis lies in the high security, combined with the planned character of the settlements, which makes them relatively spacious. Because of this, the inhabitants can build a permanent house in which they plan to live for the foreseeable future.

For the most part, they can also afford to build such a house, although many make use of the opportunity to temporize the building of their house. This temporizing, however, is effected by building parts of the house in the required shape, rather than by staged improvements in the materials from which the house is built. Instead of a development from a reed hut to a mud house thence to a house of concrete blocks, here, we see a development where, e.g. first the reed hut is surrounded by a compound wall of concrete blocks, secondly, the walls of the house are rebuilt with concrete blocks, and finally, the reed roof is replaced by an asbestos sheet roof, or even one of reinforced concrete. Namely, in view of the high security level of these bastis, there is no need to adjust the house all the time and keep it at an assumed optimal quality-level (a balance between the requirements and possibilities of the family on the one hand, and the changing security level on the other). Instead, the inhabitants either build pakka[10] houses straightaway, or they start living in a provisional hut and build pakka when they have time and money to do so. The stages represented by house types between I (or II) and IV (or V or VI) are mostly avoided.

Figure 14 illustrates this kind of development. As can be seen from the profiles, only the initial stages show a pattern different from the previous type (as in Fig. 13). Namely, in very early stages of the bastis' life, house types IV, V and VI are represented already, indicating the high level of security from the beginning. The initially high percentages scored by house type I reflect the temporary abodes which people construct to shelter themselves as long as their more permanent home is under construction.

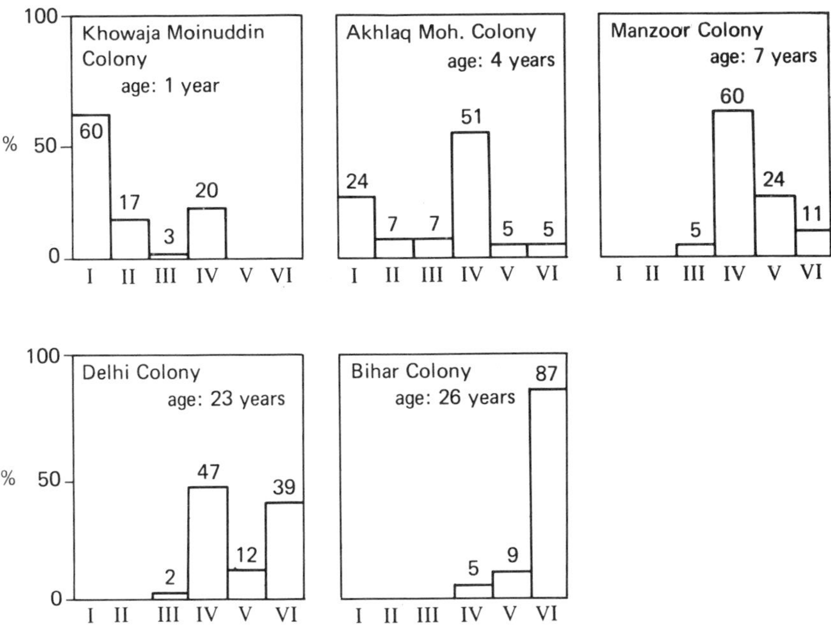

Fig. 14. House Conditions in Five Selected Bastis with Partial Initial Development

In Fig. 14, the first two examples regard bastis with one "hope-giving item" present; the third, fourth and fifth example have respectively two, three and four items present. The fact that no bastis of this type exist where there is no hope-giving item at all, is a reflection of the high security level from the beginning.

3.1.3. The two types of developing bastis compared

Some main differences between bastis with smooth development and those with partial initial development have already been dealt with in the above.

There is, in the first place, a difference in the level of security, although this difference may disappear in the long run.

Secondly, there is a difference in location in two senses. Bastis with smooth development can be found all over the city, even in central places. Quite often, however, they find themselves in areas "of second choice", e.g. alongside watercourses, etc. Illegal subdivisions by definition are created at the outskirts of the city which moreover may no longer be the outskirts after some years. Also, these subdivisions will be rarely found in danger spots.

Thirdly, over time there has been a shift in the frequency of both types. Some 30 years ago, "unorganized invasion", giving rise to bastis with smooth development, was the most common system, although illegal subdivision was also practiced from the time of Partition onwards. But this second system greatly gained in importance. Reasons for this include the - albeit unofficial - recognition of the system and even the active participation in it on the part of authorities and influential persons. At the same time, many people living in "unorganized invasion" bastis saw their attempts to improve their houses and environment frustrated and were uprooted in many instances by those same authorities that protected the creation of new bastis formed by illegal subdivision.

In the fourth place, there are some differences and similarities regarding the functions which the two basti types perform. Evidently, in illegal subdivisions, the speculation element is much stronger than in the other type, although here, speculation is not completely absent either. Although some of the smoothly developing bastis - and especially those that develop less - provide relatively cheap housing in central places of the city, they do not particularly attract the new migrants to the city, as Turner's theory would predict.[11] However, in accordance with Turner's theory, newcomers mostly start living in rented accommodation, and in places where they have access to jobs.[12] But nowadays, access to jobs is less a matter of residing in geographically central places than of having entrance to the informal job recruitment network. Therefore, settling close by friends or relatives is common amongst fresh migrants. As a result, newcomers can be found in either type of basti, as renters. Yet, there is a difference between the inhabitants of both types of basti, albeit by no means an absolute difference.[13] Illegal subdivisions have a high level of security of tenure and offer space and potential for all kinds of improvements in houses and environment. On the other hand, distances to places of work are long and expenses on transport sometimes weigh heavily on the family's budget in newly-created subdivisions in the periphery. In older, meanwhile more centrally-located subdivisions landprices have risen enormously, also as a result of the high security of tenure. Therefore, people having no job security (either having no fixed job or no well-established place in the network), or having very poorly-paid jobs, usually cannot afford to settle as owner-occupiers in the subdivisions. These subdivisions, then, typically are the residence of the consolidating poor, including both migrants and those born in Karachi. The poor without job security or with very lowly-paid jobs either remain renters or become owner-occupiers in smoothly-developing bastis.

In the fifth place, there is a difference between the two basti types with regard to the organization. Bastis with smooth development often have organizations for the basti's betterment, in which individual dwellers strongly participate, especially in the initial stages of the basti's life, when often its very survival is being threatened. In bastis with partial initial development, on the other hand, participation on the part of the residents is often very weak, or non-existent. Those who have organized the settlement continue to act as middlemen between residents and the government when further improvements are required. As by definition these middlemen are the ones who have access to the government machinery, there is little reason for the individual dwellers to participate actively in residents' organization.

It is, finally, of interest to compare pace and achievements of the development in the two basti types. The figures presented in Tables 2 and 3 reveal much of these differences.

Table 2. Average House Index, Average Distribution of House Types and Average Age, According to Type of Basti (post-Partition settlements with smooth development)

Type of basti(†)	N	Average index	House type (%)							Average age (yrs)
			I	II	III	IV	V	VI	S	
0	5	-122	6	29	18	35	7	4	-	4.2
1	27	- 27	3	9	27	46	14	2	-	12.6
2	21	- 1	1	4	14	63	15	3	-	19
3	11	+ 32	-	1	8	62	22	7	-	25
4	18	+ 67	-	3	7	47	25	16	-	24

Table 3. Average House Index, Average Distribution of House Types and Average Age, According to Type of Basti (post-Partition settlements with partial initial development)

Type of basti(†)	N	Average index	House type (%)							Average age (yrs)
			I	II	III	IV	V	VI	S	
0	non-existent									
1	21	-116	27	15	14	37	6	1	-	3
2	3	+ 40	1	1	4	53	36	5	-	7
3	14	+ 41	-	4	7	57	20	12	-	13
4	9	+114	-	1	2	35	33	28	-	21

(†)Numbers refer to the number of hope-giving items present.

Except for a few figures (mostly where N is low, so that some deviations may be attributed to chance), the figures show a pattern of steady development. The percentages found for house types I, II and III continuously decrease; those for house types V and VI continuously increase. Percentages found for house type IV increase in the first stages, and later decrease. Comparison of the tables suggests that bastis with initial partial development develop much quicker than those with smooth development. Not only are the average ages of the different basti types with initial partial development lower than comparable ages in the group of bastis with smooth development. Also the differences between figures in subsequent subgroups tend to be larger in the case of bastis with initial partial development. Finally, comparison of the figures of the last subgroup (4 hope-giving items) shows that a much higher quality in the house conditions is achieved in the case of bastis with initial partial development.

3.2. Stagnating Bastis

A number of bastis stagnate in their development. Although of considerable age, neither has the security level increased much, nor has the condition of the houses improved.

For the great majority of these bastis explicit reasons can be shown why the security levels remains so low. Some of the most prominent reasons are:
- the land belongs to any of the (semi-) public agencies (like Railway Department, Cantonment Board, Port Trust, etc.), whose policy it is not to allow squatters on their land and to try to evict them,
- the bastis find themselves on privately-owned land,
- the bastis are located on land where other destinations are planned, e.g. a hospital, a railway, a commercial area, an extension of a road,
- the bastis find themselves in river beds, and therefore are prone to flood hazards once in a couple of years.

The profile of the house conditions in these bastis somewhat resembles that of the developing bastis with no hope-providing items present. As in the case which we describe here the age of the bastis is much higher, it is justified to speak of stagnation. The inhabitants do not dare to invest in a house built of cement blocks, as "the bulldozer may appear any day."

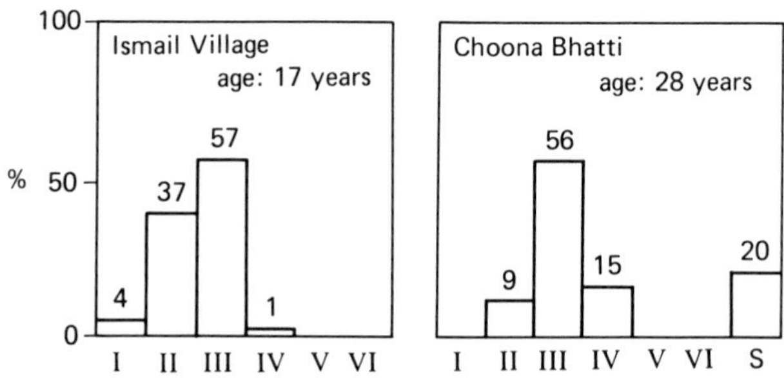

Fig. 15. House Conditions in Some Selected Stagnating Bastis.

It should be noted, however, that the reason for not developing is in many cases not inherent, but can be manipulated. Research in one such basti revealed that there was a great potential for improvement, provided security of tenure could be obtained.[14] When in one basti of this type the security status changed, the physical conditions quickly developed to such an extent that the basti could thereupon qualify for the type group of bastis with smooth development.[15]

This last example also shows that the difference between stagnating and smoothly-developing bastis is only gradual. In fact, many of the developing bastis have known periods of stagnation in their lifetime.

In a number of the stagnating bastis located close to or in the heart of the city, house type S (the double storeyed hut) occurs, which is conspicuously absent in all the other basti types. Here, the inhabitants have made an investment in their house by building a storey, but this investment has not enhanced the permanency of the house. Clearly, lack of security of tenure, combined with population pressure, gives rise to this house type.

Regarding the functions of stagnating bastis, research revealed that they do not particularly serve as transit stations to fresh migrants, but rather tend to have a fairly stable population. The hypothesis that stagnating bastis house the socially ill-adapted element of the society (like drug addicts, prostitutes and criminals) was totally refuted during research. There are, however, indications that a number of the stagnating bastis of Karachi house the economically weakest sections of the population. This is quite understandable as prices of land in these bastis tend to be relatively low, in view of the low security level.
Besides, very many of the stagnating bastis are located close to job opportunities.[16]

4. PRE-PARTITION SETTLEMENTS

Settlements dating back before Partition are - with very few exceptions - passively urbanized villages, or "goths" as they are called locally. There are some problems in subdividing them further with the help of the criteria "security", "physical development" and "age".

Obviously, in the case of goths, age has to be considered as a constant factor, as the villages are much older than the parts of the city which surround them now. Differences between, for example, a 80 years old and a 120 years old goth do not seem to be very relevant in our context.

In the same way, security of tenure has to be treated as a constant factor: the villages were established long ago and many inhabitants hold very genuine claims to the land they occupy, sometimes even supported by documentary evidence. Generally, the authorities respect these claims, which is quite understandable, as, for instance, in a number of cases the grandfathers of the present inhabitants are buried in the goth's graveyard.

Thus, in the case of the goths, from the three criteria, the condition of the houses is the only one usable for the sake of further classification.

However, again here, a complication occurs. In squatter settlements, house-types tend to cluster around the one type that is the most common in the particular basti. In the goths, however, there is a wide dispersion of the types. Quite often, all the types from I-VI are represented and the diagrams mostly show several peaks. Figure 16 illustrates our point.

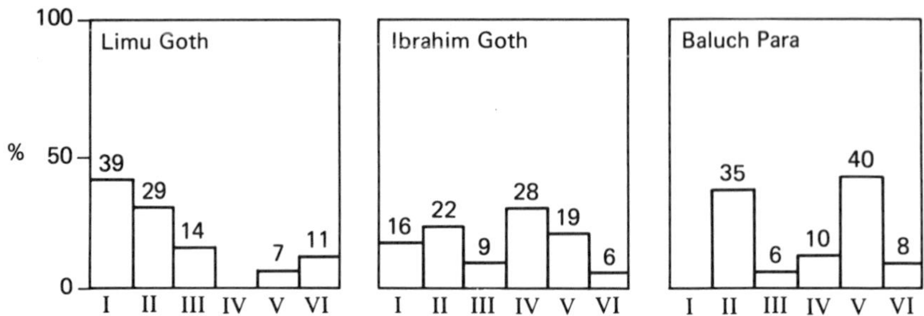

Fig. 16. House Conditions in Some Selected Goths of Karachi

Elsewhere, we have tried to explain this phenomenon.[17] What is important here, is that the index of the house conditions, which in fact represents a sort of average, is not very meaningful in the case of the goths, as it does not reveal the distribution of the different types.

We have, however, ranked the pre-Partition settlements of Karachi according to the accumulated percentages of house types IV, V and VI. By doing so, we found that the highest-ranking settlements are located in or close by the city's centre. The farther one goes from the centre, the lower is their percentage of houses of categories IV, V and VI.

We may conclude that the condition of the houses in goths has developed more, the longer these settlements have been part of the city. Thus, in a way, the age of urbanized goths still plays a role, if understood as a measurement of the time that the goths have been incorporated in the city. Although the process of development is somewhat different from what is common in squatter settlements, the goths too show a potential for improvement. What is more important, this potential is being made use of by the inhabitants, just as we found is the case of the squatter settlements.

REFERENCES

1. For information on these settlements, see: T. E. L. Van Pinxteren, Mini slum in a posh locality, Karachi, 1974.
2. For a more elaborate circumscription of the concept, vide: J. J. van der Linden, *The bastis of Karachi, Types and Dynamics*, Amsterdam 1977, pp. 40-41.
3. Institute of economic research, Osaka: Rural-urban migration and pattern of employment in Pakistan, Osaka, 1978, p. 29.
   Karachi Shehri Huquq Committee: Karachi, a city of contrasts, Karachi 1979, p. 26.
   KMC (PEM-Wing), Salient information on katchi abadis in Karachi, Karachi, 1978.
4. J. F. C. Turner, Uncontrolled urban settlement, problems and policies, in G. Breese (ed.), The city in newly developing countries, Prentice Hall, 1969.
5. See J. J. van der Linden, *op. cit.*, Ch. II, IV, V and VIII.2.

6. The index was found by attributing a negative multiplicand to the percentages of houses found in categories S (multipl. -4), I (multipl. -3), II (multipl. -2) and III (multipl. -1), and a positive multiplicand to house types V (multipl. +1) and VI (multipl. +3). House type IV was attributed a multiplicand = 0. Indices thus calculated range from -247 to +270.
7. Indices of house conditions have been clustered arbitrarily in such a way that groups of 50 bastis are formed (horizontally in the table).
8. J. van der Harst, Low income housing, Karachi, 1974, passim.
9. See, for instance, A. Ahsan, Historical development of Chanesar Goth, Karachi, 1972; R. A. Chughtai, T. E. L. van Pinxteren, H. Kiestra and M. H. Weijs, Miran Naka, Karachi, 1975; J. van der Harst, *op. cit.*, p. 16; J. J. van der Linden, *op. cit.*, pp. 168-170, 172-174, 182-185, 189-191 and 197-199.
10. Pakka: baked, solid, strong, firm, lasting, permanent.
11. J. F. C. Turner, Housing priorities, settlement patterns and urban development in modernizing countries. AIP-Journal, Vol. XXXIV, 1968, pp. 354-363.
12. See J. J. van der Linden, *op. cit.*, pp. 236-238. A. Nooyens, Immigration and intra-urban migration in Karachi, Pakistan, Tilburg, 1981.
13. Many relatively well-off inhabitants of smoothly developing - or even stagnating - bastis, who can afford to move to a subdivision, do not do so for various reasons, amongst which location, family-ties and many more factors play a role (see J. J. van der Linden, *op. cit.*, p. 251). On the other hand, many refugees from Bangladesh, apparently having nowhere else to go, bought plots in cheap but far-off subdivisions, immediately after their arrival in Karachi.
14. JRP-IV, Usmania Muhajir Colony, Karachi 1975.
15. J. J. van der Linden, *op. cit.*, p. 232-233.
16. *Ibid.* pp. 234-248, and App. V.6 - V.16.
17. See J. J. van der Linden, The squatters' house as a source of security. Elsewhere in this book.

Fig. 17. House type I.

Fig. 18. House type III.

Figs. 19,20. Streets in bastis with smooth development.

Fig. 21. Basti with partial initial development in an early stage.

Fig. 22. Basti with partial initial development.

Fig. 23. Basti with partial initial development.

Fig. 24. Basti in riverbed: the right side is stagnating in its development; houses on the left side are protected against floods by a raised floor.

Fig. 25. Stagnating basti with houses of type S.

Fig. 26. Stagnating basti in a riverbed after a wild flood.

Financing Housing in the Slums of Karachi

J. van der Harst*

One of the studies, made in the first half of the seventies within the framework of the Joint Research Project IV, concerned the housing-conditions in the slums of Karachi, the cost of housing and the way in which slum-dwellers finance their housing.[1]

1. FOUR TYPES OF HOUSING OF FREQUENT OCCURRENCE

Walking through the slums of Karachi, one can observe many types of housing. Besides dwellings which consist mainly of reed or tin, one comes across dwellings which have two or more storeys and have been built with reinforced concrete. Further, dwellings are striking which have been erected with mud, and those with wooden walls and roofing tiles.

Within this variety of housing four types of housing can be distinguished, which are of rather frequent occurrence. These are the jhuggis,[2] consisting mainly of reed-mats and cane, the mudhouses, dwellings with concrete walls and dwellings which have the walls as well as the roof consisting of concrete. The third kind is often called "semi-pakka" and the last kind "pakka".[3]

Underneath a description is given of the most important characteristics of the four types of housing. One distinguishing mark, the investment costs, has been based on data, collected in 1973. In view of the price-increases, which have occurred since then, the nominal costs are not reported, only the ratio's between them.

1.1. A Jhuggi

The construction of a jhuggi is quite simple. The most common building materials used, are cane for the frame and reed-mats for the walls and the roof. As the supply of reed-mats is diminishing, these mats are sometimes

*Some parts of this article have appeared in J. van der Harst, Factors affecting housing improvement in low-income communities, Karachi, Pakistan. In *Ekistics*, 1975, Vol. 39, no. 235, pp. 394-397.

substituted by jute, plastic, tins, metal, oil barrels or wooden planks.

Putting up a jhuggi requires no special skill; it can be built within a few days. Taking into account that the investment cost is relatively low (the cost of a jhuggi amounts roughly to a seventh part of the cost of an equally large semi-pakka dwelling), it is not surprising that new settlers mostly start with this type of housing.

Because of its building materials a jhuggi offers bad protection against fire, burglary, dust, weather conditions and impolite glances from outsiders. Another disadvantage concerns the short durability of the building materials. The durability of reed-mats, for instance, can be estimated at about one year only. This implies that the recurrent costs are rather high. A jhuggi is therefore often considered as a provisional form of housing. Its various elements are often gradually replaced by more solid building materials.

1.2. A Mudhouse

A mudhouse can be built in several ways. The following three building methods are of frequent occurrence:

(a) Wet mud is piled up to a height of 2 to 3 feet. This low wall is left to dry so as to get hard. After having dried, the wall is once more loaded with mud up to a height of 5 to 6 feet. When the second part has dried a final quantity of mud is piled up to a height of about 8 feet.

(b) The second method works with sun-baked mudbricks. The dwellers themselves prefer this method, as it makes the walls strong, erect and also looks better.

(c) The third way of constructing a mud wall consists of plastering a wall made of reed-mats and cane. The advantage of this type of construction is that in heavy rains the mud may wash off but the hut remains intact due to its frame.

Building a mudhouse is labour-consuming. The dwellers who have been interviewed about this all claimed to have built the dwelling themselves. Mostly, they spent one or two hours a day on building the house after finishing their daily work. This way it sometimes took months before the house was finished.

It is necessary to plaster the walls and the roof now and again with a mixture of mud, dung and water, especially after rain. The mudhouse originates from the rural areas, where agricultural work is irregular, thus enabling people to spend more time on the maintenance of their houses.

The investment cost is relatively low. A mudhouse costs roughly as much as an equally large jhuggi. In spite of its relatively low cost, however, this type is not as popular as a semi-pakka house. The long period of construction and the regular maintenance ask very much "do-it-yourself" labour from the dweller, who, because of his daily job hardly finds the time or the energy for it. Besides, as more houses surround a mudhouse (which is the case in an expanding city like Karachi), it becomes necessary to travel further for the mud, which again is a burden for the dweller. A mudhouse appears to ask too much time and labour from a city dweller.

1.3. A Semi-pakka House

Of all building materials cement blocks are the most important for semi-pakka houses (and also for pakka houses). The walls of rooms, verandahs, courtyards, kitchens, bathrooms and toilets are built with these blocks. The durability of a semi-pakka house is substantially extended by plastering the walls. Blocks are also used up to plinth level in the foundation. The roofs of semi-pakka houses are made of asbestos or corrugated iron sheets.

The construction procedure of a semi-pakka house differs somewhat from that of a jhuggi or a mudhouse. A jhuggi or a mudhouse is completely built by the dwellers themselves. When building a semi-pakka house, it is normal for the dwellers to hire labourers and buy the building materials themselves. The dweller rarely does the masonry himself which is by far the greatest part of the labour. He does not feel himself capable of doing this work; masonry is considered skilled labour. What does happen is that the dweller helps as an unskilled labourer. This way he has the advantage of saving labour expenses as well as being able to check the progress made with the building. As a matter of fact, the dweller is often present on the site as supervisor, so as to check the work and the supply of building materials.

When taking the investment cost into consideration, a semi-pakka house is relatively expensive. Its cost is roughly seven times as much as the cost of a jhuggi or a mudhouse of the same size.

1.4. A Pakka House

A pakka house is distinguished by its roof and its foundation. The roof is made of reinforced concrete, so that it can be used as a floor for a second storey. In order to carry these heavy elements the foundation is especially consolidated.

Building a pakka house is so complicated that the dweller prefers to leave the whole organization to a contractor. The contractor has the necessary capital goods at his disposal and knows how much labour and building material is needed. However, this does not prevent the dweller from checking the proceedings occasionally. On this point the construction procedure of a semi-pakka house differs from that of a pakka house. With the building of a semi-pakka house the dweller is organizer as well as supervisor, while with a pakka construction the dweller is supervisor, but the contractor is the organizer.

It is quite clear, that a pakka house is the most expensive of the four types of housing. The investment cost is almost twice as high as the cost of an equally large semi-pakka house.

2. FINANCING METHODS

As the incomes are low, slum-dwellers have used several methods to finance their housing. Incurring loans, membership of a bisi-committee, savings and sale of property are the most common methods used.

Distribution of the financing methods

Financing methods	
loans	48%
bisi	32%
savings	55%
sale of property	19%

Combinations of different methods are of course also applied.

2.1. Loans

Roughly one out of every two heads of the household has borrowed money to finance a relatively large investment in a house. The fact, that the money will be used for building on illegal land, makes it difficult to find institutionalized lenders. One cannot expect support from the mortgage concerns. Another difficulty is, that the lenders are reluctant to provide loans to people, who don't have a stable economic position. Amongst the borrowers almost 70% were committed to friends or relatives for a loan. Thirty percent of the borrowers could apply for a loan from their employers. Suppliers of building materials, such as blockmakers ("thala walas"), and small contractors ("mistari's") are willing to give credit to their clients. One out of every five borrowers has built his house by means of this kind of supplier credit.

2.1.1. Loans from relatives and friends

The loan taken from relatives and friends, on which almost 70% of the borrowers call, is a special kind of arrangement. Borrowing money from relatives or friends is not coupled to any specific conditions. There is no instalment schedule, not even a very rough one. Payment of interest on this loan is considered unacceptable. The philosophy behind this appears to be, that lending money to a friend or a family member is doing him a kind turn, to which conditions ought not to be linked. The borrower can pay back, when it suits him, paying interest is considered very impolite, and a guarantee is out of the question. Another part of the philosophy may be, that the borrower can return the friendly gesture, either in an immaterial form like respect and friendship, or by means of a service, or in kind. These friendly gestures may be considered the interest, which has to be paid on the loan, the duration of which is not permitted to be fixed. Redemption of these loans takes place within 3 years in the majority of cases. However, loans not paid off within 5 years, are not exceptional.

2.1.2. Loans from the employer

The loans obtained from the employer are contracted on a businesslike basis. Thirty percent of the borrowers make use of this arrangement. The borrowers receive the loan in advance. The employer deducts a fixed amount from the monthly income until the loan has been completely redeemed. In all of the cases the loans were bearing no interests. About two out of every three loans obtained from an employer are not higher than Rs 1000.- (level 1973). The instalment schedules do not exceed a period of 2 years in two thirds of the cases.

2.1.3. Loans from blockmakers or mistaris

Amongst the borrowers almost 20% finance their housing with a supplier credit given by blockmakers or mistaris (the small contractors).

The blockmakers or mistaris have their business near the borrower. There is hardly any danger, that the borrower will disappear without paying off his debt. The supply, viz. building materials or labour put into the house, forms a kind of guarantee in itself.

The procedure with these loans seems to be, that a considerable amount of the purchase, e.g. one quarter or one half of the price, has to be paid at the moment of supply, while the rest can be paid in instalments. The verbal agreement normally is, that the loan will be redeemed within 1 year or earlier, although in practice this period seems to be often exceeded.

2.2. The Bisi-committee

The bisi-committee is a pecuniary organization, which is popular amongst the low-income groups. Actually, about one out of every three respondents, used this financing method for investing in his house.

The bisi-committee is a vestige from a far past, when the society was still socio-economically static. In spite of the banks with all their branches, the saving bonds with favourable conditions and other financial facilities available nowadays, this institution is still operative.

A bisi-committee consists of members, who are related to each other in some way. For example originally belonging to the same village up country, being a member of the same baraderi,[4] living in a neighbourhood for quite some time, and contributing to the same union might be a basis for such a relationship. A firm relationship amongst the bisi-members is necessary, because a bisi requires mutual trust. Each member pays in an equal amount of money on previously fixed dates. The members agree upon the amount and the period, when starting the bisi. During each period the input (stake) of all members is paid to one of the bisi-members. The duration of the bisi is as long as the number of the members multiplied by the length of each period. If, for instance, 10 members contribute to a bisi each month, the duration of the bisi is 10 months.

The output (pot) of a bisi is equal to the number of members multiplied by the amount of money agreed upon. If, for instance, 10 members contribute Rs 10 each month, the outturn to one of the members is Rs 100 per month. All bisi-members obtain their share. Some get the output in the beginning of the committee's existence, others later on.

In some committees drawing of lots determines the lucky member. In others, the one, who needs the money most urgently at that particular time, will receive the output. When there is more than one deserving case, the members arrange a meeting to discuss the problem. The committees that pay first those who need the money most urgently, bear the marks of an insurance institution.

The member, who received the output in the beginning of the bisi's existence, is debtor until the last member has received his share. This is the reason, why the members have to trust each other. Some respondents told us, that they will never become a member of a new bisi, because the last one ended in a big quarrel. (If a member loses his job, he is often forced to withdraw, and the other members will of course disapprove.)

The one, whose payment takes place at the end of the bisi, can be considered a depositor or saver. The latter is worse off in today's society, because a bank would have paid him interest. Ninety percent of the members of various committees took care that the monthly stake did not amount to more than 25% of the household income. About one out of every two bisi-members was reluctant to pay more than 10% of the household income. Since membership of a bisi creates an obligation, which in the majority of cases lasts longer than 1 year, the members are careful not to put too heavy a burden on their income. Compared with the borrowers, of whom 33% incurred loans with instalments exceeding 25% of their household income, the monthly stakes of the bisi are a relatively lighter burden.

On the one hand, the obligation of the monthly stake is, of course, disliked. However, some respondents mentioned, that the obligation enables them to save a considerable amount of money. "Suppose, I keep the money at home. At the end of the month I am not disciplined enough not to touch the money. Without a committee I cannot save so much money". Besides, since most respondents do not have a bank account, the savings kept at home are not always safe from burglars.

A respondent in Angara Goth rented out one room for Rs 25 per month (level 1973). He contributed these Rs 25 to a bisi, which consisted of 36 members. When it was his turn to take the pot of Rs 900, he built another room with the money. He also let out the second room for Rs 30 per month, this amount he put in a second bisi. Nowadays it is no longer necessary for him to have tenants about the place. He financed a 3-room semi-pakka house by means of two bisi-committees, the stakes of which were equal to the rental value of his two rooms.

We observed, that the redemption of a loan from relatives or friends is sometimes attuned to a bisi-committee. The question: "When will the loan be paid back?", is sometimes answered with: "When it is our turn to take the bisi-output." Membership of a bisi seems to be considered a guarantee for a loan, if, of course, the pot has not yet been paid to the borrower concerned.

2.3. Saving

More than one out of every two respondents has saved for the highest investment in his housing. The data we gathered about saving are not that revealing, because three quarters of the savers could not possibly assess how much they had approximately saved for the investment. The reason they gave was, that they never kept an exact account of their savings. Since the savings as a percentage of the monthly income vary each month, it is impossible to detect a regular pattern.

2.4. Sale of Property

Almost 20% of the respondents sold property in order to be able to invest in their housing. The percentage is small, but it represents the most touching way of raising money.

In order to obtain an illegal foothold in the city, the dwellers sold their property, which had always given them financial security, for instance, ornaments, legal real estate up country, part of a business, or a provident fund. As the occupation of the land concerned is illegal, they took a risk when selling their property for housing.

3. CONCLUSION

Regarding the cost of housing, there appears to exist an enormous variety from the inexpensive jhuggi to the pakka house. Within this range, practically everybody can somehow or other house himself, provided he can avail of a piece of land.

Summarizing some main findings on the way of financing housing, the most important fact perhaps is that absolutely no use is made - or even can be made - of institutionalized lenders. Yet, one out of every two interviewers has managed to obtain a loan.

Amounts borrowed generally are of a modest size and redemption periods are relatively short, especially when compared with institutionalized mortgaging periods. One obvious reason for the relatively small loans taken for relatively short periods, is their informal nature. Having no officially recognized collateral, it is difficult - if not impossible - for poor people to secure substantial and/or long-term loans. Besides, however, it can also be assumed that the nature of the loans taken also fits the squatters' circumstances better. As many of them live in great insecurity, engaging in long-term and/or heavy strictly-to-be-observed obligations would entail too great a risk and would undo the flexibility in spending which probably is one of the very means through which the poor can survive.

REFERENCES

1. J. van der Harst, Cost of residing of low-income groups (mimeo.) Karachi, 1974; *idem*, Low-income housing (mimeo.), Karachi, 1974.
2. Jhuggi - hut.
3. Pakka - baked, strong, solid, firm, lasting, permanent.
4. Baraderi - brotherhood, small community, patrilinear group of relatives.

The Squatter's House as a Source of Security*

J. J. van der Linden

"House-ownership has both economic and psychological functions in the social mobility and social consolidation processes which go into urbanization and industrialization."[1]

1. INTRODUCTION

In connection with a survey of low-income settlements in Karachi, Pakistan, a typology of houses has been developed. As a criterion for the typology the quality of the building materials has been used. From the six house types proposed in the typology, type I represents a very temporary shack, made of e.g. reed matting, and type VI represents a completely permanent house, built of concrete blocks or bricks, and with reinforced concrete roofing; types II through V represent types - with increasing permanency - in between these extremes.

Samples were taken from most squatter settlements and passively urbanized villages in Karachi,[2] so that a profile of the house conditions in each of these settlements could be constructed on the basis of the distribution of the different house types. Amongst the things that can be learned from these profiles is a remarkable difference between the condition of houses in squatter settlements and passively urbanized villages, or "goths" as they are called locally.

When the profiles are represented in diagrams, those of the squatter settlements mostly show a rather narrow and steep curve, having one peak. This peak tends to move from left to right according to the age of the settlement. The curves of the goths, on the other hand, are much flatter, and show more than one peak in most of the cases. The following diagrams illustrate this point.

The diagrams of the squatter settlements suggest steady development, whereas in the goths, development seems to take place in sudden bursts. It is also remarkable that some houses in the goths are of a very good quality (type VI), which is indicative of a very highly perceived level of security: people do not invest in relatively expensive houses as long as there is a threat that their houses may be bulldozed. However, it looks as though not all the goth dwellers are able or willing to translate this feeling of security into investments in their houses, as the squatters do. To explain this difference, some hypotheses could be formulated and tested.

*Earlier, this article appeared in *Ekistics*, 1981, Vol. 48, pp. 44-48.

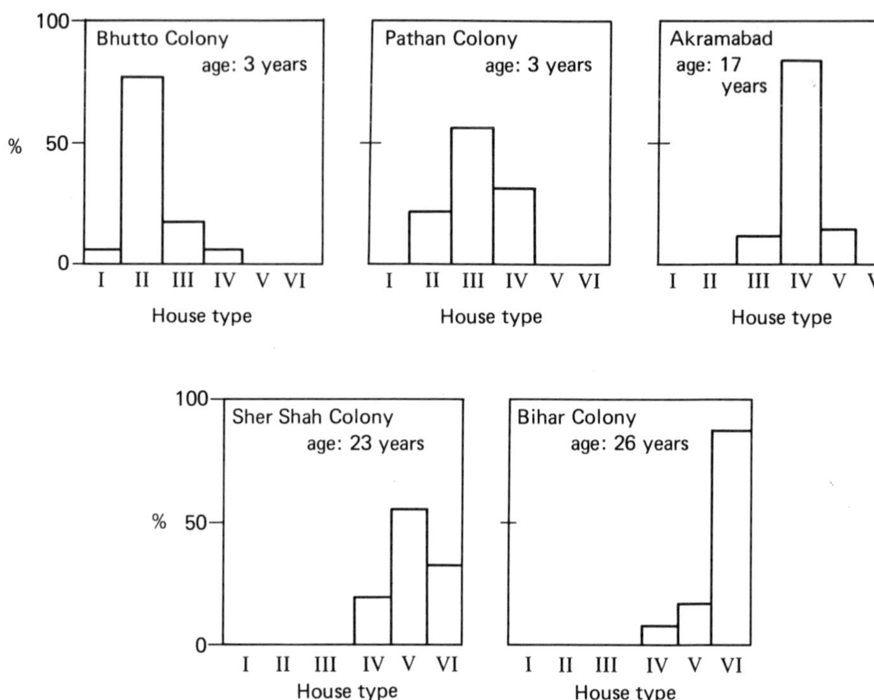

Fig. 27. Distribution of house types in selected settlements in Karachi.*

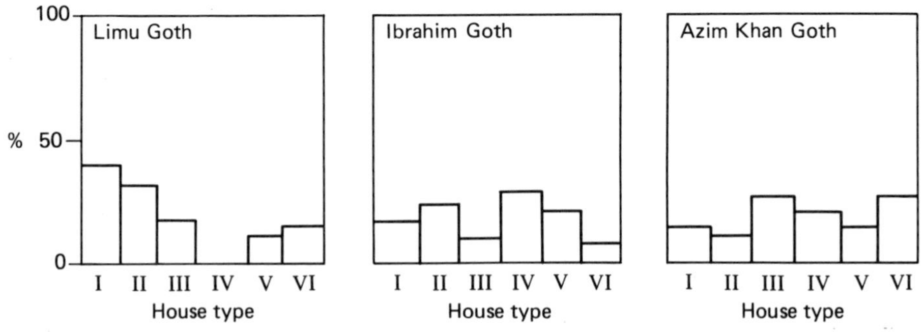

Fig. 28. House conditions in selected goths of Karachi.

*Conditions of security in Pathan Colony are relatively favourable which explains its quicker development compared with Bhutto Colony, which is as old.

2. THE HYPOTHESES

A most obvious explanation for the difference found could be the economic position of those goth dwellers who live in relatively poor houses. Indeed, the goth dwellers themselves, when asked to explain the occurrence of sometimes very primitive huts alongside rather sophisticated houses, invariably argued that difference in income explained this situation. Although, upon investigation, these differences proved to be real, it also appeared that incomes of the hut dwellers in goths were not prohibitive of more investments in housing. Many squatters, having equal or even lower incomes made much higher investments, even under less favourable circumstances of tenure. Thus, rather than an absolute shortage of financial means on the part of some goth dwellers, it would seem that their priorities are different.
This assumption would also explain the bursts of improvements to which we referred above. Namely, if the house of the goth dweller has no high priority, we may assume that those who do decide to improve their houses are comparatively "rich", and therefore in a position to make substantial improvements all at once. The squatters, on the other hand, both "rich" and poor,[3] appear to constantly invest every little bit they can save, and their houses continually improve. This squatters' investment behaviour is quite common and is widely reported from other places[4] as well as from Karachi itself.[5]

In view, however, of the different behaviour of the goth dwellers, the squatters' behaviour may not be as self-evident as is sometimes suggested.[6] In the literature, some reasons are stipulated why squatters take so much interest in their houses. Several authors[7] have suggested that, to the squatter, the house serves as "a substitute for the loss of the traditional security of the local kinship network ..... and the inaccessibility of institutionalized insurance, enjoyed only by the relatively wealthy".[8] Besides, it is sometimes suggested that squatters, lacking other visible (e.g. cattle, implements) or invisible (ancestry) symbols, need the house as a symbol of status and/or achievement more than villagers do.[9] Based on these indications, we have hypothesized that migrant squatters in Karachi attach a higher priority to their houses than natives do, because the house enhances the security of the dweller and because it is an important symbol of his status and achievement.

3. THE RESEARCH

We will describe here our findings upon investigations amongst a small sample of 25 migrant squatters and an equal number of goth dwellers.[10]

In order to find evidence about the difference in priority which goth dwellers and migrant squatters attach to their houses, we asked our interviewees the following question:

> "Some people live in a kachcha house or a hut although they can (afford to) build a pakka house.[11] They find other things more important. Are there - in your opinion - such people in this area? If yes, what then is the more important thing in their opinion?"

Both categories - goth dwellers and squatters - agreed that such people lived in their areas, although standards of the meaning "can afford to" may widely differ. Replies to the second half of the question (regarding alternative ways of spending money) are quite revealing of the different priorities attached to the house.

Table 1. Frequency of Replies Regarding Alternative Ways of Spending Money by "Rich" People Living in "Inferior" Houses

Category		Reply	Frequency of the reply by	
			Goth dwellers	Squatters
Negative + Unable to imagine		Miserliness	1	5
		Spends on women	-	1
		Is illiterate	1	-
		No idea	-	7
	total		2	13
Neutral		Matter of custom	-	2
		No lease	7	2
		Not planning to live permanently	-	5
	total		7	9
Real alternative spending		Save for hard times	5	1
		Business	4	-
		Wedding	4	-
		Education children	1	-
		Cattle	1	-
		Gold	1	-
		Send home	-	2
	total		16	3

The figures of this table convincingly support our expectation that squatters find it natural to attach a high priority to investing in their houses. They have no high regard for those who could but do not invest in their houses. In many cases, it seems as though they admit that the phenomenon occurs, but they cannot imagine why anybody should behave that way. In the goths, the phenomenon is regarded as normal, with only very few exceptions.

Regarding "status" and "achievement" our research has not led to an unambiguous result, although tendencies found point in the direction of the hypothesis. Probably a main shortcoming of this part of the research has been that we have not been able to find the right expressions to circumscribe concepts like "status", "position", etc. Further investigation in this field is required.

The three questions pertaining to security, however, have resulted in replies which can enhance our insight in this matter. One question was about the respondent's possibility to obtain a loan, if he should need one for a special purpose, and - if the reply was in the affirmative - from what source he would get it. Replies to this question are recorded in Table 2.

Apparently, squatters can obtain loans as easily as goth dwellers.[12] This is contrary to what could be predicted on the basis of our hypothesis. However, when looking at the sources of loans, we can see that goth dwellers can get loans more often from traditional kinship sources: these score 2½ times higher than for the squatters. Squatters appear to rely more frequently on non-kinship sources which we may assume to require some kind of security, at least more often than would be the case when kinship sources are relied upon.[13] Here, it is of interest to note that the "non-kinship sources" of loans are still very much informal. Squatters cannot just mortgage their house, since they are illegal occupants of the place they live in. Therefore, when the expression "on basis of the house" is used, this indicates that the house serves as a security, against which some "rich" people, or professional informal money-lenders are willing to give a loan. Sometimes, it is not easy to distinguish between borrowing from neighbours and borrowing on the basis of the house, as a quotation from an interview on the subject may illustrate.

"Everybody around knows that I have spent Rs 3000,- on this house. So my neighbours know that I would not run away, and when my wife had to be admitted in the hospital, I could borrow from my neighbours."

Table 2. Possibility of Obtaining Loans and Sources of Loans

Possibility		Source	Frequency of the reply by Goth dwellers	Squatters
No		-	8	8
Yes		Relatives	5	5
		Baraderi (community of relatives)	8	1
		Qaum (tribe)	2	-
	total	Relatives, Baraderi, Qaum	15	6
		Neighbours/friends	1	4
		Employer	-	3
		On basis of house	1	4
	Total	Neighbours, employers, house	2	11

Our second question regarding the house as a source of security was about the safest way for low-income people to keep money. Table 3 gives a review of the respondents' first choices.

Table 3. Opinions on Safest Way to Keep Money, First Choices Only

Way of keeping money	Frequency of the reply by Goth dwellers	Squatters
Build a house	13	19
Invest in business	9	3
Keep in a bank	2	3
Buy animals	1	-

Although the result is not very decisive, it can be seen that squatters have a higher preference for investing in their houses than goth dwellers, who, in their turn, invest as readily in business or keep their money in a bank. Perhaps, the most clear indication of the house's function as a source of security can be found from the replies to a third question on this matter, namely the question how a family would deal with a crisis situation. To this end we asked our respondents what their families would do if the respondent fell seriously ill. The next table shows the result.

It can be easily seen from this table that the squatters rely on self help in an emergency situation much more than the goth dwellers. Apparently, the goth dwellers can get help more often from informal sources than the squatters. Very clearly, in the great majority of the cases, the self help of squatters takes the shape of relying on the house as an asset of security to a far greater extent than the goth dwellers do.

Table 4. Frequencies of Replies to the Question What Respondent's Family Would Do If Respondent Fell Seriously Ill

Category		Reply	Frequency of the reply* by Goth dwellers	Squatters
Self help		Sell house	1	17
		Mortgage house	1	-
	total	Relying on house	2	17
		Sell savings	3	4
		Wife will work	-	3
	total	Self help	5	24
Help from others		Loan/help relatives	19	4
		Loan/help neighbours	3	1
		Loan/help friends	1	1
	total	Loan/help from informal sources	23	6
		Loan/help employer	1	2
		Loan/not specified	-	2
	total	Help from others	24	10

*Total replies in both categories (Goth dwellers and Squatters) add up to over 25, as sometimes more than one answer was given.

4. CONCLUSIONS AND SOME TENTATIVE IMPLICATIONS

Although the research described was limited in scope: the sample was very small and problems have not been dealt with in a very exhaustive way, it has, however, given sufficient evidence to show that to migrant squatters their house is much more than a mere shelter.

We may safely conclude that in many cases, to the migrant squatter the house serves also as a source of socio-economic security. If this proposition is valid, at least three tentative implications are worth considering.

(a) Firstly, this function of the squatter's house is just one more cause of the failure of so many officially launched "low-cost housing schemes". Namely, as long as the dweller cannot call his abode (however modest it may be) his own, and especially as long as he is under long-term financial obligations (however "soft" these may be), he lacks the security he would otherwise derive from his house. A quotation from an interview may underline this point.[14]
"We were given a quarter in New Karachi (official low-cost housing scheme, JL) on rent, but after some time, I fell ill and we had no savings, so after a few months, we had to leave that house, and now we are back again in an illegal settlement."

(b) Secondly, the squatters' eagerness to save and invest his savings in his house could be one more reason for authorities to respect and support the existing informal systems, rather than opposing them, as quite often is the case.[15] No doubt, in the existing informal systems there are many injustices - e.g. in the allocation and distribution of scarce resources. Here, the Government could take a regulatory role without destroying the system which at least performs some basic functions which cannot be easily replaced.

(c) In the third place, there is reason to raise some doubts about the effectiveness of loan schemes for building purposes. Van der Harst has shown that about 50% of the Karachi squatters take informal loans when building their houses.[16] These loans, however, tend to be rather small.

Both the informal nature and the small amounts of loans are in ance with our findings on the house's security function. It i doubtful if squatters - and especially the most needy among the take much interest in formal loans. In fact, instead of helpin borrower, the ultimate result of taking such a loan might be tha it diminishes his security position. Since many squatters seem to obtain the kind of loan which they feel they can manage without too much of a problem, the result of an official loan scheme might well be that only somewhat better-off people can afford the risk of taking such a loan. Consequently, it would be the relatively wealthy sections of the population who would ultimately profit from subsidized interest rates, which are a common feature of such loan schemes.

REFERENCES

1. L. R. Peattie, Social issues in housing. In B. J. Frieden and W. W. Nash (eds.): *Shaping an urban future*, MIT-Press '69, p. 26.
2. The total sample comprises of 20,310 houses in 190 squatter settlements and 60 passively urbanized villages of Karachi. For more detailed methodological notes, see J. J. van der Linden: *The bastis of Karachi, Types and Dynamics*, Amsterdam, 1977, pp. 84-109.
3. Interestingly, a survey in a Karachi squatter settlement revealed that the relation between household income and type of house is much weaker than the relation between housetype and the hope the dweller has that his house will not be demolished. See *JRP IV: Usmania Mohajir Colony*, Karachi, 1975, pp. 50-51.
4. See among many others:
   L. A. Eyre, The shantytowns of Montego Bay, Jamaica, *Ekistics* Vol. XXXVI, 1973, pp. 132-138. J. F. C. Turner, *Housing by people*, London, 1976.
   W. Mangin, Squatter settlements. In: *Scientific American*, Vol. CCXVII, 1967, pp. 21-29. R. S. McNamara, Annual speech of the President of the World Bank, 1975, Washington.
5. A. P. van Huyck, Towards a housing policy for Karachi. In: *Morning News*, Saturday, 18-III-'72, Karachi.
   Master Plan Department K.D.A.: *Karachi Development Plan 1974-1985*, p. 24, 1974, Karachi.
   J. J. van der Linden, *op. cit.* Chapter VII, IX and XI.
6. For example, H. Fathy, *Architecture for the poor*, p. 33, Chicago, 1973.
7. J. F. C. Turner and R. Goetze, Environmental security and housing input, 1967, *Ekistics*, Vol. XXIII, pp. 123-128. W. Mangin, Latin American squatter settlements, a problem and a solution, 1967, In: *Latin American Research Review*, Vol. II, pp. 65-98. L. R. Peattie, *op. cit.* G. Vernez, *A housing services policy for low income urban families in underdeveloped countries*, New York, 1976.
8. H. Caminos, J. F. C. Turner and I. A. Steffian, *Urban dwelling environments*, 1969, Cambridge, p. vii.
9. A. E. Alcock, K. N. Misra, J. L. McGairl and G. B. Patel, Self help housing 1962, Methods and practices, *Ekistics*, Vol. XVI, pp. 81-87,
   W. Alonso, The form of cities in developing countries, *Regional Science*, 1964, *Association papers*, Vol. XIII, pp. 165-173.
   J. F. C. Turner, Housing as a support system, *Architectural Design*, 4/76 pp. 222-226.
10. For more details on sampling: see van der Linden, *op. cit.*, pp. 134-135.
11. Kachcha: clay-built, half done, without use of cement, Pakka: solid, lasting, permanent.
12. See J. van der Harst, *Low income housing*, Karachi, 1974, p. 57.

13. Apparently, also squatters do rely upon their kinship network, albeit to a much lesser degree than do the goth dwellers. Therefore, the statement quoted in 2 (see note 8) appears to be exaggerated, although Table 2 also indicates that it contains a substantial amount of truth.
14. See also J. F. C. Turner, Housing as a support system, *op. cit.* and T. L. Sudra, *Low income housing system in Mexico City*, Cambridge, 1976.
15. R. Martin, Comments in Architectural design 4/76, 1976, p. 223,
16. J. van der Harst, *op. cit.*, pp. 57-67.

Class Structure in a Basti, the Relation Between Resistance on the Urban District Level and Class Struggle*

H. Meyerink and R. Vekemans

1. INTRODUCTION

This article is a much-abridged account of a field study which we carried out in a small popular district of Karachi, in 1978. The integration of the basti in the urban system, the conflicts this integration entailed and the residents' reaction, constitute the central theme of this article.

First, we will give a brief review of the basti's history, with special attention to its relation with the city. After this, we shall analyze the class structure,[1] the labour conditions and the consequences for social struggle of the basti's inhabitants. In the next paragraph, we shall describe how these inhabitants view the social reality of which they are a part. Finally, we return to the kind of resistance on urban district level as we found it was offered by the basti dwellers and indicate the relationship with class struggle.

Figures mentioned were collected in a survey which we carried out on 6 October, 1978, amongst approximately 80% of the households. Also, we took twenty in-depth interviews from different residents. Quotations are from these interviews.

2. THE BASTI AND THE CITY

The study took place in Arababad, a small popular district ("basti") on the edge of the large central city area. It is a basti where some 1275 inhabitants, or 220 households, live on one hectare of land. Including the area of the narrow lanes, the average area per dwelling is slightly over 40 m^2. There is, of course, substantial crowding. In the basti, there are five community standposts. Streets are unpaved and mostly have a dead end (see map).

---

*A Dutch version of this article was published earlier in *Zone*, no. 11, 1979, pp. 31-59.

The first houses of Arababad were built shortly after Partition, i.e. in 1947. With the departure of the colonial rulers, the cantonment areas located just outside the then city boundaries, were also deserted. A part of the hundreds of thousands of refugees from India settled in those vacated areas. During the first years after Partition, refugees chaotically squatted wherever they could find a place in their desperate struggle for shelter. In this period squatting and self-help building took place quite unhampered. From 1947-1958, Arababad was a more or less independent settlement on "useless" land at the outskirts of the city.

After 10 years, there were some 150 reed hutments (jhuggis). The residents' life was relatively peaceful and unthreatened. However, Karachi's rapid growth all around Arababad could not go unnoticed. A belt of residential areas for middle and higher-income groups was developed around the British colonial city. One of the elite housing societies, Sindi Muslim Cooperative Housing Society, made a claim on the land on which Arababad was built. In this area, the Housing Society wanted to develop a playground and a park, rather than tolerate the eyesore called "Arababad" within their "posh" district.[2]

On several occasions in the basti's history, upon insistence of the Housing Society, the urban authorities Karachi Metropolitan Corporation (KMC) attempted to evict the basti dwellers and sent in the bulldozers of the demolition squad. However, again and again, the inhabitants managed to postpone the execution through demonstrations and legal steps, in which the help of politicians and other influential people was involved. Until this day, the basti is inhabited illegally and the threat of the bulldozer is very real.

What is important is that, with the rapid expansion of the city, claims to the land of the basti became stronger. The old city's periphery was opened up and incorporated in the city. The urban population kept growing and the shortage of houses and land close to the city's centre increased.

At the time of our study, spatially, Arababad is fully incorporated in the urban network. From a peripheral area it has now become part of the centre. This can be observed from maps 1, 2 and 3 of Meyerink's article on Karachi's development. On these maps, the location of Arababad has been marked by a black dot.

Along with this development, pressure on the land of Arababad has increased enormously. The poor, especially, are forced to live close to their jobs. In Arababad, it appeared that 30% of the inhabitants had previously lived in the city's periphery. However, distance to jobs (in the centre) was too great, and, as a consequence, expenses on transport were too high. Because of the high price of land in or close to the centre, these people are now forced to live in miserable and very insecure circumstances. There is no more room in the basti. It can be observed that during Arababad's history, less and less plots were squatted upon by fresh inhabitants, and more and more plots were bought at gradually higher prices. The land rent mechanism results in enormous rises in prices, especially in the neighbouring districts, like the area of the Cooperative Housing Society. In 25 years, land prices here rose from Rs 3.50 to Rs 500,- per square yard.[3] Because of its illegal status and the resulting risks of living in Arababad, the rise in land prices was relatively less here. Because of this only, the basti is still the residence of very low-income people.

3. THE PHYSICAL STRUCTURE OF THE BASTI

Initially, all the houses were built of reed matting. Especially during the past 15 years, the houses have been rebuilt of more solid material. Because of the high sums involved in improving a house and because of the low and unstable incomes, only a few people can afford to rebuild their houses all at once. Mostly, improvements are brought about bit by bit. This is a never-ending process, as by the time a house is more or less finished, the older parts have to be replaced again. Nowadays, concrete blocks and corrugated iron roof-sheets are the most common building materials. The quality of the blocks is very poor, however. Because of the extremely high sand/cement ratio applied, the blocks are affected during rains. Plastering would give a better protection, but few people in the basti can afford this extra investment. The enormous rises in the cement price (on the black market, the price increased 2,5 fold since last year), have now almost halted the improvement process.

The first public standpost was constructed only in 1975, i.e. 28 years after the area became inhabited. Many applications, bribes and support of politicians (during election campaigns) have finally resulted in five community standposts. Initially, water would run from 12 p.m. to 4 a.m. only, so that the inhabitants had to wake up late at night and await their turn in line. In 1976, the Minister of Local Bodies agreed to a constant water supply. Sewerage is almost completely lacking. For waste water, most inhabitants have a soakpit which is easily overburdened; nightsoil is collected in an empty battery-box which has to be emptied somewhere in the neighbourhood. About 20 houses are connected to an informally-constructed sewerage system. Only a few households have electricity in their houses. To most families, the costs of a connection and the necessary bribe are prohibitive. The inhabitants themselves take care of the maintenance of the lanes. Waste is dumped in two garbage dumps just outside Arababad.

4. THE BASTI DWELLER'S SOCIO-ECONOMIC SITUATION

In order to gain some perspective, we have drawn comparisons regarding occupational and income-structure, between Arababad and Karachi as a whole. From the figures, it appears that in Arababad a relatively larger part of the working population is employed in the secondary sector than in the city as a whole. Although relatively fewer men work in the large-scale industries, there are more job opportunities in the small-scale sector and building industry for Arababad than for Karachi. However, a lower percentage from Arababad finds employment in the tertiary sector than from the whole city. It should be noted in this connection, that a large part of the tertiary sector in Arababad consists of informal activities, like hawking and lowly-qualified jobs in the formal sector (e.g. the "peons" in the bureaucracy).

Generally speaking, employment of Arababad's workforce is in the low ranks of the city's employment structure.

Estimates of unemployment provide a grim picture. From the men over 17 years of age, 20% is openly unemployed. In addition, there is much hidden employment[4] and many women do not work.[5] Almost 13% of the women over 17 years of age are single, but do not work outdoors. A comparison between incomes in Arababad and the city, for 1973, shows that incomes in the basti are substantially lower than in the city as a whole.[6] Based on this comparison, the Arababad population can be classified amongst the lowest strata of the urban population. Despite this, there is no question of there being only one social class in Arababad. There are a number of differences in the way the workers participate in the labour process. This fact also has serious consequences for the life in the basti and for the ways in which social struggle takes place.

5. THE ANALYSIS OF CLASSES

In order to clarify the relation between the way of participation in the labour process and the labour- and social circumstances of the basti's population, we have carried out a class analysis in Arababad. In this analysis, we have continually taken account of the particular circumstances that characterize capitalistic countries in the Third World.

Typically, capitalistic development in the Thirld World brought about many changes and in fact upset the whole social structure, but the population of these countries was incorporated in the process in many very different ways. Besides the capitalistic relations in the production process, which were introduced from outside, also pre-capitalistic relations have survived and several new modes of production came into existence in which relations other than capitalistic, prevail. Craftsmen's workshops, home industries, multinational enterprises and local industries with a capitalistic set-up can be found side by side in a chaotic mixture. In fact, the whole population has not been incorporated in relations of wage-labour and capital, or, in other words, only part of the population has been proletarized. However, the capitalist way of production is dominant and it determines the direction of development. Capitalistic enterprises hold the strongest competitive positions. Only here, there is substantial growth, concentration and monopolizing. Multinationals operating in these countries alongside petty craftsmen's workshops, are visible evidence of this. Competitive relations are of course rather unequal.

The results of such a complex production apparatus are extreme differences in the development of production techniques (from very primitive to highly-sophisticated techniques), differences in production capacity, productivity and rentability, but also in labour- and social circumstances. The rough distinction between self-employment and wage-labour is inadequate to describe phenomena of this kind. As a result of the incomplete proletarization, there is a mixture of different classes and fractions of classes. This mixture is recognizable on the basti-level, even though economic activities of the basti dwellers are within the lowest strata of the division of labour and although the basti dwellers figure amongst the lowest strata of the urban society.

6. THE CLASS STRUCTURE OF ARABABAD

In the class model, the primary distinction is based upon the relations with the means of production: self-employed/dependent on wage/industrial reserve army. Secondary distinctions for a further categorization are:
- differences in the degree of proletarization,
- differences in levels of technology of the means of production,
- differences in the degree of division of labour,
- differences according to economic sectors: productive, administrative.

The result of such a categorization into classes for the case of Arababad is as follows:[7]

	(N)	(%)
A. Higher specialized proletariat	67	29.5
1. Labourers in modern industry	11	16.4
2. Supervisors/foremen in private enterprises	2	2.3
3. Personnel in Government service	42	62.7
4. Medium-level administrative personnel	3	4.5
5. Drivers in large firms	9	13.4
B. Lower specialized proletariat	62	27.9
1. Labourers in traditional industry	21	33.9
2. Labourers in craftmen's workshops	2	3.3
3. Lower administrative personnel	21	33.9
4. Personnel in shops	13	21.0
5. Drivers in private service	5	8.1
C. The independent petty bourgeoisie	25	11.0
1. Shopkeepers	13	52.0
2. Merchants and Jobbers	3	12.0
3. Owners of craftmen's workshops	9	36.0
D. The industrial reserve army	71	31.3
1. Loose specialized labourers	25	35.2
2. Loose unskilled labourers	17	23.9
3. Street vendors	15	21.1
4. Domestic servants	14	19.7

Category A comprises the so-called labour elite, employed in industries with more than 50 labourers, where modern means of production are used. The productivity of labour and the production capacity are high. In this sector, often multinational capital is involved. Owners of such industries belong to the upper level of the national and international class of capitalists. The fact that some of this "elite" live in a slum like Arababad indicates how relative, and in fact false, the term "elite" is, when used in this context. Another important group within category A is the government personnel. The government apparatus in Karachi consists of a large number of poorly-coordinated bodies,[8] in which there is a range of lowly-qualified labour to be performed. Although a post with the government provides more security than with a private enterprise, wages in the government service are much lower. In Arababad, we came across several government employees who have taken up a side-job in the night in order to survive. Organization and promotion of interests of the government employees is suppressed.

Category B comprises the proletariat employed in small enterprises. Within this class fraction, relations are not always of a capitalist nature. For instance, master-servant relations and family-relations also occur. Production techniques used are old fashioned and much more labour intensive than in modern industry. The productivity is considerably lower. The position of competition with modern industry is very bad. Low wages, long working days and poor labour conditions are the circumstances under which this branch can survive. Other components of this category are the lowly-trained administrative and shop personnel. Labour conditions of especially this last group are extremely poor.

Category C is the group of petty capitalists, the lowest stratum of the urban capitalist class. With some caution, this group can be labelled as the richer and more influential part of the basti's population. Not only do they occupy an economic key position (e.g. regarding the provision of credit to other basti dwellers), but also very often this group plays a role in creating the internal relations of dependence as we have found existing in Arababad.

Category D. An industrial reserve army can be regarded as the rest category of redundant labour that is excluded from the labour process. This group is the reserve of the productive apparatus. As a result, it is either permanently or temporarily outside the sphere of wage-dependency relations. Labour in this category can be characterized as a severe struggle. Labourers in this group try to survive without having any substantial means of production.[9] There is no choice but to accept the dirtiest and lowest-paid jobs under often very insecure circumstances. Examples are street vendors of bric-a-brac, shoe shiners and coolies who offer their services to jobbers in the seaport and who have to see every day whether there is work or not, but also painters, carpenters, plumbers, etc., who cannot find a fixed job and therefore just wait at certain spots in the city, where anybody can come and hire them.

7. THE LABOUR CONDITIONS

For our investigations into the differences between these classes and class fractions, we have confronted the above class model with 6 factors which determine life and labour of the basti dwellers:

1. The income level.
2. The labour stability (in terms of the number of months in 1978 (up to November) during which labour was done).
3. The occupational stability (in terms of the number of years the same occupation was held).
4. The length of the labour day.
5. The basis of the contract (in terms of monthly, weekly or daily payment of wages).
6. Membership of a labour union.

The results of this exercise can be summarized as follows: The highest incomes are scored by the independent petty bourgeoisie, the lowest by the industrial reserve army. For the proletariat and the reserve army, the degree of specialization influences the income level. Generally speaking, the higher specialized proletariat earns higher wages than the lower specialized proletariat. A similar difference is found between specialized and unskilled labourers within the industrial reserve army. The higher specialized personnel in government services earns very low wages compared with other groups in the category "higher specialized proletariat". A similar relation can be concluded from the basis of the contract and membership of a labour union. The higher specialized proletariat scores highest for monthly payment and also is the most organized group. Regarding this last aspect, however, again, the government employees are an exception.

Moreover, formal labour contracts and social insurance hardly exist. The industrial reserve army is the least organized group. It is also this group which scores highest for daily payment. These data indicate the relation between labour security and organization. Also significant is that the higher specialized proletariat has the most regular labour periods, mostly of 8 or 9 hours per day, while the lower specialized proletariat makes much longer working days. The poor position of competition with modern industry, the weak organization of the labourers and their low wages are thus interrelated. To compensate for the difference in wages, longer days have to be made. Amongst the industrial reserve army, very different and irregular working periods were found. Here, much depends on the way self-employed individuals manage to earn their living.

Data on the labour- and occupational stability again reveal the high degree of insecurity which many have to live with. From "elite" to reserve army, the labour stability is very low (except for the government service employees who often earn so little, that they have to take up a side-job). Change of jobs is the most frequent amongst the lower specialized proletariat, and especially amongst personnel in shops. Occupational stability is very high for government employees, but not for labourers in modern industry: again it appears that the label "elite" is not much justified in their case. Labour stability is high amongst the independent petty bourgeoisie, but also amongst the industrial reserve army. For this last group, the stability is an indication of the degree of consolidation of this reserve army. It reflects the difficulty, if not impossibility, for this group to find other jobs. Thus, this stability is very negative: it is only for the lack of something better that some continue to do the lowly-paid and very insecure jobs.

The most striking features of the labour conditions of Arababad's inhabitants are the high degree of labour insecurity and the low incomes. The tone of many of the interviews we took, was gloomy. Many live close to a mere subsistence level, and incomes tend to decrease. Life, work and future are insecure. Not being able to save in fact means working for staying alive. Again and again this has struck us, and we were often deeply impressed by what we heard during such interviews.

> "During the past five years, I have been a painter. Although during this period, my income has increased substantially, life has become more difficult. In the same period, prices have risen fourfold. The question of saving does not arise. Sometimes, I even have to borrow, because we cannot make ends meet when I have found no work for some time. We have to economize on everything. Only twice in a week, we have some meat, milk we take only in tea and eggs we practically never eat. I do not take breakfast, I just take some tea in the morning, in the afternoon, mostly I eat roti-dal, and in the evening roti-sabzi.[10] If things get still worse, we shall have to eat less. I am afraid that prices will keep rising. We shall be in trouble. I can say nothing regarding my income. There is so much unemployment. It is difficult to find work. If you ask too much, they take somebody else. Previously, painters used to stand up for each other. If one painter was engaged by somebody who thought that the wage was too high, or that the work was not fast or good enough, and he wanted to kick such a painter out, then there was no other painter to replace him. Now everybody is forced to take whatever he can. It's the prices sahib.[11] There are few chances, one has to struggle hard, there are many unemployed. Finding a different job is hardly possible. How can I pay the bribes for that? And how do I get recommendations? I have no influential acquaintances. Practically all people in Arababad live this way. You ask whether changes will take place? I can say nothing about that, I do not know. The rises in prices have hit us badly, especially mentally. We cannot bring up our children properly, we cannot give them food and clothes. This is worrying us a lot. We are afraid of the future."

Characteristic of all the inhabitants of Arababad is their low position in the urban social stratification and in the divison of labour. Yet, not all the inhabitants belong to one and the same class. When classes are distinguished according to the way of participation in the labour process, there are differences which result in different social adversaries: some have no boss or patron, others continually change bosses. Regarding class positions, then, the Arababad dwellers have very little in common. There are, however, similarities resulting from the labour conditions. Very general is the insecure situation in life. Except for those in established government posts, no one enjoys institutionalized social insurance. The inhabitants are poorly organized, they work long days and earn a low wage. Because of these common labour conditions, there are also similarities in the life circumstances, e.g. in terms of consumption levels. All have to struggle for their daily survival, on the edge of subsistence. A number of the social shortcomings are crystallized on the basti level: the illegality, the continuous threat of being evicted, the low level of facilities, the poor quality of the houses, etc. etc.

8. THE IMAGE OF SOCIETY AND CHANGE

It is of importance to investigate how the shared life circumstances affect the inhabitants' awareness of their own situation. In this way, it can be seen how the dominant ideology manages to mould the inhabitants' social awareness, how it subjects them, and how it makes them adapt themselves to their "fate" of continuous discrimination. Knowledge of this social awareness can lead to an interpretation of the form of resistance, of social struggle fought from the basti. With a number of quotations from interviews, we will now try and clarify the relations between social contrasts, the perceivedly shared suppression in the urban power structure, domination and the basti dwellers' attitude towards domination.

> "Five years ago, I earned Rs 100.- per day as a jobber. I always had contracts running. We could afford much. Nowadays, things are bad, and we have to borrow. I will repay, when I have contracts again. When in business, one has to accept such things. Sometimes, you make large profits, sometimes you lose. This also happens to the big industrialists. But those big industrialists have good relations with the government. Therefore, I think they can better cope with rising prices, for instance of cement. Industrialists have acquaintances and relatives on high government posts. We do not have such contacts ...
> ... I am a religious person, I believe in God. This is the system as God wants it to be. We should not oppose it. The Prophet was poor, He lived like a beggar. This is the way we should also be. The rich are not very religious, because if they were, they would share their wealth with others, and they would be more sincere in paying taxes."

> "It is very difficult to live here in great insecurity. I cannot tell how much chance there is for getting a lease, but as far as I am concerned, I have not "one anna" hope.[12] They can evict you at any moment. In this way, we have lived here for twenty years. Still, we live here illegally. We do not have hope for the future. Everything is in vain. People of the bungalows around us think that here, it is dirty and crowded. They can easily say so from their nice spacious houses. They think that we have to move. But KMC does not do a thing for us, and that is why it is dirty here. During Bhutto, at least something was moving.[13] We got water, and some have got electricity. But the new government does not listen to us. Last year, they said that all katchi abadis would be regularized.[14] But they only promise. They lie. We can do nothing about it. We are powerless. We do not know where to go. We

are not even allowed to have our committee anymore. Because of Martial Law, everybody is afraid. Nobody dares to organize anything. (...). Wealth is there for the rich and poverty for the poor. The rich live in beautiful bungalows, while the poor have to accommodate themselves in katchi abadis. We cannot bring up our children properly. Our children will be poor too. It is logical that things are as they are, but it is bad. When it rains, I get wet while the richman is sleeping in his bed. That is bad. What to do when my child falls ill, and when I cannot find work? How shall I carry on if my son dies and I shall be left alone? The government should provide more jobs, and more factories. I don't understand why the government does not do that. But they know what is best for us."

"People live in katchi abadis because of sheer poverty. While the rich make much profit, we are poor. We have to work very hard to stay alive. The whole family is dependent upon one person. Every now and then, we even have to borrow to keep our family alive. When later I earn slightly more, I have to repay what I borrowed. This way we can never save. At the same time, the capitalists make much profit from our labour, and they become ever richer. Look at my hands. They are rough. I work for 12 hours per day and with that I earn Rs 30.- to Rs 35.-. Every other week, I am in the night shift. When I change from night-to day-shift, I work 24 hours on a stretch, because I work every day of the week. We work like horses, and yet we cannot fill stomachs. Always, when at work, there is fear in our hearts that something will happen at home, that they come to chase us away from our houses, that they will destroy everything we have built here ourselves with hard labour. While we work, our bosses take all the profits. We are like stones on the road. We are being kicked from one side to the other, but together, we form the road on which the car goes. The government always promises us all kinds of things, and always we hope that they will do something for us. But every government finishes its term and disappears. And after each term, nothing has changed in our situation. We can no more trust any government. We can no more believe that the government will do something for us. During election campaigns they always promise. Several times, they have promised us that they would regularize our colony, but nothing ever happened. They only say so to gain votes. Much in this country needs to be changed. We can have no more hope for a new government with again fresh promises. The change will be difficult. Every day, people are being murdered, the newspapers are full of it. If we try to change something, there is blood in the streets. Labourers are always victimized. Has ever a leader died in such a conflict? It is always the men of the street. Therefore, everybody is afraid to fight. None of the strikes which we organized, have succeeded. When we strike for 5 days, we cannot work 5 days. By the end of the 5 days, we have no more money and we are hungry. Meanwhile, the capitalist in his bungalow just waits until we come back. Or he engages other labourers. That is no problem because of the present-day unemployment. If we try to found a labour union, we are sacked immediately. How then can we fight, sahib? Now the time has come we can only think of working and eating. If there is not enough to eat, we skip one meal. Getting sufficient food is now our only concern. We have given up. And all around us we see the rich spending lots of money. We can only think what it would be like if we too had so much money to send our children to school."

A large part of the basti dwellers does not share the more radical awareness apparent in the last quotation. From the results of twenty interviews, we may conclude that the large majority of the basti dwellers recognizes a number of social antagonisms, of which, after all, they are the subjects. In most cases, however, no step is taken beyond the mere recognition of the results of these antagonisms, like the contrast between rich and poor which is considered almost as an unavoidable phenomenon, and a bad government that will not listen. Relations between labour- and living conditions, class antagonism and exploitation of labour, and the resulting antagonism in terms of consumption, are mostly not made conscious. Moreover, those who are conscious of these relations and who mention structural causes of the situation in which they are caught, show much fear of a confrontation with the dominating class.[15] The powerlessness perceived is very great and most interviewees are hardly aware that they could play a role in a process of change.

In this way, there is an effective system of control on the ideological level, in which the existing hierarchical structure manifests itself as the people's dependent awareness. The subjection is not so strong that the lower classes fully resign themselves to the state of affairs, but resistance manifests itself by again and again betting on points of application within the system. "Solutions" are of an ad-hoc, pragmatic, short-term nature. Necessarily, for such solutions, continuous appeals are made to the urban hierarchy. When there is a threat of demolition of the basti, politicians are approached, and appeals are made to the highest authorities. The mere fact that this course of action is taken, reinforces the power, influence, position of the authorities, and it provides them with the opportunity to show how benevolent they are. In its turn, to the basti dwellers, this again is the "proof" that pragmatic solutions are feasible.

Illustrative in this connection is also the manipulating of the basti dwellers with promises during election campaigns, and characteristic of the basti dwellers' pragmatism is the fact that they wholeheartedly make use of events like election campaigns in order to obtain the needed facilities.

9. RESISTANCE AND ORGANIZATION ON THE BASTI LEVEL

Resistance on the basti dwellers' part is manifest in different forms:
- resistance against demolition,
- struggle for facilities,
- struggle for legalization.

The danger of demolition is a result of the struggle for urban space. Other social groups make claims to the land on which the basti's inhabitants live. In the case of Arababad, these claims are being made by Housing Societies around the basti, and by a Christian organization which claims that the basti has been built on their graveyard. This last organization brought a court case against one of the basti's leaders. However, the case was lost because of lack of evidence. The Sindhi Muslim Cooperative Housing Society, on whose land the larger part of Arabadad is located (a small part of it belongs to another Cooperative Housing Society) has invoked government help three times with the aim of evicting the dwellers. These threats were the immediate cause of the founding of a basti dwellers' organization. In a united action, processions were taken out to the (Provincial) Assembly, and appeals were made to a number of Ministers, with whose influence a stay order was obtained. When the most direct threat was averted, the resistance collapsed.

The struggle for urban facilities is of a much less explosive nature, and is undertaken almost exclusively by some prominent basti dwellers, who have assumed the role of leaders. Success in this struggle is achieved via contacts with politicians. Moreover, the few successes are concentrated in periods of elections. During election campaigns, politicians regularly visit the basti and make promises. On such occasions, much money is spent on the organization of a tea-party, in order to "win" such politicians' favour.

As regards legalization, the basti dwellers have very little hope. The last bits of hope evaporated soon after Martial Law was installed in July 1977. Feelings of helplessness and bitterness are now dominant.

> "We live here for the last thirty years. And still we live illegally and unsafely. We are being considered as garbage. No government does a thing for the poor. Our only hope is God. The government only gives land far away, in the desert. We cannot live there. There is no water, there are no buses. We have told them that we live here for thirty years already. They throw us back thirty years. Why do not they allow us to live here? The government is always against the poor and does not do a thing for the poor. We have voted for them, during the elections, when they promised so much. Once they have the power, we never see them again.
>
> This will not change. New people, new promises. But they do not care about us, there are no poor people in the Assembly."

The different forms of resistance, as existing in Arababad, illustrate how effective the control mechanism is. The unity coming about under the most direct threat of eviction, disappears once the danger has vanished for the time being. The status of dependence to which the basti dwellers resign themselves, takes shape in the organizations which exist(ed) in Arababad. These organizations are always characterized by a strong internal hierarchy, in which some prominent persons from the basti figure as natural leaders on whom the basti dwellers fully rely. One result of a poorly functioning democratic control on these leaders is that they use their position to reinforce and enlarge their influence in the basti. Also in their contacts with the outside world, these organizations reinforce dependence, for the leaders always run behind those having high positions in politics or administration. Besides, the leaders are involved in a personal struggle for power which is fought on the backs of the common basti dwellers. Different leaders have contacts with different politicians and high government employees. In this way, party-political antagonisms on the urban level are introduced into the basti. Sometimes a confusing competition between leaders with their personal followings dominates the basti scene.

A rather eye-catching aspect of leadership in Arababad is that regarding class position, all leaders belong to the independent petty bourgeoisie. By continuously betting on high politicians, the basti is being manoeuvred into a kind of blackmail position. The politician grants certain favours to the basti in exchange for votes. The rendering of this service is so much expatiated on, that it seems as though the politician is on the side of the basti dwellers and as though he is concerned about them. Thus, the control over the distribution of public facilities is a main instrument of the government to control the basti itself.

Regarding resistance, it appears that the main pattern is one of being incorporated and controlled, which leads to an even greater dependence. The background of this mechanism is the position of Arababad and its inhabitants within the urban structure, a position that cannot fail to create all kinds of conflicts. Organization on the basti level is, no doubt, one of the main weapons in such conflicts, but at the same time, organization is both the result and affirmation of the control mechanism.

Yet, we believe that his dependent thinking does not necessarily imply that every form of resistance is bound to be incorporated and to end in a failure. The continuous threat to the very existence of the basti is the logical result of developments in the urban growth process. Recognition of the structural character of this threat is certainly possible and resistance on the urban district level provides a main organizational framework to channel social struggle. Spontaneous actions can issue into more durable forms of resistance, which can play a role in the overall social struggle and indeed are an indispensable aspect of it.

10. CONCLUSION: THE BASTI'S STRUGGLE AND CLASS STRUGGLE

Although in this article, the central focus is on dwelling environment and struggle on the district level, it is important to determine the place of such a struggle within the overall social struggle. The effects of basti resistance on social change should not be overrated. Struggle on the district level finds its roots in consumptive demands and therefore is a limited struggle. In this struggle, the issue is not the appropriation of the means of production, but the distribution of consumptive items. The question of the division of social power is not directly raised.

The main social antagonism is the direct result of production relations characteristic of the dependent capitalist mode of production. This antagonism finds its roots in the extraction of surplus value. The surplus value created by free wage-labourers is expropriated directly by the owner of the means of production, in exchange for wage. Therefore the relation between the two classes is one of exploitation which constitutes the main antagonism within the social relations. This antagonism is so fundamental that it cannot be solved within the capitalist social structure. Only when the system of private property of the means of production is abolished, and with it, capitalism as a social system has disappeared, would this antagonism also vanish. Dwelling environments and housing problems are fields where social antagonisms are manifested very sharply, and where they are easily recognizable by the people. Yet, these are only secondary antagonisms.

The distribution of the scarce product "housing" is extremely unequal. In Karachi, only a privileged minority has access to the formal market of the capitalist building sector. Spatial segregation is a direct expression of the antagonism between social groups. In Karachi, the different class positions are very accurately reflected in the different locations. In the struggle against this situation - i.e. for instance, the struggle against demolition and for urban facilities - the main elements of the exploitation mechanism are not being attacked. This does not imply that the housing conditions cannot improve under the existing social structure. Practice in Karachi and Arababad shows that indeed under pressure of basti inhabitants certain improvements can be extorted without the whole society shaking on its foundations. On the contrary, we consider it as one of the government's functions to maintain law and order, and the social structure, in exchange for certain improvements. Logically, in these processes, the urban power structure is not being questioned. This is the limitation of the struggle for urban space as a means of obtaining social power.

Viewed from the basti dwellers' point, however, the role that struggle on the basti level could play, should not be underrated either. We have concluded in the above that the basti dwellers' class positions do not automatically lead to a clear recognition of the causes of social problems or even of the direct social adversaries. Many of the basti dwellers have temporary, irregular and/or very insecure jobs. Not all work within relations of wage-dependence and not all belong to the industrial reserve army. Several have to subsist as independent labourers. A rather large part of the basti's population is not permanently dependent on wages and hardly has access to formal ways of earning a living. This position, however, does provide a common starting point on which a social movement can be based, namely the common direct interests of the basti dwellers in their role as users of urban space. The community aspects are implied on the one hand in similarities in housing- and living conditions, in the physical environment, on the other hand, in the daily efforts which all have to make in order to survive. All are subject to the threats to the existence of the basti. Such aspects are the direct consequences of the inhabitants' labour conditions: insecure and/or temporary jobs against low wages, or no work at all.

However, not the labour conditions as such are shared, but the derived collective consumption (public facilities) and private consumption (housing, food, clothing). Urban segregation results in the formation of districts in which people cluster who share the same problems. In other words, the shared problems are to a great extent geographically determined. The clustering of interest groups, in its turn, makes the occurrence of clashes between those groups very probable, if not unavoidable. Basti dwellers are not the only category of users of urban space. There are other social groups, more powerful than the basti dwellers. There are project developers, land owners and speculators. It is clear that these can bank on government's support, because the accumulation of capital is involved in the use of urban space that touches upon the necessary conditions for production (like office-space, roads). Sometimes, the government itself assumes the role of the land owner and disputes the use of land against both capitalist groups and basti dwellers.

Thus, resistance on the basti level is needed. As in these conflicts the opposed interests are direct results of the social positions of groups within the urban class structure, it is justified to speak of class struggle for the use of space.[16] Dependent on conjunctural or political circumstances, the interest antagonisms can assume the shape of organized resistance by urban social groups. With this, we mean somewhat long-term organized and collective actions. These actions can have manifold aims, but somehow or other the established urban order is being questioned because of the direct interests of the lowest social classes in the city. In this way, on the spatial level, district resistance can achieve the very important binding elements which cannot be achieved on the level of labour conditions. Therefore, district resistance forms the necessary basis to the basti dwellers to rid themselves of their dependent position and to reach open protest and open struggle against the consequences of class society, and ultimately against class society itself. Thus, resistance on the district level can assume the form of a protest movement against the total established urban order.

REFERENCES

1. For this, we made use of the class model which R. Janssen used in Bogota, following Castells in Santiago de Chile.
   See R. Janssen. Wij hebben zelfs geen recht op de stad, Amsterdam, 1978, pp. 142-146.
   M. Castells, La Luche de clases en Chile, Buenos Aires, 1974.
2. In the words of a spokesman of the Society: "We cannot allow those people in the heart of the city, where land is so precious and valuable (....) Arababad is the black spot in our decent society."
3. Rs 1.-- is equal to approximately U.S. $0.10.
   One square yard is approximately 0.94 m^2.
4. This is apparent, for instance, from the relatively large numbers of personnel in minuscule shops and workshops. Underpayment is often a concomitant phenomenon.
5. Women - especially in the lower classes - are not expected to work outside the house. Older, but not yet married women who have no household tasks, can in the cultural context be considered as redundant labour. Deeper investigations into the field of household and other female labour was impossible to us, since we are males.
6. In 1973, almost 45% of the households in Karachi had an income below Rs 300.-- in Arababad, this percentage was slightly over 60.80% of the Karachi households was under the Rs 500.-- line; in Arababad 85%. Apparently, the income situation in Arababad was worse than in the city as a whole.
7. Data on which this class analysis is based were collected during interviews of 83% of the heads of households in Arababad. Use was made of a questionnaire. Demographic and technical data on the basti were also obtained from these interviews. Twenty free in-depth interviews have provided us the necessary insight into living- and labour conditions, basti life and struggle and into ideological aspects.
8. In fact, it is not correct to speak of "the" government apparatus in Karachi, because there are dozens of government organizations with more or less power which operate with a fair degree of autonomy. The division of functions amongst these institutions is very shady. As, in our view, these institutions cannot possibly enjoy complete autonomy towards the existing social structures, but instead perform a supportive and reaffirmative function towards these structures, we believe that it is justified to call the much fragmented institutions with one name. See for instance: T. J. Segaar, *Karachi en de basti*, Amsterdam, 1975, pp. 60-64.
9. In fact, in this connection, the term "redundant" is not completely justified, because the reserve army has important functions to the established system. Precisely because the reserve army is a source of labour from which it can be tapped at will, it provides a brake to the development of wages. Large monopolies can gear their policy to this situation. Also, the reserve army provides goods and services utile to the system. Thus, the concepts of "marginality" and "informal sector", which refer to a group that exist completely outside the system, are in our view incorrect.
10. Roti: bread, dal: pulses, sabzi: vegetables.
11. Sahib: sir.
12. One anna is equal to 1/16 part of a Rupee.
13. Former Prime Minister Z. A. Bhutto was jailed in July 1977 and later executed.
14. Katchi abadis: irregular settlements. One of the announcements made shortly after introduction of Martial Law pertained the regularization of these settlements. Such promises, however, had been made earlier as

well. Bhutto, too, had this issue on his programme.

15. Insight in class antagonisms was somewhat more frequent amongst wage-dependent labourers; a "liberal" ideology was more common amongst the petty bourgeoisie.
16. To avoid misunderstandings, it should be noted that this does not necessarily imply a struggle to the death. The existence of the described structural interest conflicts, in itself implies class struggle. This struggle may be latent for long periods of time and large differences may occur from place to place, even between urban districts of the same city.
    Karachi is an illustrative example of this, since much confrontation can here be easily avoided because of the practically unlimited possibility of horizontal expansion of the city and the consequent liberal use of land. Of course, this does in no way diminish the existence of the interest conflicts.

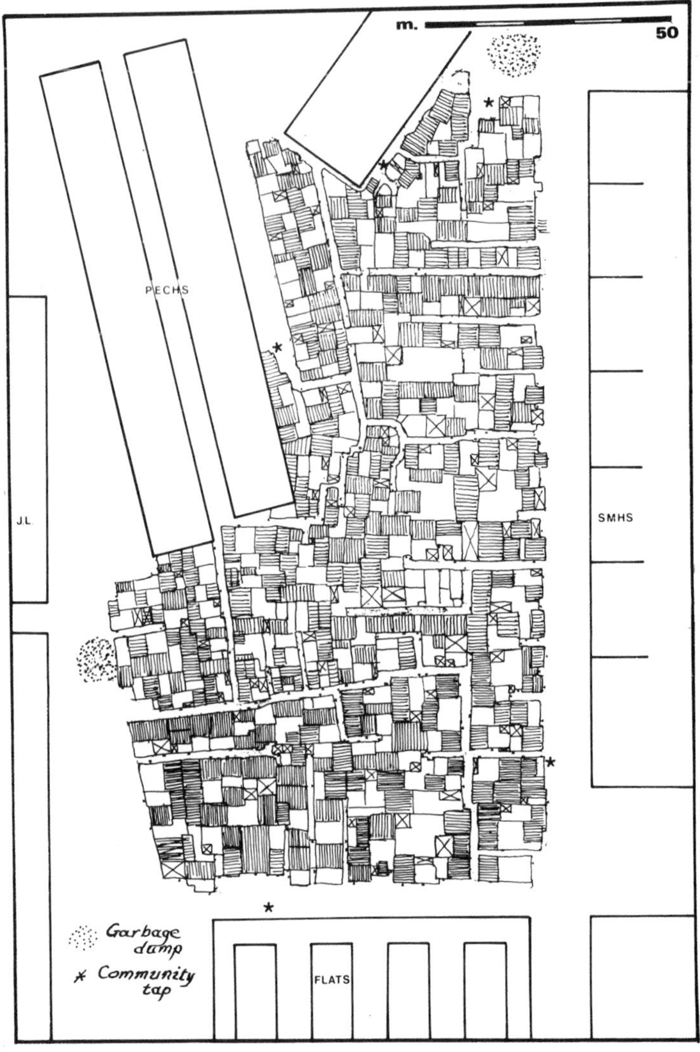

Fig. 29. Sketch plan of Arabadad.

Fig. 30. View of Arabadad.

Part III

Government Housing Policies for Low-income Groups in Karachi

K. S. Yap

The first important government housing programme launched in Karachi after independence was a response to the massive influx of refugees from India. As capital of the new Islamic republic and as main commercial and industrial centre of the country, Karachi attracted large numbers of muslim refugees ("Muhajirs"), who fled an expected domination by Hindus in India. At the time of Partition Karachi had a population of about 300,000 inhabitants, but within 5 years after independence the population went up 5 times.

To shelter these refugees, the authorities in Karachi constructed emergency refugee houses, displaced persons colonies and public servant quarters in areas like Lalukhet, Nazimabad and Landhi. However, the supply (more than 50,000 dwelling units in the period 1947-1958) always lagged behind the enormous demand. Numerous poor refugee families, who could not find shelter in one of these housing projects and could not afford a house in any other area, were forced to squat on vacant land and to construct their own houses.

According to a survey conducted on Karachi in 1959, there were approximately 120,000 shelterless families in the city. Almost 55% of them lived in jhuggi's (structures made of straw) 28% lived in semi-permanent kacha structures of mud and wood, while 15% occupied semi-permanent pakka structures built of bricks.[1] The remaining 2% did not have a house at all. The bulk of the shelterless families (85%) consisted of refugees from India.

After independence, rural-urban migration to Karachi also gained momentum. In particular since the 1960s, numerous migrants from the interior or Pakistan (mainly from Punjab and North-West Frontier Province) have joined the hundreds of thousands of shelterless refugees from India in their search for decent housing in Karachi. The present growth rate of Karachi due to migration is estimated at 2.5% per year, in addition to a similar growth rate due to natural growth. A large portion of this growing population of Karachi lives in vast and rapidly expanding spontaneous settlements, all over the city.

In an attempt to clear the many spontaneous settlements in the centre of Karachi and to resettle the inhabitants in decent houses, the military government of General Ayub Khan invited a Greek firm, Doxiades Associates, to plan and develop low-income residential areas at the outskirts of the city.

This "Greater Karachi Resettlement Programme" was designed at the end of 1959 and comprised the planning and construction of two large satellite towns: Korangi (in the South) and New Karachi (in the North). These two towns, at a distance of 10 and 15 miles from the city centre, would have to become the domicile of 400,000 and 200,000 people respectively, who were expected to be resettled from spontaneous settlements in the centre of Karachi.

The idea behind the programme was to develop these two areas into new towns with all necessary infrastructural facilities and employment opportunities, completely independent from Karachi. In Korangi and New Karachi people could obtain a plot on lease and a (core-) house, which they could further develop according to their needs and resources. The programme was intended to be basically self-financing, as all development costs were supposed to be recovered through the leasing of the plots and the sale of the houses.

In 1964, when about 45,000 of the intended 100,000 dwelling units had been completed, the Greater Karachi Resettlement Programme was discontinued. A number of reasons were mentioned for the termination of the programme.

First of all, the two areas did not develop into independent towns as intended, because many of the planned facilities were not or only insufficiently provided. Schools and medical centres were not completed or only sparsely equipped; the number of job opportunities remained below the anticipated level, because the area did not attract enough industry; and the commercial infrastructure lagged behind the population growth, since investment costs were high.

As a consequence, many inhabitants of Korangi and New Karachi had to travel to Karachi for work and services, and the transport costs weighed heavily on their income. Some of them were eventually forced to sell their house and plot and to return to Karachi to settle again in spontaneous settlements in the city centre. Others did not pay their debts and as a result in Korangi and New Karachi only 70 million rupees have been realized and Rs 116.2 million are in default in spite of the fact that both projects were heavily subsidized. The default in payment by the residents and the heavy subsidies to the programme made it impossible for the government to continue to finance the projects.

Although the Greater Karachi Resettlement Programme was discontinued by the government, the two areas have been further developed and in 1974 Korangi and New Karachi had an estimated population of 500,000 and 200,000 people respectively. The two areas have not become independent satellite towns; they are not predominantly inhabited by low-income families from spontaneous settlements; and although they have definitely contributed to an increase in the housing stock in Karachi, this has not tangibly resulted in a reduction or reduced growth of the spontaneous settlements in Karachi.

In 1965, while looking for a more feasible solution to the housing crisis in Karachi, the government adopted a policy of "plottownship" development. In these plottownships families from spontaneous settlements in Karachi could be resettled. Three major areas were designed and planned for in this programme: Orangi, Baldia and Qasbah, all situated at the northern fringe of the city.

Contrary to the Greater Karachi Resettlement Programme, where serviced plots-plus-core-house were provided, in the plottownships only plots were leased out and basic infrastructure provided, while the residents were expected to construct their entire house themselves. The plots in these areas were also smaller than those in Korangi and New Karachi and the level of infrastructure was lower: e.g. water was supplied through public taps instead of private house connections.

The principle behind the plottownships corresponded to a large extent to the present-day ideas about assisted self-help as advocated by John Turner: the government only provides the basic framework for the low-income groups to cater for their own houses. However, this programme also proved to be only a partial success.

Many people were (forcefully) shifted from inner-city bastis in Karachi to the plottownships long before infrastructure, and in particular drinking water, was supplied to the areas. Moreover, many of the open plots became a prey to speculators, while other parts were encroached upon by squatters. Although the allotment of plots is still going on, the number of plots available is largely insufficient to relieve the acute housing shortage for low-income groups in the city and the programme has remained restricted to the three areas mentioned above.

During the 1970s, two other housing policies for low-income groups were attempted in Karachi. One consisted of a plan to demolish the two major inner-city squatter settlements of Karachi, Lyari and Jacob Lines, and to resettle the occupants in multistoreyed buildings at site. In both areas, some spontaneous settlements were actually demolished and replaced by blocks of flats, but these remained empty or were occupied by higher-income groups. The prices of these flats were far too high for the basti-dwellers they were intended for, and the basti-dwellers also disliked the idea of living in a flat, which requires a completely different life style.

In 1974, the Karachi Development Authority launched the Metroville Programme. Under this programme, people could obtain a plot-plus-utility-wall with connections for water, sewerage, gas and electricity, but were supposed to build their houses themselves according to their needs and resources. Since the start of the programme, one Metroville of 5000 plots near Baldia and Orangi Township has been completed, for which many illegally constructed houses had to be demolished. The area is however only sparsely occupied, while all around Metroville I the illegal settlements are rapidly expanding.

One of the reasons why Metroville has not (yet) been successful is the shortage of water in the area, which makes Metroville I a rather unattractive place to live. Another reason is the price of the plots, about 40 rupees per square yard, which makes plots in Metroville more expensive than a plot in a spontaneous settlement. Thirdly, Metroville has also to some extent fallen prey to speculators.

From the above can be concluded that the authorities in Karachi have gone through a whole range of policies in their attempt to solve the housing crisis for the low-income groups in the city. The policies ranged from resettlement of basti dwellers in flats (Lyari, Jacob Lines) and low-cost houses (Korangi, New Karachi) to various forms of site-and-services projects (Metroville, Baldia, Orangi and Qasbah Township).

All these programmes have definitely contributed towards an expansion of the housing stock in Karachi, but they could not solve the housing problems of the urban poor. On the one hand, the costs of residing in these areas (inclusive of transport costs to work, schools, etc.) were usually too high for the basti dwellers. On the other hand, the number of dwelling units constructed under these programmes was too small in proportion to the enormous housing needs in the city to have a positive effect on demand and prices of houses.

Basic component of all programmes was clearance, i.e. the demolition, of the illegally constructed houses in the bastis and resettlement of the occupants at site or elsewhere. Clearance implies that houses, however rudimentary and illegal, are demolished and capital invested in these houses, however small, is wasted; resettlement implies that the government and the occupants have to invest again in the new housing project and thereby burden the private and public capital and construction market.

In JRP-IV, an attempt was made to calculate the cost of shifting of a population of 6000 people from a basti in Karachi (Usmania Muhajir Colony) to a resettlement area in the north of the city. It appeared that clearance of Usmania Muhajir Colony meant the demolition of residential buildings worth Rs 750,000. For resettlement in the new area, the population would have to pay Rs 100,000 to Rs 400,000 for new plots, dependent on the size of the plot and the number of families per plot. Moreover, transport costs to schools and work would double (figures for 1973).[2]

The only approach which utilizes the investments made by the basti dwellers to a maximum and which minimizes extra contributions by government and individual families is legalization and upgrading of spontaneous settlements. However, cases of legalization and upgrading of bastis were rare in Karachi until the 1970s. Where they took place, they did not form part of an overall programme, but they were *ad hoc* decisions by the authorities due to the political pressure the population of these bastis could exert on the government.

In this way, Khudadad Colony, Hyderabad Colony, Delhi Colony, Mahmoodabad and some parts of Lyari were legalized and upgraded. Basic to this approach was the issue of leases to the occupants and the provision of infrastructure. As a result of legalization and upgrading, none of the above-mentioned bastis can be called a slum any more.

Once they had obtained complete security of tenure, the residents in these areas started to improve their houses, which almost all became completely pakka structures. The improved housing conditions and the infrastructures provided to the areas by the authorities further contributed to an overall improvement of the living conditions in the erstwhile spontaneous settlements, so that they no longer created dangers for the physical health of the residents. In view of the unsuccessful attempts of the government to clear the bastis and resettle the basti dwellers and on the basis of research in legalized and non-legalized spontaneous settlements in Karachi, JRP-IV recommended the authorities in Karachi to abandon the idea of slum-clearance and to start a programme of regularization and improvement of spontaneous settlements. These recommendations, together with similar suggestions from other sides, eventually led to the establishment of the Central Planning Team, the formulation of the Improvement Policy for Sub-standard Urban Areas and the KMC programme of katchi abadi regularization and improvement.

REFERENCES

1. Kachcha - unbaked, clay-built, below a fixed standard, half-done.
   Pakka - baked, strong, solid, firm, lasting, permanent.
   Jhuggi - hut.
2. JRP-IV: Usmania Muhajir Colony - Karachi 1975, pp. 109-113.

The Implementation of the Metroville I Project in Karachi; a Study of the Perception of Various Interest Groups*

Islamuddin Siddiqi

1. THE GENERAL PERSPECTIVE

On 17 March 1970, the Government of Pakistan and the United Nations Development Programme (UNDP/Planning and Development Collaboration International (PADCO) signed a Plan of Operations for the creation of a Master Plan Project in the Karachi Metropolitan Region. The Master Plan Project became operative on 1 February 1971 and had the following objectives:

(a) To prepare an overall development plan for the Karachi metropolitan area, a programme that is to be maintained and modified as necessary, as part of the government's permanent planning activity.
(b) To establish a permanent governmental planning machinery for the guidance of growth in the metropolitan area and the region.
(c) To train the planning staff necessary to sustain such planning.
(d) To identify specific programmes and projects necessary for implementing the overall plan, as a basis for subsequent feasibility studies and project preparation.

To fulfil the above-cited purposes, the roles of the participating agencies in carrying out the project were clearly defined. The United Nations was the executive agency for the project, while the Karachi Development Authority (KDA) acted as the cooperating government agency.[1]

A team of foreign and local professionals were engaged in a vigorous interdisciplinary exercise. As a result, the final report, Karachi Development Plan 1974-1985, was prepared and submitted to the government in August 1974. This voluminous document describes in detail the policies, programmes, and projects recommended for the comprehensive planning and development of Karachi Metropolitan Region.

*This article is an abridged version of the author's M.Sc. Thesis, Bangkok, 1980.

1.2. Metroville Programme

The Master Plan Department (MPD) suggested a new and comprehensive housing policy, together with a programme to implement the policy in Karachi. It included four basic residential development programmes, namely (a) Improvement and Regularization of Unauthorized Areas (IRP), (b) Utility Wall Development (UWD), (c) Open Plot Development (OPD) and (d) High Standard Development (HSD).[2] The Metroville Programme was specifically designed to demonstrate in practice all four housing programmes and the strategy cited above in a single project.

According to the planning and implementing agency, Metroville is defined as a comprehensive programme for developing fully-integrated and viable self-sustaining urban communities. The programme is based on several innovative concepts, new designs and special building techniques. It introduces the new development concept of providing a utility wall with connections for water, sewerage, electricity and gas on smaller plots, to ensure better standards of environmental sanitation, and to offer possibilities of incremental building to match the resources of the low-income target groups, without disturbing their family budget for the higher priorities of food, clothing, etc.

This programme is not aimed at just increasing the housing stock; it is strengthened with a whole series of support programmes. All the agencies responsible for different parts of urban development and related public facilities have made coordinated efforts to ensure the availability of utilities, services and public facilities to the Metroville population. This programme is one of the components of the overall housing programme to be undertaken between 1974-1985 under the recommended Karachi Development Plan, with an emphasis on aided, guided, self-help with the ultimate aim of providing the proper environment for people.[3]

1.2.1. Metroville Programme Objectives[4]

The following are the objectives of the Metroville Programme:

1. To provide the proper range of plot types matching the paying capacity of different income groups, particularly responding to the demand of the lower income groups.
2. To put more emphasis on environmental sanitation conditions by providing water, sewerage, electricity and gas connections, on a utility wall in the kitchen, bath and toilet.
3. To encourage incremental building to match the family budget priorities and family needs; and discourage forced housing standards through built-up houses requiring more payment for housing, and thereby further curtailing the already deficient food budgets.
4. To arrange readily available house building loans to the lower-income groups, to enable them to finance their own housing.
5. To extend technical assistance to self-help builders, train construction labour, and guide building research into low-cost building methods and materials.
6. To provide electricity, gas, treated water supply and proper sewerage system; organize refuse collection, ditch cleaning, street maintenance, police and fire protection.
7. To organize proper health services and population planning programmes to create healthy, planned and prosperous families.
8. To support mother and child care and other social welfare programmes for community development.

9. To conduct adult literacy and public education programmes through mass communication media to develop a sense of civic awareness and community responsibility.
10. To provide sufficient general education and training facilities for the local school age population within the Metroville site.
11. To enhance family incomes by promoting local employment activities, particularly household handicrafts and small industries with loan facilities and vocational training.
12. To provide 40% of the resident labour force, employment opportunities within or nearby the Metroville site, so as to minimize commuting trips, cut down transportation time and cost and reduce the load on the transportation system.

1.2.2. Scope of the Programme[5]

The Metroville Programme is a major component of the Karachi Development Plan 1974-1985, and combined with its integral part - the Slum Improvement Programme - it will play a vital role in guiding future growth and shaping the environmental form of the entire Karachi urban area. The programme will be instrumental in controlling the urban sprawl which continues under heavy squatting thrust, jeopardizing planned development, and threatening the urban environment of this metropolis of over 5 million people.

As spelled out in the Housing Programme of the Karachi Development Plan, about 40,000 dwelling units will be required for housing 200,000 persons added to the city each year according to rather modest population projections. It demands annually 4 Metrovilles for 50,000 persons each, to accommodate the additional population alone. Proper housing for the already existing 1 million squatters may require at least one more Metroville per year under the Slum Improvement Programme.

1.2.3. Future Metrovilles

In order to meet the target of providing 4 Metrovilles each year as per Karachi Development Plan, the Metroville Cell of the Master Plan and Environmental Control Department (MPECD-KDA) has already prepared site plans for new Metrovilles in Karachi.

According to the brochure issued by MPECD-KDA, the preliminary planning studies have been completed for ten new Metrovilles to be located in the following areas of Karachi: Landhi, Qasba, Korangi, Baldia, Khanto, Pipri, Orangi, KDA Scheme 33, near Steel Mill Township and near Port Qasim. These Metrovilles, to be undertaken during the next 5 years, will provide fully serviced plots with utility walls having water, sewerage, gas and electric connections for a population of about half a million, at a cost of about Rs 500 million (US$ 50 million).[6]

The latest information on progress in this regard is that following Metroville I, Qasba Metroville has also been executed. On 1 September 1979, Metroville III was publicly announced with two other KDA schemes, through all local newspapers.

1.3. The Metroville I

1.3.1. Location

After a careful examination of various possible sites, the best was selected for Metroville I. The selected site is South of Orangi Township, very close to Sind Industrial Trading Estate (SITE). It is an excellent site, being nearest to major employment centres in SITE, not very far from the central area of Liaqatabad, Nazimabad and Golimar. It is a location where small firms can easily procure materials and sell their products. The Metroville I market will serve not only the local population but also the surrounding areas; the Metroville I can be linked easily to the adjacent communities of Orangi and Baldia. As a result of its excellent location, the Metroville project will develop rapidly and may command very high land values.[7]

The selected site covers an area of 204 acres, surrounded by panoramic ridges protecting the area from dust storms. The ridge in the south forms the boundary separating it from SITE, but a gap in this ridge connects them together, thus giving easy access to the industrial area.

1.3.2. Project Description[8]

The site has been carefully planned for an ultimate population of 35,000 persons. It provides a maximum number of small plots for low-income families, grouped around 9 small parks and playgrounds and served by 9 schools for children. One large playground is placed in the centre. Larger plots are planned along wider roads to provide easy access for private cars and to improve the aesthetic look of major traffic routes. A site for flats is planned on the 120-feet wide major through traffic road. Cinemas, petrol pumps, and other commercial plots are also to be placed on the major road to get maximum advantage of location and to provide easy access. The main market, health and community centres, police station, post office, site offices and administrative block are to be located near the major road, as one enters the Metroville.

The street network is designed to reinforce the focal points which are potential sites for commercial plots; bus stops are chosen to serve these focal points.

1.3.3. Housing Types[9]

The basic design criterion of Metroville development is the adoption of housing and building techniques that provide adequate services and a flexible community lay-out, while enabling the family to build incrementally using self-help techniques.

Financial assistance in terms of readily available building loans and technical assistance in low-cost building techniques shall be provided to self-builders under the Metroville programme . The capacity to make housing payments and repayment of house building loans will be raised by increasing family incomes through the promotion of local economic activities, particularly household industry, with technical support and vocational training.

The Metroville programme provides a full range of housing types, including open-plot development on 80 and 120 square yard plots and utility-wall development with water, sewerage, electricity and gas connections on a wall and a cemented floor in the kitchen, bath and toilet area. The family would be encouraged to add semi-pakka or pakka structures in accordance with their family budgets and family needs.[10] There will be also high standard development on larger plots of 240 and 400 square yards, with full utilities.

2. OBJECTIVES AND METHODOLOGY

2.1. Objectives and Scope of the Study

The main objective of the study is to assess the perception of the target group and other interest groups regarding the implementation of Metroville I programme, in order to arrive at policy recommendations for future schemes of MPECD-KDA. More specifically, the study addresses the following questions

1. To what extent has the project been implemented as compared to the stated objectives?
2. What has been the response of the target group (selected/allottee households) with respect to their participation and cooperation in the programme?
3. What problems, constraints and bottlenecks are encountered by the concerned agency in the implementation of the project?
4. What is the perception of the residents of adjoining unauthorized settlements about the Metroville I programme?
5. What is the professional planners' assessment of the programme?

2.2. Data Collection

This study is focused on Metroville I only, hence the total area of 200 acres has been covered. For the purpose of drawing a representative sample from the various interest groups involved in the project, various methods and techniques ranging from census, random sample, quota to judgement sample were employed. Information was gathered through mailed questionnaires, interview schedules, free interviews as well as the relevant material available in the library, official reports and records, and local newspaper reports.

The groups directly or indirectly concerned with the Metroville project, and which were contacted, included the following: (a) the resident allottees of the scheme, (b) allottees living elsewhere in Karachi, (c) the residents living in adjoining settlements and (d) the professional planners representing the Pakistan Institute of City and Regional Planning (PICRP), Karachi Chapter. These groups were represented by 11 respondents, i.e. 100%, in the case of the first group (a); 40 respondents, i.e. 1.2% in the case of the second group (b) which comprised altogether 3,385 members; 50 respondents from the third group (c); and 10 planners out of the 20 members of the PICRP, who were present in Karachi at the time of the survey.

3. EXISTING CONDITIONS IN METROVILLE I*

3.1. Occupancy in the Area

Although the first allottee moved to the site in the year 1974, the occupancy rate has in fact been extremely poor. By the end of October 1979, only 11 allottee households were found living in Metroville I. Besides them, there are 137 repatriate families of widows from Bangladesh who are rehabilitated in sector 1 as a special case. The Directorate of Social Welfare, Government of Sind, Red Crescent Society of Pakistan and other voluntary social welfare agencies worked jointly and provided one-room row houses/quarters to these 137 families in November 1976. On humanitarian grounds, the allottee families were not charged the cost of plots and houses. At the time of the survey, 3 more houses were under construction and the owners were scheduled to move in within 2 to 3 months.

3.2. Provision of Utilities and Civic Facilities

From every angle, progress in this regard has not been satisfactory. According to the KDA physical development was completed at the end of 1977, but the target group in general has numerous complaints. The following is a brief account of the existing conditions with regard to the various utilities and facilities.

(a) Water supply. A 500,000 gallon capacity water reservoir has been constructed to meet the need of the area. But due to the shortage of water in Karachi as a whole, the supply of water to Metroville is gravely short. Some water is available in some parts of the Metroville only, and even these are without supply on Fridays. Other parts are completely deprived of water supply. According to KDA sources, "...water was pumped from the Benaras Pumping House only for two hours between 1 to 3 a.m. This would mean about 40,000 gallons which is not enough to fill the reservoir. People have to be patient until the overall water supply situation is improved in Karachi."

(b) Electricity. Only street lights are provided whereas the individual house connections, for which the allottees already have paid fully, have not been extended so far. This is mainly due to a dispute between the KDA and the Karachi Electric Supply Corporation (KESC) on the issue of escalation of rates.

(c) Natural gas. In all the utility walls pipes for water supply and gas connection have been provided, but due to a dispute similar to that of the electricity issue, in this case with the Karachi Gas Company (KGC), no gas could be provided so far.

(d) Sewerage. This facility has been provided in all the plots throughout the scheme.

(e) Roads. All the roads, major and minor, within the entire scheme have been metalled and completed.

(f) Schools. Only one school building was under construction.

(g) Miscellaneous. The administration block was under construction and the site-office of MPECD-KDA has been functioning in a part of the building. Three blocks of townhouses have been completed with another block constructed by the Building Research Station for demonstration of low-cost building units.

---

*At the time of data collection, i.e. from September-November 1979.

There were two blocks of double-storey flats nearing completion, managed by the Ebrahim Alibhoy Charitable Trust for their members. The same charitable trust was also busy constructing a community facility building in the area. It is necessary to mention here the commitment of the Royal Netherlands Government to assist financially in the construction of the community facility building. Formal arrangements were being finalized in this respect.

So far, no parks or playgrounds could be developed in the area, perhaps due to the acute shortage of water. Similarly there is no dispensary, police station or post office in the area. The House Building Finance Corporation (HBFC) which was supposed to open a site office, has for some reason not been able to do so.

In conclusion, it can be said that the implementation of the Metroville I programme is lagging far behind the original schedule. The same is also true for support programmes involving adult education, cottage/small industry development and technical training to self-help builders.

4. COMPARISON AND ANALYSIS OF RELEVANT CHARACTERISTICS AND OPINIONS

This part attempts a comparison of relevant characteristics and opinions of Metroville residents, Metroville allottees living elsewhere in Karachi, residents of adjoining settlements and professional planners.

For the sake of maintaining uniformity in the presentation of tables and to avoid repetition of lengthy names and titles of these groups studied, short names and titles have been used, as follows: "Residents" for the resident allottees at the Metroville I, "Allottees" for those Allottees who had not moved to the site at the time the survey was conducted, "Neighbours" for residents of adjoining settlements, and "Planners" for the professional planners of PICRP.

4.1. Pressure to Move: Rental Status and Insecurity of Tenure Encourage Movement to the Metroville I Site

The active cooperation and participation of the target group is the key to the success of any programme. An adequate degree of participation cannot be achieved without cultivating the desire to do so, which ultimately depends on the intensity of need felt by the people.

More than 2 years have passed since the completion and handing over of the plots to the allottees of the Metroville I scheme. Yet the majority of the allottees, comprising a target group of more than 3,400 households, have not moved to the site so far due to various problems encountered in the area. There is a very small minority of only 11 Allottees who have moved to the site voluntarily and they are presently living in their newly constructed houses. Besides this group, another group of 137 repatriated families of widows from Bangladesh are also living in the Metroville I. As mentioned earlier, this group has been given special treatment and does not fall within the scope of the present study.

Considering the four study groups only, the following question was asked: "What are the main reasons convincing these 11 households to move to Metroville earlier, as compared to the huge majority of Allottees who prefer to hold back?"

In order to find possible answers to the above question, a comparison of occupancy status and legal status of dwelling and plots of Residents and Allottees is presented in Table 1.

Table 1. Occupancy Status and Legal Status of Dwellings and Plots of Residents (past situation) and Allottees (present situation) (in percentages, absolutes in brackets)

Group	Occupancy Status			Legal status of plot	
	Owned	Rented	Other	Authorized	Unauthorized
Residents (11)	-	63.7 (7)	36.3 (4)	63.7 (7)	36.3 (4)
Allottees (40)	47.5 (19)	27.5 (11)	25.0 (10)	100.0 (40)	-

In addition, Table 2 below shows the range of the rents paid by Residents and Allottees who live, or lived in the past, in rented accommodation.

Table 2. Amount of Rent Paid by Residents (in the past) and Allottees (at present) (in percentages, absolutes in brackets)

Group	Monthly rent paid, in Rupees				
	up to 100	101-300	301-500	501-700	above 700
Residents (7)	-	28.6 (2)	42.8 (3)	14.3 (1)	14.4 (1)
Allottees (11)	45.4 (5)	36.4 (4)	9.1 (1)	9.1 (1)	-

It is important to note here that none of the Residents owned a house before they moved to the Metroville; in comparison, 47.5% of the Allottees own houses. On the basis of personal experience, the researcher feels that in household surveys where allotment or the possibility to own public land is involved, respondents tend to conceal the fact that they own land. Perhaps the reason for this is that it is illegal for a single person to apply for or hold more than one plot of land in any public housing or sites and services scheme. Considering such a tendency, therefore, there is some possibility that the actual number of Allottees owning their houses and/or plots would even rise above the percentage shown in Table 1.

The same table shows that the majority (63.7%) of the Residents lived in rented houses as compared to only 27.5% of the Allottees. The remaining 36.3% of the former group had some other arrangements not requiring payment, as compared to 25% of the latter.

It is interesting to note that all the Residents (36.3%) who neither owned nor rented houses but lived under some other arrangements, come from unauthorized settlements. On the other hand, all the Allottees live in residences on authorized plots of land.

Further investigation of 7 Residents and 11 Allottees renting houses, revealed that the rent they paid greatly differed. As evident from Table 2, the majority of the Residents (71.4%) used to pay rent ranging from Rs 301 to 800 as compared to the Allottees, of whom only 18.2% pay rent of Rs 300 to 700; the majority (81.8%) are paying less than Rs 300 per month. Almost half of those in the less than Rs 300 range pay only up to Rs 100 per month.

This makes it clear that the feeling of insecurity and rental status, combined with comparatively higher rental rates pressurized the Residents into moving to the site earlier than the Allottees. The Allottees on the other hand, generally do not experience insecurity of tenure and rental status as intensely and therefore they do not feel the need to move to the site.

4.2. No Urgency to Move: The Majority of the Allottees Do Not Have the Urgent Need for Houses in Metroville I

It has been established in the previous paragraphs that the Allottees do not feel any pressure to move to the Metroville site. Some additional data presented in Table 3 throws more light in this regard. The table shows that the Allottees are living in better and more comfortable conditions than the Residents of Metroville I. The majority of the Allottees (72.5%) live in pakka houses constructed on plots of land measuring more than 80 square yards. As far as the number of rooms are concerned, a high proportion of

Table 3. Allottees by Type of House, Size of Plot, Number of Rooms and Utilities Available in the Present House

	Frequency (n)	Percentage (%)
1. House type		
pakka	29	72.5
semi-pakka	11	27.5
2. Plot size (square yard)*		
up to 80	14	40
80 - 120	13	37.1
above 120	8	22.9
3. Number of rooms		
one	6	15
two	16	40
three	13	32.5
more than three	5	12.5
4. Utilities		
water	29	82.5
electricity	37	92.5
gas	23	57.5
sewerage	26	65.5

*Excluded were 4 Allottees who had sold their plots and 1 who did not respond to the question.

Allottees have more than two rooms to live in. Apart from house size, the main difference is in the degree of comfort enjoyed by Allottees as compared to Residents with regard to the availability of water supply, electricity, natural gas and sewerage system. From the 40 Allottees, 29 have water supply connected to their houses, 37 enjoy electricity connection, 23 use natural gas to cook with, and 26 are served with a sewerage system. We also learned that the majority of the Allottee respondents (55%) are among those fortunate enough to have all the four public utilities available to them. It is natural, therefore, that the majority of the Allottees, particularly those living in comparatively more comfortable conditions, do not feel the urgency to move to the Metroville site. Perhaps they would move if equally comfortable conditions were made available at Metroville.

4.3. Missing the Target Group: the Majority of the Metroville Residents and Allottees have Higher Incomes than the Originally Planned Target Group

In the year 1974, when the Metroville programme was conceived, the target group was defined as those "persons who already have a job, craft or business and who are looking for secured land tenure and a chance to improve their standard of living. In terms of income, the main target group covers those households with income of Rs 700 per month and below."[11] It is in this context that an examination of the present situation is attempted.

The data presented in Table 4 below suggests that the households involved in the programme have incomes higher than that originally planned for the target group.

Table 4. Distribution of Residents, Allottees and Neighbours According to Income (percentages, absolutes in brackets)

Income (Rs)	Residents (11)	Allottees (40)	Neighbours (50)	All groups (101)
1 - 700	18.2 (2)	7.5 (3)	78.0 (39)	43.5 (44)
701 - 1000	36.4 (4)	50.0 (20)	18.0 (9)	32.7 (33)
1001 - 2000	9.1 (1)	30.3 (12)	2.0 (1)	13.6 (14)
2001 - 3000	27.2 (3)	2.5 (1)	-	3.9 (4)
above 3000	9.1 (1)	-	-	0.9 (1)
no income/no response	-	10.4 (4)	2.0 (1)	4.9 (5)

A comparison of incomes of the three groups clearly shows that a very low percentage of Residents (18.2%) and Allottees (7.5%) fall in the income group of up to Rs 700 per month. The Neighbours, however, appear better justified to fit in the target group, with a majority of them (78%) earning Rs 700 or less.

Two things need to be noted here: first, in the present study, income is based on the monthly earning of the respondents/heads of households only, whereas the Rs 700 income group originally targeted was fixed on the household income basis. Obviously, the income of the whole household is often higher than that of the household head only. Secondly, it is a common tendency of respondents in such household surveys to mention incomes lower than the actual and to inflate their expenses. It is safe to assume, therefore, that some more respondents in each income group would have joined the next higher income group if it had been possible to gather the actual household incomes.

In order to examine the situation further, the following table is reproduced from the Karachi Development Plan 1974-1985. It shows a break down of the target income groups.

Table 5. First Metroville Project: Population and Household Income Groups[12]

Income group (Rs)	Number of households	Population	Percentage of households	Percentage of population
0 - 299	1,174	5,295	20.0	14.0
300 - 499	2,994	18,982	51.0	51.0
500 - 999	1,468	10,849	25.0	29.0
1000 - 1999	176	1,699	3.0	5.0
2000 and above	59	468	1.0	1.0
Total	5,871	37,293	100	100

Table 5 shows that 94% of the selected households should be earning an income of below Rs 1000 per month. Yet the survey has revealed that only 56.8% belong to this category. The remaining 43.2%, instead of only 6%, as planned, belong to the Rs 1000 and above income groups.

The impressions of Fr. Anzorena also support this finding. He reports that the "Metroville sites and services projects are available at very reasonable prices, they are near the sources of work in the industrial zone, they have basic facilities available in a service wall, but they are stocked and the allocation to the target groups seems a question mark."[13] Hence it can be concluded that there had been something wrong somewhere in the selection procedure due to which the actual target group did not get proper attention and representation.

4.4. Beyond the Reach of Neighbours: A Large Majority of Neighbours Who Fall in the Target Group do not Want to Own Land at Metroville

The Neighbours were asked whether they ever desired to own a plot in Metroville. An absolute majority (90%) of the Neighbours shows a negative attitude. This is very important to consider. These people have been living just adjacent to the Metroville site for several years; most of them witnessed the birth of this scheme and a very high majority (90%) cross through the Metroville on their way to and from work. Their opinion is also important for the reason that they are truly representative of the planned target group.

Now the point to consider is why these people, who know the Metroville I better than many others, have outrightly rejected the possibility of becoming plot holders in the scheme. Does this prove the failure and unattractiveness of the Metroville programme to the lower-income groups? Or are there some other reasons for this attitude? It is worthwhile mentioning here that among the 50 Neighbours interviewed, 3 already have plots at Metroville I, but all of them are "fed up" and want to sell their plots.

In order to look into this matter more deeply, a comparison of the income of this group and those of the Residents and Allottees is presented in Table 6.

Table 6. Income of Neighbours, Allottees and Residents (percentages, absolutes in brackets)

Income (Rs)	Neighbours	Allottees	Residents
Nil	2.0 (1)	-	-
up to 500	58.0 (29)	7.5 (3)	-
501 - 1000	38.0 (19)	58.0 (20)	63.6 (7)
1001 - 1500	2.0 (1)	27.5 (11)	-
1501 - 2000	-	2.5 (1)	-
2001 - 2500	-	-	-
2501 - 3000	-	2.5 (1)	27.3 (3)
3001 - 3500	-	-	9.1 (1)
No response	-	10.0 (4)	-
Total	(50)	(40)	(11)

The differences in income are very obvious: the majority of the Neighbours are earning less than Rs 500; only one earns more than Rs 1500 per month.

Differentials in educational background are also marked: unlike the other two groups, 48% of the Neighbours are illiterate. Among the remaining 52%, no one went higher than matric or formal technical and vocational training. Among the other two groups, literacy is comparatively higher.

Considering that the Neighbours are less educated and comparatively poorer than the present Allottees and Residents, they exhibit a very negative attitude. This attitude, manifested in their disapproval of owning plots at the Metroville, is perhaps based on their perception that the Metroville scheme is designed only for the upper income and elite class, and not for them. This assumption is further supported by the discussion on "speculation" in a later section of this article, where it is shown that a huge majority of the Neighbours are of the opinion that the main reason why Allottees do not move to the site is that they are not really needy, but are speculators.

4.5. Affordability House Construction Costs at Metroville I are Beyond the Reach of Lower Income Groups

The data gathered from all the 11 Residents who have completed or partly completed construction of their houses shows that construction costs are generally very high. The Residents, most of whom definitely belong to middle and high income groups, preferred to construct their houses in one stretch. None of the Residents adopted the incremental or gradual construction approach. In most cases, construction costs were higher than 2 to 2.5 times one's annual income, which is a standard accepted internationally for moderate housing.

Table 7. Residents: Household Size, Annual Income and Construction Cost

Serial No.	Household size	Annual income (X Rs 1000)	Construction cost		
			Total (X Rs 1000)	per sq. yard	as % of income
1	10	33	61	763	184
2	5	30	75	625	250
3	6	12	65	542	542
4	4	7.2	35	438	486
5	9	19.2	45	375	234
6	10	9.6	50	625	521
7	6	36	72	900	200
8	6	11.5	23	288	200
9	8	12	65	813	541
10	12	42	165	1375	393
11	8	7.2	10	125	139

Among the Residents, 5, or 45.5% expended more than twice their annual income (ranging from 2.5 to 5.4 times). Their main source of finance were loans from the House Building Finance Corporation (HBFC) or employer organizations, banks, relatives/friends. Some savings were also mentioned together with loans as sources of funds.

There seems to be no apparent explanation for these high construction costs other than the unavailability or shortage of cement and other construction materials as well as the shortage of skilled construction workers. Another factor which could be adding to the overall cost is the shortage of water. According to some Residents and office bearers of the Metroville Welfare Centre (MWC), about Rs 5000 is added to construction costs due to lack of water in the area.

Now if we assume the affordability level of lower or even middle-income groups earning Rs 500 or 700 per month to be about Rs 15,000 and Rs 21,000 respectively (2.5 times the annual income), then there seems to be no hope for them as the costs demand income proportions higher than they can afford. However, it has been noted in several household surveys conducted in Karachi slums that respondents tend to inflate expenditure, contrary to their response in the case of income. If such is also the case with the respondents of Metroville, then there is a possibility for middle-income people, provided they have access to loan facilities, to afford houses in the area. But even then it remains beyond the reach of low-income people.

4.6. Attractions of Metroville: the Majority of Residents and Allottees Were Attracted to Metroville Because of the Basic Utilities and Good Location

Residents and Allottees were requested to give three reasons that attracted them most into applying for plots and land in this scheme.

Most of the respondents could not give three reasons but a good number of them gave more than one; therefore tabulation of the data has not been done on percentage basis. Only the frequency with which each reason was mentioned has been recorded in Table 8.

Table 8. Main Reasons for Obtaining Plots in Metroville I

Reasons	Residents	Allottees	Total
MPECD-KDA promised basic utilities	7	23	30
Good location/open environment	3	17	20
Proximity to place of work/CBD	3	16	19
Cheap land/plots	3	5	8
Did not have any plot elsewhere	1	6	7

Although the first three reasons shown in the table have been mentioned as the main reasons (in the same order of importance), one wonders why the last item, i.e. "did not have a plot elsewhere", was seldom cited. The reason could be an earlier finding showing a good number of the Allottees owning their own houses and plots. Perhaps quite deliberately a large majority tried to avoid mentioning this reason, because they had plots elsewhere. Although this is not enough evidence to draw such a strong conclusion, it does indicate the possibility of latent multiple ownership of land by the Allottees.

4.7. No Problem with Bureaucracy

Like many other developing countries, Pakistan's bureaucracy does not have a good reputation. Malpractice, inefficiency and corruption are rampant in more or less all quarters of government and semi-government departments. The existence of anti-corruption squads or vigilance wings in these departments for the purpose of eradicating such evils from society stand witness to the existence and acknowledgement of these phenomena.

Bureaucracy, in general, is much criticized; and in particular the agencies responsible for the provision of public services and civic amenities are strongly abused. Under such circumstances, the above-cited finding of the study appears all the more unusual and important.

All the respondents in the Resident and Allottee groups were asked if they faced any problems in obtaining allotment, lease or transfer of plots.

All but one of the respondents from the two groups did not face any kind of problem in dealing with the MPECD-KDA staff in negotiating for allotment/lease/transfers of plots. Only one respondent among the Residents mentioned having paid a small amount (Rs 30) to some lower employee of the KDA for the favour of a quick approval of a site plan. Unlike the findings of some other social household surveys where the people of Karachi freely availed of such opportunities to air complaints, this study shows a trend that demands explanation.

Also, this finding contradicts the complaints and allegations made by the office bearers of MWC and some press reports. However, it supports the claim of the official in charge of Metroville Cell KDA that all red tape had been removed and direct access to the authorities was provided to the target population. According to this officer, the success of the programme depended entirely on fair dealings which could be facilitated only by eliminating the barriers between the people and the decision makers. He explained that: "We are doing our best to carry out this project as honestly as possible. But because the people have accepted corruption as a way of life, therefore they hardly believe that things can go well without bribes - especially at the KDA. So instead of choosing the right path......they prefer to pay money and get rid of the problem...... I have opened my office to all the allottees of Metroville in order to know directly about their problems, and to solve them if I can. But they tend to see the lower staff to resolve their problems in their own way."[14]

Despite allegations made by some people, office bearers of MWC and journalists, it is clear in the light of data available that there is no evidence to support such allegations.

4.8. Worse Than Before: The Majority of the Metroville Residents Consider Their Present Living Conditions Worse Than Before

To ascertain the Residents' level of satisfaction, they were asked, "how do you compare your present living conditions with your previous residence?"

A great majority (9 out of 11) consider their present living conditions worse than before. The basic reason for their discontent is the lack of public utilities and civic amenities.

4.9. Better Than Surrounding Areas, According to Residents and Neighbours

Among the Residents, 72.6% find the living conditions in Metroville better, or much better, than in the adjoining areas, though worse than in their previous residences. Two of the Residents, however, feel that conditions in Metroville are even worse than in the adjoining areas. These two residents perhaps had in mind the acute water shortage problem, which is not so serious in the adjoining areas.

Among the Neighbours, a significant number of respondents (22%) did not find any difference in living conditions of Metroville and their settlements. Among the rest, 50% felt that living conditions were better in Metroville.

On an aggregate, out of 61 respondents from two groups, 33 or 54% held opinions in favour of Metroville. There is agreement between the two groups on this issue. However, it is not possible to ignore the fact that of the Neighbours, 26% felt that living conditions in Metroville were worse than in their own areas. Besides, another 22% did not find any difference between the two.

This gives an indication that the Neighbours have some reservations and they do not find many good points about Metroville to unanimously declare it a better area.

4.10. Waiting for Water

For life, the need for water is inevitable. This is felt and realized by the Residents, Allottees, as well as the MPECD-KDA.

When the Allottees were asked to say when it would be suitable for them to start construction on the site, the most frequent response was "as soon as water is supplied". Improvement of financial position, sanction of loans and the provision of lacking utilities and amenities in the area are also stressed, in that order.

Another possibility, "when other allottees of my group move", though mentioned only four times, needs elaboration. The majority of the plots in Metroville were allotted on group basis representing various industries, government and semi-government departments, etc. The basic idea was to settle them in clusters or groups of their own choice. A few respondents informally said that some groups are now negotiating with their employers through their labour unions for the sanction of house building loans, preferably without interest, or mass construction of prototype houses by employers for them. Later on the construction costs may be deducted from their salaries on easy instalment terms. This information indicates yet another reason for the Allottees' delay in moving to the Metroville site.

4.11. No Local Services

Water is partly available domestically to 3 Residents only; the rest buy water from water sellers who come in mobile water tankers. In summer, one water tanker costs about Rs 200, in winter Rs 100. Some Residents have constructed water reservoirs in which to store water.

The Residents were asked to say where they went for services for which there is little or no supply in the area, e.g. water, markets, medical care and schooling.

For shopping, medical care and education, Residents depend heavily on other areas in the city or adjoining areas.

4.12. Allottees' Plans

The Allottees were asked the question: "What are your plans for your plot in Metroville?"

Out of 36 Allottees (i.e. excluding 4 who had sold their plots), 16 or 44% are undetermined or do not have immediate plans in mind. They are followed by 22% who are waiting for others to move in first. Four Allottees are waiting for good offers to sell their plots. There are only 4 who have some kind of plan to start construction as soon as water is provided or loan/ financial assistance is made available.

4.13. Water or Speculation?

Shortage of water in the area has obviously been acknowledged at official and public levels as the main reason keeping Allottees from moving to the site. To gauge the influence of this problem and to explore if there were some other reasons involved, all the respondents in the three study groups were asked to state three possible reasons discouraging Allottees.

Table 9. Reasons Discouraging Allottees from Moving to Metroville, as Stated by Residents, Allottees and Neighbours

Reason	Frequency of mentioning by			
	Residents	Allottees	Neighbours	Total
Shortage of water	10	22	16	48
Lack of gas, electricity, transport	6	10	22	38
Speculation	3	–	27	30
High cost of construction	3	2	4	9
Financial constraints	–	16	–	16
Waiting for others to move	–	5	6	11
Waiting for loan/assistance	–	2	–	2
Construction after retirement	–	2	–	2
Insecurity of life and property	–	1	1	2
Security of tenure/ownership	–	–	8	8
Allottees are not needy people	–	–	6	6
Other and no reply	3	2	3	8

There is a high degree of agreement between the Residents and Allottees as far as the top two reasons, i.e. water problem and absence of utilities and amenities, are concerned. There are some significant differences with regard to the other reasons, however.

Financial constraints experienced by Allottees is a reason frequently mentioned by the Allottees themselves, whereas the other two groups are silent on this issue. A possible reason may be the fact that the Allottees are directly concerned.

"Speculation" as a reason holding back Allottees is mentioned by many of the Neighbours who feel that the Allottees are not really needy people. This reason is lightly supported by the Residents as well. On the other hand, it is interesting to note that none of the Allottees touched on this matter.

If we examine this in the light of some other findings, i.e. that the majority of Allottees own their houses, have secured tenure, pay low rents, belong to the middle or even upper-income groups and have more comfortable living conditions than the Residents and Neighbours, then it seems logical to think that speculation may be one important reason keeping them from moving in. The Allottees, being the group involved in speculation, would obviously have avoided mentioning this reason.

4.14. Recommending Metroville

Residents and Allottees were asked whether they would recommend a relative or friend to buy a plot in any Metroville scheme. A related question asked only of Allottees was whether they thought their decision to own a plot in Metroville I was right or wrong.

The majority of Residents and Allottees (63.8% and 47% respectively) are in favour of recommending the scheme. Despite their expressed grievances, the Residents are even more willing to recommend the scheme than Allottees. An explanation of this attitude may be that Residents feel that development will ultimately take place in the area or that it is always good to invest in land whenever there is an opportunity to do so.

At this point, it is relevant to present some figures on the response of the Karachi population to a public announcement on the opening of three new sites and services plot townships of KDA in Karachi. These schemes, viz. Gulistan-e-Jouhar, Metroville III and Shah Latif Town, were announced by KDA on 1 September 1979 through all local newspapers.[15] Altogether, 12,210 plots were offered for allotment by computer balloting, the schemes having 2735, 1475 and 7000 plots respectively. The sizes of plots varied from 60 to 400 square yards.

Interested citizens of Pakistan were required to submit their applications on prescribed forms through commercial banks, depositing in advance an amount equal to 10% of the cost of the plot within 6 weeks.

According to a press release, a record number of 224,587 applications was received for the 12,210 plots, a ratio of 18.4 to 1. The sum deposited was to the tune of Rs 45,972,000.[16] This overall ratio of 18:1 (31:1 in the case of the 1475 plots in Metroville III) is quite amazing. In view of the experience from Metroville I, however, it is questionable to what degree the low-income groups are represented amongst the applicants.

5. CONCLUSIONS AND RECOMMENDATIONS

5.1. Conclusions

1. Judging from the extent to which the 12 basic objectives of the Metroville I scheme were accomplished, the concerned agency has failed in that the implementation of the scheme was not proper and timely. In reality there is no evidence to contradict the fact that so far none of the 12 objectives could be fully achieved.
2. Except for the initial positive response in getting allotted plots of land, the target group (i.e. the selected allottees) in general have shown indifference or negative response in respect of post-allotment cooperation and participation in the programme.
3. The Master Plan Department and the Environmental Control Department of KDA has encountered a number of major problems and constraints that hampered the effective implementation of the Metroville I programme. They were:
- lack of intra-departmental and inter-agencies coordination,
- shortage of water supply,
- indifference of target group,
- inadequate number of trained and qualified staff,
- speculation by allottees.

4. Despite their sufficient knowledge about Metroville I, the residents of neighbouring areas, people who are truly representative of the planned target group, perceive that this scheme is beyond their reach and is actually meant for the middle and upper classes of society. This indicates that the Metroville programme has widely drifted from its initial track and is now catering only to middle and upper-middle income groups, instead of the lower-income people.
5. The professional planners appreciate the planning of Metroville I, are critical of the implementation phase and recommend that the programme be continued, subject to some basic amendments.

5.2. Recommendations

Apart from various reasons responsible for holding back the progress of Metroville I project indicated by the study, the writer feels that there are some other reasons too. Those reasons fall in the direction as pointed out by Angel and Benjamin in their article; "Seventeen reasons why the squatter problem can't be solved". "Third World societies are faced with a difficult challenge - shelter - the task of assuring that everyone is adequately housed. Are we really willing to confront this challenge - to solve the housing problem? Many believe that we are solving the housing problem. We are not." "The current approach to the housing problem is crowded with myths, principles, and beliefs that are in fact obstacles to its solutions."[17]

The Metroville I has also been a victim of the myths of "large projects", "completeness", "professionalism" and the attitude of "somebody else's problem". The writer feels that if it were possible to get rid of such myths, beliefs or principles, it would have been much easier for the decision makers and planners to come up with better and practical solutions in general, and in the case of Metroville I in particular.

In the light of the above discussion and the findings of the study, the following recommendations are made:
1. Change in attitude: Decision makers and planners should gradually amend their attitudes and approaches in order to get rid of the deep-rooted myths and principles which form the real hurdles in their endeavours to solve the problem of low-income housing.
2. Adopt smaller projects: This is very necessary especially while experimenting on new schemes and concepts like Metroville, so that management and implementation can be effectively controlled by the limited professional manpower within the available time and resources. Such an approach would hopefully not lead to a situation like the present one, where it is still difficult to decide whether the concept of Metroville failed, or the implementing agency, or both.
3. Better and effective coordination: The coordination especially of the support programme is extremely important. For this purpose a permanent coordination, evaluation and monitoring cell within the structural framework of MPECD-KDA should be formed.
4. If the MPECD-KDA sincerely intends to pursue the original plan of Metroville to use the utility wall development concept for future Metrovilles, the importance of a proper and fair selection procedure should not be undermined. A fair and objective selection of the needy and deserving people representing the desired target group will definitely ensure better participation and cooperation with the implementation team. This will enhance the progress of the programme.

5. New Metrovilles should only be undertaken after attaining considerable progress in old Metrovilles. This is essential in view of the limited number of experienced, capable and qualified personnel available. Moreover, there is a need to provide more encouragement and incentives to whatever qualified professionals are available for the programme. Further enhancement of their salary scales or increasing allowances etc., is desirable.

6. In order to induce the target group to cooperate and participate fully, closer rapport with them should be established by the planning and implementing agency. Right from the initial phase of planning as well as during the implementation, an on-site community relations office should be operative, manned by adequate and experienced personnel.

REFERENCES

1. Master Plan Department, KDA, *Karachi Development Plan 1974-1985*, Karachi, 1974, p. 1.
2. *Ibid.*, p. 24.
3. Karachi Development Authority, Metroville, An experiment in human settlement at Karachi, Pakistan, *Karachi*, undated, p. 7.
4. *Ibid.*, p. 8.
5. *Ibid.*, p. 9.
6. *Ibid.*, p. 10.
7. Karachi Development Authority, Brochure "Metroville", *Karachi*, undated, p. 4.
8. *Ibid.*
9. *Ibid.*, p. 5.
10. Pakka: solid, firm, lasting, permanent.
11. Government of Pakistan, *National Pilot Project 3*, Final report on low-income settlements in Karachi, 1977, p. 4.
12. Master Plan Department, KDA, *op. cit.*, p. 344.
13. J. Anzorena, S.J., Report to SELAVIP-members, Santiago de Chile, 1980, pp. 1-2.
14. Free interviews with the officers in charge of the Metroville Cell, MPECD-KDA, *Karachi*, October 1979.
15. *Dawn*, Karachi, 1 September 1979.
16. *Dawn*, Karachi, 11 October 1979.
17. S. Angel and S. Benjamin, Seventeen reasons why the squatter problem can't be solved, *Ekistics*, Vol. 41, 1976, pp. 20-26.

Fig. 31.

Fig. 32.

LOW COST EXPERIMENTAL HOUSE
BEING BUILT BY
BUILDING RESEARCH STATION KARACHI
ZUBAIR ASSOCIATES
(ENGINEERS BUILDERS DEVELOPERS)
K.D.A (MASTER PLAN DEPT)

Fig. 33.

Fig. 34.

Jacob Lines; a Development Policy Considered

M. H. Weijs

1. THE JACOB LINES STUDY AS A PART OF THE JRP-IV PROGRAMME

At the time the Joint Research Project IV (JRP-IV) started, an enormous lack of knowledge existed about the inner-city slums and the squatter areas as well as the urban system of Karachi as a whole. The governmental approach to the slum and squatter areas restricted itself to clearing the more visible parts and the places that were intended to be devoted to other uses.

To gain more insight in the situation JRP-IV concentrated during the first years on two interrelated fields of study.

- problem oriented or sectoral studies. Studies were made for example on building costs, intra-city migration, housing typology, sewerage, etc.,
- area oriented studies, conducted in areas for which no improvement-programmes existed. Based on these studies recommendations were made for development policies, for the benefit and with the participation of the residing population. (Chanesar Goth, Usmania Muhajir Colony, Miran Naka).

During discussions between the JRP-IV staff and the Pakistani authorities about possible fields of study, which would be useful to and were wanted by the authorities, an evaluation of the redevelopment scheme of the Jacob Lines Area was mentioned. National, regional and local authorities were all involved in plans aimed at the renewal of this downtown city area, inhabited without authorization and in poor conditions by a large population. As a result, the study of the Jacob Lines Area became part of JRP-IV's programme for 1974-1975.[1]

A rehousing and flat construction programme had already started in March 1974, in advance of the redevelopment scheme for the area. The proposed evaluation of the redevelopment scheme had to be restricted to the study of the question, whether continuing construction of flats in the area solved the problems of the residents - which had to be one of the aims of the scheme - or just created new ones.

This area-oriented study is unlike the other ones also something of a problem-oriented study, in as much as it does not give an all-encompassing picture of the area, but restricts itself to information relevant to the above-mentioned question. At the same time it was the first one in which an active development policy could be evaluated.

2. SKETCH OF THE AREA AND THE DEVELOPMENT POLICY

2.1. The Area

The so-called Jacob Lines Area comprises 700 acres. Formerly the area was the border area of the city and predominantly in use as a military encampment with barracks and rifle-ranges. After Partition additional quarters were built in the area to accommodate more refugee people.

Nowdays different parts can be distinguished in the Jacob Lines Area. A large part is still military cantonment area, but the rest is mainly residential. The unauthorized settlements are restricted to 200 acres, mostly inside the area. In some parts only squatters reside, in other places squatters live mixed with the residents of the government quarters and barracks. In total 3/4 of the total population of the Jacob Lines Area (about 125,000 persons) live on these 200 acres.

The Jacob Lines Area is well located next to the city core. It lies between the commercial city centre of Saddar and the middle-class Housing Societies. On its verge are the central market and bus station of Empress Market. The external connections are mostly good, the area being bordered by thoroughfares. Thus the industrial area of Landhi-Korangi is easy to reach, but the industrial area of SITE (Sind Industrial Trading Estate) less so. Passing through the area is not easy. Only a few streets are paved and all are winding and narrow. This restricts the internal circulation, and there is no congestion of the traffic.

2.2. Forces Behind the Development Policy for Jacob Lines

While the urban area of Karachi increased and the land use in the central parts of the city intensified the development of the Jacob Lines Area lagged behind. While the rest of the centrally-located areas was used to its fullest economic possibilities the Jacob Lines Area became only a densely settled, chaotically built-up area. There was little incentive for the population to improve the quality of their houses beyond a modest level, because of lack of security of tenure and there was no possibility to use the obvious commercial qualities of this central area, because the land was owned by various government agencies.

But some forces are at work to change the situation, as in other places. Seen by a city-planner the Jacob Lines Area is a nuisance for the creation of a functional and physically well-integrated inner-city pattern along Western guidelines. Authorities normally prefer a good-looking modern city centre and try to remove too visible slum areas. Governmental and commercial agencies see the profitable possibilities of the integration of the area in the urban landmarket and its redevelopment. And, at the same time, to rehouse the present population from a slum environment into decent modern constructions can politically be a good move. Together these forces led to the proposition of different plans and schemes for redevelopment.

2.3. Formulation and Implementation of Development Plans up to 1975

In 1972 the then Prime Minister of Pakistan, Mr. Bhutto, ordered the Karachi Development Authority (KDA) to undertake a comprehensive redevelopment scheme of the Jacob Lines Area for construction of multi-storeyed flats where the present occupants of the plots would be given preference of rehabilitation on a minimum charge. In accordance with this directive the KDA-Masterplan Department published in 1972 a report[2] containing proposals for a complete redevelopment of Jacob Lines by private enterprises into a modern high-rise city area with mixed commercial and residential land use.

Following the outline of this report the National Construction Company (NCC) was charged with the preparation of an integrated plan providing low-cost housing facilities for the population and a plan ensuring minimal shifting of the residents. An inventory of the residing population was made, and a pre-planning report of a redevelopment scheme was published[3] which sketched the construction of an impressive new urban centre "... which will not only lead the way for any future development in the city of Karachi and Pakistan, but will be a shining example to urbanists and planners all over the world."[3]

As a first step into this new era the authorities cleared a 10 acres plot in Jacob Lines for the construction by the NCC of 1200 flats in 4-storeyed apartment-buildings.

This starting place was a relatively easy one. The residents of this part were mostly quarter dwellers who were rehoused in other government projects (e.g. Federal C Area). The few squatters were permitted to build a temporary shelter in another part of Jacob Lines. In this way no problem arose with the relocation of the residents. The 1200 flats had to be finished during 1974 and augmented to 3000 at the time of the JRP-IV evaluation study. In fact, at that time only 475 flats were slowly nearing completion.

It was a well-known fact that persons at higher government levels were dissatisfied with the plans and the flats as developed so far. Wanted was a more spacious, varied, good-looking inner-city residential area with apartment buildings. Therefore another firm, Pakistan Environmental Planning and Architectural Consultants Ltd., was directed to make a lay-out plan and building designs for the rest of this partially built-up area, in combination with an overall plan. No master-plan for the total area was accepted up to 1975, nor any sectoral plans for water and sewerage systems, to be used as a guideline for further developments. In addition, no other plots could be made available for the intended construction of more flats. About the way the nearly finished flats would be distributed among squatters, government servants and non-residents, and about prices to be paid, nothing was known.

3. THE EVALUATION STUDY OF THE DEVELOPMENT PROJECTS

3.1. Execution of the Study

As in most studies, different phases and various approaches connected to these phases can be distinguished. Fundamentally we first tried to obtain background information about the development policy proposed for the area. From there we tried to acquire information about the flats to be constructed (3.1.1.) and attempted an assessment of the needs and ideas of the Jacob

Lines population (3.1.2.) and of the possibility of matching them with the future availability of flats in the area (3.2.).

3.1.1. Background Information

When we started the study, next to nothing was known about factual development strategy for the Jacob Lines Area. So at first we made an inventory of the fragmented information in official speeches, statements, plans and actions and of the way the NCC put the directives given into a plan of action, in order to get an idea of the applied development policy. We learnt that the present occupants of the plots would be given preference for rehabilitation on a minimum charge. The residential flats would be transferred to the residents. But up to that moment no flat had been completed and nothing was known about the way they would be distributed, nor at what cost. In this way we were unable to see how the policy of rehabilitation was put into action or to derive yardsticks to measure its aptitude.

We were restricted to gathering information about the 475 flats nearing completion. These consisted of two types. Type A has an area of approximately 550 square feet, has three rooms, a semi-separated kitchen, a w.c. and shower, and a balcony. The staircase is located inside the building which rises four storeys. These flats were meant for the lower-income groups and costed about Rs 24,000 to construct in 1975. Type B is approximately 800 square feet, has four spacious rooms and a larger kitchen as well as two bathrooms. Construction costs were about Rs 40,000. It can be described as a pure middle-class dwelling. It was proposed to add to these costs a price for the land arbitrarily set at around Rs 10 per square yard. This price was far below the free market value of the land, as was shown by sales in the adjacent areas. In fact, the value assigned to the land depends on the government strategy, because the land is government-owned. Therefore we excluded in our financial calculations the cost of land. At the NCC the intention was to sell the flats, after completion, to the future residents, on an instalment basis. The House Building Finance Corporation (HBFC) would take over the mortgage debts. At the normal procedure people would have to pay a part - thought to be Rs 6000-8000 - in advance and Rs 155-175 monthly for an A-type flat, to cover only the construction costs.

It was unknown to what extent the government wanted to provide the Jacob Lines population with subsidies conducive to ownership. In our opinion the government is unable to extend really substantial subsidies to the Jacob Lines Area on a large scale, as would be the case with the 30,000 flats to be constructed in the area, without neglecting its other tasks. Therefore we will refer to the actual construction costs and the instalments needed to cover these. The figures mentioned above, however, will have to be considered as minima. The next flats to be constructed needed to be better-looking and more spaciously built. This means that these flats would become more expensive.

3.1.2. The Research

Next to inquiring into what was to be offered, we studied the population that was to receive the offer. The NCC had carried out a population survey before, but no results could be obtained. So after some time of personal observation and free interviewing in the area, we prepared a questionnaire for further structured interviewing.

We restricted ourselves to the squatter population of the Jacob Lines Area and left aside the minority of government servants, living in authorized quarters and barracks. We assumed their problems to be of a different kind from those of the squatters, and expected that extra government aid would be more readily available to them. The part of the Jacob Lines Area where unauthorized settlements are a common phenomenon was subdivided into 54 more or less homogeneous sectors. These we used to stratify our sample for the survey. By this sample survey we collected the data about the squatter population we present below.

Many people entered the area in the years following Partition. Attracted by its location and the presence of relatives most people stayed on in the area. Thus in our population sample, more than 40% have lived for more than 25 years in the area. Most of the people live together with their families. Deras (residences of single men) are relatively few in number and are usually located in the border regions. About one-fourth of the households comprizes more than 6 members. The rest has less and is therefore able to live in medium-sized dwellings, when there is only one household to a dwelling . At the moment of the survey this was the situation of 80% of the households.

No less than 40% of the household heads are self-employed, mostly in the hawker and salesmen groups. Most people working in the area (25% of the total) belong to the same groups. Only 10% of the informants have a higher or administrative profession. The places of work are often not far away: 40% of the workers are able to do without transport costs whatsoever. For many this is an important fact because their income is low. The arithmetic means of incomes, earned by household heads and total households are Rs 350 and Rs 480 per month respectively. The modal class of the household heads and total households earns Rs 201 to 300, comprising 40% and 25% respectively of both groups. Despite the fact that saving is difficult, 80% of the sample population have improved their house by at least one category in the 6 point housing typology used in Karachi.[4] While a majority (70%) started with a dwelling of a very temporary nature in category I, 60% of the households now live in a semi-permanent dwelling of category IV or better. Visible is the willingness and ability of the people to improve their dwelling little by little. In total a very high amount of money has been invested in the area in this way, although the willingness to invest is hampered by the insecurity of tenure.

3.2. Confrontation of the People and the Proposed Solution

Three quarters of the population of the Jacob Lines Area do more or less like the place in which they live; the reasons usually relate to the situation rather than to the site itself: central location and proximity to work. Certain aspects of the site dominate the reasons for disliking the area: poor facilities and uncleanliness. But on the whole, 90% of the people would like to stay in the area if the land is allotted to them and are of the opinion that they can solve their problems, if the government takes care of the general environment. Only 40% is in favour of a flat if given an equal choice between a flat and allotment of a plot. Without alternatives, 80% would be willing to move to a flat.

Because only about half of the population has ever visited a flat, their reasons to opt for and against flats were compared with the experiences and opinions of a population in existing low-cost flats in another area of Karachi. In that way we tried to get a better idea of the validity of the opinions expressed in connection with flats. In order to do so we interviewed 50 inhabitants of the government-owned flats in Federal C Area.

One of the main reasons given by the respondents in the Jacob Lines Area for *liking* a flat is that it will become their property. In our opinion this aim to get property, and with it the right to stay, will also be served by the allotment of plots to the residents of the area. Some other main reasons are the same as those given for disliking the area in its present state: flats have better facilities and are cleaner. Again we think that these improvements may be achieved also through land regularization and allotment. On the other hand, residents of the existing low-cost government flats often complain about unsanitary conditions in their area - people throw garbage out of windows and sweepers take away only a fraction. Sewerage is a constant source of trouble and electricity problems annoy a large number of people. Only the supply of water is sufficient in most cases, although it is sometimes scarce and for just a few hours. The existence of facilities does not guarantee their functioning.

On the whole, we can say that the reasons mentioned by the people in the Jacob Lines Area in favour of flats do not necessarily hold true, whereas they do in the case of allotment. Only the provision of a completed, pakka[5] constructed, flat is a really compelling reason for those squatters in low category dwellings.

Respondents in the Jacob Lines Area gave reasons for *disliking* a flat. These reasons related mostly to the rigid and inconvenient construction of the flats: no courtyard: no extension possible, lack of privacy (pardah).[6] Among the interviewed flatdwellers these dislikes were even more prominent.

It is understandable that nearly all people would want to stay in the area they have invested in and are attached to by relatives and/or memories. They live in a community which has grown spontaneously and do not like to be put together with strangers in an apartment building.

Up to 1975 only one uniform type of three-room flat had been constructed. In fact, smaller dwellings are wanted and are sufficient for some of the households (e.g. 1-3 member households, 13.5%); on the other land, the three-room flat may be too small for households of, say, 8 members and more (20%). Financially the rehousing does away with important investments made up till now. People will have to start over again.

The government considers 7.5% of the income of its low-paid servants as a reasonable part for expenditure on housing. We used this percentage and double (15%) to calculate which amounts could be spent by which parts of the population on instalments. If we compare these with the amounts people say they are able to spend, we get roughly the following picture:

Amounts available for instalments calculated as percentages of income and as given by respondents

Instalment amount	As part of the income of				Given by respondents
	head		household		
	7.5%	15%	7.5%	15%	
up to Rs 30	72.5	15	52	10	55
Rs 31-60	15	58	30	42	25
Rs 61-100	5	15	12	27	7.5
over Rs 100	2	6.5	4.5	20.5	12.5
no answer	5.5	5.5	0.5	0.5	-
Total	100	100	100	100	100

Whatever the great differences between the figures of the different columns, it is quite obvious that, even if we take the column with the highest amounts, no more than 20% of the residents are able to pay more than Rs 100 a month. Because this is a household income which often comprises also of the incomes of relatives who may leave the household this percentage seems high. The estimate made by our interviewees seems more reasonable.

We have seen what the normal conditions of the HBFC loans are. Even if we disregard the advance amount asked on the bold assumption that people can arrange this by borrowing money from relatives or by selling jewellery, the conclusion remains that at most 5% of the residents will be able to pay the instalments of Rs 155-175 accompanying the advance amount and move into and stay in the flats. The rest will at most move into a flat only to sell it quickly at a profit (although not many intend doing this at the moment) or will not move into one at all. The group most in need of government aid will be ousted. We reach this conclusion in the most reasonable assumption that the price will not be a free-market one including the land value, but just the total of construction costs.

If the government wants to allow everyone to move into a flat and subsidizes every resident for that part of the instalment he is not capable of paying, then the government will have to provide a subsidy of Rs 1,340,000 a month taking into account prices of 1975, over a period of 20 years. All this for the residents of the Jacob Lines Area only. If the advance amounts also have to be paid by the government, then the total subsidy is increased by Rs 70 million!

Along with this, we still have to reckon with another factor which may minimize the amounts that people will be able to spend. A quarter of the household heads work in the area itself. The place of work will not in every case change when people move, but when it does, some will find it difficult to find work or a (work)shop nearby under the same conditions. A reduction of income may result at a time when it is most difficult to cope with it.

With these facts in mind it seems incredible that 7-8 of our respondents think they are financially able to obtain a flat with the instalments mentioned by them.

4. THE REPORT OF THE IN-DEPTH STUDY OF THE JACOB LINES AREA

4.1. Evaluation and Recommendations

The data gathered in the in-depth study of the Jacob Lines Area provided the opportunity to conclude the report of the study with an evaluation of the used development policy and with recommendations for a new approach.[1]

One of the aims of the redevelopment scheme was to give the resident population a "preference for rehabilitation on a minimum charge."[2] The great majority of the resident population consisted of squatters. This group will be more difficult to rehabilitate than the minority of government servants, who can be lodged in other government-owned flat buildings.

Most of the unauthorized settlers had a strong preference to stay in the area and to get the ownership of their plot. Some 40% prefer a flat, but their arguments are not always valid as was shown. Also, some of the arguments in favour of flats would hold for allotment of the land and regularization as well. A still more serious problem is the inability of more than 90% of the squatter population to pay the normal instalmets for these flats, while it will be undesirable - perhaps even impossible - to devote the needed, extremely large amounts of government money to such a project over a long period of time. Therefore we had to conclude that this kind of redevelopment scheme will not solve the problems of the majority of inhabitants of the Jacob Lines Area, in fact it creates considerable new problems and does not fulfil the above-mentioned aim. With the preferences and possibilities of the residing population as a starting point we developed some guidelines for a development policy better adapted to the situation.

In the existing plans, the minimum charges will be beyond the people's paying capacity. Therefore we recommended that the investments made by the population be tampered with as little as possible and that endeavours be made to link the plans up with the existing improvement tendency.

Rehabilitation of the main squatter areas should be considered step by step in accordance with the overall redevelopment plans for the Jacob Lines Area, by allotment and regularization. The land use can be improved by allowing interested residents to enter flats on easy conditions, and then using the space they leave behind for rearrangements. The quarters left by the government servants can serve the same purpose: for squatters from other plots or, after clearance, for some other use. The main squatter areas occupy at most 200 acres of the Jacob Lines Area; thus at least 400 acres are left for new flats construction etc. This implies that contrary to existing trends, the other part of the Jacob Lines Area with its military land use should be used at an early stage for rehousing government servants and interested squatters, to allow for the improvement of squatter areas at the same time.

If these other plans are looked into and started with in time, the dwellings in squatter areas can step by step be improved by their inhabitants without further government assistance. In fact, the commercially most interesting parts of the Jacob Lines Area, (e.g. near Saddar), remain available for new flats and commercial blocks. The government can develop these parts at a profit and use the revenue for physical improvements of the squatter areas.

4.2. Impact of the Report

The position of JRP-IV as a research institute outside the Government Departments offered the advantage to conduct studies in a more or less independent way. At the time JRP-IV had to promote the resulting reports itself, and to bring these to the attention of the authorities concerned. JRP-IV reports gave evaluations and recommended courses of action; the follow-up and implementation had to be done by the government agencies.

The study of the Jacob Lines Area was carried out in the last year of the five-year period of the existence of JRP-IV and the report was published at the end of the last year. Because it was decided to end the joint project, we were only able to present the report to the government and interested persons, such as some members of the Provincial Assembly. In the nearly-stagnating situation around the Jacob Lines development at that time nobody else was able to carry on or interested in carrying on the proposed line of action. Only much later was reference sometimes made to the report.

REFERENCES

1. M. H. Weijs, *Jacob Lines Survey*, An outline, Karachi, March, 1975.
   M. H. Weijs, *Report indepth study of Jacob Lines Area*, Karachi, 1975.
2. *KDA-Masterplan-Department-Redevelopment of Jacob Lines*, 2 Volumes, Karachi, 1972.
3. Y. Lari, (National Construction Company), *Pre-planning report on Jacob Lines*, Karachi, August, 1974.
4. J. J. van der Linden, *The bastis of Karachi, Types and Dynamics*, Amsterdam, 1977, pp. 92-93.
5. Pakka: baked, strong, solid, firm, lasting, permanent.
6. Pardah: veil, curtain, cover, privacy. The word is also used to indicate the system by which women are secluded from the outside world.

The Karachi Master Plan and Housing the Poor

T. J. Segaar

1. INTRODUCTION

In 1968, the United Nations Development Programme (UNDP) agreed to assist the Government of Pakistan in the preparation of a development plan for the Karachi city and its region.[1] The actual start of the project was in the beginning of 1971.

The participating parties were UNDP as the donor agency and the Karachi Development Authority (KDA) as the counterpart government agency in Pakistan. UNDP provided six experts, including the project manager, and appointed an American-Czechoslovakian planning firm (PADCO/TERPLAN) as subcontractor to execute the work together with KDA. KDA established a semi-autonomous Master Plan Department (MPD) with about 30 staff members and 10 draughtsmen. The duration of the assignment for the UN - and PADCO-TERPLAN staff covered 144 man months and 292 man months respectively within a three-year period.

The specific objectives of the Master Plan Project (MPP) were:
(a) To prepare an overall development plan and programme for Karachi city and its region;
(b) To establish a permanent governmental planning machinery for the guidance of growth in the Karachi city and region;
(c) To train the professional Pakistani staff to sustain such planning;
(d) To outline the specific programmes and projects necessary for implementing the overall plan.

This overall plan should formulate guidelines for the development in the period up to the year 2000 with a sequence of investments to be made for a short term, i.e. in the period 1974-1985. This plan represented a comprehensive approach in the sense that it was not only concerned with physical aspects, but also with the social and economic development (such as employment, housing, health, education), transport, public utilities (water, sewerage, etc.) and the legal, financial and institutional framework required for implementing the plan. Actually, the physical plan was an outcome of the social and economic planning objectives rather than the other way around.

The work was organized in four phases, viz.:

(a) Preparatory activities and studies (September 1968-January 1971);
(b) First planning cycle: preparation of preliminary, alternative development plans for 1985 and 2000, including somewhat more detailed programmes for 1985 and recommendations for immediate action programmes (February 1971-June 1972);
(c) Second planning cycle: further development and evaluation of two alternative plans, prepared during the first cycle, and the selection of one final plan (July 1972-June 1973);
(d) Final planning phase: detailed planning and budgeting of specific programmes to be implemented first (July 1973-December 1973).

In their 1967 request for United Nations assistance, the Pakistani authorities considered the problem of the "shelterless people" - as people living in self-made hutments and simple houses on unauthorized land were called at that time - a major issue to be dealt with by the project. In spite of the many efforts that had been made since 1947 to provide sufficient and adequate housing to the fast increasing Karachi population (430,000 inhabitants in 1941, 1.1 million in 1951 and 3.5 million in 1971), the number of "shelterless people" increased every year.

This article will focus on two questions, viz.:

- What kind of work was done by the project in the field of housing the poor?
- How far could this work be considered worthwhile and successful?

2. PLANNING FOR HOUSING THE POOR

The work done by the MPP in this field included:

- identification of the scope of the housing problem and the future housing need of the lower-income groups,
- identification of the major housing issues affecting the poor,
- preparation of various low-income housing proposals,
- reacting to immediate requests for advice on urgent housing matters.

2.1. Scope of the Housing Problem

Based on various existing reports and on a socio-economic survey executed by the MPP during the preparatory phase among 11,000 randomly selected households in Karachi, a rough estimate could be made about the scope of the housing problem by applying a number of key-indicators, such as land tenure, public utilities standards and population density of the dwelling units. In 1972, it appeared that there were about 1.5 million low-income people (i.e. those having a household income up to Rs 300 per month) in Karachi, of which about 800,000 lived in "unauthorized areas", without any secure land tenure. In 1958, this number was about 500,000. In this income category, the average number of persons per habitable room was 4.7. More than 50% of all dwelling units in Karachi had only one room and only 16% of all households had the public utilities water, sewerage and electricity in their house.

The reliability of these data had to be checked through careful interpretation and through a post-enumeration survey.

This kind of figure indicates the "objective" housing problem. It does not tell anything of how people feel about their situation, i.e. the "subjective" housing problem. The few research findings about slums in Karachi available at the time,[2] confirms their positive role for the inhabitants as well as for the city as a whole, a role also mentioned in the international housing literature. Slum improvement rather than demolition was therefore strongly supported by the MPP.

The MPP prepared demographic and income projections for 1985 which indicated that in 1985 an estimated 590,000 new households would need shelter and services, from which about 250,000 households would fall within the lower income groups (up to Rs 400 household income per month). This meant that between 1972 and 1985, about 20,000 small plots with basic services would have to be provided yearly, whereas in the 1960-1970 decade, KDA was able to provide only 5000 small plots per year on average.

2.2. Housing Issues

The detrimental housing situation in Karachi could be reduced to three basic issues, viz. housing policy, land policy and housing finance.

(a) Housing policy In spite of the critical housing situation, the Pakistan government did not have a clear housing policy and did not define housing programmes on a continuing base with a regular allocation of funds to implement them.

There had been major allocations of funds for housing in the fifties and sixties, both for new residents and for resettlement of "slumdwellers" from the inner city into flats, individual houses and "nucleus" (i.e. uncompleted) houses, but they were all *ad hoc* projects and many of them did not respond to the needs of the lower-income people. The housing provided by these projects was too expensive, often too far from the employment sites and often without adequate public utilities.

This was, for instance, indicated by the two resettlement schemes at the outskirts of Karachi, planned to ultimately house 600,000 people, from where about 50% of the resettled households returned to the inner city within a few years.

Moreover, these projects were not well conceived with regard to financial planning. None of them could be occupied by low-income people without high government subsidies. However, subsidy could not form the basis for continuous housing programmes because the governmental financial resources were too limited. The lack of funds was partly due to the large number of arrears in existing projects where no solid regulations for collecting rents and instalments had been made. The result was decapitalization of lower-income housing schemes and a failure to sustain an adequate construction programme.

In spite of some voices indicating the socio-economic causes of the existence of slums, the positive functions for their inhabitants and the financial advantages of slum improvement versus slum clearance,[3] the negative attitude towards slums generally prevailed in government circles during the sixties and the beginning of the seventies. Slums were considered a disease rather than an opportunity and therefore clearance rather than improvement was the overall accepted policy.

(b) Land policy The MPP felt that the housing problem in Karachi was particularly a result of the land policy with regard to land leasing, land speculation and land tenure.

Karachi is one of the few cities in the world where most of the land is owned by the government. But this fact was not used to influence the urban development positively.

By leasing the land for a 99-year period, the government lost the opportunity to tackle problems like land speculation, and promoted large scale housing developments for higher-income groups. KDA itself contributed to this speculation by providing some first phasing of infrastructure into new areas before land already developed elsewhere was fully utilized. Hardly any penalty was applied for non-utilization of land. In the early seventies, about 15% of all developed land was vacant - an area on which at least 1.4 million people could have been settled.

The prevailing land tenure pattern favoured the relatively few well-to-do, who could occupy land through their relations and money. It did not respond to the rapidly changing conditions in the city since 1947, where the ever increasing squatter settlements reflected insecure land tenure for thousands of families.

(c) Housing finance At the time of the MPP, there was no private or public institution that was willing to provide housing loans to individual low-income people. The only existing government agency in the field of housing loans, the House Building Finance Corporation (HBFC), only lent to middle- and higher-income people.

The HBFC was also incapable of supporting some major low-income housing projects as it lacked the capital to do so. This lack of capital was partly due to serious management problems causing a high default rate on invested money.

Very complicated administrative procedures also hampered the HBFC from providing adequate services.

2.3. Housing Proposals

(a) Objectives In the development alternative finally selected for Karachi, the housing programme aimed at:

- provision of an adequate plot or rental accommodation for every household at a price which takes into account the limited household incomes,
- increase of the water supply and sanitation from 16% of the households (1973) to 60% by 1985,
- prevention of unauthorized and unplanned squatting,
- increase of the housing stock to the maximum feasible level (see (b)).

With regard to the low-income groups, these objectives imply the improvement and regularization of unauthorized settlements, the expansion of open plot development schemes (see (b)) and the prevention of the clearance of existing houses.

The housing programme refers to the entire residential environment of the household, i.e. not only to the shelter as such, but also to the plot area, the public open space, the access to public utilities and to places of work, education and health facilities. It also includes concern with the financial and administrative aspects of the housing delivery system.

(b) Housing programmes Three basic housing development programmes were recommended for the lower-income groups, viz.:
- improvement and regularization programme of unauthorized areas (IRP),
- open plot development (OPD),
- utility wall development (UWD).

The IRP is meant to serve the lowest target group (household income up to Rs 300 per month). The programme consists of four parts: a survey of all existing unauthorized areas to determine whether they could be regularized and improved; provision of secure land tenure; implementation of improvements according to minimum established standards for public utilities; development of an administrative and financial plan.

The OPD is a programme directed to the same target group as in the IRP programme. It provides 80 square yard plots, secure land tenure, a minimum level of public utilities, community facilities (school, health centre), workshops and market places. People have to organize the construction of their houses themselves.

The OPD might initially have the features of the IRP, but it has the advantage of proper site planning and it encourages gradual private housing investment, so that much lower public cost is involved.

Some 80,000 open plots were foreseen for the period up to 1980 and an additional 36,000 by 1985.

The UWD programme is one stage above the OPD scheme and directed to the target group with household incomes between Rs 300 and Rs 1000 per month. It provides public utilities inside the plot in a utility core wall and a small plinth area. No house construction is provided, but a variety of houses of different types and quality would be possible.

The major advantage of the programme is its flexibility to respond to the needs of a wide spectrum of incomes at a relatively low cost. Site planning and community facilities would be very similar to those of the OPD scheme.

For the period up to 1980, some 11,000 plots were planned and an additional 20,000 by 1985.

Estimates were prepared about the total cost of developing land and infrastructure for these three programmes. These costs would have to be provided for, if a sound financing policy was to be developed.

Extensive proposals were made for the set-up of a National Housing Bank, by greatly expanding the resources of the HBFC and by streamlining its administrative procedures.

It was mentioned that the government would have to contribute itself by making available the money which it used to invest in specialized government housing programmes (e.g. for government officers and industrial workers). Moreover, the HBFC should begin to attract private deposits, so taking on a savings bank function. This might also include a forced savings programme for employees with fixed incomes.

Within this new HBFC, an independent low-income housing subsidiary was proposed. Its purpose would be to make available small loans to lower income people participating in the OPD and UWD programmes. This lending programme required a subsidy element in order to achieve lower interest rates and to make up for the greater administration costs, likely to be involved.

KDA would have the full responsibility to lay out plots and develop the infrastructure, either with their own staff or through contractors. KDA did not have the responsibility for any house construction. It would not finance its own construction activities, but should seek to arrange finance from construction financing agencies. KDA would have to dispose of its plots on a differential pricing policy, in order to create a surplus from the upper-income groups thus reducing the cost of plots to lower-income groups.

2.4. Immediate Actions

During a long plan preparation, as is the case with the MPP, it makes sense to react and advise on urgent matters which occur meanwhile and which do not allow any delay. This happened in the field of low-income housing with regard to two matters, viz. the regularization of unauthorized areas and the national housing policy.

In 1972, KDA's Townplanning Department had identified 35 unauthorized colonies all over Karachi, for which advice was asked from the MPP team on their authorization or clearance.[4] Based on the housing policy developed, there was, in the MPP, a strong preference for regularization and improvement of those colonies.

However, more than anything else, this was a sensitive political issue. Strong practical arguments had to be found to convince the KDA that regularization made sense. In fact, it meant that the Director General of KDA had to be convinced. The existing link between KDA and MPP - the Director General of KDA was administratively the head of MPP - made it easier to achieve this. Nevertheless, the game had to be played. A game, in which existing political feelings and considerations had to be known; sound academic ("objective") arguments did not appear to be automatically adequate to settle the matter.

Therefore, the outcome was a compromise, accepted by both the MPP team and KDA. A compromise basically in the shape of criteria to be applied for the evaluation of the unauthorized colonies, since these could at least be partly recognized by the KDA authorities. These criteria were:
(a) Desire of the residents for regularization;
(b) Safety for life and property;
(c) Existing level of utility services;
(d) Land-use conformity with the proposed Master Plan;
(e) Socio-economic viability of the community, based on the availability of:
   - work opportunities in or near the area,
   - transport to work,

- health and educational facilities,
- socially cohesive community structure.

If all five of these criteria were fulfilled positively, authorization and improvement of the area should be carried out. If any of the criteria were not fulfilled, an evaluation should try to reach the most feasible conclusion.

After the evaluation, altogether 6 colonies were excluded from authorization, 18 colonies were indicated for authorization and 9 colonies required further study.

Resettlement of the people in the 6 colonies to new sites could, however, only be considered if at the new site the following conditions were met:
(a) Secure land tenure;
(b) Location near work opportunities;
(c) Good accessibility to transport;
(d) Better public utility services than in the unauthorized area, i.e. at least at the level established for the IRP and OPD programme;
(e) Basic health and educational services.

The inventory made by MPP of these 35 colonies was necessarily a rather quick and superficial one. Unfortunately, some more formalized link between MPP and the Joint Research Project for Slum Improvement and Urban Development (JRP-IV) was never established. The latter would have been the most obvious organization to provide useful data about the unauthorized areas. However, JRP-IV made it clear that it wanted to remain independent from MPP in order to be able to continue its own programme of scientific in-depth studies of selected slums. The consequences of this choice were that even after several years, JRP-IV could not yet provide an overall picture of the unauthorized areas in Karachi. So this project remained outside the planning work that was under way in their specific field of interest, at a level and intensity that had never before occurred in Karachi.

In 1972, the Ministry of Production and Presidential Affairs, in the Government of Pakistan, appointed a Housing Committee to examine the national housing problem and to advise the government on an appropriate housing policy. A sub-committee was set up to prepare a comprehensive housing policy. Its report was published in April 1973[5] and reflected to large extent the ideas of MPP at that time, both with regard to the analysis of the causes of the housing problem and to the strategy to tackle it.

3. STRENGTH AND WEAKNESS OF THE MPP

In urban and regional planning, some people question the sense of preparing a comprehensive master plan. Some consider it too much of a theoretical exercise because the possibilities for implementation are assumed to be low. Others feel that the reliability of the data on which future developments are projected, is doubtful or that the plan preparation takes too much time, so that the plan is already out of date at the time its implementation should start. Still others have the opinion that it is useful to prepare a short-term plan, but that it makes little sense to plan for a period of 20 to 25 years ahead.

Somehow, all these thoughts were considered at the start of MPP. Much emphasis was put on preparing a plan which could really be implemented in financial, organizational, institutional and legal terms. A plan to be discussed at all relevant administrative levels - national, provincial, and municipal - during various stages of the planning work. A plan that provided some general development framework for the year 2000, but at the same time stressed the short-term planning and plan implementation through developing programmes for the period 1974-1980-1985. A plan that included all basic, relevant development items, and was in that sense comprehensive; because leaving out of some of them would imply a denial of the fact that development requires at least some integrated approach. The housing sector is just one example that shows how many interlinked aspects are involved. A plan which was based on the most reliable data available at the time, but recognized the dialectical fact that planning with incomplete and less reliable data is the actual situation and challenge for every planner in a developing country.

Recognizing the need and importance of developing a realistic master plan does not imply a denial of the fact that it does have several weaknesses. Both the importance and the weaknesses of a master plan will be briefly discussed now, as far as housing the poor is concerned.

3.1. The Need and Importance of MPP

The contribution and importance of the MPP with regard to housing the poor has been in four fields:
(a) Analysis of the actual housing situation and housing problem;
(b) Projection of the housing demand;
(c) Preparation of housing programmes;
(d) Assistance in immediate action programmes.

(a) Actual housing situation One of the most striking facts at the time the MPP started, was the lack of basic data available in some organized form from the authorities who were dealing with housing. A first and essential piece of work was to bring together existing housing data into a useful form, to interpret them and to collect additional data, so that at least some general insight could be gained about the housing situation and the scope of the housing problem. This overall picture included the size of the housing stock, the housing types, room occupancy, house construction capacity, construction costs, consumer's capacity to pay for housing and housing financing. As was mentioned in par. 2.4., information on the unauthorized areas in some more detail than could be collected by the MPP staff should have come from JRP-IV.

Such an inventory is, in scientific terms, not a very exciting exercise, but it is required to show government officials the actual situation, and a condition for starting some action in the field of planning, decision making and implementation. All kinds of case studies are not enough to achieve this. After De Goede and I had finished the Azam Basti study,[6] including recommendations and cost estimates for the improvement of this "slum area", the report was well received by the Pakistani officials, but they asked why this particular area was selected, how far it could be considered representative and they expressed the need for an overall study of "the slums" in Karachi. This does not mean that such an overall picture should always precede any implementation at a small scale - the Azam Basti recommendations should anyhow have been implemented straightaway, in order to learn from experiences in actual slum improvement (a "trial field") - but an overall picture is surely required for initiating action in a planned way, at some significant scale.

The analysis of the actual housing situation also indicated the causes of the housing problem, i.e. it was shown how the poor have become the victim of government policies with regard to housing, land and finance (see para. 2.2).

Finally, it was felt that one should learn from planning efforts made in the past as an imput for settlement schemes to be planned in future. Therefore, an evaluation was made of one of the two resettlement schemes (see para. 2.2) to investigate how successful this kind of settlement planning had been, how people felt about it, how they used space and facilities, how they had changed, or made additions to, the original housing and settlement lay-out, etc. From a few existing studies of improving "slum areas", information was gathered on how people in unplanned areas gradually changed their housing and environmental situation themselves.

The importance of the MPP in describing the actual housing situation and in identifying the causes of the housing problem was not only that facts were arranged in a systematic and useful way for planning, but also that they were published and discussed. Many of these facts were politically sensitive and therefore were not usually discussed publicly. The authority and prestige of the MPP, due to its affiliation with the United Nations and the participation of so many foreign experts, made it relatively easy to express and discuss everything with all relevant officials at all government levels, many times.

(b) Housing demand Planning for housing in the near future requires information about the housing demand, i.e. how many houses have to be built, for whom, of what type? To answer these questions, an insight is required in the present housing situation and household income distribution as well as in the population growth and the future household income distribution. The MPP has prepared alternative population projections based on demographic data (fertility, mortality and migration) and on economic development assumptions for Karachi. Afterwards, household income projections were made, based on the development possibilities which were foreseen for various economic sectors and on an income distribution policy which was proposed by the MPP. Both the population and income projections were made for 1985.

The importance of this piece of work was that through MPP, the government officials have got some realistic idea about the need for houses in the period 1974-1985 for various income categories. Prior to the MPP, nobody knew anything about it.

The housing demand had to be translated into housing programmes. Based on the capacity to invest in housing and the housing costs, two lower-income categories were defined, for which three different housing programmes were proposed (see para. 2.3).

(c) Housing programmes The three housing programmes for low-income people (see para. 2.3) were realistic programmes in the sense that they were adjusted to the needs of the people and their limited capacity to invest in housing. The type of houses, public utilities and community facilities reflected minimum levels and a high degree of self-help. They were therefore feasible at a large scale over a ten-year period and might avoid the *ad hoc* features of previous low-income housing projects. The more so, as proposals for the financial and institutional set-up were attached to these housing programmes.

The importance of the MPP is that it has indicated the way to solve the present housing crisis and to prevent the future one, by implementing these housing programmes and by abandoning the policy of the past with regard to housing, land, finance and administration.

(d) Immediate action programmes The most direct contribution of the MPP was provided through advice on urgent issues that required immediate action, when the planning work was not yet complete. Two examples were mentioned in para. 2.4., which concern the housing problem of the poor directly.

3.2. The Weakness of MPP

There are two major weaknesses of the MPP. The first one concerns the lack of integration between planning and implementation. Preparing a plan is one thing (and relatively simple), implementing it is something else (and relatively hard). Even if concrete programmes are made for immediate implementation that appear to be feasible, actual implementation may be very hard because of political and economic interests, rigid institutional arrangements, etc. Therefore, assistance in implementation is as much required as in planning.

Obviously there are financial limitations which prohibit a too long involvement of foreign assistance and, of course, Paksitan wants to make its own decisions and to prevent too much foreign interference in "internal matters". However, it is no testimony of realism when a distinction is made between separate planning- and implementation phases. In MPP, these two phases only coincided occasionally in the immediate action programmes (para. 2.4).

In the field of housing, the implementation of the proposed programmes for the lower-income groups has been little successful up to now,[7] not because the original planning was bad, but because there was a lack of guidance during the implementation and there were major deviations from the original plans. The point is that the political, economic and institutional issues that often prevent successful implementation should be dealt with in an integrated planning-implementation development approach, and not only during a planning stage. The high status of the MPP at the time might not have been a guarantee that some successful implementation would have occurred should this approach have been followed, but it might have increased the chance for it.

The second weakness concerns the lack of training in planning approaches and planning techniques. Planning might be relatively easy compared with implementation, the western, modern planning approach of the MPP in a non-western world with a limited number of professional planners is complicated and can only be understood if enough time for training is available. Actually, this time was limited. Much more time should have been reserved in the work programme for both on the job training and additional forms of training. It once happened that Pakistani staff members commented on the work programme and time schedule, which were on the wall in the Conference Room, with, "there hangs Washington on the Wall!" (PADCO had its home office in Washington). Was it really understood by all, by some or by very few of the Pakistani? Were the presentations and discussions at the weekly progress meetings, and the major reports understood? The result of the limited training was that two of the objectives of the MPP, viz. to establish a permanent government planning machinery and to train Pakistani professional staff to make this possible, did not adequately materialize.

But at the same time, the question can be asked: how much time was available for the Pakistani to express their opinions? According to western norms, maybe enough opportunities were provided: did not the MPP period cover 4 years altogether? But how far were the feelings, opinions and unspoken thoughts of the Pakistani understood by the expatriate staff?

Sometimes, I had to recall the verse I once read somewhere, which could reflect the opinion of the expatriates versus the Pakistani, as well as vice versa:

"I know you believe
you understood
what you think I said,
but
I am not sure you realize
that what you heard
is not what I meant."

REFERENCES

1. Master Plan Department KDA, *Master Plan for Karachi Metropolitan Region*, First Cycle Report, Vol. I, II and III, Karachi, 1972.
   Second Cycle Report, Part I, II, III-a and III-b, Karachi, 1973.
   Karachi Development Plan 1974-1985, Karachi, 1974.
2. In 1972, only the Azam Basti report (see para. 3) and some limited information from JRP-IV was available, with regard to the slums of Karachi.
3. See, for example: K. Shibli, Low income housing policy for urban areas, in: *The problem of shelterless people and squatters in Pakistan*, Karachi, 1966, pp. 49-54.
4. Master Plan Department KDA, *Regularization of unauthorized colonies* (mimeo), Karachi, 1972.
5. Subcommittee on Housing, *National Housing Policy*, Islamabad, 1973.
6. J. H. De Goede and T. J. Segaar, *Report Azam Basti*, Amsterdam, 1969.
7. See Islamuddin Siddiqi's article on the Metroville. Elsewhere in this book.

Part IV

Translating Policy into Action

K. S. Yap

In the previous chapters we saw how various attempts by the Pakistani authorities to solve the housing crisis of low-income groups failed, because the target groups could not afford to buy or rent the dwelling units constructed for them. We also saw that on the other hand research conducted in the bastis of Karachi by the team of JRP-IV generated interesting and encouraging results with regard to the capacity of the basti dwellers to improve their housing conditions on a self-help basis. In particular the finding that basti dwellers can and will invest (more of) their savings into improvement of their houses, if they obtain security of tenure, opened new perspectives for a solution of the housing crisis for the urban poor in Karachi.

The conjunction of three events around 1975 stimulated a final breakthrough in the government policy on the low-income housing and squatter settlements in Karachi.

First of all, the government of Prime Minister Zulfiqar Ali Bhutto as well as the officials of the Karachi Metropolitan Corporation (KMC) were anxiously looking for ways to help the residents of Karachi's oldest, most densely populated and environmentally worst squatter settlement, Lyari, a known rampart of the ruling Pakistan People's Party (PPP). Legalization and upgrading of the settlement with 600,000 inhabitants would definitely be a positive and politically advantageous affair.

Simultaneously, the World Bank had reached the conclusion that even site-and-service projects alone could not solve the housing crisis of the urban poor and that for many years to come squatter settlement upgrading projects would be necessary to meet the demands for housing of low-income groups in urban areas. Within the framework of this policy, the World Bank offered Pakistan financial aid to upgrade squatter settlements in Karachi.

Thirdly, 5 years of research by the Joint Research Project IV had produced a fairly accurate inventory of the numerous bastis in Karachi, an appreciation of the amplitude of the problem, and a profound knowledge of the ability for self-improvement of living conditions by the basti dwellers. In the last years of the Project, the results of this research were translated into general policy recommendations and presented to the Pakistani authorities on both municipal and national level.

The research findings of the Joint Research Project combined with the World Bank's offer for financial aid and the eagerness of the Pakistani authorities to start some government programme in Lyari would eventually lead to the Karachi Slum Improvement Project.

However, the World Bank set a number of conditions on its financial aid to the Karachi Metropolitan Corporation for squatter settlement upgrading. It was prepared to provide a substantial loan to the Corporation on the condition that it would be utilized for a city-wide squatter settlement upgrading programme by means of a revolving fund. For the city-wide programme, KMC would have to formulate a general policy on squatter settlement upgrading and this policy would have to be adopted and approved by the Provincial Government of Sind. For the execution of the policy, a separate department for squatter settlement upgrading would have to be created within KMC.

The United Nations Development Programme (UNDP) was found prepared to send a team of experts, who could advise and assist KMC to meet these conditions. Once the policy had been formulated and approved and the department established, a Dutch team of advisers from the Amsterdam Free University would succeed the UNDP team in helping the KMC to implement the policy in a city-wide programme.

The policy formulated by KMC and the UNDP experts on the basis of their first experiences with planning the regularization and improvement of Lyari, was entitled "Improvement Policy for Sub-standard Urban Areas" and was founded on the following principles:

- KMC provides security of tenure to the occupants of plots in the squatter settlements by granting 99-year lease titles for these plots against payment of lease charges to a revolving squatter settlement upgrading fund,
- KMC provides the regularized settlements with basic infrastructure and finances this operation with money from the revolving squatter settlement upgrading fund,
- improvement of the individual houses is left to the occupants, who will be encouraged to invest in their property by the increased security of tenure,
- each squatter settlement upgrading project is in principle self-financing, as the expenditures for the provision of infrastructure in the area are to be equilibrated by the revenues from leasing of plots in that area,
- for regularization and upgrading some re-planning of the settlement is unavoidable, but demolition of structures and relocation of residents is to be kept to a minimum,
- in planning and implementation of regularization and improvement, residents' participation is maximized.

While these principles appear to be very solid in theory, their application in the field proved to pose some problems, as was shown in KMC's first upgrading project in Karachi: the Lyari Improvement Scheme. This scheme prepared with assistance from UNDP and to be financed by the World Bank failed, basically because the cost of infrastructure and consequently the level of lease rates to be paid exceeded by far the paying capacity of most Lyari residents and were therefore politically unacceptable to the government.

So, when the Dutch team of advisers arrived in Karachi in June 1977 to replace the UNDP team, it was clear that the "Improvement Policy for Sub-standard Urban Areas" needed an elaborate translation into practical action guidelines. It appeared that numerous obstacles in the realm of planning and implementation still had to be overcome and that many questions still required an answer. Some of the problems the team had to face were:

How to maintain a balance between costs and revenues, when the paying capacity of most basti dwellers is low, while the settlement needs extensive and expensive infrastructural works to upgrade the living conditions to a level, where they no longer endanger the physical health of the residents?

How to plan an existing spontaneously created settlement with minimal demolition and relocation without perpetuating it as a slum for the next 99 years?

How to overcome the profound mistrust of squatters in the intentions of the authorities after years of government menaces and attempts to demolish the illegal settlements?

How to persuade residents to pay charges for a lease title, when the selection of their settlement for regularization and improvement has already provided them with almost complete security of tenure?

How to involve the many residents of a squatter settlement in planning and implementation without giving too much power to the intermediaries?

It should be clear from the above that the answer to each of these questions could not be found within the area of one discipline alone. All these questions had to be approached simultaneously from various sides and therefore required a multi-disciplinary effort by economists, sociologists, engineers and physical planners. Take for instance the problem of the type of infrastructure, and in particular that of an excreta disposal system to be provided to Baldia Township, the first squatter settlement to be taken up for planning after the arrival of the Dutch team.

The design of an excreta disposal system for a regularized katchi abadi (i.e. unauthorized settlement) is primarily an assignment for a civil engineer, but the contributions of economists, sociologists and physical planners are indispensable. A main constraint for the system to be designed is a technical one: water supply in Baldia Township is restricted to 2 hours on alternative days and as a result in the area only 2 gallons (9 litres) of water per head per day are available on average. This low quantity of water per head excludes the construction of an underground waterborne sewerage system in Baldia Township.

But the availability of water is only one constraint. As the residents of the settlement have to pay for the improvement themselves, the cost of the system has to bear a relation to the paying capacity of the residents. Consequently, the engineer has to remain in close contact with economists and sociologists, while designing the system.

In addition, it is the physical planner's concern that the system should be able to be laid out easily without requiring excessive demolition in order not to disturb the existing settlement. Moreover, various socio-cultural factors have to be taken into account, like values of purity, methods of anal cleaning, ignorance about hygiene among the population, etc.

In one of its documents, the Dutch Advisory Mission (DAM) therefore stated that the excreta disposal system for regularized katchi abadis should meet the following conditions: "it should be inexpensive and easy to construct, it should require little and easy maintenance and cleaning, it should be adapted to local physical and socio-cultural conditions and it should be incrementally improvable", a sheer impossible instruction for an engineer.

In the following four articles, the Economic Planning Adviser, the Physical Planning Adviser and the Community Relations Adviser of the Dutch team and a British civil engineering consultant to KMC/DAM discuss some of the problems they faced, while trying to translate the policy principles of the Improvement Policy for Sub-standard Urban Areas into well-defined actions for execution in a factual situation.

Physical Planning of Baldia Township

H. Meyerink

1. INTRODUCTION

1.1. Squatter Settlements

Squatter settlements mainly develop at the periphery of a city, that is to say, at those places where land values are low. However, because of the urban growth, these settlements initially located at the urban fringe, gradually become a part of the city itself. And as a result of its growing potential for utilization in the production process, the value of the land rises.

The more the squatter settlements are incorporated in the city, the more they start to obstruct the optimal functioning of the large-scale production process. For, the land cannot be utilized for other, productive purposes, like the construction of offices, hotels and apartment buildings or the construction of roads, which although in themselves not productive, are a necessary prerequisite for the satisfactory functioning of the production process.

1.2. Squatter Settlement Upgrading

For years, various governments have therefore done their best to cut these "cancerspots" out of the city life. In those days bulldozing of squatter settlements was a common phenomenon.

However, it resulted in vehement conflicts between government and residents, and the more so, because the government did not offer an adequate housing alternative to those who were dislocated. In order to resist dislocation, residents reinforced their local organization even more and exercised political pressure on the government.

In an attempt to de-escalate this confrontation over the utilization of space, the government was forced to tolerate squatter settlements. However, tolerance could not solve the problems, for simultaneously industrial capital interests continued to exercise pressure on government planning departments to remove the obstacles to the production process. Moreover, squatter settlement organizations tried to secure legal rights to the land they occupied and to force the government into upgrading the facilities in their area.

Eventually, legalization and improvement programmes for squatter settlements became an instrument for the government to increase its popularity among large portions of the population. Such social projects became a necessary evil to maintain law and order and thereby the social system. Urban planning departments were faced with the task of organizing urban space without stirring up antagonism amongst the various interest groups. One of the main components of the planner's task is to replan existing squatter settlements so that they are integrated in the urban system and do not obstruct the functioning of the production process any longer. This refers not only to infrastructural integration (such as the construction of wide thoroughfares), but to legal integration as well. The costs of these projects had to burden the government budget as little as possible, because other projects like capital intensive enterprises which attract foreign currency and military projects kept their priority.

As a consequence, the cost of the integration into the city has to be paid by the residents themselves as much as possible. This is feasible because the threat of clearance still exists. Residents are eager to obtain security of tenure, so that they can stay in the area, and the government exploits this eagerness to make the residents finance the upgrading project. Residents obtain legal rights to their plots which are thereby integrated in the legal free land market. At the same time, plots and owners are registered.

An important point is also the increase of property values after legalization. To owners of more than one plot, the prospects are bright. One can find speculators in each settlement and very often they constitute a powerful group in the area. They are the richer people in the neighbourhood, who often are in touch with politicians and the government. They are in a position to grant jobs and lend money.

2. PLANNING

The Dutch Advisory Mission (DAM) had been requested to assist local government in planning and execution of a squatter settlement upgrading programme in Karachi. Sociologists, economists, physical planners and engineers had to prepare plans which were supposed to fit into the above context of divergent and sometimes opposite interests.

As this proved to be impossible, the Dutch contribution to the Karachi Slum Improvement Project was terminated after 2 years.

2.1. General Approach

The general approach for squatter settlement upgrading in Karachi consists of:

- provision of security of tenure to the residents through legalization of their occupancy (=regularization),
- upgrading of overall conditions in the settlement through provision of basic infrastructure (=improvement).

The work of the physical planner is concentrated primarily on the preparation of a concept plan and a detailed plan, for which physical surveys provide the basic data. Before and during the preparation of plans, data from other disciplines are also utilized and together these define the way space is organized.

3.1. The Selection of Baldia

Although the Karachi Metropolitan Corporation (KMC) was involved in the planning of other areas like Golimar/Gulbahar and Bhutta Village as well, I shall only discuss the planning work on Baldia, because work on this settlement attained the most-advanced stage.

The selection of Baldia as a settlemnet to be upgraded fell outside the scope of the work of the physical planner. The priority of Baldia is not based on physical standards or criteria, but has a mainly political background.

The more political pressure a squatter settlement organization can exercise on the government, the higher the priority of that settlement in the upgrading programme. This situation results in a competition between settlements for selection in the legalization and improvement programme.

When a certain organization has achieved its aim, the other squatter settlement organizations accuse the government officials concerned immediately of political favouritism. Usually, these accusations are correct, for government officials risk losing their position when opposing the ruling group.

The period in which Baldia was selected was quite chaotic; it was the time just before the elections. The extensive upgrading programme for Lyari had come to a deadlock and work on another area had to be started. Baldia was probably selected because the government officials concerned did not run any risk by choosing this remote and politically rather heterogeneous area.

3.2. Baldia

Baldia is situated at the extreme western fringe of Karachi, behind the Sind Industrial Trading Estate (SITE) and near a Pakistan Airforce base. The settlement stretches out along the Hub River Road which connects Karachi with Baluchistan. The distance from Baldia to the centre of Karachi is 10 to 15 kilometres.

About 25 years ago, the area was still a desert with some scattered habitation. In view of its rather favourable location near an industrial zone, the area was utilized by local authorities to resettle people from the city centre.

In 1954, for instance, potters from Lyari were relocated in this area and in 1965 plots were allotted to inhabitants of a settlement which had been burnt down. Simultaneously, other parts were illegally occupied by people looking for shelter.

In 1965, the Karachi Development Authority (KDA) decided to mark part of the desert for the construction of one of its plot townships. Within a rectangular street pattern, plots of 80 and 120 square yards were marked out and plans for the provision of infrastructure were prepared.

However, only a part of these plans has been implemented and infrastructure has been provided slowly and inadequately. West of the area developed by KDA, a police training centre has been built, which forms the boundary of our project area. In the desert west of the police training centre, some large graveyards are situated and speculators have tried to demarcate illegal plots.

At present the built-up area covers approximately 1000 acres and is inhabited by about 180,000 people. The majority of the population lives on illegally occupied land. Nobody has a legal title, which proves that he has the land in free- or leasehold. The general level of infrastructure is rather low and consequently there is a constant threat to the health of the population.

A human waste disposal system is lacking. Water shortage is enormous: there are only very few public water standposts, which supply water on alternate days for 2 hours. Garbage is collected only occasionally.

There are only few schools and health centres in Baldia, which usually work on a commercial basis. The roads mainly lead from the hills north of Baldia to the Hub River Road in the south. During the monsoon rains, roads and streets serve as stormwater drains.

3.3. Preparations for Planning

For Baldia, as for most squatter settlements, maps were not available, mapping was a prerequisite. Early 1977, this work was carried out for KMC by a private firm. Aerial photographs of Baldia did not exist either and consequently a check on the mapping was hardly possible. In a latter stage, during the detailed planning, a number of inaccuracies in the survey maps were detected.

An additional problem was a dispute between KMC and the survey firm over the payment of the bill. The firm refused to hand over the original maps to KMC and KMC refused to fully pay the firm. Most likely the true reason behind the dispute was a refusal by the firm to pay a "commission" to the concerned KMC officials.

The mapped spatial structure of Baldia represented the point of departure for the replanning of the settlement.

On the one hand, the settlement had to be linked and adjusted to the urban system, or at least it had to meet certain minimal requirements, which had to avoid conflicts with the functioning of the large-scale production process.

On the other hand, the internal structure had to be adapted, without provoking conflicts with the residents.

In order to connect the settlement with the urban system, data had to be collected, like existing plans for the area, long-term plans for Karachi (like the City Master Plan) and urban planning standards and requirements.

To get a better view of the settlement, data about the physical structure of the settlement, the functions of the various zones and buildings, the shortage of amenities and the wishes of the residents also had to be gathered.

3.3.1. Some Main Requirements in Planning for Baldia

(a) According to the Karachi Master Plan, the Hub River Road at present 24 ft. wide had to be widened to 200 ft. The road forms a part of the future Asian Highway and has some strategic importance.

(b) In the days of the plot township programme. KDA had prepared physical development plans for Baldia. According to these plans very wide and straight roads with large roundabouts would intersect the area. Hundreds of dwellings would have to be demolished for the implementation of the plans.

(c) While preparing plans for the built-up part of Baldia, the future extension of the area to the west had to be taken into account. One of the alternatives for future development of this zone was the creation of a new industrial area.

(d) The experience of local planners with the planning of housing projects for low-income groups is poor; and re-planning of existing squatter settlements is completely new to them. The standards they tend to apply are similar to those applied to new housing projects for middle-income groups; the training of physical planners is also oriented towards planning for these sort of projects. Besides, most planners are middle-class people themselves, who spend their life in a middle-class environment.

(e) In the above, we have mainly discussed standards and plans for the road network. Standards for services like water supply, sewerage, and also for schools, health centres, recreation and green belts have not been fixed and cannot be fixed. Everybody agrees that the service level in squatter settlements is abominable, but that is true for most residential areas in Karachi.

3.3.2. Information About the Settlement Itself

(a) To gain a better understanding of the structure of the settlement a land use map was first prepared. Almost all officers of the Central Planning Team of KMC (CPT) participated in this work. Street after street was visited and the function of each building plot was marked on a map: residence, small workshop, factory, shop, school, clinic, etc.

(b) In a next phase, more information was collected about the schools and health centres. Regarding the schools, data were gathered about the number of students, the number of classes and class rooms, the type of education and the controlling authority (public or private); regarding the health centres, the type of treatment and the financial basis (commercial or non-profit) were established.

(c) An inventory of infrastructure in the settlement was made: water supply, human waste disposal, garbage collection, etc.

4. CONCEPT PLANNING

While preparing the concept plan, a number of other aspects besides the above-mentioned data were taken into account. In DAM's view, as many houses as possible would have to be preserved. From the financial point of view, adjustments and improvements had to be as inexpensive as possible, since residents had to pay the cost of improvement themselves. The lower the cost, the better the chance of success.

This principle implied that the new lay-out of the settlement had to be in accordance with the existing situation, wherever possible. The former KDA plans for the settlement ran completely counter to this principle. So, it became the task of CPT to convince the KDA townplanners of the feasibility of opening up a settlement while preserving most of the existing structures.

For this purpose, alternative plans had to be developed, which corresponded better with the existing situation. All internal roads of Baldia were examined to see whether they could be developed for west-east traffic, without requiring too much demolition. In order to explore these possibilities, all public open space was coloured black on a map, so that a structure emerged which showed possible connecting roads.

It appeared that a west-east connection for motorized traffic could be constructed without too much demolition. In the field, the proposal was checked and measurements were made to determine the minimal width of the road. Eventually, a 54 ft. wide road twisting through the settlement was selected.

The municipal planners were not completely convinced that the capacity of this "narrow" road with its many bends would be sufficient to absorb all traffic, especially if the future development west of Baldia was taken into account.

To meet this objection, a 200 ft. wide road was planned in the hills north of Baldia. It would be connected to the main road in the SITE industrial zone. The KMC planners agreed to this plan.

As the construction of the road would be very expensive and the road would not directly serve the interests of the residents, it was decided to keep the cost of construction of this road outside the project budget and to construct the road only when the new industrial zone was being developed. In the meantime, an effort would be made to keep the alignment of the road free from new structures.

Another problem was the Hub River Road, which had to be widened for military reasons. To attain the width proposed in the Master Plan, many houses, shops and small-scale industry would have to be demolished. However, a study of the alternatives showed that one could meet the requirements with a somewhat narrower road: a width of 175 ft. would be sufficient.

While planning the internal road network, existing road widths were maintained, wherever possible. Only for the construction of some roads which were intended to open up neighbourhoods for traffic, would parts of a few houses have to be demolished.

4.1. Amenities, Schools, Health Centres, Green Belts

After the inventory of schools and health centres in Baldia had been completed, it appeared that Baldia had considerable arrears in this regard, compared to the city average. Moreover, even the city average is far below the level the Master Plan considers minimally necessary.

Clear standards with regard to amenities have never been fixed; it is up to the planners to decide. In view of the arrears in Baldia compared to the city as a whole, it was decided to take the present city average as point of departure and go beyond this level whenever possible.

In order to determine the spatial distribution of amenities in Baldia, quite a simple approach was followed. All schools and health centres (including their capacity) were marked on a map. Next, all open public space minus the streets was marked. With a list of the amenities to be provided, a number of alternative locations for amenities was developed.

The alternative with the best distribution over Baldia was eventually selected and the location of the amenities was marked on the concept plan. All remaining open public space was proposed as park.

However, the actual construction of schools and health centres falls outside the framework of the improvement programme. It is the concern of other government departments. In view of the malfunctioning of these departments, it is quite unlikely that anything will happen in the next decade.

4.2. The Concept Plan

Once completed, the concept plan of Baldia showed the future land use of occupied and unoccupied space in the settlement. It showed the future development of the Baldia road network and its linkage to the city road network. It presented a general sketch of Baldia and formed the point of departure for further planning on a neighbourhood level.

On the basis of concept plan and inventory, a budget was prepared. This budget is necessary to fix the level of lease rates, and also to obtain approval for the upgrading programme from the central government.

After eight months, the concept plan of Baldia was officially approved, but its limited status became apparent very soon. SITE started the allotment of plots for a housing project in a part of its area, where according to the concept plan the northern loop road would be constructed.

To KMC, SITE is a much-too-powerful agency against which to start a court case, and therefore the alignment of the planned loop road was changed.

5. DETAILED PLANNING

At detailed planning, the existing road network on a neighbourhood level is brought in line with the planned road network in the concept plan. The remaining internal road network of each neighbourhood is planned, the exact location of the amenities from the concept plan is determined and a land use is proposed for the remaining open space.

All the information is marked on a map (scale 1:500), on which the existing plots and the road network also have been indicated. In this way it becomes apparent which structures (or parts of structures) will have to be demolished.

The plans serve as a basis for the issuing of lease titles to the occupants of plots and they therefore have a legal status. Before leases can be issued, the plots have to be measured again to determine the lease charges to be paid by the occupants. So, it is obvious that the plans have to be as accurate as possible.

5.1. The Field Work

Checking and updating of the original maps from 1977 was a prerequisite. Not only had mistakes been made while mapping the area in 1977, but also changes had taken place in the built-up area in the meantime.

Some plots had been extended, while other plots had been subdivided; new plots had been occupied. These new encroachments especially are a frequent problem in the relatively young settlements at the periphery of the city. Every year, a new portion of vacant land is being occupied.

Consequently, each map is already out of date upon its completion. A clear decision or agreement about a date which determines the "final existing situation" has never been reached. Aerial photography would have been very useful in this respect to fix the situation at a certain moment.

During the field work for Baldia, a number of holes in the policy and approach were detected. As mentioned above, the maps of the existing situation form the legal basis for the issuing of lease titles to the individual occupants. It is therefore essential to determine the exact dimensions of each plot.

Often, more than one family (for instance two brothers) live on one plot and "own" the plot together. A decision has never been taken whether to mark one or two plots on the map, in such a case.

An even more complicated problem is encountered in areas, where Kutchis live. Many Kutchi families live as a sort of collective community on one large plot; sometimes altogether 60 people. The application of usual legal norms on these communities would do harm to the socio-cultural nature of this group.

It is possible, of course, to mark just one plot on the map and to adjourn the legal problem of property relations to a later date, but this would create a legally unfair situation. The lease rates per square yard increase as plots are larger: lessees of small plots pay Rs 15 per square yard, while lessees of large plots pay up to Rs 40 per square yard.

If, for instance, a community of 10 families lives on a plot of 800 square yards and this compound is marked as one plot on the map, the occupants have to pay (800 x Rs 40 =) Rs 32,000 or Rs 3200 per family for a lease title. If, however, the compound is mapped as 10 plots of 80 square yards, each family has to pay only (80 x Rs 15 =) Rs 1200, or in total Rs 12,000 for a lease title.

On the other hand, if this method of calculating lease charges is applied for all large plots, the entire system of increasing lease rates for larger plots becomes senseless. Every occupant will pretend that he shares his plot with several families.

The absence of decisions on this sort of matter made realization of a number of (DAM) objectives rather doubtful.

5.2. The Planning

As soon as the existing situation has been mapped, the data from the concept plan (scale 1:2500) are transferred to the detailed plans (scale 1:500).

The planning of the road network poses relatively very few problems. The only difficulty is that usually more demolition is required than had been anticipated originally. This concerns mainly parts of houses along main roads. Sometimes it is decided to deviate from the concept plan and make a road a couple of feet narrower.

Very often another location for proposed schools and health centres has to be found, as the places indicated on the concept plan have been occupied in the meanwhile.

The actual detailed planning concerns the design of the remaining road network and the defining of land use for public open space.

Streets which have become superfluous, because the houses along those streets can also be reached from other streets are not incorporated in the planned road network. The occupants of the houses along such "superfluous streets" can have this space allotted to their plots, so that they can extend their houses. Such an approach yields more revenues for the improvement programme from leasing, while costs are reduced, because fewer streets have to be metalled (map).

Fig. 35.

Problems which arose during the detailed planning of Baldia mainly concerned differences of opinion between CPT and DAM planning about the application of minimum standards.

A minimum street width is determined by calculating the functions and requirements of a typical street. Consequently, the narrowest house access lane has to be 8 ft. wide, wide enough to construct a water pipe line and a sewer line, to carry the sick or dead on a stretcher from the house to the main road and to let the cart of a fruit seller pass through.

However, in many instances, streets do not have to meet all these functions and requirements. A water pipeline or a sewer line may, for instance, be laid out in an adjacent street; sometimes a dead-end street has a rather private character. In such cases, a street narrower than 8 ft. is feasible.

Still, the standard of 8 ft. is strictly applied by KMC planners and as a result parts of often very small houses have to be demolished. But it is absurd that 6 ft. streets which function will have to be widened to 8 ft. and that occupants of houses on both sides of those streets have to pull down their compound wall and rebuild it one foot inwards. A very high and unnecessary expense for them.

The strict application of these planning standards provoked many a discussion, but the results were negligible. During the last 2 months of the project, the minimum street width was even raised to 10 ft. without any obvious reason.

5.3. Residents' Participation

Once plans have been completed and approved by the department, they are officially published. An announcement is made in the newspapers and the plans are displayed at the KMC office. Local leaders from the area concerned receive a copy of the plans and in the afternoon or evening meetings are organized, where community relations officers explain the plans to the residents.

Residents have the opportunity to raise objections to the plans and planners prepare comments on these objections. Objections and comments are examined by the Public Objections Hearing Committee. This is called residents' participation.

However, objections to wide thoroughfares in the concept plan are dismissed, because the concept plan has already been approved, although the construction of these roads in particular requires the most demolition. Also the lease rates have already been fixed and cannot be amended.

Moreover, the information the residents receive is very incomplete and concealing. The plans give the impression that schools and health centres will actually be built under the improvement programme. People are also told that water supply and waste disposal will be improved. In fact, it is rather unlikely that these improvements can be financed out of the lease proceeds.

The plans are being used to give the residents the impression that KMC is doing something for their area and to convince them to pay lease charges. This happened at a moment when it was not even sure that the improvement project for Baldia could be implemented. Approval from central government had not yet been obtained and the transfer of the Baldia land from the provincial authorities to KMC had not yet been arranged.

In this way, residents' participation is being reduced in an attempt to make the residents responsible for the plans, while they have no control over their preparation. In the participation process, local leaders act as intermediaries between government planners and residents. All this allows the government to dismiss objections from residents at the implementation stage.

The government's argument is: "You have had an opportunity to raise objections to the plans. If you didn't, it is your own fault."

6. IMPROVEMENT PLANS

The very unhygienic conditions are mainly caused by the inadequate functioning of water supply, sewerage, drainage and garbage collection. Improvement of these services obviously has the highest priority in squatter settlement upgrading programmes. During the entire project period, numerous efforts have been made to find methods to upgrade infrastructure in the settlement.

6.1. Water

The shortage of water in Baldia is enormous. Public standposts supply water only for 2 hours on alternate days. Pressure on the water is very low and consequently the amount of water supplied is rather small. In the hottest months of the year (April, May, June) the situation is even worse: sometimes no water is supplied for a whole week. At such instances, private water carriers make huge profits and residents have to pay dearly for their water.

The water shortage is, of course, the result of a general shortage of water in Karachi, but it is aggravated by the unequal distribution of available water over the city.

The location of Baldia at the periphery of Karachi, its hills and the quality of the water supply network contribute to a further deterioration of the situation.

For a rapid increase in water supply to Baldia, the available water will have to be distributed more equitably over the city. It is obvious that such a decision falls outside the scope of work of the CPT planners. Improvements under the programme are limited to an upgrading of the water supply network in Baldia, but this will not increase water supply to the area.

6.2. Sewerage

The absence of a sewerage system is about the most important cause of unhygienic conditions in Baldia. At present, many of the inhabitants use open battery boxes to defecate. These boxes have to be emptied daily by a sweeper who throws the contents on vacant land outside the area.

Some residents have dug a deep pit on their compound. The pit is covered by a slab and connected to a latrine. Excreta fall into the pit. This is a much more hygienic system of human waste disposal.

The design of a human waste disposal system which could end the unhygienic situation in Baldia was one of the most important items of the improvement programme.

Initially, the feasibility of an underground waterborne sewerage system was examined. However, besides its very high cost, the disadvantage of a waterborne system is that it will get blocked, unless enough water is available to flush the system. And Baldia does not have sufficient water.

A system of open drains also gets rapidly blocked, but these blockages can be more easily removed. On the other hand, the hygienic conditions in the settlement will hardly be improved with such a system.

Eventually, a sanitary engineering consultant from England was engaged to study alternative solutions for human waste disposal systems. He developed the "improved water-sealed soakpit", based on the soakpit system already used by some residents of Baldia.

The existing system is improved by the extension of the pit, which increases its volume (so that the pit is full only after about 20 years) and by a better closure of the top of the pit. The system has the advantage that it is cheap to build, that it is familiar to the people of Baldia and that it functions well. Each dwelling would need such a pit on the plot.

KMC was unwilling, however, to include this human waste disposal system in its improvement package for Baldia. The pits have to be dug on the private compound and this falls outside the scope of work of KMC.

6.3. Garbage Collection

Another cause of bad hygienic conditions in Baldia is the inadequacy of the garbage collection system. All over the city the garbage collection system functions very badly, but the low-income settlements obviously suffer most.

To improve the garbage collection, it was proposed to purchase some additional garbage vans and to reorganize the collection system. Whether this leads to an improvement in garbage collection in Baldia remains to be seen.

6.4. Storm Water Drainage

During the monsoon rains, large parts of Baldia are flooded, because the rain water is not easily drained away. The improvement programme proposed to widen the existing drains and provide a cemented lining.

7. SUMMARY AND CONCLUSIONS

If we look back at the results of 2 years planning for Baldia, we see that not much is left of the original improvement programme. Construction of schools and health centres in an early stage of the project has proved to be impossible. Improvements in water supply, sewerage and garbage collection have been abandoned one after the other. The only component in the programme which remains is the improvement of the road network.

The improvement and extension of the road network and the consequent integration of the settlement in the city has been the basic demand of the urban planning departments, a demand, which is a logical consequence of the function of these departments. They have to organize urban space in such a way that the production process can function smoothly.

Despite the abandonment of many improvement items in the programme and despite the way residents' participation functioned, the people of Baldia remained willing to participate in the execution of the programme, which had boiled down to mere legalization.

After legalization, the market value of land in Baldia will undoubtedly rise considerably. The price an occupant will receive upon sale of his plot will be much higher than the present market value. In fact, only speculators owning several plots will profit by this price increase.

The owner-occupier will have to look for another house, if he sells his present property. And if he wants to save some money from the amount he receives at sale, he will have to change his living conditions: he will have to buy a new house with less or worse facilities, or a house which is far away from employment opportunities, or a house with a low security of tenure.

Despite the reduction of the improvement programme to a level at which only the requirements of the planners are met, and despite the willingness of the residents to cooperate, approval of the squatter settlement upgrading programme could not be obtained. That was the reason the Dutch contribution to the project was stopped. Approval could not be obtained because of the hierarchy of the various government departments and their differences of opinion about squatter settlement upgrading.

The Economics of Land Tenure Regularization in Katchi Abadi Improvement*

E. A. Wegelin

1. INTRODUCTION

The slum improvement policy of Karachi Metropolitan Corporation (KMC) recognizes two major areas of government intervention in the process of katchi abadi improvement:

- environmental upgrading of katchi abadis through the provision/improvement of basic infrastructure, such as water supply, roads, drainage, waste water - and solid waste disposal, electricity supply,
- regularization of (illegal) land tenure of the residents in katchi abadis (slum areas).

It is felt that regularization of tenure would enhance residents' security of tenure to such an extent that they would be stimulated to invest in improving their dwellings themselves, without much involvement from the government side.

This contribution examines the effectiveness of land tenure regularization in katchi abadis as an instrument of resource mobilization and attempts to assess its redistributional implications.

The following section sets forth KMC's slum improvement policy and its implementation to date. This is followed by an extensive discussion of the resource mobilization potential of its land tenure regularization component both in terms of infrastructure cost recovery and dwelling upgrading. A number of constraints are identified, on the demand as well as on the supply side. Redistributional aspects are discussed in terms of wealth transfers and access to urban land in favour of the urban poor.

*Comments on an earlier draft by Dr. M. J. Rodell and Mr. R. Skinner (Bouwcentrum International Education, Rotterdam) are gratefully acknowledged.

2. LAND TENURE REGULARIZATION IN KARACHI

Contrary to the land ownership position in many metropolitan cities in Asia, public land ownership is the rule rather than the exception in Karachi. This not only applies to land ownership generally, but also, more specifically, to those areas housing low-income families. In 1978 approx. 300,000 low-income families or 1.65 million people (30% of Karachi's population) lived in spontaneous settlements, the katchi abadis of Karachi, generally without any title to the land. It was estimated that in 1978 these settlements covered a total area of approximately 9,900 acres, of which three quarters are under the jurisdiction of the Karachi Metropolitan Corporation. The remaining land is under the control of the Karachi Development Authority (KDA), the Cantonment Board (military land), the Karachi Port Trust and Pakistan Railways. A sizeable proportion of land controlled by KMC and KDA is owned by the Provincial Government of Sind (GOS).

This public ownership and control of squatted land means that land tenure regularization is possible on a large scale without having to resort to cumbersome and costly expropriation procedures which so often preclude legalization of squatters' land tenure in other major cities in Asia.

Since the bulk of Karachi's squatters live on land controlled by the KMC, it is not surprising that when (by sheer force of numbers) the emphasis of the government's low-income housing policy changed from slum clearance and construction of low-cost flats (the all-too-familiar story of too few and too expensive) to slum upgrading, KMC had to accept a substantial responsibility. This resulted in the development of a KMC slum improvement policy[1] and attempts at implementation of this policy in a number of large slum areas under KMC control (such as Lyari, Baldia Township, Golimar/Gulbahar, Bhutta Village and some smaller areas).* Even prior to the adoption of this policy KMC had already made scattered efforts at regularizing land tenure (in some parts of Lyari, in Liaquat Ashraf Colony, Mahmoodabad, Azam Basti, Chanesar Goth), while in some areas tenure had been regularized by other controlling agencies such as KDA (Khudadad Colony) and the Cantonment Board (Delhi Colony).

The improvement policy recognized that neither the residents nor KMC had the resources to carry out upgrading single-handedly. It also appreciated that joining governmental and residents' resources would have the potential of utilizing these resources far more efficiently, if infrastructural improvements and regularization of tenure were intimately linked. Full cost recovery in infrastructure provision (except for health and educational facilities which were considered government responsibilities to be provided free of charge) through payment of improvement charges and lease charges by the residents was anticipated. Lease charges were to be related to the market price of the land, but were also supposed to be in line with land lease charges the government had hitherto been charging in selected areas.

Residents were to participate in planning and decision making on infrastructural improvements. This participation, coupled with the expected provision of legal land tenure, was thought to be sufficient incentive for the residents to pay both improvements and lease charges. Upon full payment of both, leases would be provided. Infrastructural improvements were initially to be financed from funds partly provided by KMC and GOS and partly from external sources. These funds would serve as seed capital for a

---

*See map on next page.

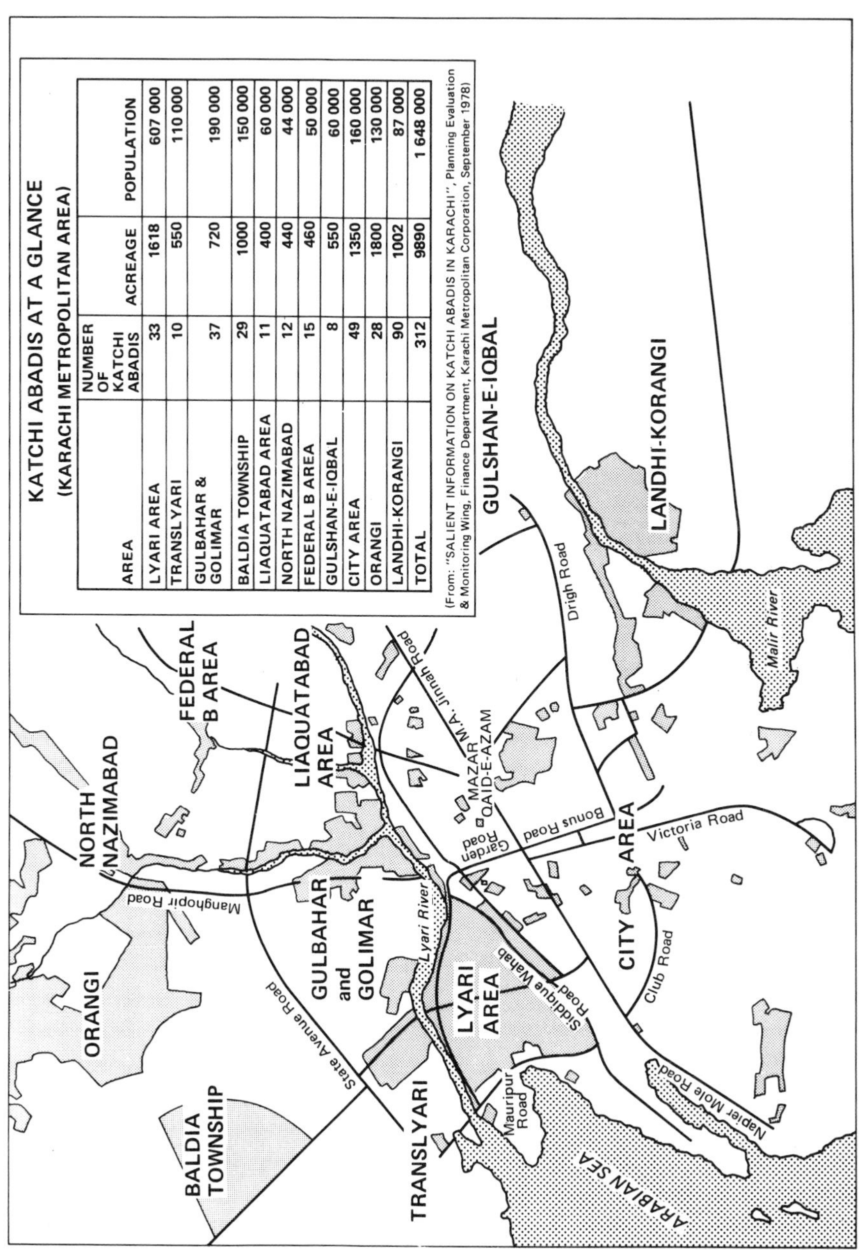

KATCHI ABADIS AT A GLANCE
(KARACHI METROPOLITAN AREA)

AREA	NUMBER OF KATCHI ABADIS	ACREAGE	POPULATION
LYARI AREA	33	1618	607 000
TRANSLYARI	10	550	110 000
GULBAHAR & GOLIMAR	37	720	190 000
BALDIA TOWNSHIP	29	1000	150 000
LIAQUATABAD AREA	11	400	60 000
NORTH NAZIMABAD	12	440	44 000
FEDERAL B AREA	15	460	50 000
GULSHAN-E-IQBAL	8	550	60 000
CITY AREA	49	1350	160 000
ORANGI	28	1800	130 000
LANDHI-KORANGI	90	1002	87 000
TOTAL	312	9890	1 648 000

(From: "SALIENT INFORMATION ON KATCHI ABADIS IN KARACHI", Planning Evaluation & Monitoring Wing, Finance Department, Karachi Metropolitan Corporation, September 1978)

Fig. 36.

revolving slum upgrading fund into which lease-and-improvement charges were to be paid. Availability of seed capital made an approach of simultaneous improvement and regularization technically possible. It was felt that both the existence of the fund and the fact that regularization and improvement would be carried out side by side would act as a further incentive for the residents to pay the charges.

The revolving fund mechanism would make it possible to sustain katchi abadi regularization and improvement over a long term period. The policy prescribed differential lease charges according to plot size and land use and anticipated periodic adjustment to compensate for inflation. Rates, moreover, would vary between areas according to locational advantages. Leases issued were to be transferable subject only to payment of all KMC dues.

The policy assumed that provision of legal tenure would stimulate residents to mobilize additional resources to improve their own houses. Not only would this become less risky than before, but the title deeds could be used as collateral to raise loans for home improvements.

Although the policy does not specify this, the standard KMC practice had been (and still is) to provide leases for a period of 99 years, for which a once-and-for-all lease charge is to be paid, whereas the plotholder is subsequently supposed to pay a marginal annual amount in land rent. Lease agreements restrict type of land use and subject land subdivision and amalgamation to approval by and payment of a fee to KMC.

These conditions (particularly the period of 99 years and unrestricted transferability) provide the plotholder with virtual ownership rights, which was expected to make it very attractive to get one's tenure legalized. The snag in the policy lay in the improvement charge: this was supposed to ensure full recovery of the improvement costs. The charges would be levied in proportion to the standard lease rates. The improvement charges, of course, depended also on the proposed standards of improvement.

The first project in which these rates were to be applied was the Lyari Improvement Project. Lyari, with a population of about 600,000 is Karachi's largest and oldest slum area. The proposed improvement charges were a multiple (sometimes even ten times) of the proposed lease charges, which in themselves were not much higher than what residents had hitherto been paying in those parts of Lyari where regularization had been going on for some time. It appeared that the new system, under which residents would have to pay both improvement and lease charges before their tenure was officially regularized, overtaxed the willingness of the people to pay. The charges to be paid in Lyari became an issue in the 1977 general election campaign and on 20 February 1977, the then Chief Minister of Sind, at an election rally in Lyari: "told the cheering crowd that the rates would be fixed at Rs 4 (per square yard, E.W.) for residential and Rs 6 for commercial and he also warned the KMC officials that if all the leases are not completed and handed over to the residents by June 30, they will be sacked"[2].*

These rates, which were subsequently notified in the Government Gazette were very close to the rates people had been paying before, but only a fraction of the market price. The implication of the Chief Minister's statement was that no improvement charges could be levied. This undermined the very basis of the project's finances.

---

*US $1 = Pakistan Rupees (Rs) 10.

Subsequently, in other areas (notably Baldia Township, Gulbahar/Golimar and Bhutta Village) KMC demonstrated it had learned some lessons from the fate of the Lyari Improvement Project. In the Baldia Township Regularization and Improvement Project, for instance, proposed infrastructural improvements were at much lower standards and an all inclusive lease-charge was proposed, which was about twice as high as the now prevailing rates in Lyari and only marginally higher than those in areas such as Mahmoodabad and Azam Basti. As in the case of Lyari, charges (in this case lease charges only) payable by the beneficiaries were the main way in which the costs of infrastructural improvements were expected to be recovered. Otherwise the proposal for rate structure and lease conditions was very similar to that of the Lyari leases: larger plots as well as non-residential land use would be subject to higher rates, leases were transferable and a once-and-for-all payment would entitle the occupant to a 99-year lease.

This changed in May 1978 when the provincial Martial Law Government issued a directive,[3] restricting transferability of leases to inheritance. These limitations had a direct impact on the willingness to take up leases, particularly in Lyari, being the only area where the process of issuing leases had been going on for a considerable time and in relatively large numbers, i.e. at a rate of several thousand per year. At that time a total number of 11,450 leases had been issued in Lyari since 1972, yielding a total revenue of Rs 5.3 million. The number of lease applications dropped considerably.

In other large areas the impact of this restriction was not immediately felt, mainly because disputes between the KMC and the Government of Sind (GOS), which owns large tracts of squatted land in Karachi (e.g. the entire area of Baldia Township and sizeable sections of Golimar/Gulbahar) on the price to be paid by KMC to GOS for the land ownership transfer to KMC had prevented the issue of any leases until then.

Both these problems were potentially solved in December 1979 when the earlier Martial Law Order (MLO) was reconstituted to limit non-transferability of leases to a period of 5 years following issue and to allow transferability during this period for the purpose of mortgage to the House Building Finance Corporation (HBFC) or a scheduled Bank as collateral against approved building loans. The new MLO (no. 110) also provided for the transfer of Government land to KMC for the purpose of katchi abadi regularization at the price of 10% of lease charges recoverable from the occupants. The MLO 110 also allowed the possibility of a different land lease period than 99 years.[4]

Yet, by mid-February 1980 the total number of leases issued in Lyari had barely crossed the 12,000 mark, although about 25,000 applications were in various stages of processing. Ownership transfer of Baldia Township and Golimar/Gulbahar Land from GOS to KMC was officially effected in September 1980, after which issue of leases could start in these areas.

While, in principle, the ideas laid down in KMC's slum improvement policy were reasonable, and certainly embodied a more realistic approach to low-income housing problems than earlier resettlement attempts, the policy was based on a set of assumptions, which - with the benefit of hindsight - do not appear to be completely correct. Some assumptions related to the land tenure regularization aspect of the policy are discussed in the following sections.

3. RESOURCE MOBILIZATION THROUGH LAND TENURE REGULARIZATION: CONSTRAINTS ON THE DEMAND SIDE

A central demand constraint on resource mobilization recognized in the policy consists of the generally below average income levels of katchi abadi residents. The policy therefore stipulated that standards of infrastructural improvement be set at such levels and in such ways that residents would be *able* and *willing* to pay lease- and improvement charges high enough to cover full costs of such improvements.

In as far as ability to pay goes, the low level of the charges and the provision to pay these in instalments, if necessary, were thought to ensure that residents would not face substantial hardships in paying.

Proposed charges were certainly low as compared to informal market prices in most areas. A limited survey carried out in various parts of Baldia Township in May 1978 indicated that the proposed residential lease rate of Rs 15.-- per square yard amounted to 25 to 30% of informal land transaction prices (depending on exact location).* A more selective survey in a centrally-located part of Baldia Township (Ghaus Nagar, Muslim Mujahid Colony, Medina Colony) in October 1978 indicated average property prices in those areas of Rs 120 per square yard for built-up properties and Rs 75-100 per square yard for vacant plots. Prices for 43 vacant plots located in a potentially attractive commercial area of Baldia Township (major road separating sectors 3 and 5, Saeedabad), which were auctioned officially (but technically illegally!) by KMC during 1974-1976 were Rs 92.-- per square yard on average. (Average value for 16 plots auctioned in 1976 was Rs 112.-- per square yard).

Based on data collected in a larger-scale sample survey, average residential property values in Baldia Township are estimated at approx. Rs 200.-- per square yard in 1979 as compared to Rs 155.-- in 1977 for the same sample.[5]

In other areas, too, charges are substantially below prevailing informal market prices,[6] but obviously this does not automatically imply that charges are within the paying capacity of all residents. After all, in many cases such charges would have to be paid *in addition* to prices paid when the plot was acquired on the informal market. In the above survey only 32% of the interviewed residents indicated they had settled in the area without paying any money to acquire their plot. Tables 1 and 2 provide a comparison of charges with income levels for Baldia Township. The average plot size is 117.3 square yard and the typical plot size range is 70-130 square yards. In the project proposal owners of residential and residential-cum-commercial plots of less than 150 square yards were given the option of paying in four interest free annual instalments, annual payments ranging from Rs 188.-- for a residential plot of 50 square yards to Rs 1,125.-- for a residential-cum-commercial plot of 150 square yards. It was felt that, except for the very lowest income bracket (up to Rs 300 per month) this would not be a problem.

---

*With the exception of one area - Rasheedabad - far from the main road without any access to water supply, where informal land prices were substantially lower than in other parts of Baldia Township.

Table 1. Proposed Lease Charges, Baldia Township Regularization and Improvement Project (in Rs)

		Land use							
Plot size in sq. yds.	Percentage of plots below	Residential		Residential - cum-commercial		Commercial		Industrial	
		Rate per sq. yds.	Total charge	Rate per sq. yds.	Total charge	Rate per sq. yds.	Total charge	Rate per sq. yds.	Total charge
50	7.5	15	750	30	1,500	100	5,000	100	5,000
80	(30.0)	15	2,200	30	2,400	100	8,000	100	8,000
100	(48.2)	15	1,500	30	3,000	100	10,000	150	15,000
120	(64.6)	15	1,800	30	3,600	100	12,000	150	18,000
150	83.1	15	2,250	30	4,500	100	15,000	150	22,500
200	92.0	25	5,000	50	10,000	100	20,000	150	30,000
250	n.a.	50	12,000	70	17,000	100	25,000	300	75,000

Sources: *PC I Baldia Township Regularization and Improvement Project* (Revised, May 1979), *Annex VI and Baldia Evaluation Survey Report*, 1979, Table 4.11 (p. 56). Figures between brackets are interpolations.

Table 2. Distribution of Monthly Household Income in Rs, Baldia Township, Spring 1979

Income	Percentage of Sample
0-300	6.1
301-500	19.1
501-700	23.4
701-900	15.7
901-1,100	12.7
1,101-1,300	7.7
1,301 and above	15.3
	100.0

Average: Rs 865. Median: Rs 750. Sample of 720 households.

Source: M. Schuringa *et al.*, 1979, p. 39.

As for residents' willingness to pay, it was assumed that this would be high because:

(a) Obtaining a lease would increase *de-facto* security of tenure substantially.
(b) Residents would feel they were getting their money's worth because infrastructural improvement of their area would be carried out simultaneously with preparations for regularization (such as physical surveys, individual cadastral plot measurements, administrative procedures.
(c) A high level of residents' participation in improvement and regularization planning would ensure agreement of the residents with the plans ultimately adopted.
(d) There was the prospect of being able to use lease titles as collateral for loans.

The assumption of willingness to pay for these reasons has proved to be a tenuous one. Regularization of land tenure and actual issue of leases are only the final stages in the process of consolidating *de-facto* security of tenure. In Karachi particularly, large scale evictions had already become unlikely before KMC introduced its slum improvement policy. This was further reinforced by the Government announcement on 1 January 1978 that all katchi abadis in existence at that time would be regularized unless the area was subject to hazards like frequent floods or was otherwise required for public purposes. This announcement may have taken away some of the incentive for residents to spend money on obtaining a lease, particularly because, as noted, the Government shortly afterwards directed that lease titles of regularized plots would be non-transferable, thus preventing their use as collateral.

This means that not much can be expected from regularization as a mechanism to stimulate private home improvement. Although it has been shown in a number of studies that the level of *de-facto* security of tenure is positively related to residents' investments in home improvement,[7] regularization in the circumstances described above means only a marginal increase in the level of *de-facto* security of tenure. Moreover, a potential stimulus for home improvement, namely the use of the lease title as collateral for improvement loans was precluded by the non-transferability clause (however, this possibility was restored in December 1979).

As for area improvement, KMC was not perceived by the residents as being particularly concerned with this: in a survey early in 1979 it was found that only 15% of residents in Baldia Township had witnessed any (marginal) improvement activity on the part of KMC.[8] Indeed, area improvement activities of KMC in the area until that time had been *ad-hoc*, resulting from incidental pressure from area leaders rather than from the improvement plan.

Planned area improvement actually militates against the interests of some of these leaders who act as brokers between residents and the government.[9] This also limits practical possibilities of residents' participation in regularization and improvement planning: channels of communication between executing agencies such as KMC and KDA and ordinary katchi abadi residents are blocked by area leaders and local politicians, whose interests are different from those of ordinary residents. The middleman role of such leaders is endangered by systematic planning and active residents' participation. Therefore it is not surprising that area leaders refused to be co-responsible for area improvement plans initiated by KMC and did not form an effective channel of communication between KMC and ordinary residents.[10]

It must also be noted that political circumstances after the declaration of Martial Law in July 1977 were hardly conducive to residents' participation, for prolonged periods of time public meetings were prohibited. This situation improved markedly after the local bodies elections in November 1979. The elected members of the Karachi Metropolitan Council (four for Baldia Township) appear more successful in communicating between the residents and KMC officials.

In the fiscal year 1980-1981 Rs 2.8 million worth of road improvement will be carried out in Baldia Township. This has been made financially possible through a federal government grant to KMC for the purpose of katchi abadi improvement, totalling Rs 20 million.

Up to November 1980, 1,500 applications for lease have been received by KMC's Baldia Township office. 200 applicants out of these had paid their charges in full. Monthly recovery of lease charges was at the level of Rs 100,000 during July-October 1980 (during fiscal year 1979-1980 a total amount of Rs 500,000 had been recovered).

These positive changes were largely due to the activities of the four councillors, but yet willingness to pay on the residents' part may be considerably less than necessary for full cost recovery. The survey carried out early in 1979 indicated that only 51% of the residents in Baldia Township were willing to pay the lease charges, but even this figure may be too optimistic: the same survey showed that only one quarter of the respondents could mention the correct lease rate they would be expected to pay![11] According to the project proposal, a default rate of more than 20% would upset full cost-recovery.

4. SUPPLY CONSTRAINTS IN LAND TENURE REGULARIZATION

4.1. Prevailing Lease Rates in Other Areas

KMC's slum upgrading policy devoted considerable attention to the determination of lease rates. As noted above, these were to vary according to location, plotsize, land use and to be adjustable for inflation. Based on overall full cost-recovery, rates would be set following a dialogue between KMC and the residents regarding the detailed area improvement plan.[12] In addition: "The basic structure of the rates for leasing by KMC of land in irregular areas, is to be the same as that of the rates sanctioned in the past for application by KMC to various irregular areas".[13] This last provision - which incidentally was inconsistent with some of the other criteria noted - assumed much more weight than was anticipated. Sanctioned lease rates in areas under KMC control other than Baldia Township are shown in Table 3. Not only the structure, but also the absolute level of these rates acted as precedents in determining rates for Baldia Township in the sense that they reflected what had previously been politically acceptable. KMC could not deviate much from this, particularly in respect of residential and residential-cum-commercial rates which were considered most sensitive. Yet KMC could have argued that all these rates were fixed nominal amounts established at different points in time, with no possibilities of adjustment for inflation, and that locational advantages would be different for each area. The precedents of prevailing rates in combination with limited administrative capability of KMC (see below) motivated the KMC in April 1978 to propose uniform lease rates throughout the city, thus depriving it of a major instrument for resource mobilization and guidance of development planning.* However, the Martial Law Order (MLO) No. 67 (May 1978) stipulated existing rates as the lower limit, whereas MLO 110 (December 1979) revised this lower limit upwards to Rs 15.-. The above goes to show that in the prevailing circumstances existing rates were important bench marks for the setting of new rates, rather independently from financial or affordability considerations.

Table 3. Lease Rates Per Square Yard Charged by KMC in Various Katchi Abadis in Karachi (1978)†

Area	Land use and plot size		
	Residential	Residential - cum-commercial	Commercial
Hyderabad Colony	Rs 8.50	-	Rs 60.-
Bihar Colony	Rs 10.-	-	Rs 60.-
Liaquatabad and Orangabad	Rs 7.-	-	RS 25.-
Lyari	Rs 4.- (up to 200 sq. yds.)	-	Rs 6.- (up to 200 sq. yds.)
Mahmoodabad/ Chanesar Goth/ Azam Basti	Rs 8.- (up to 240 sq. yds.) Rs 16.- (42-400 sq. yds.) Rs 25.- (401-600 sq. yds.)	Rs 14.- (up to 100 sq. yds.) Rs 30.- (101-200 sq. yds.) Rs 50.- (201-400 sq. yds.)	- -

4.2. Land Ownership Disputes

It is generally assumed that private ownership of land on which slum areas have been built (illegally) constitutes an impediment to governmental efforts at slum upgrading, particularly so if these efforts include some attempt at increasing slum residents' security of tenure. Indeed, there is abundant evidence that this is a major problem area in slum upgrading all over Asia.[14]

*The lease period of 99 years itself imposes a similar constraint, but, unlike in other cities in Asia, this has never generated a significant extent of professional or public debate.

†Note that lease rates for different areas were established in different years as a once-and-for-all nominal charge. In an inflationay climate, this is an incentive to postpone taking up a lease.

Yet, the experience in Karachi indicates that large-scale public land ownership in itself is not a sufficient guarantee for a smooth and rapid legalization of tenure, even when the government has decided upon this as a matter of policy. Initially, in a situation where land was owned and controlled by a multitude of government organizations and in which no accepted policy of land tenure regularization existed, legalization had been achieved in various areas largely through incidental influence and bribing. Van der Linden[15] presents three illuminating case studies of katchi abadis where these instruments in the hands of the residents were extremely important. All three colonies discussed by him are located on government land. In each case it took some 20 years to conclude an accommodation with the various government agencies concerned and to reach a situation in which leases could be issued by the executing agency. Conflicts between various government agencies regarding ownership and administrative control of the land figure prominently in the history of two of these areas (in the third case KMC land ownership was never disputed, but KDA's lack of concurrence to upgrading plans was a major cause of delay).

Even after the government adopted a policy of legalization of tenure, disputes over land ownership continued to form a major supply constraint, particularly so for a large number of slum areas located at the (one time) fringe of the city. Karachi is largely surrounded by arid, desert-like land on which agricultural land use is virtually excluded due to lack of rain, structure and salinity of the soil. As a result of this, very little land outside the city had been claimed and utilized by private individuals during the centuries in which Karachi's growth was relatively slow and land title registration unknown. This vested land ownership of large tracts of land in the Government of Sind by default.[16]

During the colonial era this presented relatively few problems, but after Partition of British India and independence of Pakistan in 1947 this situation changed. Partition and independence brought about a rapid growth of the city during 1947-1951 (more than 10% population growth p.a.), after which the flow of migrants from India gradually tapered off until 1971 when an additional inflow of migrants came from newly-independent Bangladesh. Apart from these incidental factors, natural population increase and rural-urban migration alone accounted for an average annual population growth rate of approximately 5% in the post-independence period. As the city expanded, the municipal (metropolitan) area has been extended from time to time and a development agency was set up to develop Karachi's fringe localities (Karachi Development Authority - KDA). This meant that KMC and KDA received administrative control over substantial tracts of land from time to time but, in many cases, the Government of Sind, through its provincial Board of Revenue, resisted transferring ownership of these lands to such bodies. The land ownership-and-control situation of Baldia Township is a typical case in point.

The first inhabitants settled in what is now Baldia Township in 1953, whereas the name Baldia Colony dates from 1956. In 1964 administrative control was assumed by the Baldia Town Committee. Baldia Township area was officially gazetted for development purposes in 1965. Administrative control was transferred to KDA, which prepared a so-called plot-township plan for the area. After several years of disagreement between KDA and KMC, administrative control of Baldia Township was transferred to KMC in 1974. Land ownership, however, was still vested in the Government of Sind. Provincial land matters are handled by its Board of Revenue which, in conjunction with the provincial Finance Department, generally seeks to maximize land revenue. Consequently, the debate on the price for transfer of land ownership between

GOS and KDA (during 1965-1974) or KMC (from mid 1974 onwards) had been protracted in the absence of a policy guideline for such cases. The Board of Revenue and the provincial Finance Department insisted that the transfer price should come close to unofficial market prices paid in the area, whereas KMC, supported by its controlling authority (the Commissioner of Karachi and Local Government Secretary, GOS) effectively argued the case of low opportunity costs of land, since it would be impossible to evict the squatters from the land.[17] After the Federal Government's directive to regularize katchi abadis in existence on 1 January 1978 this latter argument became particularly difficult to defeat. Moreover, local bodies like KMC which face pressures to regularize and improve katchi abadis at relatively low lease rates and which otherwise have a chronic lack of resources, can ill afford to pay substantial amounts to the provincial government to acquire squatted land.

The policy guideline issued by the provincial Martial Law Administrator in April 1979 largely endorsed the local bodies' viewpoint, linking the expected lease proceeds to the transfer price of the land. It was decided that this transfer price would amount to 10% of the lease charge payable by the occupant, which amount would be treated as the provincial Government's contribution to the development of the katchi abadi concerned in the form of a soft loan to the local government. As mentioned, this guideline was subsequently enacted in the Regularization and Development of katchi abadis Order (MLO No. 110) in December 1979. Establishment of this guideline was doubtless an important improvement, but in spite of this, land ownership of Baldia Township was only transferred to KMC by September 1980, delaying legal issue of leases by KMC considerably. At the time of writing no leases had been legally issued yet, due to flaws in the procedural arrangements necessary in the area. Neither the actual amount to be paid by KMC to GOS, nor the terms and conditions on which this would be re-lent to KMC have yet been established.

4.3. Inadequate Administrative Machinery

The fact that, in spite of official readiness on the part of GOS to transfer land ownership to KMC, the method of this transfer had still not yet been worked out completely more than a year after principles had been decided on, points to another supply bottleneck in the process of regularization of katchi abadis - the lack of adequate administrative machinery. This applies to the Government of Sind, but much more so to KMC.

The experiences in regularizable KMC-owned and controlled areas cast strong doubts on KMC's administrative ability to regularize efficiently and expeditiously. Regularization is a complex, time-consuming activity, involving plot boundary surveys, tuning proposed regularization to area improvement plans, effectuating lease payments by the residents and preparation of lease documents. This is aggravated by the lengthy and cumbersome procedure the applicant has to work through to obtain his lease. This procedure not only involves a large number of steps, offices and officials but, moreover, it has never been designed specifically for regularization. As a result, the applicant is required to produce documents he cannot produce by definition, namely a sales deed or a gift deed.* For the same reason the procedure fails

*After the newly-elected councillors became involved in leasing in 1980, leading to increased numbers of applications to be processed, this requirement has been waived in cases where it would be obviously inapplicable.

to incorporate elements which stimulate an efficient leasing process, such as block surveying, publicity campaigns, delegation of responsibilities to mobile lease offices (incorporating the presence of all necessary officials) or financial incentives to residents to take an early lease. In some cases, the reverse seems to be in evidence: residents sometimes complain it is necessary to bribe officials to carry out their duties in the procedure, thereby raising the effective lease charge payable. In the presence of established *de-facto* security of tenure, this tends to reduce the interest of the residents to go through with the entire lease procedure. While the lengthy procedure is commonly justified as providing safeguards against corruption, this is far from certain: apart from difficulties in persuading officials to play their part, residents are easily tempted to connive with the KMC surveyor to register a smaller than actual plot area or a different land use. The large number of plots to be surveyed together with a general reluctance on the part of officials to check back on site strongly reduces the likelihood of detection.

More generally, KMC's internal organization is not as yet geared towards project implementation on a reasonable scale: many functions are handled centrally by specialized departments (e.g. the Land Department, Finance Department, Engineering Department, Health Department) without an organizational formula for coordination at the project level. Where a start has been made on such coordination (in Lyari, for instance), insufficient delegation of powers to the Project Coordinator severely limits its utility. Minor decisions on individual plots have to be referred to the KMC head office, resulting in delays, additional money-making opportunities and sometimes the relevant files are lost altogether.

Here, again, the intentions at the policy level are laudable: a special Directorate of katchi abadis and evaluation has been created in KMC under MLO 110, and a coordinating katchi abadi cell has been set up in the Local Government Department, GOS. However, this has so far had little impact in expediting actual regularization and improvement work. This is partly because of staffing difficulties in the Directorate, which, in a departure from previous practice, will have responsibility not only for planning, but also for implementation of regularization and improvement of katchi abadis.

The MLO 110 provides for the establishment of a revolving fund, but its organizational position *vis-a-vis* the Directorate and operational capability have not yet become clear.

5. REDISTRIBUTIONAL ASPECTS OF LAND TENURE REGULARIZATION

5.1. Characteristics of the Land Market

The redistributional impact of legalizing land tenure depends to a large extent on the degree of imperfection in the urban land market. In the case of a perfectly competitive land market, this would be very clear: market rates would reflect opportunity costs; consequently, in case of government land lease issues below market value only the government loses and the occupant gains to the amount of the government's loss. In the case of a subsequent transfer of the lease, the occupant would charge the market value and retain the full redistributional surplus.

In actual fact, of course, the urban land market is highly imperfect. First of all, it is a highly-dynamic market. In a city like Karachi, in which population grows by 5% per annum while the ultimate supply potential of land is fixed, an equilibrium land price is unthinkable. A long-run upward price trend is inevitable. In the short-run, prices may fluctuate considerably, affected by changes in short-run demand or supply positions. The potential for volatile fluctuations is high, because at any point in time only a fraction of potential demand and supply is exercised in the market.

Secondly, the urban land market is heterogeneous by nature: each piece of urban land is unique in terms of its location and soil constitution. Properties are not fungible (not interchangeable like loaves of bread or notes of currency). Of course, some pieces of land are more comparable to each other than others: it is generally possible to identify sub-markets in which different groups of buyers and sellers operate. Non-fungibility, however, violates two conditions for a perfect market namely the condition of large numbers of buyers and sellers and the condition of transparency of the market. Violation of these conditions introduces the possibility of restrictive practices and coercion.

Thirdly, transparency of the market is further reduced by imperfect knowledge and foresight on the part of potential buyers or sellers regarding present and future market conditions.

Fourthly, further market imperfections result from government interventions. Land use regulations, differences in levels of urban services and in tenure conditions all stimulate fragmentation of the land market. In Karachi, this is reinforced by the unusual pattern of land ownership, in which a limited number of government bodies own most urban land. In theory, this should give the government an unusually strong hold on the land market, but, as noted in previous sections, this does not apply in practice: there is as yet no overall governmental land disposal policy to which all government bodies concerned adhere.* Consequently, resulting market distortions tend to be erratic rather than systematic.

The market imperfections noted above make it extremely difficult to fully identify the beneficiaries of below-market value leasing in a particular katchi abadi. Generalization is even more difficult because different conditions obtain in different areas. The following discussion, therefore, is of necessity somewhat speculative.

Conceptually, the following issues seem to merit discussion:

(a) What is the direct redistributional impact of the change in government policy embodied in the Chief Martial Law Administrator's announcement in January 1978 and subsequent enactments in MLO 67 and MLO 110?

(b) Apart from that, is there any direct redistributional impact of issuing leases as such within such a policy environment?

---

*The Regularization and Development of katchi abadis Order (MLO 110) provides a legal framework for such a policy in as far as squatted provincial government and local government land goes, but unfortunately excludes land owned by federal government agencies, such as Pakistan Railways. Moreover, under this order the provincial Government is given the discretionary power to declare such land a katchi abadi (bringing it under the purview of the order's land disposal provisions). As demonstrated in Section 4.2 above, this makes it possible to delay land ownership transfers for a considerable period.

(c) What is the impact of the policy change and the issue of leases on land values in the project area itself, in other (adjacent) katchi abadis and on urban land market prices in general? Who gains and who loses as a result of this?
(d) What additional redistribution takes place through government intervention as a result of the area becoming part of the formal urban land market? In particular, what is the impact of property taxation and municipal rates being levied?
(e) How does regularization influence the urban future and what is the redistributional impact of this? More particularly, how does legalization influence access to urban land for different income groups in future?

5.2. The Direct Redistributional Impact of Regularization

5.2.1. The Impact of the Policy Change

With the policy change, the government has officially renounced its powers to evict occupants of katchi abadis in existence before January 1978 on provincial and local government land and to auction off such land. While it may be argued that its effective powers to do so on a large scale were already limited substantially before the policy change (see para 4.2 and below), such powers have now become even more restricted. In those areas officially notified as katchi abadis under the provisions of article 2 of MLO 110 (such as Baldia Township and Golimar/Gulbahar), eviction of residents living there as of 1 January 1978 has become completely impossible. In such cases the existing situation and the informal land market is legitimized.*

To fully understand the redistributional impact of the change in policy, however, two important matters should be pointed out. Firstly, levels of *de-facto* security of tenure vary considerably in Karachi's katchi abadis. Such levels are determined by factors such as land ownership, location and age, level of infrastructure provision, protection by government officials or politicians, government pronouncements and the availability of (provisional) land titles.[18] The change in policy adds only marginally to *de-facto* security levels in many cases. Baldia Township is a case in point. As far back as 1972, the late Prime Minister of Pakistan, Z. A. Bhutto held a speech in the area, in which he promised that the area would be regularized.[19] In some parts of Baldia Township residents were issued (provisional) allotment slips from KDA in anticipation of leases at a future date.[20] Following transfer of land control to KMC in mid-1974, KMC repeatedly expressed its intention to regularize and improve the area.[21] In these circumstances the announcement of the Chief Martial Law Administrator, General Zia-ul-Haq on 1 January 1978 and subsequent enactments of MLO 67 and 110 in Sind really added only marginally to *de-facto* security of tenure. In Lyari (see Section 2 above) the change of policy initially even had a perverse effect: leases

---

*An interesting feature of the notification of Baldia Township as a katchi abadi under MLO 110 (implying land ownership transfer to KMC) is that the entire area of 7,200 acres has been included, not just the project area of 1000 acres considered under KMC's slum upgrading programme. A large part of the remaining 6200 acres is still unoccupied. In principle, this provides KMC with the attractive option to develop the unoccupied portion with serviced plots to be leased to overspill households from the project area and other areas to be upgraded under its improvement programme.

to be issued under MLO 67 would be non-transferable, whereas leases issued previously were transferable. As a result residents submitted a petition to KMC requesting that Lyari be excluded from the list of katchi abadis. In Golimar/Gulbahar a situation very similar to Baldia Township prevailed. Substantial provision of infrastructure, political and bureaucratic patronage as well as political promises had made eviction extremely unlikely already before the policy change. In other areas, however, the change may have added substantially to *de-facto* security.

However, the MLO 110 is far less wide-ranging than the initial sweeping announcement made by the Chief Martial Law Administrator on 1 January 1978. Article 2 provides for provincial government discretion to declare an area a katchi abadi for the purpose of the order, which, moreover, only extends to provincial or local government-owned land. Article 8(V) provides a long list of exceptions: "No katchi abadi, or a portion thereof situated on land which is not safe from flood hazards or is required or reserved for roads, hospitals, schools, colleges, libraries, playground, garden, park, community centre, mosques, graveyards, railway, high tension line or such other purposes and is otherwise in conflict with the planned land use of approved schemes shall be regularizable."[22] These provisions enable the government to be almost as selective as before in deciding which areas to regularize and which not.

The impact of the policy change as enacted in MLO 110 is primarily that it has provided a framework within which the struggle for land tenure consolidation will take place. This is important, but its impact should not be exaggerated. In view of the often very organized manner in which katchi abadi formation and consolidation takes place[23] and the high *de-facto* level of tenure-security in some major slum areas prior to the policy change, claims by Pakistan Government officials that the policy change led to massive land invasions[24] must be dismissed as an unrealistic simplification, at least in as far as katchi abadi development in Karachi goes.

To the extent that the policy change limits the government's option to evict, enhancing *de-facto* security of tenure to the residents the government clearly loses and residents clearly gain, particularly so because the costs of eviction were largely borne by the residents: the government did not normally provide more than marginal assistance by way of compensation and/or provision of alternative sites. This meant that land auction values were realised by the government at little costs. Moreover, in areas to be regularized under MLO 110 there is as yet no compulsion to take up (and pay for) a lease and there is no threat of eviction if one does not do so. Hence, residents in such areas acquire (marginally?) increased security of tenure, reducing the risk of eviction with its attendant costs, without having to pay anything in exchange.

If the original occupants are low-income households and if they capture these gains fully, such a direct redistributional impact can be judged highly favourable on equity grounds: redistribution of wealth from the government to the poor takes place.

As shown in Table 2 above, Baldia Township certainly does not exclusively house low-income families. A comparison of earlier (and somewhat less reliable) income distributional data of Baldia Township, Golimar and Lyari indicates that income levels in the latter two large katchi abadis are somewhat lower than in Baldia Township.[25]

An important point to note is that the current practice in Karachi is to issue leases to property owners, not to plotholders as such. This means that in the case of plotholders renting a plot from absentee landlords, the primary redistributional benefit accrues to the landlord who, moreover, is likely to gain twice: his rented property, with greater security of tenure can now also command a higher rent in the market. This may bring about a regressive equity impact on two counts: firstly, landlords are generally richer than tenants; secondly, poor tenants would possibly be forced out if they cannot afford to pay the higher rent.* However, in Baldia Township, the percentage of plotholders who were renting is quite low: 13.6% in 1977 and 11.1% in 1979. In the much more centrally-located area of Lyari, the percentage was substantially higher, 33.2% in 1975.[27] In both areas renters were more recent settlers than owner-occupiers. In Baldia Township, household incomes of renters were lower than those of owner-occupiers (data for Lyari are not available).

As to the question whether poor tenants will be forced out, there is as yet little evidence on this in Karachi. To date there has been only one systematic attempt to trace socio-economic changes in residents' composition over time in a katchi abadi as *de-facto* security of tenure increases.[28] This study brought out some interesting facts related to the above question:

- during a 1½ year period from late 1977 to early 1979, overall mobility was low: only 11% of residents moved (or 7.5% on annual basis); of those whose place of destination was known, 62% stayed in Baldia Township (44% of all movers),
- people who left were generally poorer than those who stayed, but so were new arrivals who, however, earned a little more than the leavers,
- both among leavers and among new arrivals the percentage of renters was high, 57% and 45% respectively (much higher than the overall percentage of 11.1). Rents paid increased substantially during this period.

The above data seems to lend support to the hypothesis that poor tenants will be forced to move out if security of tenure in the area increases. However, the limited quantitative importance of renters, combined with low overall mobility during the period, precluded an in-depth analysis of socio-economic and mobility patterns of this group. The percentage of renters among the new arrivals was lower than among leavers, indicating that some landlords took physical possession of their property in anticipation of impending regularization (possibly to be on the safe side in case the government decided to issue leases to occupants irrespective of occupancy status). As to owner-occupiers who sold and left (about 5% of all plotholders during the 1½ year period), there is no evidence on their selling price compared with prevailing market value. One cannot entirely exclude the possibility of low sale value as a result of coercion or lack of knowledge of market prices, but this would seem to have a very limited quantitative impact in any case.

Summarizing, the scanty evidence seems to indicate that the direct redistributional impact of the policy change could be highly favourable, but that the actual outcome depends on whether tenure would be granted to occupants or to owners and on the pre-regularization income distribution of occupants.

---

*It should be noted that, in the case of the landlord acquiring official tenure, the potential for additional resource mobilization through home improvement discussed above may also be less. It seems reasonable to assume that additional resources invested by the landlord would otherwise have been invested elsewhere anyway, whereas the incentive on the part of the tenant cannot possibly be very substantial. However, no evidence on this is available.

5.2.2. The Impact of Issuing Leases as Such

In areas where security of tenure is assured and where there is no compulsion to take up a lease, it is very doubtful if the actual issue of leases will bring about any substantial redistributional impact. Eligible residents (or landlords) would probably weigh the pro's and con's of taking up a lease under such circumstances. Taking up a lease means payment of official lease rates, going through the complex lease procedure, sometimes including paying bribes to officials concerned (see Section 4.3). The lease title issued carries some restrictions on alternative land use and the provision of non-transferability during the first 5 years. Against these disadvantages, a resident would weigh the advantage of minimal additional security of tenure and the possibility of using the lease title as collateral for a building loan (excluded specifically from the non-transferability clause). Residents may or may not take up a lease; but in view of the circumstances the net benefits of doing so are not likely to be more than marginal, particularly so because there is as yet no effective formal credit institution which extends small housing improvement loans, even with the lease title as collateral. Commercial banks in Pakistan do not generally finance housing; if at all, this is confined to upper and middle-class housing. The House Building Finance Corporation so far has been primarily extending housing loans to middle-class families. Although it would be a logical institution to finance house improvement in legalized slums, it has not yet undertaken such activities in Karachi (it did finance a katchi abadi Development Scheme in Faisalabad, Punjab through the Faisalabad Development Authority during 1976-1977, under which each allottee could take out Rs 10,000, presumably for house building or extension).[29]

Summarizing, once an area is declared a katchi abadi for the purpose of MLO 110 and when it is notified as such in the Government Gazette, the actual lease issue is not likely to have a substantial redistributional impact. Many residents, in fact, may not want to take up a lease: the costs of doing so may well outweigh the benefits.

This would be different if not taking up a lease within a certain period would forfeit the right of regularization and bring the demolition squad back in. For revenue boosting purposes the Government or KMC may want to introduce such a provision in future, in which case residents would stand to gain much more substantially from actually taking up a lease, particularly so if suitable credit mechanisms are evolved. In such cases the net redistributional outcome would depend on the same factors as noted in the previous section, namely on whether tenure will be granted to occupants or owners and on the preregularization income distribution of occupants.

5.3. Indirect Redistributional Impacts

5.3.1. Land Value Changes and Access to Urban Land

Urban land value increases are generally high, often higher than the overall rate of inflation. This is partly caused by an underestimation of future urban growth by the market. This myopia of the market means that future land scarcity is not adequately reflected in present market prices, which, therefore are subject to strong upward pressure over time. However, this general tendency cannot really be considered to be a result of regularization *per se*. This impact is reflected in the extent to which specific value increases differ from the general trend resulting from urban growth. For analytical

purposes impacts on the following areas may be considered:
- the project area itself,
- other non-regularized katchi abadis particularly those in the vicinity of the project area,
- the urban land market in general.

As to the impact that regularization has on property values in the project area itself, it is generally assumed that regularization tends to accelerate the increase in land values as a result of enhanced security of tenure, increased pressure on the government to provide urban services and (in case of transferable titles) increased access to (future) serviced urban land for different segments of market demand. Testing this assumption is a vital aspect of a longitudinal study now in progress in several katchi abadis in Karachi.[30] Base-line data of the study are now established, but only an analysis of the time series data to be generated will throw some further light on the validity of the above hypothesis.

However, if regularization leads to accelerated property value increases in the area, these will accrue to whoever obtains the lease and therefore the resulting redistributional impact is likely to be the same as for the direct impact discussed in the previous section. It may be noted, however, that rapidly increasing land values may have the additional impact of effectively barring low-income groups from settling in the project area.

As for other (adjacent) non-regularized katchi abadis, the net impact is difficult to assess. Regularization of the project area may cause rising expectations in other areas or the reverse. Because of this, land in these areas may become more or less attractive with a concomitant acceleration or slowdown in land value increases. Regarding the urban land market in general, the impact of regularization on values will most likely depend on the magnitude of the expected addition to the formal land market. If the project area is small and no impact on other katchi abadis is expected, there will be virtually no impact on overall land prices. If project area regularization on the other hand is part and parcel of a government policy affecting a large proportion of urban land (as is the case in Karachi), overall land value increases are likely to experience a deceleration as a result of regularization. This would have the tendency to reduce land access problems for the urban poor.

A recurrent assessment difficulty in the above is the extent to which expectations of regularization influence present market prices and in which areas. Where it may be assumed that the impact of anticipated regularization is already fully incorporated in present prices, not much influence on future value increases can be expected. This, however, is not very likely: again the market may be expected to suffer from myopia.

By virtue of large-scale government ownership of present and future urban land (by law, all waste and desert land is vested in the provincial government), provincial and local authorities in Karachi have a unique opportunity to ensure that the urban poor will not be denied access to serviced urban land.

5.3.2. *Taxation*

Regularization implies that owners of regularized plots in principle are liable to pay government land charges. In Karachi, the most important of these are property tax, water-, fire-, and conservancy charges.* Property tax, as well as the three municipal rates, are charged as a percentage of the Net Annual Rental Value (NARV) of the property as follows:

Property tax	20-25%	(higher NARV's are taxed more heavily)
Water charge	6.5%	
Fire charge	1.5%	
Conservancy charge	5.0%	
Total	33-38%	

NARV is calculated at 90% of Gross Annual Rental Value or GARV, (allowing for 10% in depreciation and maintenance costs). The assessment formula used to compute GARV is complicated and arbitrary. Assessment is carried out infrequently: the last comprehensive assessment of properties in Karachi dates back to 1968-1969. Properties in new rating areas are assessed *ad hoc*, when areas are designated as such. As a result of all this, the assessed-to-market rental value ratio had declined to less than one-third by 1974-1975[31] and this ratio is probably much lower at present.

Consequently, it may be assumed that, at present, annual property tax and municipal rates generally comprise less than 10% of actual annual rental value. In newly regularized katchi abadis this is likely to be even less because the property tax allows for considerable exemptions. A NARV of up to Rs 1000 is not taxable, and neither are properties built on a plot area of less than 100 square yards (as shown in Table 1 almost 50% of plots in Baldia Township are smaller than this; in more centrally located katchi abadis, this percentage is likely to be even higher). New properties are exempted for 3 years and, in addition, objections and appeals regarding initial assessment may be granted at the discretion of the assessing officials. So plot owners in regularized katchi abadis are likely to end up paying only municipal rates at 13% of a NARV substantially below actual annual rental value. Limited collection capability on the part of KMC is likely to reduce the effective rate burden even further.

Finally, it may be argued that municipal rates, in contrast to property taxation, are charges for services rendered and as such only have redistributional implications to the extent that charges are not equal to the value of these services.

All in all, the redistributional impact of property taxation and municipal rates seems to be negligible at present. Only if a more realistic and regular assessment of properties were undertaken and exemption limits reduced simultaneously with an increase in collection capability could it be expected that this type of government intervention will have any impact.

---

*In addition there are several provincial taxes, municipal licences and fees, which are property related, but these are quantitatively insignificant.

5.3.3. Lease Terms and Access to Urban Land in Future

At present, regularization in Karachi generally provides the owner of the plot to be regularized with a lease of 99 years duration, with limited transferability during the first 5 years and full transferability thereafter. Conversion of land use is only possible with the express consent of the lessor (KMC) and upon payment of a conversion fee. Sub-division and amalgamation of plots is allowed only with the express sanction of KMC at charges of Rs 2 and Rs 200 per square yard respectively.[32] No change of land use or reversibility is allowed in case of sub-division or amalgamation.[33] KMC's power to reacquire the plot before the expiry of the lease period can only be involved in cases of breach of lease conditions or rules and bye-laws.

Obviously, in case of large areas of land being regularized on these terms and conditions, the long-run effect would be a tendency to freeze land-use patterns over long periods of time, thereby reducing planning flexibility, but enhancing continued possibilities of access to urban land to the urban poor. Changes in land use, amalgamation or reacquisition during the lease period generally favour the rich more than the poor.

6. CONCLUSION

Large-scale government ownership of urban land offers a unique opportunity to use land tenure regularization as an instrument for resource mobilization and redistributional justice. Largely due to problems of inter-agency cooperation and administrative- and political constraints, this potential has been realized only to a very limited extent.

In order to make land tenure regularization a more effective instrument, substantial departures from previous practices would be necessary:
- leases should be issued to occupants rather than to plot owners,
- a simplified and more aggressive lease procedure with more decentralized powers to approve and to initiate action should be adopted,
- a mechanism should be established to enable early implementation of land transfer policy decisions,
- infrastructural area improvement should be carried out hand in hand with regularization and effective credit mechanisms for home improvement should be set up,
- property value assessment should be regularly conducted, assessment appeal possibilities reduced and property taxation exemptions critically reviewed; this would not only reduce the need for lease charges geared to full cost recovery, but also increase the potential of property taxation as a redistributional instrument.

KMC's slum improvement policy has provided a framework for thought on slum improvement potential. It has become clear that the document suffered from omission in some areas, notably the lack of a coherent land transfer and disposal policy. This gap has been partially filled by the enactment of MLO 110. What is more serious, however, is that both these policy documents assume the existence of an operational capacity of implementing agencies, especially KMC, which is far beyond realistic administrative capabilities for the years to come.

In the prevailing uncertain situation in Pakistan it is not likely that the necessary administrative reforms will be carried out by GOS and KMC. It is more likely that the present state of affairs will continue, with marginal adjustments from time to time. In the inherent trade-off between considerations of land productivity and equity, this has favoured equity by default. A continuation of this is not an altogether bleak prospect for the urban poor.

REFERENCES

1. KMC, An improvement policy for Sub-standard Urban areas, Karachi, 1977. This policy document was the first attempt to systematize the approach KMC utilized in its slum improvement programme. In as far as land tenure regularization is concerned, the policy operated under the provisions of the Sind Peoples Local Government Ordinance (1972, modified in 1979) and the Sind Peoples Local Councils (Land) Rules, 1975.
2. Daily *Dawn*, Monday, 21 February 1977.
3. Martial Law Order No. 67, "Regularisation and Development of Katchi Abadis", May 1978.
4. Martial Law Order No. 110, "Regularisation and Development of Katchi Abadis Order", *The Sind Government Gazette-extraordinary*, 20 December 1979.
5. Calculated from: M. Schuringa, S. A. Khan, E. Meyer and K. S. Yap (ed.), *Baldia Evaluation Survey Report*, 1979, tables 4.11 (p. 56) and 4.20 (p. 63). Exact magnitude of figures is somewhat unreliable, because non-response was different in each area, so averages did not cover exactly the same plot.
6. Compare, for example: J. J. van der Linden, *The Bastis of Karachi, Types and Dynamics*, 1977, pp. 276, 283 and J. van der Harst, "Land policy for spontaneous settlements", *Joint Research Project* - IV (mimeo.), September 1974, p. 3.
7. See, for example: J. van der Harst, "Low Income Housing", *Joint Research Project IV* (mimeo.), 1974, p. 10, van der Linden, *op. cit.*, 1977, pp. 114-119.
8. Schuringa *et al.*, *op. cit.*, p. 68.
9. See, for example: K. S. Yap, "Resident's participation in katchi abadi improvement", in: *Pakistan Economist*, Vol. 19, No. 2, 13 January 1979, pp. 21-24, E. A. Wegelin, "Slum improvement in Karachi: look back in despair", *Pakistan Economist*, Vol. 19, No. 26, 30 June, 1979, p. 9, and J. J. van der Linden, "Slumupgrading in Karachi, Necessities, Possibilities and Constraints", paper read at the Congress of the International Federation for Housing and Planning, Göteborg, 1979.
10. See Schuringa *et al.*, *op. cit.*, p. 66 and contributions by Schuringa and Yap in this volume.
11. Schuringa *et al.*, *op. cit.*, pp. 65-70.
12. KMC, *op. cit.*, pp. 28-31.
13. *Ibid.*, p. 28.
14. See, for example: M. Sarin, ed., "Progress and problems relating to slums and squatter settlements in the ESCAP region" (mimeo.), 1978 (ESCAP, forthcoming, 1980), pp. 24-25, 2.10-2.24.
15. Van der Linden, *op. cit.*, 1977, pp. 253-284.
16. Major exceptions were land owned by the State Railways, the military (Cantonment Boards) and the Karachi Port Trust. See A. F. Baillie, *Kurrachee, past, present and future*, 1890 (reprinted 1975), p. 87.
17. For example:
    - Minutes of the meeting held on 29th May 1975 between Board of Revenue, Local Government Department (both GOS), KMC and Commissioner, Karachi.
    - Minutes of meeting held on 26 February 1979, in the office of the Additional Chief Secretary (Dev.), G.O.S. to discuss the price of land in Baldia Development Projects.

18. See references in note 9, and in addition: van der Linden, 1977, pp. 55-83, 253-284.
19. Schuringa *et al.*, 1979, p. 25.
20. *Ibid.*, p. 23.
21. This was brought out clearly in the early discussions between KMC and GOS regarding the landownership transfer. See, for example: minutes of the meeting held on 29 May 1975 referred to in note 17.
22. The Sind Government Gazette-extraordinary, 20 December, 1979, part I, p. 1120.
23. Van derLinden, *op. cit.*, 1979, pp. 2-5.
24. Quoted in: S. Angel: "Land tenure for the urban poor", working paper no. 1, Human Settlements Division, Asian Institute of Technology, May 1980, pp. 47-48.
25. N. S. M. Ahmed, "Regularisation and improvement of katchi abadis in Karachi", *BIE Bulletin* No. 9, April 1980, pp. 23-24.
26. Schuringa *et al.*, *op. cit.*, p. 48.
27. N. S. H. Ahmed, *op. cit.*, p. 18.
28. Schuringa *et al.*, *op. cit.*, pp. 36-44. See also the contribution of E. Meyer in this volume, where a more in-depth analysis of the survey data is offered.
29. - House Building Finance Corporation, "A house for every household", September 1978.
    - *Ibid*, "Loaning during 1977-78" (mimeo.), June 1978.
    - F. H. J. Nierstrasz and H. M. J. van Gogh, *Housing Finance for Pakistan*, Bouwcentrum, Rotterdam, July 1979, pp. 8-10, pp. 65-84.
30. See: Applied Economics Research Centre, University of Karachi, "Cost-Benefit Analysis of Regularisation and Improvement of Katchi Abadis in Karachi: First Round Report", April 1980. The study *inter alia* aims to determine changes in property values resulting from regularization and improvement over a three-year period. Property values are estimated periodically in ten katchi abadis, and value changes are attributed by applying test control analysis as well as multiple regression analysis.
31. H. A. Pasha, "Is the local tax base adequate? A case study of the Karachi Metropolitan Corporation", Applied Economics Research Centre, University of Karachi (mimeo.), April 1978, pp. 12-14.
32. Sind Peoples Local Councils (Land) Rules, 1975, rule No. 17.
33. KMC, Corporation resolutions 2701 (dated 17 July 1978) and 2426 (dated 17 October 1977).

Community Participation in Katchi Abadi Upgrading

K. S. Yap

1. IMPROVEMENT POLICY

In its policy document entitled "An Improvement Policy for Sub-standard Urban Areas", the Central Planning Team (CPT) of the Karachi Metropolitan Corporation (KMC) mentions the necessity for people's participation in any katchi abadi (i.e. unauthorized settlement) regularization and improvement programme as one of the vital lessons it has learnt from recent experiences.[1]

"The residents of a (Sub-standard Urban) area ("SUA") are directly affected by its conditions, so no SUA improvement project can succeed without the initiative and participation of its residents. KMC should carry planning to the people and with them should define their means and needs for improvement. Successful people's participation will be a boom to all concerned, as it will encourage collaboration instead of conflict."[2]

The document continues: "KMC has therefore evolved a programme to maximize utilization of the enormous potential for self-improvement available in the SUAs themselves. This potential will be tapped if the roles of KMC and each SUA community are defined so that each does what it can do best. KMC will provide a suitable organizational framework, technical skills and legal and administrative capabilities. The people in each SUA will invest their resources of manpower, capital and intimate knowledge of their own needs and possibilities."[3]

According to the policy document, the role of SUA residents in the regularization and improvement programme for their area should be to:

(a) Request improvement assistance, including regularization, if required.
(b) Organize themselves in such a way to permit a dialogue between KMC and the community as a whole.
(c) Participate in preparation, and initially review the concept plan developed by professionals of KMC's CPT.
(d) Develop, with professional assistance from KMC, the improvement programme and financing plan for their area.
(e) Prepare the detailed regularization plans for review by the planners of KMC.
(f) Make the necessary physical re-alignment to implement the detailed plans.

(g) Pay the improvement costs and the price of land if leasing is required, so that the construction of public facilities which they have agreed upon may start.

The people should also seek:
(a) To collect funds from private persons who wish to help.
(b) To participate in construction work to reduce their cost burden.
(c) To reduce operating costs of public services, so that more services may be supplied in their area."

What KMC (or at least the authors of the policy document) obviously had in mind was a regularization and improvement programme for katchi abadis along the lines of John Turner's recommendations for an autonomous housing system.

In Turner's view the common people possess the bulk of the nation's human and material resources for housing and their collective entrepreneurial and managerial skills surpass the financial and administrative capacity of even the most highly-planned and centralized institutional system. Consequently, the government's task in housing is mainly to guarantee access to resources (land, materials, credit, technology, etc.) to low-income groups, so that they can supply their own houses.

The policy document explicitly states: "KMC cannot provide improvement, but they (the katchi abadi residents) can achieve improvement with KMC help. They, the people, and not KMC are the improvers, the motive force for improvement".[5]

KMC realized however that people's participation in planning and implementation requires some form of community organization in the katchi abadis concerned.

"To use this service (of KMC) efficiently, the community must speak with one voice. For that purpose, the leaders of the community must ensure that there is a community consensus before the key decisions are taken, as to nature, scope and costs of development to be undertaken. It is probable that many communities will not have, at the outset, the necessary level of organization to act. In such cases, KMC may approach some third party to act as community organizer. KMC itself will not directly undertake that task as doing so will handicap its future dialogue with the community. There is here a positive role for either political leadership or professional assistance, or both." [6]

Outcome of this process of community organization is an "Area Self-Improvement Working Party" and several "Muhallah Self-Improvement Working Parties" to represent the population of the entire area and the various muhallahs (i.e. the quarters of the area) respectively, in the dialogue with the KMC planners.

Although the exact role and authority of the working parties are not explicitly described in the policy document, their most likely function is to participate in the planning and decision-making process and to guide implementation where self-help activities are involved.

2. SELECTION OF AREAS

The principles and procedures outlined in the policy document had been based upon the experience of the Lyari Improvement Planning Team (LIPT). In the period 1975-1977, the team had, with technical assistance from UNDP (the United Nations Development Programme), prepared regularization and improvement plans for Lyari, Karachi's oldest spontaneous settlement near the city centre, with a population of about 600,000.

As Lyari had been the first katchi abadi to be upgraded according to the new KMC policy for squatter settlements, plan preparation and implementation had been undertaken on a rather experimental basis. When the Dutch Advisory Mission (DAM) replaced the UNDP team to advise and assist CPT in planning regularization and improvement of a second cycle of katchi abadis in Karachi, one of its first tasks therefore was to develop a systematic planning procedure and define the role of katchi abadi residents in the upgrading programme.

On paper, the policy of KMC for squatter settlement upgrading seemed to provide ample room for a large amount of residents involvement in planning, decision-making and implementation. However, translation of the general policy into feasible procedures proved to be rather difficult, as a result of the different conditions in the other Katchi abadis and of the changed political situation.

Lyari had been selected as first area to be regularized and improved according to the new policy, not only because it was the oldest and most densely populated katchi abadi of Karachi, but also because it was an area politically dominated by the ruling Pakistan People's Party (PPP) of Prime Minister Zulfiqar Ali Bhutto. On account of its age and size, Lyari urgently needed regularization and improvement, but its selection also has to be seen as a friendly gesture of PPP and Government towards its supporters in the area.

These circumstances had largely enhanced the possibilities of people's participation in planning and implementation of the Lyari upgrading project. First of all, KMC did not have to worry about the presence or absence of a strong community based organization in Lyari, which could undertake the planning dialogue with KMC. The Pakistan People's Party had an elaborate and well-established network of community workers in the settlement, who could represent the population and organize residents for community activities.

Secondly, the representatives of the Lyari population were important and powerful local leaders of the Lyari PPP. As a result, they were not only tough partners in the dialogue with KMC, but also had close connections with the (PPP) ministers in the Government of Sind, the controlling authority of KMC. Consequently, what these representatives could not bring off in direct negotiations with KMC planners and administrators, they could always try to achieve by establishing contact with kindred politicians in provincial government and assembly.

A clear example of such contact was the announcement by Chief Minister of Sind, Jatoi, that Sind Government had fixed the lease rates for Lyari at Rs 4 and Rs 6 per square yard for residential and commercial plots respectively, KMC had proposed much more elevated lease rates for Lyari in order to make the Lyari Improvement Project self-financing (a condition of the World Bank for a $40 million loan to the project).

This announcement of Chief Minister Jatoi swept away the self-financing basis under the project and as a reaction the World Bank withdrew its support and the project collapsed, just before the arrival of the Dutch team.

With Dutch advisors to replace the UNDP team, KMC decided to start afresh by selecting new areas for regularization and improvement. Residents of dozens of katchi abadis visited KMC to submit petitions in which they requested the Metropolitan Corporation to give priority to their settlement.

Upon receipt of such requests, community relations officers of CPT would make a reconnaissance visit to the area to assess the feasibility of its regularization and improvement. If both seemed to be feasible, the area was put on a list of regularizable katchi abadis.

Areas taken up for planning were in general picked from that list, but neither in the order of receipt of the request, nor according to the urgency of its improvement. Selection of areas was a completely political issue, like it had been for Lyari.

Political parties and politicians have their followers in the katchi abadis. In order to extend and strengthen their (patronage) relationship with local leaders and common residents and to draw votes in times of election, politicians would urge KMC to select specific areas for regularization and improvement.

These requests were not directed to KMC or CPT (as were the requests for regularization and improvement by common residents), but they were addressed to some high government official, who would pass them on to KMC and CPT with his personal recommendations. Thereby, these requests would get the character of an official government order rather than a request to KMC.

Because these requests came from persons with apparently considerable political influence and were supported by highly-placed government officials, KMC was usually forced to give first priority to katchi abadis mentioned in these requests, in spite of all criteria for selection mentioned in the policy document.

There was, of course, support from within the area for such a decision by KMC, as most residents liked to see their settlement regularized and improved. However, for obvious reasons politicians in general requested regularization and improvement of rather large areas and these are by nature normally both politically and ethnically heterogeneous.

It was therefore difficult to organize the population of such areas and to establish one working party with the various local leaders to represent the entire population. Moreover, such a request for regularization and improvement could hardly be seen as an expression of a strong willingness and motivation of residents to collaborate with KMC for upgrading of their settlement.

The situation was further complicated by the overthrow of the PPP government by the armed forces in July 1977. Following this *coup d'état*, Martial Law was declared, political parties, political meetings and all political activities were banned. Main victim was of course the Pakistan People's Party: many party officials were arrested, others went underground.

Soon the Pakistan National Alliance (PNA), the former opposition party, which had welcomed the military take-over, gained in importance and influence and tried to press KMC into regularization and improvement of its "own" katchi abadis. It succeeded in persuading KMC to give priority to the planning of two basically PNA areas: Gulbahar and Liaquatabad.

However, their relationship with the military rulers could never match the good connections the PPP had maintained with the previous government. The PNA was not sufficiently mass-based either to be able to organize large sections of the population, like the PPP had been able to do in Lyari. And once the PPP had been removed from power, the PNA soon fell apart and split up into competing parties each with its own following in the katchi abadis.

All this had important repercussions on the possibilities to involve katchi abadi residents in planning, decision-making and implementation of the regularization and improvement programme.

First of all, as under political pressure rather highly-populated and politically heterogeneous katchi abadis were selected for regularization, these areas usually did not have a solid community organization which could represent the population in a dialogue with KMC.

The policy document suggested that in such cases KMC could ask a "third party" to organize the community and assist in the establishment of one "Area Self-Improvement Working Party". The policy document did not specify however what kind of "third party" it had in mind for such a difficult (and highly political) job. Besides, freed from political pressure by the PPP to take the interests of the population into account, KMC eagerly recaptured its power to plan and decide in its own way.

But most importantly, the military rulers issued several Martial Law Orders which banned the exercise of official functions by politicians and thereby excluded the possibility of local katchi abadi leaders taking part in the decision-making process.

So, people's participation in implementation by self-help activities through a community organization and in decision-making by an official area representation became impossible. What was left, was the possibility of people's participation in planning.

Here, the utmost KMC was willing to offer was to consult the population in certain aspects of the plans for its area and to invite public objections to these plans upon completion.

3. THE NEED FOR PEOPLE'S PARTICIPATION IN PLANNING[7]

DAM realized that without a proper community organization self-help activities within the framework of a regularization and improvement project would be rather difficult. On the other hand, implementation of plans, on a self-help basis or by KMC, was still far away. The first task faced by CPT and DAM was to prepare the regularization and improvement plans for katchi abadis.

People's participation in decision-making would be impossible in view of the restrictions on activities of politicians in official functions, DAM realized. However, participation in decision-making could become less important, if during plan preparation the CPT planners would work in close collaboration with the population of the area under planning.

The necessity of residents' involvement in plan preparation for their settlement can be justified on various grounds.

Squatter settlements are by nature dynamic and juridically complex areas. They have been created without proper planning and coordination and they continue to develop and grow rapidly in a spontaneous way. Ownership of plots, if one may speak of ownership in a squatter settlement, is defined by verbal and informal agreements, patronage relationships and traditional norms which are difficult to translate into modern legal terms.

Without proper residents' assistance, surveyors and physical planners have an arduous, almost impossible job to record the existing situation and especially the boundaries of each plot on their maps and to prepare a detailed regularization plan for legal purposes.

Besides, dimensions, land use and ownership of plots and houses continuously change, even in the period between the preparation of the detailed regularization plan and the issuing of leases in that area. Open plots are occupied; houses are turned into shops and shops into houses; plots and houses are rented or sold and people extend their plot by encroaching on roads and open land.

Once the location of major infrastructural works and the width of roads and streets have been fixed and detailed regularization plans have been prepared and approved, new encroachments and occupations may create serious problems for the implementation of the plans.

Consequently, plans would have to be modified or cannot be implemented at all, or the new structures have to be demolished resulting in a financial loss for the residents and a waste of money and materials.

It is impossible for physical planners to check an area under planning continuously, after the detailed plans have been prepared. It is also inadvisable to assign this task to the local chauki dars (watchmen) of KMC in view of their corruptibility.

Only residents in the neighbourhood, in whose interests the improvements are carried out, can see to it that changes in the situation do not jeopardize the regularization and improvement of the area. They will be ready to do so, provided they know the plans for their neighbourhood and agree to them. The best way to achieve this is to involve these residents in the planning work.

Residents' participation in implementation was expected to remain limited, but was at the same time crucial for a successful execution of the projects. KMC and its contractors would probably carry out all or most of the improvement work, but the residents have to bear the cost of regularization and improvement through payment of lease charges. If residents would not apply for a lease and pay lease charges for their plot, improvement would become impossible.

In the years before the adoption of the Improvement Policy, threats of demolition and false promises of improvement on the one hand, illegal occupations and encroachments on the other hand, created great mistrust between residents and government about each others' intentions.

A better relationship between residents and KMC was therefore considered to be essential for a successful execution of the policy. Only if residents believe that KMC will utilize the lease proceeds for the improvement of their area, will they be ready to pay lease charges. And only if KMC is convinced that residents will pay lease charges, will it start any improvement work. Residents' participation in planning was believed to be an instrument to bridge the credibility gap between residents and KMC.

4. PROCEDURE

With the above considerations in mind, CPT and DAM developed the following procedure for people's participation in planning:

(a) Reconnaissance and socio-economic survey Before planning starts, community relations officers of CPT visit the area to identify local leaders and community organizations and to approach the population to discuss general needs and problems of the settlement. Simultaneously, general information about the settlement and its population is collected.

A detailed checklist has been prepared for this purpose. Items on the checklist refer to age and size of the settlement, land ownership, existing infrastructure, needs and priorities for improvement and names of local leaders and community organizations.

Next, a socio-economic survey is conducted in the area, on the basis of a 5% sample from the plots indicated on the physical survey map. Data collected during this survey relate to family and population size, income and employment status, length of stay, education, etc. and to the size, quality and occupancy status of the dwelling.

(b) Concept planning and budgeting On the basis of these data, physical planners and engineers of CPT prepare the comprehensive concept plan, while economic planners draw the financial plan for the regularization and improvement project.

Meanwhile, community relations officers request the local leaders identified during the reconnaissance survey to form a committee of representatives from the area. Once concept plan and financial plan have been completed, these are presented to the committee, so that the local leaders can apprehend content and constraints of both plans.

During the meetings with the local leaders, copies of the plans are handed over to the leaders, with a request to discuss these with the residents of their muhallah. Simultaneously, pamphlets in Urdu explaining plans and procedures are distributed in the area. In addition, the local leaders are informed that CPT is ready to discuss the plans at muhallah meetings with the residents.

When these meetings have been held and concept plan and financial plan have been thoroughly discussed, public objections are invited during the "public objections period". The period lasts two to four weeks and during that time the plans are displayed at KMC offices inside and outside the area, so that individuals and organizations can see them and send their objections to KMC.

After closure of the "public objections period", the objections are discussed in a meeting of the "Public Objections Hearing Committee". In principle, this committee should be composed of equal numbers of representatives of KMC and the population.

After the plans have been amended in accordance with the decisions of the "Public Objections Hearing Committee", they are sent to the Government of Sind for final approval.

(c) Detailed regularization planning As soon as concept plan and financial plan have been approved, physical planners start the preparation of the detailed regularization plans. For the detailed planning, the area is divided into planning units, which coincide as much as possible with the muhallahs, the socio-ethnic communities in the settlement.

Basis for the detailed regularization plan of each planning unit is the detailed physical survey map (scale 1:500). Physical planners enter all elements of the officially approved concept plan on this map, and also prepare a list of issues to be settled for completion of the detailed regularization plan.

The survey plan with concept plan elements and the list of issues are handed over and explained to the local leader(s) of the muhallah under planning, with the request to discuss these with the residents of the muhallah.

At the same time, appointments are made for a meeting between local leaders and residents of the muhallah and physical planners and community relations officers of CPT to discuss issues and plan. A week or more later, the meeting is held, preferably at an open and public space in the muhallah.

Having heard the views of the residents, the physical planners return to their office and draft a final version of the detailed regularization plan for the muhallah. Subsequently, the plan is officially published and objections are invited. These objections are discussed in the public objections hearing committee meeting, before the plan is submitted to the Government of Sind. Once the Government of Sind has approved the plan, leases can be issued to the residents.

(d) Improvement planning and implementation Procedures for involvement of residents in detailed improvement planning and plan implementation have not been developed during the Karachi Slum Improvement Project. The work of CPT on the various katchi abadis under planning never reached these stages during the project period.

5. PEOPLE'S PARTICIPATION IN PRACTICE

During the Karachi Slum Improvement Project CPT was mainly involved in the planning for regularization and, to a much lesser extent, improvement of four large katchi abadis (Lyari, Baldia Township, Golimar/Gulbahar and Bhutta Village) and two small areas (Taru Lane and Hijrat Colony).

The Dutch team concentrated its attention on the planning of Baldia Township and in at least some Baldia muhallahs residents participated in the planning according to the procedure outlined in the previous section. In fact, the procedure was largely formulated on the basis of experiences in the planning of Baldia Township.

In the other katchi abadis under planning, people's participation was on the whole restricted to surveys and public objections periods. Hijrat Colony was the only exception: in this katchi abadi, local leaders obtained funds for the physical survey from the community itself. However, work on Hijrat Colony never went beyond the survey stage.

In this section we will therefore only discuss people's participation in the planning of Baldia Township, as this provides the best illustration of the possibilities and limitations of residents' involvement in plan preparation.

In 1976, a private surveying firm had conducted the physical survey of Baldia Township, as the area already appeared on the list of regularizable katchi abadis of KMC.

When in June 1977, it looked as though Prime Minister Bhutto would be forced by political riots in the country to call for new elections, the PPP candidate for the constituency which included Baldia Township, urged KMC to give top priority to the regularization and improvement of this settlement.

However, before the community relations officers of CPT, following the request, could complete the reconnaissance survey of the area, the Bhutto Government was overthrown by the armed forces and Martial Law was declared throughout the country. The PPP candidate of Baldia Township, Minister of Health in the Government of Sind, was removed from office.

When a couple of weeks later the reconnaissance visits were resumed, all local leaders of the Baldia PPP had been arrested or gone underground. The only local leaders left in Baldia were members of the PNA and some independent politicians.

Initially about ten leaders could be identified and when concept plan and financial plan neared completion, these local leaders were requested to form a group of representatives from the area. Eventually, about 40 local leaders (all PNA members or independent politicians) from almost all muhallahs of Baldia Township constituted the "Anjuman-e-Ittehad Baldia Township" to represent the population in the dialogue with KMC.

With this group, the comprehensive concept plan and the financial plan were discussed; copies of the plans were distributed among the leaders; and a number of meetings were arranged in the area to explain the plans to the residents. To shun any reference to the Pakistan People's Party and Zulfiqar Ali Bhutto, the term "people's participation" was superseded by "public participation" or "residents' participation".

During the muhallah meetings and public objections period, residents and local leaders showed remarkably little interest in the proposals of the concept plan, which they considered too general and too abstract. The leaders mainly objected to the level of the proposed lease rates (Rs 15 per square yard for the smallest residential plots) and reminded KMC of promises made by Prime Minister Bhutto of lease rates of Rs 5 per square yard.

The majority of the common residents were mainly interested to see whether their plot or house would be affected by the regularization and improvement programme. However, the scale of the concept plan (1:2500) did not allow for any definite answers in this respect.

Some months later, the public objections to concept plan and financial plan were discussed by the "Public Objections Hearing Committee". The concept plan was approved without major amendments, as almost all public objections were rejected by the Committee, which consisted of KMC officials only. Objections to the proposed lease rates were referred to a later meeting, when KMC would have given the detailed lease rate schedule for public objections.

Next, physical planners of CPT started the detailed regularization planning. The first muhallah taken up for planning was Muslim Mujahid Colony. This muhallah has a rather regular street pattern and was therefore easy to plan. It is located in the heart of Baldia Township and is the domicile of an important local PNA leader.

For the detailed regularization planning of Muslim Mujahid Colony CPT followed the procedure outlined in the previous section. The issues discussed related to the selection of streets to be widened, straightened and metalled for traffic, the location of a clinic and a pedestrian bridge over a nala (watercourse). Planners and residents easily reached agreement on these issues.

When public objections to the detailed regularization plans of Muslim Mujahid Colony were invited by KMC, only two minor objections were received. One objection was accepted by the "Public Objections Hearing Committee"; the other was kept pending until the applicants would produce evidence of their case.

Simultaneously with the detailed plan of Muslim Mujahid Colony, the detailed lease rate schedule for Baldia Township was presented for public objections. Numerous objections to the proposed lease rates were received, in particular to the rate of Rs 15 per square yard for the smallest residential plots. Almost all objection letters quoted statements by former Prime Minister Bhutto that the Baldia land would be leased at Rs 5 per square yard.

Local PNA leaders found themselves in a difficult position: could they agree to higher rates than had been proposed by the previous PPP Government? The only answer KMC could give was that Rs 15 per square yard was necessary to finance the improvement of Baldia Township, and that the PPP Government had made promises, but had not improved the area.

During the meeting of the "Public Objections Hearing Committee" three local leaders of Baldia Township were present to explain and defend the objections to the lease rates: the president and joint secretary of the Anjuman-e-Ittehad (both PNA) and a local PPP leader who had been released from prison earlier that year. After a long discussion, in which the PPP leader was the main spokesman for the population, the proposed lease rate schedule was approved with only minor amendments.

All other local leaders kept aloof of this meeting and refused to publicly accept its outcome. Many PNA leaders feared loss of popularity among the Baldia population, if they agreed to the lease rates. Local leaders of parties which had broken away from the PNA opposed any government decision or proposal. Both groups of local leaders apparently hoped to reverse the decision at a later stage, by exerting political pressure on the Government of Sind (with hopefully a result similar to the one for Lyari).

The Government of Sind nevertheless approved the detailed plan of Muslim Mujahid Colony and the lease rates of Baldia Township and leasing could start in this muhallah. But then it turned out that many plot boundaries had been incorrectly indicated on the regularization plan of the muhallah.

The survey maps proved to be quite unreliable and despite muhallah meetings and public objection periods residents appeared to have been unable to detect mistakes on survey maps and regularization plans. A number of errors had to be corrected in already officially approved plans.

On 21 December 1978, the Governor of Sind handed the first 21 lease documents over to the residents of Baldia Township. Because of the high lease rates and out of discontent over the course of affairs, local leaders of former PNA parties threatened to disturb the official ceremony, but nothing happened.

After Muslim Mujahid Colony, CPT prepared regularization plans for other muhallahs of Baldia Township. In some muhallahs residents participated in the planning in the same manner as people had done in Muslim Mujahid Colony. In other muhallahs the population was hardly involved in the plan preparation. The Karachi Slum Improvement Project was closed down before these plans could be published for public objections.

6. CONCLUSIONS

In her article "People power: community participation in the planning of human settlements", Mary Hollnsteiner cites several reasons why it is significant to involve people in the decisions that affect their own lives.[8]

First of all, people's participation is important, because it may rectify misconceptions of architects, planners and administrators and thereby provide re-education to these specialists, who are directly involved in the project, but often have lost their capacity to empathize with the viewpoint of lower-income people.

People's participation rectifies planning errors by making it possible for the population to point out to technicians and managers what will work and what will not. It is a wise listener, Hollnsteiner writes, who takes these points seriously and revises plans and programmes accordingly.

As we have seen in the previous sections of this article, this consideration played an important role in the planning approach for Baldia Township. It was felt that only if plans were prepared in close collaboration between CPT planners and Baldia residents, could various sorts of errors be avoided and could the chances of a successful plan implementation be improved. The experiences in Muslim Mujahid Colony showed that even much more and much closer collaboration between planners and residents is required than could be accomplished in this muhallah.

A second reason for people's participation mentioned by Hollnsteiner is that programme results are more successful if the intended beneficiaries take part in their design and implementation. If people like living in their community, they will more readily take care of it and express their interest in action.

This reason covers DAM's argument that people's participation in planning is necessary to see that new encroachments do not jeopardize implementation of plans and to persuade residents to apply for a lease and pay lease charges. Confidence in and knowledge about each others' intentions and willingness to collaborate is a necessary condition for the success of the programme.

Besides these two arguments - rectification of misconceptions and increased residents' interest in the project - which present people's participation mainly as a device to improve the chances of a successful programme, Hollnsteiner also makes reference to the democratic ideology.

The right of citizens to express their views and share especially in decisions that affect them is a mark of modern society, she says. People's participation springs from guarantees cited in most national constitutions of the world.

The rest of the article makes clear that to Hollnsteiner the only real form of people's participation in the planning of human settlements therefore is a representation (preferably in a majority position) of residents' groups on a decision-making board.[9] As we have seen, people's participation to this extent did not occur during the Karachi Slum Improvement Project.

The main reason why representives from the Baldia population did not have a share in the decision-making process (e.g. in the Public Objections Hearing Committee) was of course the Martial Law Order which banned the exercise of official functions by politicians and thereby excluded local leaders from a position on a decision-making board.

Although Hollnsteiner's reference to the democratic ideology is almost indisputable, there are however some arguments to question the desirability of a people's representation on a decision-making body within the framework of the katchi abadi upgrading programme in Karachi. A share for residents' representatives in the decision-making process can only be justified, if there is something to decide upon. By isolating human settlement projects from the rest of society, Hollnsteiner has unfortunately neglected this issue in her otherwise eloquent advocacy for people's participation.

Regularization and improvement of katchi abadis means integration of erstwhile spontaneously developed settlements in the overall urban system by legalizing land tenure and provision of basic infrastructure. In order to be able to provide infrastructure, planners have to adapt and re-plan the physical lay-out of the settlement so that it can be connected to the existing infrastructural network of the city. However, basic principle for any squatter settlement upgrading project is the preservation, wherever possible, of the existing situation and as a result planners and residents are left with only a very limited number of alternative options for planning.[10]

An important principle of the katchi abadi policy of KMC is also the self-financing character of any improvement project: people in the area have to finance the upgrading of their settlement. Because the paying capacity of the residents is low, only a minimal level of infrastructure can be provided; because all settlements have the same priorities for improvement (water supply, sanitation, roads), the infrastructure provided is similar for almost all settlements.

Consequently the margins for decision-making during the planning process are in general rather small. The example of the detailed planning of Muslim Mujahid Colony showed that residents could decide on the location of a pedestrian bridge over a nala, but that levels of lease rates could not be a point of discussion, because they were determined by the paying capacity of residents, the required infrastructure and the cost of improvement.

Besides the margins of decision-making, the power of the decision-making board is relevant for a discussion on the desirability of residents' representatives on that board.

In a "democratic" society, people's representatives are elected by the population and the authority of a decision-making body on an area level is legally defined in relation to the authority of elected representatives on municipal, provincial and national levels. Provided the election of representatives and the decision-making powers take place correctly, higher government levels will endorse decisions on an area level without any problem.

In basically one-party political sytsems, area representatives almost by rule belong to the ruling political party and are subject to party programme and party discipline. Therefore power relations are clearly defined and decision-making becomes a negotiation process between party and government (see Lyari).

In Karachi, the situation during the Karachi Slum Improvement Project was fundamentally different. The power relations of the various political parties and politicians were mostly obscured by the ban on political activities. During the entire project period, there were no municipal councils, no provincial assembly, no national assembly, but politicians still exercised influence on the decision-making process of the government.

The influence of politicians on government decisions was partly based on their popular support, but mainly on patronage and other forms of relationship with government officials. So, even if agreement could have been reached between KMC officials and population representatives on important issues like lease rates, there would have been no guarantee that these decisions would have been endorsed by higher government levels and executed by KMC. Decisions could well have been rejected by higher government officials under pressure of politicians who did not have sufficient support in the area concerned, but still had influence in the government.

A crucial position in this regard is occupied by local leaders in katchi abadis. They are supposed to represent the population of the area, but because of their special position in the settlements, they often have personal interests different from those of the common people. Besides, they usually maintain patronage relationships with influential politicians, so that even their minority viewpoint on an area level can ultimately become the final decision on the provincial level.[11]

Under these circumstances, with little to decide and no guarantee that decisions are endorsed and executed, there seems to be little point in forcing KMC into accepting (majority) residents' representation in a decision-making board on an area level. Instead of this token form of democracy, it is definitely better to give all attention to an intensive consultation with residents on muhallah level during plan preparation.

REFERENCES

1. KMC, "An Improvement Policy for Sub-standard Urban Areas", Karachi, 1977, p. 2.
2. *Ibid.*, p. 2.
3. *Ibid.*, p. 2.
4. *Ibid.*, p. 20.
5. *Ibid.*, p. 21.
6. *Ibid.*, p. 19.
7. See K. S. Yap: "Leases, land and local leaders. An analysis of a squatter settlement upgrading programme in Karachi" Amsterdam 1982.

8. M. R. Hollnsteiner, "People power: community participation in the planning of human settlements". In: *Assignment Children*, No. 40, October-December 1977, pp. 13-15.
9. *Ibid.*, p. 23 and 27.
10. See H. Meyerink: The Physical Planning of Baldia Township. Elsewhere in this book.
11. K. S. Yap, "On possibilities left". Elsewhere in this book.

Planning for Improved Sanitation

J. Pickford

1. INTRODUCTION

High infant mortality rates and widespread disease are characteristic of people with bad living conditions throughout the world. These curves show the number of people surviving to various ages as a percentage of births. The full line is typical of poor developing countries and the broken line is typical of industrial countries. In the Third World many of the deaths, particularly of infants, are due to dysenteries and gastro-enteritis. The major cause of these illnesses is the contamination of food and water by microorganisms which come from the excreta of someone who already has the disease. Malnutrition is often associated with deaths from other diseases such as measles, and in an insanitary environment malnutrition is as likely to be due to worm infestation as to a low calorie intake.

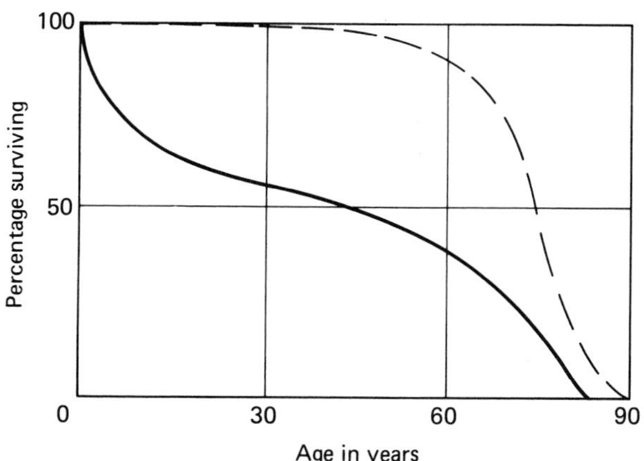

Fig. 37.

2. SANITATION IN BALDIA IN 1978

Between December 1978 and February 1979 a survey of the existing sanitation in Baldia was carried out by the WEDC Group,* who also made recommendations for improvements. Although no reliable statistics were available, there was no reason to suppose that the health/disease pattern was any different from what it is in other similar places. All the distinguishing features of an unhealthy environment were present. An inadequate and irregular supply of water was delivered at points where it would be easily contaminated. Accumulations of excreta, sullage and solid waste were to be seen all over the area. Their removal, if at all, and final disposal were done in such a way that fly nuisance was inevitable.

2.1. Excreta Disposal

The most obvious reservoir of faecal infection is human excreta if it is accessible to flies or is handled by the householder or by sweepers. In the majority of Baldia's homes excreta disposal was found to be crude, aesthetically disgusting, and carried out with the maximum risk of spreading disease. Even where the reasonably satisfactory system of pour-flush latrines and soakpits was in use, the actual construction of the soakpits was thoroughly unsatisfactory.

2.2. Dry Latrines and Conservancy

At the time of the WEDC survey up to 70-80% of the houses in some muhallahs quarters of Baldia used dry latrines, many of which were of the crudest imaginable type. In the latrine the user placed his feet on concrete steps and excreted into a trough between them. From time to time a sweeper visited the latrine. The accumulated excreta were transferred from the latrine through an opening behind the trough to a kerosene tin whose top had been removed. From this they were tipped into a larger container, which was usually carried on a bicycle. These containers were then emptied in nalas (watercourses) or on vacant land. Two sites in the hills to the north of the inhabited parts of Baldia were the main dumping grounds. The excreta were simply tipped in low-lying places, fresh material on top of old. The third main tip was on the bank of a flowing nala in the Sind Industrial Trading Estate (SITE) area to the south of Baldia. In addition to the excreta this nala was grossly polluted with household refuse and industrial waste.

In some of the latrines a container was placed in the trough. Discarded car battery cases were commonly used. Their capacity was insufficient for the interval between sweepers' visits, so they overflowed. Their small size also inevitably caused fouling of the sides of the container and of the trough.

Whether a container was used or not, the trough was often washed out after a sweeper had removed the main part of the excreta. The householder poured some water into the trough and this with the washed-out excreta usually trickled down the outside wall of the latrine into the street or vacant land. Some householders had built shallow lined open tanks outside their latrines, usually in the street, and discharged their wastewater (sullage) to this. The sullage was collected by sweepers from time to time.

---

*The WEDC (water and waste engineering for developing countries) Group at Loughborough University of Technology, England.

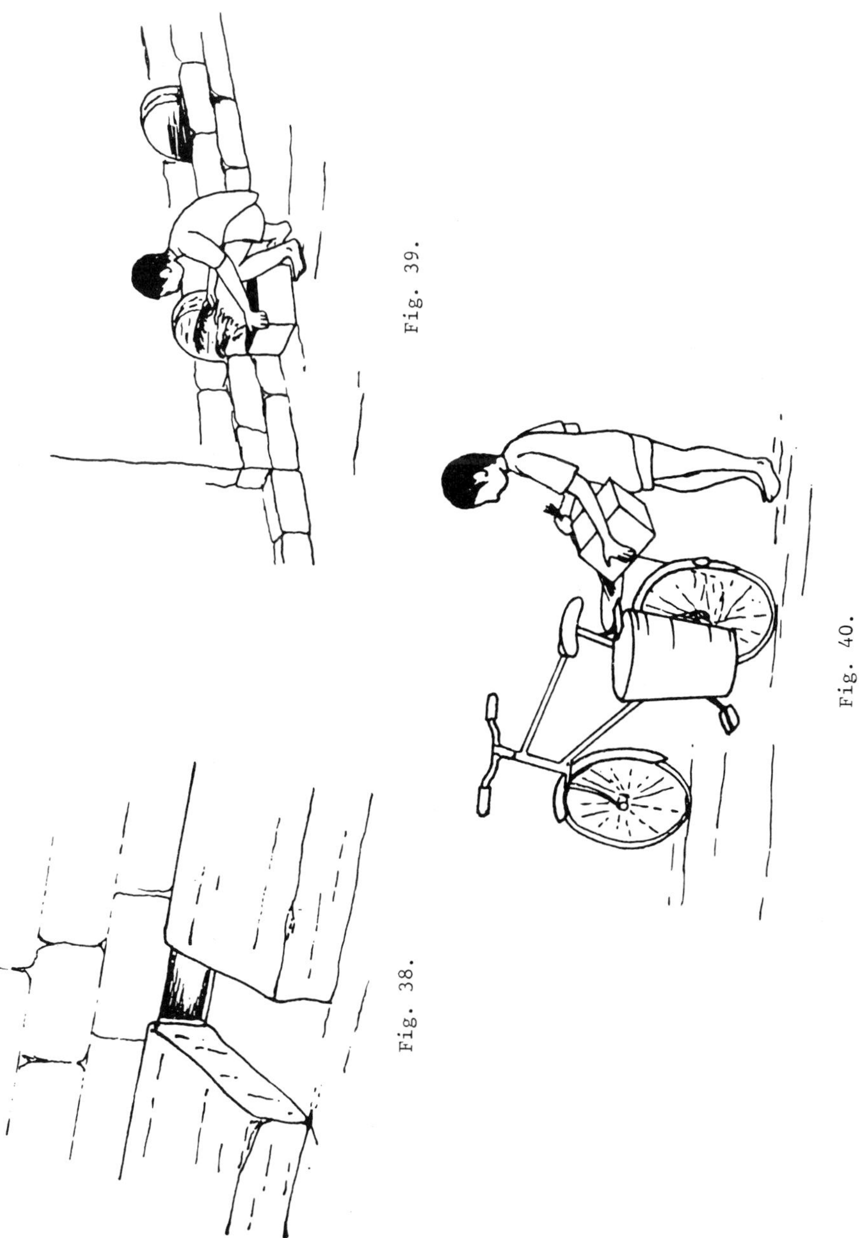

Fig. 38.

Fig. 39.

Fig. 40.

About forty self-employed sweepers collected the excreta, charging the householders Rs 7-20 (US $0.80-2.1) per month. Most of the collection was carried out between 6 am and 2 pm. Although contracts were normally for daily collection, householders complained that sweepers did not come regularly.

Latrines and disposal areas were malodourous and were surrounded by millions of flies.

2.3. Pour-flush Latrines and Soakpits

Most of the remaining houses had pour-flush latrines which were usually of the type shown here. Pits were commonly about 1.2 metres diameter. They varied in depth from 2 to 8 metres depending on the ground conditions and the owners' inclinations or resources. Stones were put in the pits to support the walls and prevent collapse when vehicles pass over. These stones filled up the whole of some pits, but in others holes were left in the centre. Generally large stones were placed at the top of the pit and these were covered by a thin layer of cement mortar. A few pits had concrete slabs on top, and in some the slabs were built up above the road level, usually with removeable access covers. The object of raising the tops above the streets was said to be to prevent vehicles passing over the pits. In narrow streets vehicles could not pass at all because of the raised pits.

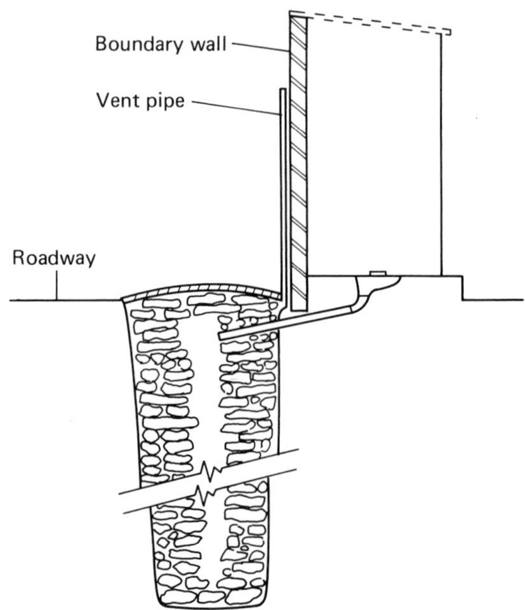

Fig. 41.

The vent pipes when provided were usually made of sand and cement and so were brittle. They were normally 75 mm diameter and about 2 metres high. Even when they remained intact they did not seem to provide good ventilation and the tops were below the house roof level.

Almost all the sqatting slabs were made of concrete and most latrines were clean and tidy. Normally only faeces, urine and water used for anal cleaning were put in the latrines, but in a few areas bath and kitchen wastewaters were also thrown in. The pits seemed able to deal with this without difficulty. In general the pits were reported to last for about 6 years, but their life obviously depended on their size, the number of users and the porosity of the soil. There was no evidence of fly-breeding in the pits.

2.4. Septic Tank, Communal Latrines and Open Defaecation

A few properties with water supply and wcs had small septic tanks whose effluent was discharged to open drains. One property, a clinic, had a septic tank and drainage field which seemed to work satisfactorily. There was one very bad communal latrine at the bus terminus; it appeared that it was never cleaned.

The occupants of the few houses which had no latrines and some children from houses with latrines, resorted to open defaecation. People near the hills went there. Elsewhere men used banks of nalas and open areas. Some women and children squatted on two stones in the compound; faeces were covered with a handful of soil and later thrown into the roadway or a nala.

2.5. Sullage Disposal

In large plots sullage (wastewater from bathing, laundry and cooking) soaked into the open ground around the house. Sullage from other plots was discharged into the streets or open ground. Where the discharge was small it soaked into the ground, but in areas with high density and small plots and where water was easily obtained, open drains were formed with gradients towards nalas. Some drains had been lined, especially in the older areas where the roads were narrow or where there was a bazaar. Although the Karachi Metropolitan Corporation (KMC) employed a number of sweepers, part of whose job was to keep drains clean, clearing was usually done by householders past whose plots the drains ran. Drains crossing open land or behind properties were generally unattended and were blocked with refuse.

In most nalas there was no flow, even though many of the drains and standpipes discharged into them. This was because they were choked with refuse which dammed them and absorbed the liquid, providing a breeding place for flies. Water which did not soak into the refuse or the ground formed very septic and malodourous pools.

2.6. Refuse Collection and Disposal

One truck was under contract to the KMC to collect household refuse in Baldia, but it was not seen at all during the 2 months of the WEDC sanitation survey. Refuse was dumped, and left, on vacant land and in drains and and nalas, where it attracted vermin, stray animals, birds, flies and mosquitoes, besides preventing the flow of water in drains and nalas. The official dumping ground for all Karachi refuse was at North Karachi, 24 kilometres from Baldia. However, most of the refuse removed from Baldia was dumped and burned to the north-west of the township on the site of the proposed hospital.

3. FACTORS AFFECTING THE SANITATION OF BALDIA

3.1. Geology and Hydrogeology

Baldia is situated on rocks which are mostly fissured limestones, sandstones and shales. They outcrop in the east, as shown on the map, which also gives the position of seven hand-dug holes which were examined.

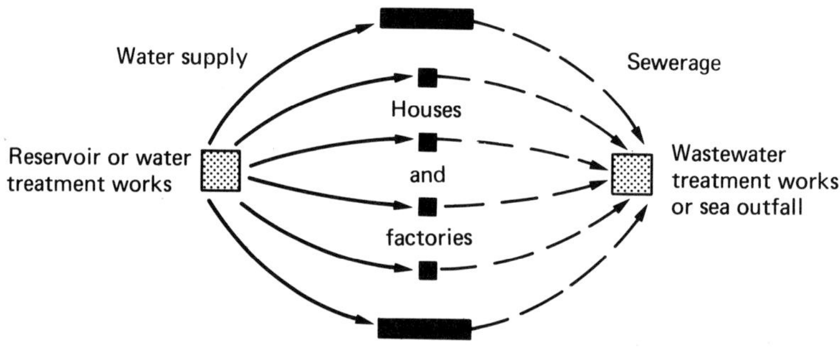

Fig. 42.

Most of the area is overlaid by recent alluvial deposits of marine origin of a clayey matrix with sand, silt and gravel. There is no distinct stratification; the alluvium varies irregularly throughout the area although the clay content tends to be higher in the north and south.

The permeability of the soil is generally low, but there are isolated pockets where it is more absorbent. Excavation causes little difficulty as the alluvium is firm, dry and self-supporting. Local opinion considered that a free-standing soil-face would not be stable if wet, but it was not possible for the WEDC team to check this.

Towards the east, rocks are found within 4 metres of the ground level. They are hard and highly fissured, and can be removed using hammer and chisel. The porosity of the rocks is negligible, but many of the fissures are quite large and some contain water.

Generally groundwater is at greater depths than 5 metres except for small quantities in some of the rock fissures. There is a slow accumulation of water in some excavations which appear to be dry when first dug. All groundwater is saline and not fit for drinking. Five wells were examined during the WEDC survey. In two the water rose to less than a metre below ground level following rain; in two others the water was about 5 metres below the ground; in the fifth the water in an 11-metre deep well stood about 1.5 metres below the ground.

3.2. Water Supply

In 1970 about 900 cubic metres of water was provided in bulk to Baldia each day. Some additional water was brought in by tanker and part of the piped water was passed on to areas outside Baldia. Allowing for expected losses of 30% in the system, the average water consumed by the 68,000 people then living in Baldia was about 9 litres per day. By 1977 the bulk supply had increased fourfold, but the population had risen to 150,000, and the estimated daily supply per person was 19 litres. At the time of the WEDC survey a network of mains fed standpipes from a KMC pumping station, which delivered water for about 5 hours a day. Most standpipes were open-ended 12 mm diameter pipes. The area was zoned and each zone received water for about 2 hours every 2 days. The pressure was low, and water was only available in the lower west and south-west of Baldia. By cooperative effort some people in higher areas built tanks which were filled by tankers and donkey carts. About a quarter of a rupee (US 3¢) was charged for each 18-litre tinful. Twenty-one properties were connected to the public supply, but no further connections were approved.

There were proposals for improved bulk supplies to Karachi from the Hub reservoir scheme and part IV of the Indus river scheme. However, it seemed unlikely that water delivered in Baldia would exceed about 45 l/pd (litres per person per day) up to 1985, and the most optimistic forecast for the end of the century was 68 l/pd. Any increase in the number of house-connections would decrease the water available at standpipes.

3.3. Socio-economic Situation

Although many of the houses in Baldia are well-built of modern materials, the resources of the people are stretched by the cost of providing houses. The usual building method around cities in developing countries is followed. Houses are built in stages as funds become available, so there exist side by side a building for which only the foundation has been dug, another with two floors completed and fully occupied and a third in which a few rooms are completed and occupied while construction of the remainder of the building continues whenever there is money to spare to buy cement and other building materials. Most houses are built by the owner assisted by relatives and friends.

In general householders would rather spend any spare cash on extending their houses than on building a satisfactory latrine. Payment of sweepers for emptying dry latrines is a continuous burden on household budgets, but few families can afford to pay out a lump sum for a new and better latrine.

Communal latrines are not an acceptable option even if they satisfied the necessary prerequisite of continuous attendance by a sweeper. The accepted tradition is for each house to have its own latrine.

When water is available, virtually everyone uses it for anal cleaning. It had been reported that some sections of the Baldia community were in the practice of using stones and sand, but this was thought to be the result of water-shortage. If water is available it is likely that these groups would conform to the common practice of anal washing.

The dry latrines were the cause of strongly-expressed complaints throughout Baldia. It was recognized that the exposed excreta and the method of removal resulted in health risks. Overflowing latrines and pools of foul liquid were a nuisance to pedestrians. Householders grumbled about the irregularity and unreliability of scavengers and the cost of collection. However, no-one wanted to use communal latrines as privacy was considered important.

Pour-flush latrines were regarded as much more satisfactory. In particular the squatting slab could be kept clean. Householders mentioned some difficulties. One was the common location of pits in streets, some of which were effectively blocked up by cover slabs above the street level. Some people spoke about the trouble they had when pits were full.

4. RECOMMENDATIONS FOR IMPROVED SANITATION

A wide spectrum of methods of dealing with excreta is available. The WEDC advisers considered all known methods, assessing their suitability for Baldia. Limitations to the application of any system were the very severe shortage of water, small plot sizes and the inability of the public authorities to provide any service to householders. It was noted in connection with the last-mentioned point that neither refuse nor night-soil was collected regularly by the KMC, and that householders had to pay for private contractors for these services. Any system has to be low-cost, although it was likely that the government of the Netherlands would provide substantial aid towards the cost of an appropriate system.

Water-carried sewerage has been the traditional method of dealing with excreta in cities. Parts of Karachi are sewered and there are two well-designed and well-built but badly-maintained sewage treatment works.

The sewerage network was known to be inadequate for existing flow partly due to poor maintenance which had resulted in the partial blockage of trunk sewers. The principal reasons for the rejection of sewerage for Baldia were the low water supply and the very high cost, which is often ten or twenty times as great as simple on-site systems. Conventional sewerage requires something like 50 l/pd of water, and there is no possibility of this amount of water being available for the remainder of the century.

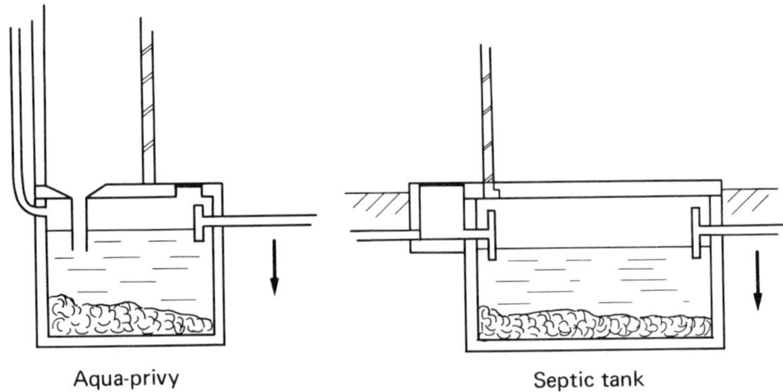

Fig. 43.

A number of systems proposed in North America and Scandinavia to avoid the wasteful use of water for transportation of excreta were clearly unsuitable because their cost is even higher than water-carried sewerage. These include vacuum sewerage and some on-site methods such as incineration.

Improvement of the night-soil system had attractions because it was the method already widely used in Baldia. Current practice was so bad that almost any change would be an improvement. An adequate night-soil system would have to include the replacement of the private contractors by a public collection system, and this was ruled out. However, some changes could be introduced to eliminate some of the worst features of the present system.

Septic tanks and aqua-privies had to be rejected for the majority of households because the size of the plots was far too small. Septic tanks were deemed to be particularly unsuitable because they require water-flushed drains with water closets having a demand for water similar to that for conventional sewerage.

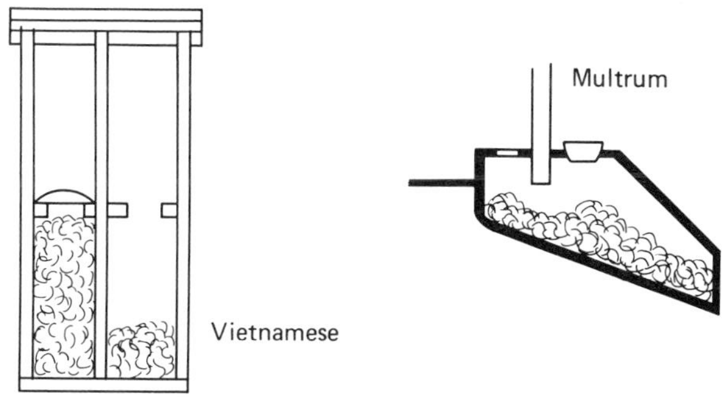

Fig. 44.

Compost latrines, which have been successfully used in parts of East Asia, have two requirements which could not be satisfied in Baldia. One is the need for vegetable matter which has to be placed in the container with excreta. Something like three times as much vegetable matter as excreta has to be deposited and this would not be available in Baldia where the plots are too small to grow any foodstuffs. The second requirement was not satisfied for the same reason. Compost latrines require disciplined attendance to add the vegetable matter regularly and to ensure that the composting material does not become wet. This can only reasonably be achieved when the latrine owners acknowledge the need for compost to improve soil used for growing crops.

4.1. Selection of the Most Appropriate System

And so the solution had to be some form of pit latrine. Where water is used for anal cleaning and the size of the plot and the position of the latrine on the plot are suitable, the pour-flush water-seal latrine has many advantages. It is widely used in India and other parts of Asia. In Bihar and some other States in India there have been very successful programmes for the conversion of dry latrines to pour-flush latrines.

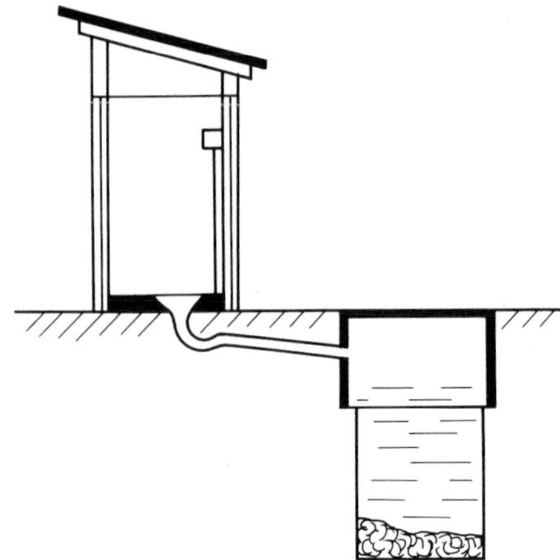

Fig. 45.

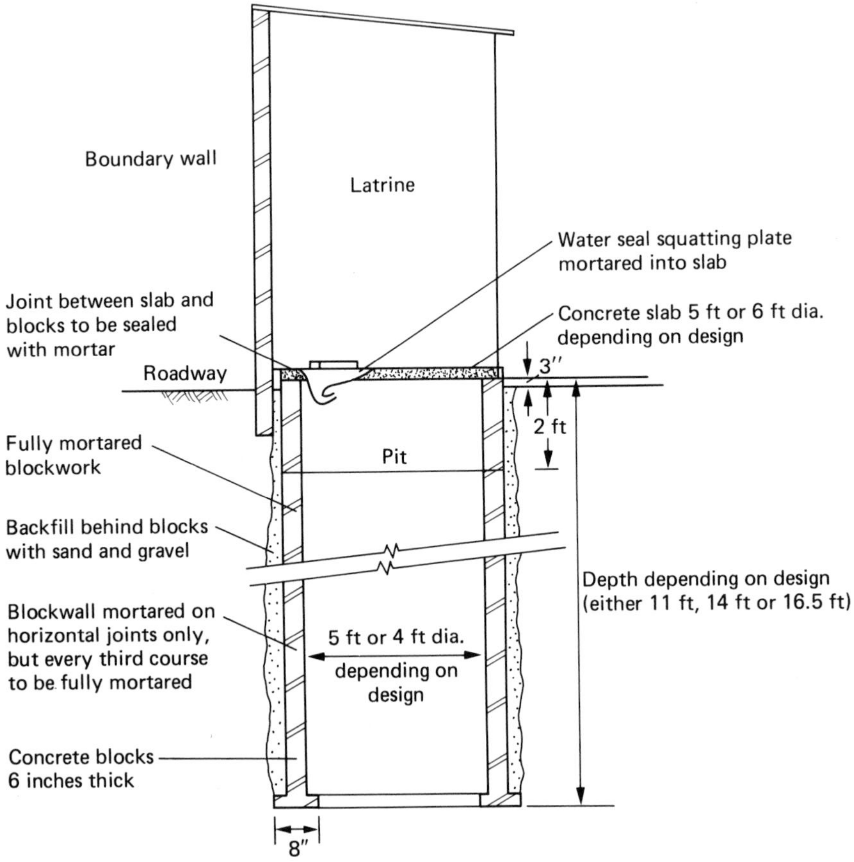

Boundary wall

Latrine

Water seal squatting plate mortared into slab

Joint between slab and blocks to be sealed with mortar

Concrete slab 5 ft or 6 ft dia. depending on design

Roadway

3″

2 ft

Fully mortared blockwork

Pit

Backfill behind blocks with sand and gravel

Depth depending on design (either 11 ft, 14 ft or 16.5 ft)

Blockwall mortared on horizontal joints only, but every third course to be fully mortared

5 ft or 4 ft dia.

depending on design

Concrete blocks 6 inches thick

8″

Fig. 46.

Where new latrines are to be built on plots with sufficient space and where the occupants are in the habit of using water, the use of pour-flush latrines with a soakpit within the plot has many advantages.

However, the existing practice in Baldia where pits were in use was to place the pit outside the plot (usually in the street) because there was insufficient space for an on-site offset pit. It was considered that location of pits in streets should be abandoned if other improvements to the infrastructure were to be implemented. In particular streets should be kept clear for pedestrian convenience, and in the case of wider streets for vehicular access. Consequently a pit in the usual position under the latrine was deemed to be most suitable.

One of the advantages of an offset pit is that it can be emptied from outside the latrine. However, it is the practice in Baldia to dig pits of such size that if they were not filled with stones they would last an average family for many years - certainly beyond the planned life of the proposed improvements, 1990. During the survey it became clear that many householders were aware of the unsatisfactory characteristics of the commonly-used type of offset soakpit latrine. They needed, and were unable to obtain, advice on better designs.

It was therefore decided that "standard" latrines should be designed which could be adopted by householders able to build their own latrines and which would be the basis of schemes evolved to assist householders who were unable to afford to construct pit latrines. The "standard" latrines should allow for the accumulation of faecal solids for at least 15 years. The pit should therefore be large and there should be a clear space for solids.

4.2. WEDC Designs

Study of household size showed that the average in Baldia was 6.5 persons. Less than 16% of households had more than 9 members. The size of pit should therefore be large enough for 9 persons. Two standards were proposed - one to last 15 years and the other 20. The pit walls would be lined to prevent collapse, and the filling of pits with stones was deprecated. Since most people preferred to use water for anal cleaning, a water seal could be provided to prevent nuisance from smells, flies and mosquitoes. For households where it was customary to use other anal cleaning material a straight-down chute was required and the pit would be ventilated. The following details therefore would be the basis of design.

Contributing population: 9 persons
"Life" of pit: 15 or 20 years
Location of pit: under latrine or offset (but on the householder's plot)
Type: water-seal except when water is not used for anal cleaning, in which case the pit should be under the latrine and should have an ample ventilating pipe.

It was found that a pit 5 feet in diameter inside the lining and 14 feet deep would provide a 20-year life. For a 15-year life the depth or the diameter could be reduced. Suggested details of construction were prepared. These included the structural design of reinforced concrete slabs and details of a locally-made water-seal. However, it was made clear that lining material and details of the slab and water seal were only tentative suggestions. Trials should be carried out locally to develop the most suitable design.

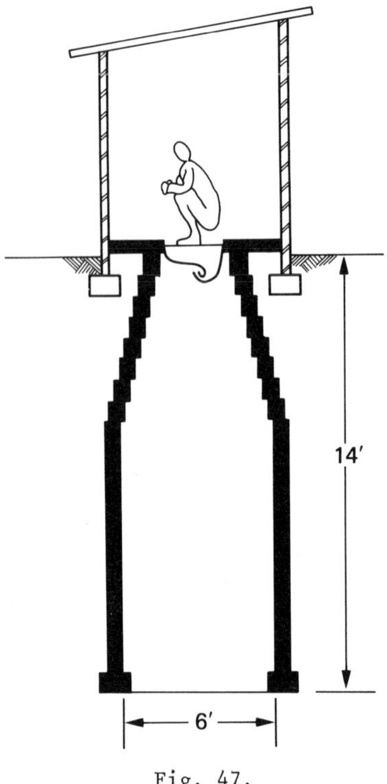

Fig. 47.

Jaycee Design

In fact a design was evolved locally which admirably used local skills, traditions and materials. The top of the pit was built like a local "tandur", i.e. oven, with corbelled brickwork. Its design was developed by Henk Meyerink, in cooperation with the Pakistan Jaycees, the national branch of an international charity organization involved in social welfare activities.

Implementation

It was recommended that the new type of latrine should be built by two methods. For householders able and willing to build their own latrines advice should be readily available. This would include providing drawings for those able to read them.

It was acknowledged that most people could not afford the lump sum required for the construction of a pit with a lining, cover and water-seal of the kind recommended. Capital could be made available from foreign aid if a satisfactory mechanism could be evolved. Several modes of implementation were suggested. These included bank loans, loans from KMC, provision of material on completion of previous stages and so on. However, the KMC were unable to accept any option offered and were unable to suggest an alternative idea.

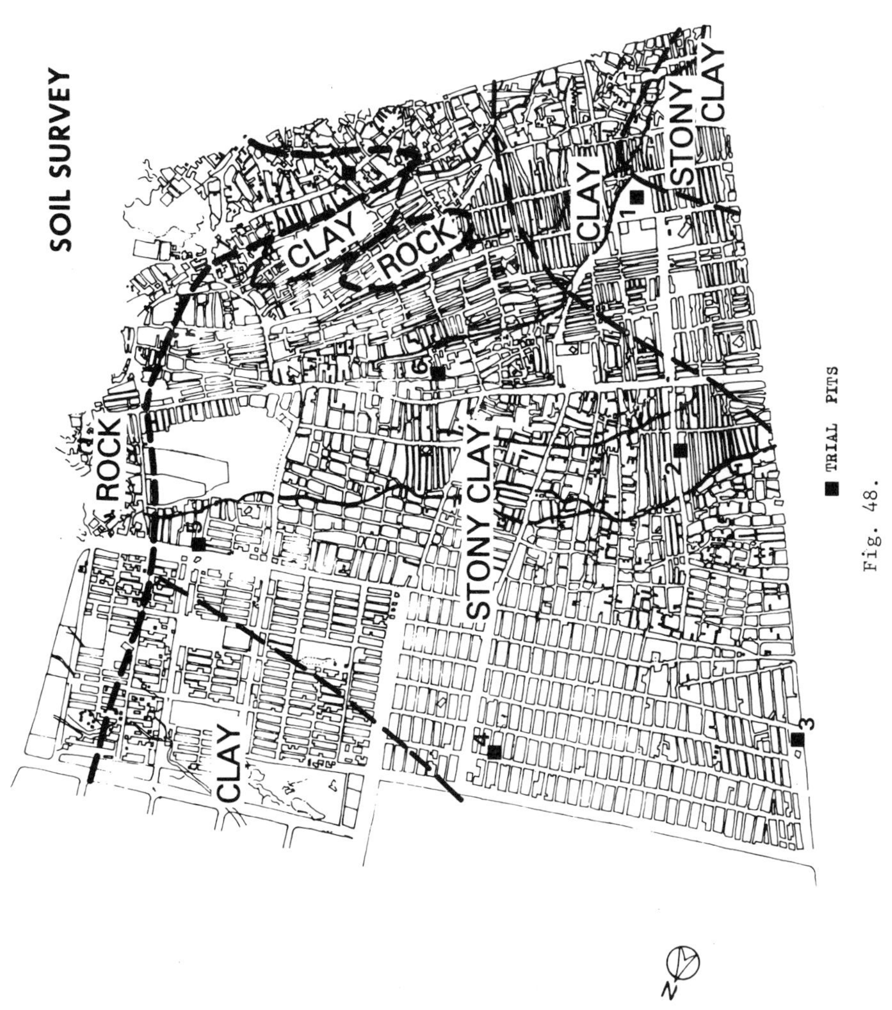
SOIL SURVEY
ROCK
CLAY
ROCK
CLAY
STONY CLAY
CLAY
STONY CLAY
CLAY
1
2
3
4
5
6
■ TRIAL PITS

Fig. 48.

Consequently latrines of the Jaycee type were built without KMC involvement. These are a peculiarly local development and are a very good example of really appropriate technology.

FURTHER READING

M. Bell and J. Pickford, People and pit latrines in Africa, In: *Proc. 6th WEDC Conf. Water and waste engineering in Africa*, LUT, Loughborough, 1980.

R. Feachem and S. Cairncross, *Small excreta disposal systems*, Ross Institute, London, 1978.

A. Pacey (Ed.), *Sanitation in developing countries*, John Wiley, Chichester, 1978.

J. Pickford, Control of pollution and disease in developing countries, *Water Pollution Control*, 1979, 78, 2, 239-249.

J. Pickford, Sanitation for buildings in hot climates, *Public Health Engineer*, 1979, 7, 4 October, 158-161.

Part V

Problems in Execution

K. S. Yap

Since it had been anticipated that translation of policy into action would not be an easy process and that execution of the policy would require continuous and careful monitoring, funds for evaluation studies had been allocated in the project budget of the Dutch Advisory Mission. One such study, a cost benefit analysis of squatter settlement upgrading, is presently being carried out by the Applied Economic Research Center (AERC) of the University of Karachi. Another evaluation study was conducted in Baldia Township during the first half of 1979 by the Baldia Evaluation Survey Team (BEST).

The objective of the cost-benefit analysis is to compare the costs mainly for the Karachi Metropolitan Corporation (KMC), and the benefits for the society of squatter settlement upgrading in Karachi, mainly expressed in increased housing values in the regularized areas. The study is carried out by means of a series of six rounds of surveys in five test areas (katchi abadis (i.e. unauthorized settlements) expected to be regularized and improved in the course of the study) and five control areas (katchi abadis not eligible for regularization or improvement). The entire study will take about 2 years and since up to now only two rounds of surveys have been completed, results are not yet available.

The original objective of the Baldia Evaluation Survey was to measure the effects of regularization and improvement on variables like the quality of houses and the composition of population. By measuring the improvement of housing conditions after regularization and provision of infrastructure and comparing these with the situation before the start of the regularization and improvement project, it was thought possible to discern whether government intervention in spontaneous settlement really encouraged residents to invest (more of) their savings in the improvement of their houses, as the research findings of JRP-IV seemed to indicate.

The improvement of housing conditions in a regularized settlement as such does not yet prove, however, that the objective of the programme has been attained. It is not unlikely that in the course of regularization and upgrading, living in the settlement becomes too expensive for the original residents and that they (are forced to) move out. They could be replaced by higher-income groups, which undertake the improvement of the housing conditions, while the original low-income groups have to find shelter elsewhere, most probably in another illegal settlement. Therefore, it is important to compare also the changes in population composition and income distribution before and after regularization.

The replacement of original low-income residents by outside higher-income groups as a result of regularization and improvement is predicted by Marxist critics of squatter settlement upgrading programmes, like Burgess and Janssen.[1] In their opinion, Third World governments are in fact not interested in improving the housing conditions of the urban poor, but merely want to incorporate the illegal settlement in the urban system (and thereby its plots and houses in the free land and housing market) to the detriment of the urban poor, who originally raised the settlement.

Despite the fact that hardly one and a half years had passed since the start of the planning work in Baldia Township, and the fact that implementation of the regularization and improvement had not yet begun, it was nevertheless decided to carry out the evaluation survey in Baldia Township and to measure the effects of (the announcement of) regularization and improvement on its housing conditions and population composition. As the data presented in Meijer's article show, no significant changes in housing conditions and population composition were found, compared with the situation in 1977, when a socio-economic survey was carried out to collect data for the planning work. It has therefore been decided to conduct a third survey in 1981 (and maybe a fourth one a couple of years later) to measure the long-term effects of the programme on Baldia Township.

Besides questions on changes in quality of housing and composition of the population, the opportunity of the survey was seized to gather also some data about the effectiveness of KMC's attempts to involve the Baldia residents in the planning work for their settlement. For this purpose questions were included about the information KMC had extended to the population in connection with the project, and about the role of local political leaders, who served as intermediaries between KMC and the common residents. Schuringa's article provides some remarkable insight into the way local leaders manipulated information in their own interest.

The role and the interests of local leaders in katchi abadi upgrading are also discussed in van der Linden's article, which tries to analyze some of the opposition the project encountered in its efforts to execute the regularization and improvement policy. This opposition was in fact so strong that following an evaluation mission in early 1979, the Government of the Netherlands and the Amsterdam Free University decided not to extend the project after the termination of the first project period, because of lack of progress in the work.

Main motive for the Dutch Government to end the project was the fact that regularization and improvement plans could not be implemented because the necessary institutional arrangements had not yet been made and funds for katchi abadi upgrading were not yet available. As early as 1977, the Netherlands government had intimated that it was prepared to consider a (soft) loan of US $5 million to KMC for upgrading of Baldia Township, if requested for by the Pakistani government. However, a KMC request for this loan never reached the annual bilateral negotiations between Pakistan and the Netherlands, because the Provincial Government of Sind refused to approve the request.

The Provincial Government gave various reasons for their refusal to approve the request and to forward it to the Federal Government. First of all, its policy was oriented towards rural rather than urban development, as the latter was thought to stimulate the rural exode. Secondly, it was feared that once infrastructure was provided to Baldia Township, residents would refuse to pay lease charges and this would turn the project into a substantial financial loss.

Within the Dutch team there was a feeling that besides these (in principle valid) arguments, there were more reasons why the provincial authorities did not give any priority to the Baldia Township Regularization and Improvement Project and why KMC did not try harder to persuade the authorities to approve the project. What seemed to be lacking was basically the "political willingness" to execute the policy.

In his article, van der Linden describes some of the reasons why local political leaders in katchi abadis and bureaucrats in government bodies would not like to see the regularization and improvement policy for katchi abadis executed. Van der Linden thereby contradicts the arguments of marxist critics (referred to above) that governments carry out squatter settlement upgrading programmes only in order to reinforce existing power structures and neutralize oppositional movements of squatters. The resistance of politicians and bureaucrats to squatter settlement upgrading seems to indicate that these programmes are in fact threatenting their position.

If the obstacles for an execution of the regularization and improvement policy are basically of a political nature, the obvious way to remove these obstacles is through political action, e.g. political pressure on the local and provincial authorities by the people most concerned, the common residents of the katchi abadis. Along these lines, the Dutch team tried to motivate residents of Baldia Township to organize themselves and demand regularization and improvement of their settlement. However, this placed the Dutch advisers in a rather awkward position, being counterparts to KMC, but having Baldia residents as their allies against KMC.

In the last article of this section, Yap tries to discern some possibilities left to set the regularization and improvement programme going again. He proposes the establishment of local organizations of katchi abadi dwellers to defend their rights, along the lines of the slum-dweller organizations in Bombay. However, in view of the lack of efficiently working local organizations in katchi abadis, the heterogenity of the katchi abadi population, and the central position local leaders occupy in katchi abadis, it is rather doubtful whether such organizations can really be established.

REFERENCE

1. R. Burgess, Petty commodity housing or dweller control? A critique of John Turner's views on housing policy, *World Development*, 1978, vol. 6, no. 9/10.
R. Janssen, Wij hebben zelf geen recht op de stad. Vogelvrij wonen in Santa Rosa da Lima: een stadssociologisch onderzoek naar de woon-en levensomstandigheden in een volksbuurt van Bogotá. Colombia, Amsterdam, 1978.

The Evaluation of Regularization and Improvement of Baldia Township

M. Schuringa

1. INTRODUCTION

In order to assess the changes which could take place as a consequence of regularization and improvement of a katchi abadi, Karachi Slum Improvement Project (KSIP) had already decided at an earlier stage to try to evaluate the effects of regularization and improvement in the first katchi abadi in the project. This unauthorized settlement (katchi abadi) was Baldia Township; planning in the area started in 1977 and it was expected that by 1979 implementation of the plans would be well on its way. Due to a number of reasons however, the programme had hardly started at that time.[1] Despite this lack of progress, it was decided to carry out an evaluation survey to assess the changes which had taken place in the area since the start of the planning work. Because it was expected that the mere announcement that Baldia Township was going to be regularized would be sufficient reason for a number of changes to take place.

The evaluation study took as its point of departure a socio-economic survey of Baldia Township which was carried out by JRP-IV in 1977 at the request of the Karachi Metropolitan Corporation (KMC), as part of the planning procedure for regularization and improvement of the area.[2] The original 850 questionnaires of this survey were still available and the same sample of plots could be visited again to interview the residents (the same or new). This would make a comparison of the sample characteristics and the individual cases of the 1977 and the 1979 survey possible. For analysis of the data, the respondents were divided in three groups:
- stayers, interviewed both in 1977 and 1979,
- leavers, interviewed only in 1977 and replaced by:
- newcomers, interviewed only in 1979.

The evaluation study focused on three issues:
1. Will the target group - the low-income households - benefit from the regularization and improvement programme? Low-income groups may be displaced by higher-income groups as a consequence of increased attractiveness of the area and the resulting rise in property prices.
2. Did the residents start improving their house and their direct surroundings as a result of the higher security of tenure? Together with the infrastructural improvements to be carried out by KMC, this would result

in living conditions which no longer endanger the health of the residents.
3. How effective is the people's participation via community leaders?

The first issue is discussed in the chapter on "Dispelling mechanisms at katchi abadi improvement". The other two issues are dealt with in this article.

1.1. Baldia Township and Its Population

Baldia Township is a katchi abadi on the north-western periphery of Karachi and covers an area of about 1000 acres. It is bordered by a large industrial area (Sind Industrial Trading Estate, SITE), an air force base and rocky hills. The only possibility of extension is into the desert in the north west. The township is divided in 32 muhallahs (divisions) inhabited mostly by people of the same ethnic background or the same place of origin. Since 1953, when the first people were moved to the area by the authorities, the population has been growing rapidly. This was among other things due to the fact that people, evicted from other parts of Karachi were told to settle there, and to the vicinity of SITE. In 1965 it was decided to make Baldia a plottownship, plots were set out according to a rectangular pattern, measuring either 80 or 120 square yards. But the "structured" part is only about 1/3 of the total area, the remaining part had already been occupied and is built up in a rather haphazard way, the plot sizes varying from 16 to 1024 square yards, (average 117.3 square yards per household). KMC took administrative control over the area in 1974. The existing infrastructure is largely insufficient; there are few metalled roads and only 500 public taps which run on alternate days for 2 hours. There is no drainage or sewerage system and no regular solid waste disposal system.

The population is estimated at 175,000 inhabitants in 1979. Most households consist of parents with their children (married or unmarried), while in 25% of the sample more distant relatives were also part of the household. The average household size is 6.72, the average number of households per plot 1.16.

The majority of the respondents (60%) had lived in Baldia Township for more than 10 years, and 91% of the respondents had lived either in Baldia Township (25%) or elsewhere in Karachi before moving to the present plot. Since the 1977 survey, 11% had left their plot but over half of these had remained in Baldia Township. These data seem to indicate that up till now, mobility of residents was rather low.

2. HOUSING

In its regularization and improvement programme KMC provides security of tenure by issuing leases and carrying out basic infrastructural improvements, whereas the improvement of the individual houses will be left to the residents themselves. It is expected that the security of tenure will stimulate the residents to improve their own houses.

The condition of houses in a katchi abadi may vary considerably, from the temporary "jhuggi" (i.e. hut), made of waste materials without any facility, to the permanent multistoreyed house, made of reinforced concrete with private water-, gas- and electricity connections. To be able to assess changes in housing conditions, a classification of housing conditions is needed. The typology developed by van der Linden[3] has been used in the evaluation survey.

2.1. Typology of Houses

This typology is based on a single criterion: the quality of building materials used. Four groups of building materials, both for roofs and for walls were distinguished and ranked according to the preferences of the residents of the katchi abadis.[4] The different combinations of building materials used result in a typology of houses with 6 categories of house types.[5]

Type	Typical materials
I	reed matting or tin sheets
II	non-permanent materials
III	non-permanent materials
IV	cement blocks
V	plastered cement blocks
VI	reinforced concrete

The advantage of this typology is, that it is easy to manage: the characteristics can be observed from the street in most cases. But a negative result is the fact that other criteria of quality have to be ignored. In practice there might be some problems in assessing the type of house: a compoundwall can be made of different materials, rooms might be constructed with different materials; sometimes plastering has been done so badly that it can hardly be considered as such, or the interior of the compound might be different from the outside, which the observer sees. Furthermore, the typology may have insufficient differentiation in the case of Baldia Township: 85% of the houses are classified in type IV and V.

A comparison of the building materials used in 1977 and 1979 shows only minor differences. There has however been a shift from type IV to type V as a result of the plastering of either housewall or compoundwall.

Table 1. Distribution of House Types and Some Income Characteristics

Type	% 1979	% 1977	Average income 1979	Distribution up to Rs 700	Household income 1979 Rs 701 and more
I	0.4	0.7	Rs 693	0.6	0.3
II	1.8	2.4	731	2.3	1.4
III	1.6	1.6	923	1.5	1.4
IV	42.9	51.9	802	46.3	39.9
V	42.5	35.1	901	40.8	44.3
VI	10.7	8.3	1002	8.5	12.7
	100%	100%		100%	100%
No response	12	22		18	
Total	720	720		341	361

One would expect a relationship between income and type of house. Average income by type of house shows indeed a higher average-income for the more permanent house types. The rather high income of the households in type III demonstrates the stagnating character of this temporary house type. Due to the limited number of houses in the categories other than IV and V far-reaching conclusions cannot be made. Moreover, if the incomes are divided in two categories only (up to Rs 700 and above Rs 700), no correlation can be found. The distribution of house types over the different muhallahs shows no obvious concentration of types. In the older muhallahs type VI is somewhat overrepresented compared to the total average, but this might be due to the fact that people have had a longer time to (gradually), improve their houses. Another reason might be that the perceived level of security is higher in some muhallahs because the people had been shifted there by the government or because it has a planned lay-out.

2.2. Improvements

In order to obtain as much information as possible on the improvements carried out in the period between the two surveys, the respondents were asked directly what they had improved in their houses. The overthrow of the government of former Prime Minister Bhutto in July 1977 was given as reference date for the start of the period between the two surveys.

Almost half the respondents (46%) stated to have improved something in their house. Painting and the improvement of a room (not further specified) accounted together for 43% of the mentioned items.

One of the hypotheses of the evaluation survey was that higher-income households will improve more than lower-income households, other things being equal. A cross-tabulation between income and improvement, however showed no significant relationship.

Table 2. Income by Improvement

	No improvement	Improvement
Rs - 300	69.8	30.2 = 100% (43)
301-500	58.8	41.2 = 100%(131)
501-700	59.1	40.9 = 100%(159)
701-900	52.8	47.2 = 100%(108)
901-1100	53.4	46.6 = 100% (88)
1101-1300	45.1	54.9 = 100% (51)
1301-	53.4	46.6 = 100%(103)
		(683)
No response 37		
Total 720		

The Pearsons product-moment correlation coefficient (r) was calculated for summarizing the strength of association between the household income and the money spent on improvement. Almost no correlation was found (r = .1293). However, there might have been some intervening variables. To exclude their effects, the partial correlation coefficients were calculated controlling for: type of house (r = .1298), estimated property value in 1979 (r = .0846) and length of stay in the area (r = .1469). Hardly any correlation was found.

There might be two reasons for this lack of relationship:
- the period between July 1977 and March 1979 was too short,
- improvements were paid out of incidental incomes, which were not measured.

The findings of this survey are confirmed by the findings of a cost-benefit analysis of regularization and improvement of katchi abadis in Karachi,[6] carried out by the Applied Economic Research Centre, Karachi. In this study it was found that there was no relationship between improvements carried out and income - over a period of 1 year. However, the cumulative investments since the acquisitions of the property cross-tabulated against income show a high significance (r = 121.24 with 96 degrees of freedom; significance 0.0397). This seems to confirm our explanation that the period between the two surveys was too short to show a significant relationship.

2.3. Facilities

The Improvement Policy for Substandard Urban Areas of the Karachi Metropolitan Corporation defines a substandard urban area, a katchi abadi, as an urban settlement where, because of low quality and lack of urban infrastructure, living conditions are such that they endanger the physical health of the residents. Key factors in the hygienic conditions prevailing in the area are the availability of water and the method of excreta disposal.

Shortage of water is a major problem in Baldia Township. The public water-taps (550 in whole Baldia Township) only provide water on alternate days for 2 hours, and even that supply is not always certain. Besides, in some areas there are hardly any taps, while pressure on the existing taps is sometimes rather low. In those areas and in other areas in case of watershortage (i.e. in summer) people have to buy water from donkey carts, watercarriers or trucks. The price paid for the water may vary from Rs 0.30 per canister (18 litres) normally to Rs 2 in the hot season, when demand rises. Officially water is delivered by KMC trucks free of cost, but some payment to the driver is often necessary to encourage him to come with the truck. These trucks only deliver water to large (private) tanks and in some areas people have jointly built a community tank in order to be able to receive water regularly. Most respondents fetched water from the public taps (77.4%), followed by delivery by truck (15%). The percentage of people taking water from the public tap is rather high, which might be due to the fact that the survey was carried out from February to April, when the taps ran regularly. There is however quite a distinction in the mode of watersupply over the different muhallahs. The muhallahs, where over 50% of the respondents did not take water from the public taps, are all located at the eastern part of Baldia Township, on the slopes of the hills: pressure on the main line is too low to provide water in these public taps, which are far away from the mains and slightly elevated.

Regarding the method of excreta disposal, there are three types of latrines used in Baldia Township. Cheapest and least hygienic is the bucket latrine. The bucket, which is mostly an empty battery box, is uncovered and has to be emptied manually and regularly by sweepers. It is used by 34.9% of the respondents, whose average household income is Rs 806 per month. The second type is the soakpit, a hole in the ground, lined with stones, covered by a cement slab, often located outside the plot, and linked with the toilet by a pipe. The liquid soaks away in the ground while the solid waste remains; this has to be removed after 5 to 10 years, depending on the size of the pit and the number of persons using the latrine. Since most of the soakpits do not have a waterseal or an appropriate ventilation pipe, they attract flies and mosquitoes and are not an optimal solution from a hygienic point of view. The soakpit is used by 61.2% of the respondents, having an average income of Rs 899 per household. In fact, a survey carried out by a consultant, showed that a modified soakpit is the best solution for Baldia Township in view of the financial and cultural constraints, as well as environmental restrictions.[7]

The third type of latrine is the septic tank, a cemented underground tank which has to be emptied after a number of years. Since this type is quite expensive to build, it is only used by 3.1% of the respondents, having an average income of Rs 943 per household.

2.4. Cost of Housing

To establish the impact of the regularization and improvement announcement on the costs of housing, a distinction between the various forms of occupancy has to be made. In a katchi abadi four types of occupancy status can be distinguished:

- renting,
- owned by
  - buying the house,
  - constructing a house on vacant land with payment for the land either to the government or to some person who claimed to have rights on the plot,
  - constructing a house on vacant land without payment for the land.

In Table 3 the occupancy status for the different categories of respondents is shown together with the occupancy status in 1977 (when only a distinction between renting and owning was made).

Table 3. Occupancy status

	Stayers		Newcomers		All respondents		1977
Renting	7.1		45.2		11.1		13.6
Owning	90.5		53.4		86.5		86.1
- bought		13.1		34.2		15.3	
- construction with payment		41.9		13.7		39.0	
- construction without payment		35.5		5.5		32.2	
Other	2.5		1.4		2.4		
	100%		100%		100%		100%
No response	5		9		15		-
Total	638		82		720		720

The new respondents who have constructed their homes on vacant land, were already owners of the plot in 1977, but let it at that time. Compared with the situation in 1977 (where different categories were distinguished) 2.5% less respondents are tenants. This seems to point to a shift from renting to owner occupancy.

It is difficult to assess the costs involved in buying and construction since the amounts mentioned by the respondents are spread over a period of many years, during which inflation played its role and improvements after initial construction might not have been included in the price. Nevertheless, it is useful to get an idea about the costs involved, even more so if these are compared with the estimated property values for 1977 and 1979, as given by the respondents. In Table 4 the cost of the house, comprising the total investment people have made in their houses and plots up till now, and estimated values for 1977 and 1979 are shown.

Table 4. Cost of House and Estimated Property Values for 1979 and 1977

Costs	House	Property value 1979	Property value 1977
- 5000	34.6	1.7	6.4
6000 - 10,000	33.2	15.7	22.6
11,000 - 20,000	24.4	42.6	42.7
21,000 - 30,000	4.3	20.3	17.0
31,000 - 40,000	2.0	9.1	5.3
41,000 - 50,000	0.7	5.1	3.3
51,000 - 75,000	0.8	3.7	2.3
76,000 - more	-	1.7	0.4
	100%	100%	100%
No information:	40	129	207
Total	642	720	720
Average in Rs	10,872	23,871	18,125

An approximation of the average increase of property values was found by asking the respondents for their own estimates of the property values for 1977 and 1979. The average increase thus found is 39.8%. This is much more than the official housing inflation figure for this period (11.9%). To what extent this rise in value is due to the announcement of regularization and improvement, and not to an overall increase in property values, is not known, since there was no control group in the study. Since renting is the least attractive occupancy status, it was expected that only people who would, financially speaking, be forced to do so, would rent a house. The average income by occupancy status shows indeed that tenants have the lowest average income per month per household (Rs 796) while buyers have the highest (Rs 924). However, the distribution of occupancy status against income group reveals another phenomenon. In the lowest-income group (up to Rs 300 per month) only 2.3% rents a house, while 90.7% has constructed their house on vacant land. This might be explained by several factors, the most important of which are:

- the households with the lowest-income cannot rent, or buy, so they have to construct their houses on vacant land. These might in the beginning be of inferior quality, but can be improved in the course of years (a cross-tabulation of income by house type shows that these households are represented in all categories of house type),
- the households with the lowest income have been living in the area for the longest period of time (81% of those have been living in the area for more than 10 years, the overall average for that period being 60%) and in addition, these people might be predominantly older people, whose financial

position used to be such, that they could afford to build semi-permanent houses initially.

3. WAYS OF COMMUNICATION AND ATTITUDES TOWARDS REGULARIZATION AND IMPROVEMENT

Regularization and improvement of a katchi abadi is a process which requires cooperation between the authorities concerned and the residents. The necessity of resident's participation in the planning process is reluctantly being recognized by KMC and it is institutionalized at three stages in the planning process: surveying, detailed plan preparation and public objection period. Before actual planning starts, information about the socio-economic characteristics of the population is collected through a sample survey. Local organizations and community leaders are identified and the problems of the area are discussed with them, while priorities of the residents for improvement are also brought to the attention of the authorities. After an outline of the detailed regularization plans has been made, a public meeting is convened where the plans are discussed and where the residents can come forward with suggestions. Finally, after completion of the plans and establishing of the lease rates, residents may object to these during the "public objections period". A "public objections hearing committee" reviews the objections and takes a decision, after which plans and a proposal for lease rates are sent to the government for final approval.

As it is impossible for the authorities to deal with each resident individually, communication between the parties will often take place via the community leaders, who are considered to be representative of the various ethnic and socio-political groups who live in the katchi abadi. The community leaders are asked to organize public meetings, to explain the plans of the authorities to the residents and to formulate a *communis opinio* of all residents. It is obvious that by assigning such a vital role to the community leaders, they may influence the regularization and improvement of the area considerably. It is therefore important to know what kind of people function as community leaders and how they have become community leaders. Unfortunately, not much research has been done on this subject in Karachi. De Goede and Segaar[8] and Streefland[9] have devoted part of their research in katchi abadis in Karachi to leadership patterns. Although the katchi abadis they studied are mainly christian communities, which may have a somewhat different social structure than moslem communities, their observations are useful to get some insight into leadership patterns. De Goede and Segaar make a distinction between traditional and modern leaders. The traditional leaders are aged people in a group of relatives (actual or perceived family ties are very strong in Pakistan) whose power is predominantly based on seniority. The modern leaders derive their position mainly from the fact that they have a certain occupation and/or some level of education. Both the traditional and the modern leaders play a role in local affairs (settling disputes, marriages etc.) within the group of relatives or outside this group within the neighbourhood. But even for the leaders, influence outside the katchi abadi will be difficult to achieve since most of them have a comparatively low socio-economic position which does not lead to contacts with people in high positions and institutions functioning at civic level. The few leaders who do have these contacts are most important and powerful in the community. The outside contacts can be a result of different types of relationships: through relatives outside the community, through their socio-economic position, through friendship, through political affiliations or, last but not least, through bribery. De Goede and Segaar note that leadership in the settlement they studied, becomes ineffective as soon as it extends beyond the group of relatives, a consequence of the egocentric nature of the leadership. Many community leaders try to benefit themselves and favour their relatives by means of their position. The reason that this kind of leadership can exist is the fact that the residents, besides being poor, are largely illiterate and therefore fully dependent on those people who have some means to achieve anything, however little this may be. Streefland who discusses the changes in leadership patterns in a christian community in Karachi in the fifties and sixties, relates that initially the extent of effective leadership mainly depended on the number of followers one had. These followers were relatives and people from "the home town" in the rural areas, where most people originally came from. This resulted in a large number of leaders in the area, none of whom had a significantly larger group of followers than the other, and who were in constant competition with each other. This pattern changed in the early sixties when - due to political reasons - one leader had to be chosen for the entire area. The selected community leader was chosen because of his education, his position and his outside contacts. Apart from this community leader, some community organizations were formed, whose leaders were also chosen on basis of their achievements and outside contacts. Thus, there is a shift from traditional to modern leadership, which is not so much person-oriented but rather interest-oriented. However, in the course of years, the community leader and the leaders of the organization became factions opposing each other and competing for followers. The result was that leadership once again became person-oriented.

In Baldia leadership is a mixture of traditional and modern patterns and is very much person-oriented. Even more so because in some areas the residents come from different ethnic backgrounds resulting in factions along ethnic lines. Quite a number of leaders have outside contacts, for instance via political parties and in that capacity have access to government officials. Moreover most are richer than the average resident. A number of leaders are "brokers", acting as middlemen between the residents and the authorities. Also sometimes the leaders are speculators who move into an area when it is only sparsely populated and set out plots which they will later sell or lease to newcomers, making a lot of money in the process and gaining influence. These leaders all compete with each othe for supporters. One would expect all residents, leaders and non-leaders alike, to have the same interests (i.e. legalization and improvement for as little money as possible) but this is quite often not the case as is explained in van der Linden's article on the roles and interests of different groups involved in katchi abadi upgrading (elsewhere in this book). As a result, the community leaders may only inform their own supporters about the plans of the authorities and will only represent their own interests to the authorities. This may go to the extent of wrong or no information at all being given to the residents. For instance, during the Baldia Evaluation Survey, all residents in one area said that the lease rate would be Rs 5.-- per square yard while the actual rate was Rs 15.-- per square yard. On further inquiry it turned out that the community leader had told the residents to answer Rs 5.-- hoping that this would strengthen his bargaining power with the authorities. The authorities, when confronted with the conflicting interests and difficulties in reaching the common residents, are sometimes at a loss. So far, no alternatives have been tried but working through the community leaders and existing organizations, even though it is known that people will very likely only pursue their own interests and that of their close supporters.

In order to get to know the extent to which the residents of Baldia Township are informed about the regularization and improvement plans, what their channels of information are and how effective these are, what their attitude towards the idea of regularization and improvement is, a number of questions on these topics were asked in the Baldia Evaluation Survey.

One way to measure the information received by the residents was to ask whether they knew what lease rate per square yard they were expected to pay and how they knew this. Of the respondents 47.3% did not know the lease rate, of the respondents who did know 23.4% gave the correct rate (Rs 15.-- per square yard) and 29.3% an incorrect rate. Five alternative channels were given through which the respondents received this information: neighbours (65.4%), community leaders (12.3%), KMC (10.4%), newspapers (6.3%) and other (5.7%).

The effectiveness of the different channels, is shown in the cross-tabulation in Table 5.

Table 5. Knowledge of Lease Rate by Way of Communication

Knowledge of lease rate	Way of Communication				
	Newspaper	KMC	Neighbours	Community leader	Other
Correct	78.3	71.1	40.8	35.6	19.0
Incorrect	21.7	28.9	59.2	64.4	81.0
	100%	100%	100%	100%	100%
Absolute	23	38	240	45	21
No information	353 (the people who did not know the lease rate)				
Total = 720					

$X^2 = 20.7$ X^2 (4,00.5) = 9.49

Both KMC and the community leaders are organizing meetings to discuss regularization plans in the area. The survey showed that the bulk of the residents (72.7%) never attended these meetings or informal discussions. To detect a possible relation between attendance at discussions and knowledge of lease rate another cross-tabulation is made:

Table 6. Knowledge of Lease Rate by Participation in Discussions

Knowledge of lease rate	Participation in discussions	
	Participation	No participation
Correct	43.5	15.9
Incorrect	17.3	33.8
Don't know	39.3	50.3
	100%	100%
Absolute	191	509
No information 20		
Total 720		

$X^2 = 61.6$ X^2 (2,0.05) = 5.99

The chi-squares in Tables 5 and 6 are both considerably higher than the values in the chi-square distribution. This means that the knowledge of lease rate is dependent on the way of communication as well as on participation in discussions. The above also shows that the community leaders are not very active in informing people about the regularization and improvement plans and if they do inform them they are often not accurate.

The attitude of the residents towards regularization and improvement was measured by asking whether they would be willing to take a lease and if not, what the reason was; 50.9% answered that they would take a lease, 32.7 % answered that they wouldn't because of lack of money, the remaining 16.4% stated various reasons like "don't know as yet" or "not interested". It is interesting that it appears that the willingness to take a lease is related to the awareness of KMC improvement activities in the area. These activities are not part of the regularization and improvement programme, which has not started as yet, but are *ad hoc* improvements on a small scale. The fact that residents who have seen some improvement activity (14.8%) are more inclined to take a lease than residents who answered that no work had been done at all (72.2%) supports the idea that regularization and improvement should be carried out in combination. This would break the vicious circle of mistrust both on the part of the residents as on KMC's part. The residents are not willing to pay the leases before improvements are carried out, believing that once they have paid, there is no guarantee that improvements will actually be implemented. The KMC, on the other hand, is not willing to improve without getting paid for the leases in advance, assuming that the residents won't pay once improvements are carried out. The real reason that people are not willing to take a lease, might well be that actual security of tenure is already so strong, that people do not see any advantage in taking the official lease, believing that improvements may be carried out anyway, though it may take much longer.

4. CONCLUSION

The results of the evaluation survey show that the announcement of regularization and improvement has so far not induced the residents of Baldia Township to improve their houses and their direct surroundings on a large scale. The only remarkable change that has taken place during the two-year-period between the two surveys is the rise in property values. Although it is not possible to measure this rise accurately with the data available, the interviewee's estimates strongly point to this tendency. It is, however, not possible to detect to what extent this rise may be caused by the announcement of regularization and improvement, because of the absence of a control area. The rise may partly correspond to a general trend in Karachi as a result of continuous immigration from the rural areas and of population growth.

There may be several reasons for the fact that little change has occurred. First of all, the period between the two surveys, was only 2 years. The changes that were expected to take place, may take much longer to materialize, it is therefore recommended that a follow-up survey be carried out after another two years.

Secondly, the residents might not be interested in improving their houses very much, because they may have other priorities in spending the (little) money they save.

Thirdly, the expected changes were to some extent based on the hypothesis that low-income households would be replaced by higher-income households, who would have more money to spend in improvements. This phenomenon, however, has not taken place. The residents who left did belong to the low-income group but they were replaced by people with low- and middle-incomes, who moreover were tenants in 45% of the cases (for detailed account see E. Meijer's article on dispelling mechanisms, elsewhere in this book).

With regard to the effectiveness of people's participation via community leaders, the survey shows that if the authorities really want the residents to take part in the planning for regularization and improvement, they should not work exclusively through the community leaders. Yap[10] proposes the institution of a (private) non-profit organization which should provide professional assistance to the residents during regularization and improvement. But this will be quite difficult to carry out without including the community leaders, who otherwise might regard it as an attempt to reduce their power and who will as a consequence oppose the organization, manipulating their supporters to do the same. So far no other alternatives have been proposed, but it will be very useful if a way could be found where residents are more directly involved in the planning process making them at the same time more aware of their rights.

REFERENCES

1. See other articles in this section.
2. JRP-IV, Socio-economic survey Baldia Township (mimeo.), Karachi, 1978.
3. J. J. van der Linden, *The bastis of Karachi, Types and Dynamics*, Ph.D. thesis, Amsterdam, 1977.
4. These groups are for walls: 1. Plastered cement blocks. 2. Unplastered cement blocks. 3. Planks, mud, stones. 4. Chatai (reed matting), canister. For roofs: 1. Reinforced concrete. 2. Tiles, asbestos sheets. 3. Corrugated iron, mud, planks. 4. Chatai, canister.
5. J. J. van der Linden defines an additional type S: the double-storeyed jhuggi, that does not exist in Baldia.
6. AERC, Cost-benefit analysis of regularization and improvement of katchi abadis in Karachi, first round report (mimeo.), Karachi, 1980.
7. J. Pickford and B. Reed, Sanitation for Baldia Township (mimeo.), Karachi, Loughborough, 1979.
8. H. J. De Goede and T. J. Segaar, *Rapport Azam Basti*, Een advies voor de ontwikkeling van een wijk in Karachi, Pakistan, gebaseerd op sociologisch onderzoek (Report Azam Basti, an advice for the development of a settlement in Karachi, Pakistan, based on sociological research), Amsterdam, 1969.
9. P. H. Streefland, The sweepers of Slaughterhouse, Conflict and survival in a Karachi neighbourhood, Assen, 1979.
10. K. S. Yap, Resident's participation in Katchi abadi improvement, *Pakistan Economist*, 13 January 1979, pp. 21-24.

Dispelling Mechanisms at Katchi Abadi Improvement

E. Meijer

1. INTRODUCTION

Katchi abadi (i.e. unauthorized settlement) improvement aims at improvement of housing conditions of low-income groups. To achieve this aim the government tries to upgrade areas with predominantly low-income residents. If the physical improvement succeeds, it is still possible that the aim has not been achieved. The original residents of the area might be dispelled and replaced by higher-income groups, because of the increased attractiveness of the area and the subsequent increase in prices of houses.

In the first part of this article the various ways in which katchi abadi improvement can act as a dispelling mechanism are discussed. The second part describes the results of the "evaluation" survey the Karachi Slum Improvement Project (KSIP) conducted in the spring of 1979 in the first katchi abadi under planning (Baldia Township), especially with regard to the possible occurrence of dispelling mechanisms.

2. THEORETICAL BACKGROUND

At the end of the 1960s a completely new approach to housing and uncontrolled urban growth developed, with John Turner as the main representative. He considered housing not as a commodity, which can be consumed by sale or rent, but as an activity; what is important is not the material object, "house", but its function in the lives of people. Turner posed in his "First Law":[1] "When dwellers control the major decisions and are free to make their own contribution to the design, construction or management of their housing, both the process and the environment produced stimulate individual and social well-being". He raised self-help to be the most suited and desirable way of housing and considered stimulation of self-help part of the solution of the housing problem. The government should create a framework for self-help with proscriptive legislation which sets limits to which people may go, instead of prescriptive laws, which set lines which people must follow. The provision of security of tenure is an important function of the government. Turner postulates that investment in housing by people who need it and have to pay for it, is a function of the security provided by the living environment.[2] The illegal squatter will only invest if his security of tenure increases.

J. J. van der Linden studied the security of tenure and its relations with housing quality in the katchi abadis (a local name for slum, or squatter settlement) of Karachi (Pakistan). He emphasized the importance of the perceived level of security of tenure and he posed that there is not a simple dichotomy; legal or illegal occupation of land. Both the residents and the government recognize a range of possibilities between these extremes. The hope that the land will be allotted to the occupants was used as operationalization of the perceived security of tenure. The inhabitants base their hope on a number of indicators, on the basis of which the level of security of tenure can be established. Next, van der Linden developed a typology of houses to determine the quality of houses in a katchi abadi. Eventually he combined the data on the security of tenure and the quality of the houses on a graph which is "strongly suggestive of a correlation between both".[3]

From figures presented by van der Harst,[4] van der Linden concluded that the effect of security explains approximately 50% of the variation in investments in housing (an operationalization of the development of the quality of houses). Though in Usmania Muhajir Colony hardly any correlation between income and the quality of the houses was found,[5] it has as yet not been sufficiently assessed whether income is not an intervening variable. It is possible that security correlates with the quality of houses because income correlates with both in the same way: people with a relatively high income have houses of good quality and live in katchi abadis with security (and vice versa). The interaction effects of income and security should therefore also be taken into account.

Besides, the correlation is a static one: katchi abadis with poor housing conditions have in general a low level of security. The question whether or not katchi abadis develop with increasing security of tenure has not yet been answered, though van der Linden was supported by several authors when he assumed that data on different katchi abadis of different ages can be used as a substitute for data obtained from longitudinal studies in some of the same katchi abadis.

Marxists in particular have critized the Turner-school fundamentally. Rod Burgess[6] considers the housing problem as the product of the general conditions of capitalist development. In his view, Turner depoliticizes the issue by locating the origins of the housing problem in the operation of a bureaucratically and technologically top-heavy system rather than in the operation of a specific mode of production. Burgess stresses the commodity status of "self-help" housing, functioning in a total system with a dominant capitalist mode of production, which produces the industrial housing object, and the dependent petty commodity form. The petty commodity production of housing has two forms: the manufactured petty commodity form and the self-help form, in which the producer and the consumer of housing are one and the same.

For several reasons the self-help form cannot be understood outside of the process for commodity formation. First of all, it consumes commercial products: cement, roofing materials and re-cycled throw-aways, which increasingly tend to be commercially valued. Secondly, the construction of the house involves a considerable labour input, giving new value to the materials used; there is an increasing use of wage-labour. Finally, the house constructed for the use of the producer has a potential commodity status: it can be brought onto the (illegal) market for sale or rent. Without prior destruction of the capitalist mode of production the recommendations of Turner will only be carried out on a limited scale to further petty commodity interests in ways that are not detrimental to the maintenance of capitalist relations of production in general. For example, the granting of legal tenure will integrate the katchi abadis into the process of capitalistic valuation of urban land and will not benefit the squatter.

Janssen[7] mentions dispelling mechanisms as parts of the urban growth process. In Santa Rosa (a squatter settlement in Bogotá, Colombia) the legalization of the water-works resulted in an increase in property prices which forced a number of dwellers to find cheaper housing elsewhere.

2.1. Katchi Abadi Improvement

International development organizations like the World Bank and United Nations Development Programme (UNDP), and the Karachi Metropolitan Corporation (KMC), have gradually adopted the plea for stimulating self-help housing. One of the consequences was the Karachi Slum Improvement Project which started in 1977 and tried to improve the built environment to standards acceptable to all concerned. Wegelin[8] distinguishes three elements that are important in the katchi abadi improvement policy.

•Land tenure. Very often the land has been illegally occupied. The lack of security prevents the residents investing in their dwellings and the illegality often makes the government reluctant to provide basic urban infrastructure. The provision of security of tenure gives the residents impulses to invest more in housing. If the land is in private hands, then legalization depends on the possibilities for expropriation. Public land will reduce this problem. Especially since the government acquires additional funds by the issue of leases (these are "sold" for a lump sum and a minor annual rent).

•Improvement of the individual houses. Costs of such improvements are left to the residents. The government's task is reduced in this respect to provision of security, credit facilities and technical advice. In addition to the freedom of the residents to choose the extent and way of improvement themselves, some guidance by community organizations or the government can prevent them from creating potential problems for other residents.

Improvement of urban basic infrastructure. The extent of existing infrastructure together with the selected standards concerned, determine the magnitude of the costs. Construction of metalled roads, an adequate water distribution network, sewer lines and drains can only be done by the government. Smallscale additional amenities, like the paving of lanes, could be built and financed by the residents themselves.

A fourth element is the financing of the improvements. KMC does not have sufficient funds - or sufficient political will to allocate the available funds to katchi abadi improvement - and provincial and federal governments give priority to development of rural areas. This implies that in the present conditions KMC has to aim at full cost recovery. Costs of improvement of the infrastructure and, if necessary, land purchases should be balanced, in the long run, by lease issues and other (possible) revenues. Consequently, the choice of standards plays an essential role. It is possible to connect the standards to the health condition. The living conditions in a katchi abadi are such that they endanger the physical health of the dwellers. The standards should be defined in such a way that the living conditions will improve to a level at which the danger to the physical health of the residents will be substantially reduced (but in practice it will be difficult to define clear standards).

Summarized: with katchi abadi improvement the government acts just as the organizer: the funds obtained from the issue of leases are used for land purchase and the improvement of the infrastructure. The residents improve their houses by their own effort and pay for the infrastructural improvements. The result is liveable housing for the low-income groups.

2.1.1. Dispelling Mechanisms

Katchi abadi improvement cannot be examined in isolation. It is necessary to consider the katchi abadi as part of the urban system. Besides, one has to take into account the diversity in katchi abadi residents. The fact that there are various (economic) interest groups obscures the results of the katchi abadi improvement ("liveable housing for the low-income groups").

(a) Widening of the real estate market A katchi abadi is not a neighbourhood where mere squatters live in their self-built houses. This may have been the case at the start of a katchi abadi, but in the course of years an "illegal real estate market" has developed for the sale of houses and land, though there are no legal property rights.[9] In many cases one or another form of paid labour has been involved in the construction of the houses. The functioning of these markets has not yet been examined sufficiently.[10] It can be expected that if the official real estate market is short of houses (the situation in almost all Third World cities), the demand on the (in this case legal) market will increase with the legalization of the squatter neighbourhood. Lower middle-class groups will become interested, especially if the infrastructure is upgraded to a level attractive to them. The higher property prices, together with the lease charges can force lowest-income groups to look for cheaper housing elsewhere. As such, with complete integration in the official real estate market, legalization can act as a dispelling mechanism for low-income groups in squatter settlements.

A government which wants to avoid this has two options. At the issue of leases, restrictive conditions with regard to sale of the plot can be set. This could reduce the land value, but in view of the many possibilities to evade the law (particularly through corruption), the issue of restricted leases will only slightly subdue the property market. Secondly the government can intervene directly in the real estate market. However, this conflicts with the capitalist mode of production and will elicit an enormous pressure on the government.

(b) Internal differences within the katchi abadi population Too often, Turner considers the katchi abadi residents a group with similar interests. Especially when the katchi abadi exists for some time the residents are dispersed in groups with sectional interests. The original invaders were interested in reaching safety with security of tenure, while what new purchasers want, is to raise the value of their property.[11] The various groups with divergent interests with regard to katchi abadi improvement will be discussed now.

The owner-resident. With regard to katchi abadi improvement owner-residents are not a homogeneous group because the economic conditions of the residents - very important with housing - vary considerably. Depending on the standards, a smaller or larger group of residents will not be able to pay lease charges. They can sell their houses and leave, or stay and hope the government will not remove scattered "illegals". Others might not take a lease because they do not feel the need to in view of the changing level of security of tenure and they do not believe that the government will utilize the lease proceeds for improvement of the infrastructure of their muhallah. If many residents act this way, full cost recovery is jeopardized.

Apart from residents who invest more in the house owing to the improved security (in accordance with Turner's theory), some residents may sell their house to squat elsewhere. They will probably belong to low-income groups. People at the minimum of existence always need money for incidental expenditures, like the marriage of a child, sickness costs, etc. It will be very difficult for them to resist a relatively high offer for the house.

> "There may be many bona fide squatters who cannot withstand the temptation created by their scarce resources on the one hand and the offer of a relatively high sum for the land they dwell upon, on the other hand."[12]

> "The offer of quick money often proves to be too much for the original inhabitants who always need money. They sell their rights and squat elsewhere."[13]

If this really happens, then poorer residents are dispelled by katchi abadi improvement to make room for relatively richer people. This process can be judged in different ways. Residents get a higher price for their house as a consequence of katchi abadi improvement. The activities of the government lead to a transfer of income which evokes a positive judgement. On the other hand, the selling-price will still be relatively low because of the poor market information. Speculants will make the biggest profits at resale, specially when the house is sold without a lease. Moreover, the acquired money will be spent on every day necessities and a shelter has to be found elsewhere under possibly even worse conditions.

If the above-mentioned assumptions prove to be true, no structural solution of the housing problem is offered to the low-income groups which was the main object of katchi abadi improvement.

The tenant versus landlord. A not insignificant part of the katchi abadi residents rent their dwelling: in Baldia, at the periphery of Karachi, 11%.[14] The tenants will benefit least by legalization because they do not obtain the lease for their house. They do profit by the improvement of the services. The landlord on the contrary profits by katchi abadi improvement on account of the increase in value of his property. In general the landlord has enough means to pay the lease charges.

He can react in different ways:
- no change; the housing conditions of the tenant improve,
- increase of rent; because of the widening of the rental market, middle-class tenants will get interested if the dwelling becomes legal and the services improve. They will be ready to pay a higher rent. If the original tenant can pay the higher rent, the result does not have to be negative. However, higher housing costs may force some low-income tenants to leave,
- sale; higher prices make it inviting for the landlord to sell and in that case the tenant has to look for shelter elsewhere,
- the improved conditions convince the landlord to live in the house himself. An attendant factor is the fear that the tenant will try to get a lease for the house he is renting. Some "petty" landlords will move in to ascertain the lease.

Once more the various possible consequences of katchi abadi improvement dispelling of low-income groups can be involved.

(c) Conclusions Regularization, by absorbing the katchi abadi in the official urban land market, and improvement of the basic infrastructure, by increasing the attractiveness of the area, will result in rises in prices that can dispel low-income groups:

- owner-residents as a consequence of relatively high offers for the land and lease charges on the one hand and their chronic need for money on the other,
- tenants by increase of rent or eviction.

The selection of high standards by technocrats strengthens these dispelling mechanisms, but standards can also be an instrument for lessening the dispelling mechanism by choosing standards conforming to the paying capacity of the residents.

3. EVALUATION OF THE ANNOUNCEMENT OF KATCHI ABADI IMPROVEMENT

To asses what the consequences of katchi abadi improvement are and whether dispelling mechanisms are a reality, one has to conduct a longitudinal survey in different katchi abadis. Observed changes can only be ascribed to a special stimulus if they can be distinguished from "normal" changes. Two more or less identical katchi abadis,[15] one about to be regularized and improved (test-group) and the other not (control-group) should be surveyed simultaneously several times in the course of time to see whether in the first area more residents from low-income groups leave than in the second. As far as we know surveys like this have not been conducted.

One of the[15] objectives for the Karachi Slum Improvement Project was to conduct an evaluation survey in Baldia at the end of the first project period, and to assess the occurrence of dispelling mechanisms. The policy of KSIP aimed at prevention of dispelling by choosing low standards.

However, there were no possibilities to have a comprehensive study design as described above. A socio-economic survey of Baldia carried out by JRP-IV[16] in 1977, could be repeated but there was no control-area. Moreover, hardly any regularization plan and no improvement plan had been implemented. But it was expected that the mere announcement of the start of the planning work for Baldia would arouse a feeling of security amongst the population and (consequently) start the processes of change. The following results should be understood in connection with the above.

The plots visited in 1977 were visited again in 1979 and the occupant (the same or a new one) was interviewed. The two questionnaires were analysed together for comparison. So there were three groups of respondents:

- stayers, interviewed both in 1977 and in 1979;
- leavers, interviewed only in 1977 and replaced by:
- newcomers, interviewed only in 1979.

With regard to the dispelling mechanisms the following hypothesis had been formulated: "After the announcement of regularization and improvement, residents from low-income groups will be replaced by higher-income groups from other parts of Karachi." The dispelling mechanisms were measured on the basis of the variable household income. Every earning member of the household was asked his monthly income to form a total household income.

After the comparison of the income in 1977 and 1979, the incomes in 1979 of the stayers and the newcomers were compared as were the 1977-incomes of the leavers and the stayers. Then it could be observed whether the leavers belonged generally to low-income groups and the newcomers to high-income groups. To eliminate the effects of the occupancy status, the differences in income between the owners and tenants were calculated.

First of all, migration in the period between the two surveys proved to be low; 11% of the respondents had moved. About half of the residents who had left their plot, had stayed in Baldia. To compare the purchasing power of the incomes in 1977 and 1979, an "inflation correction" had to be calculated. Though it was doubtful whether official figures form the Central Statistical Office in Karachi reflected the actual price-increase in Baldia, they were used for lack of an alternative. It gave an inflation rate of 10.2% (annually 7.6%), applied for calculating the "inflation corrected income 1979".[17]

Table 1 gives the distribution of household income (in seven groups) in 1977 and 1979 and the inflation corrected income in 1979. The average household income increased by 22.7% between 1977 and 1979 and inflation corrected the increase amounts to 11.3% (significant at alpha = 0.05). The median, which for income distribution is a more suitable central tendency measurement rose by 13.5% (after inflation correction).

Table 1. Household Income per Month

	1979	1979c*	1977
Rs 0 - 300	6.1	6.7	9.8
301 - 500	19.1	25.5	32.1
501 - 700	23.4	19.4	22.3
701 - 900	15.7	17.1	13.3
901 - 1100	12.7	13.0	9.9
1101 - 1300	7.7	5.8	3.9
1300 -	15.4	12.5	8.6
	100%	100%	100%
No information	18	18	26
Total number	720	720	720
Average	Rs 865	Rs 785	Rs 705
Median	Rs 750	Rs 681	Rs 600

*inflation corrected.

Various inequality measurements summarize the distribution of income in Table 2.[18] Though the measurements vary considerably, they all point to a - slight - decrease of inequality. The very minor decrease of "H" indicates that changes in the income distribution occurred least in the lower incomes (this might be due to the general nominal increase of income).

Table 2. Inequality Measurements in 1977 and 1979

	1977	1979	% decrease
Coefficient of variance C	0.663	0.609	8.1
Standard deviation of logarithms H	0.650	0.647	0.5
Gini coefficient G	0.312	0.308	1.3
Kuznets index D	0.239	0.233	2.5

The increase of the average income - after inflation correction - can be caused by "immigration" of higher-income groups (and dispelling of lower-income groups) or by a general rise in prosperity of the original residents of Baldia. To differentiate these causes Table 3 shows the distribution of the income of the stayers and newcomers in 1979 and of the stayers and leavers in 1977 separately.

It turns out that the newcomers are overrepresented in the income group Rs 301-900 and on an average earned 5.7% less than the stayers. It has sometimes been suggested that in particular the richest and the poorest people leave the area.[19] This would flatter the average income of the leavers. The figures of Table 3 do not show much evidence for this train of thought.

Table 3. Household Income Stayers, Leavers and Newcomers

	1979		1977	
	stayers	newcomers	stayers	leavers
Rs 0 - 300	6.5	2.8	9.0	16.0
301 - 500	18.6	23.6	32.4	29.6
501 - 700	22.7	29.2	22.2	23.5
701 - 900	15.1	20.8	12.7	17.3
901 - 1100	13.7	4.2	10.3	7.4
1101 - 1300	7.8	6.9	4.4	0.0
1301 -	15.7	12.5	9.0	6.2
	100%	100%	100%	100%
No information	7	10	25	1
Total number	637	82	637	81
Average	Rs 871	Rs 821	Rs 704	Rs 634

However, to test the hypothesis, the comparison has to be refined. The hypothesis can be split up into two predictions to be tested:
1. The residents that were replaced belonged to lower-income groups.
2. The replaced belonged to higher-income groups.

ad.1. The average incomes in 1977 of the leavers and the stayers have to be compared. The average income of the leavers (Rs 634) proved indeed to be lower than the average income of the stayers (Rs 704; the difference is significant at 0.05-level).

ad.2. The difference between the average income of the newcomers in 1979 and that of the leavers in 1977 was larger than the difference between the average income of the stayers in 1979 and 1977. Thus, the newcomers belonged to the relatively high-income groups (compared with the leavers).

However, the first difference and thus the comparison too, are not significant at the 0.05-level.

A factor which might be important in this respect is the occupancy status. Many newcomers rented their houses (45%) while in the total sample only 11% of the respondents were tenants. The average incomes of the three groups of respondents were compared separately for owners and tenants. The difference of income between the staying and leaving tenants in 1977 was especially substantial, this may indicate that in the sample particularly the poorest tenants have left. Again these differences are not significant, partly due to very limited numbers of respondents in the various groups.

In Table 4 the above has been summarized by showing the average incomes with the percentages difference and, between brackets, the one-tailed probability (which for significancy should be lower than the chosen level 0.05).

Table 4. The Average Incomes Compared

	1977	% difference	1970^{+}
all respondents	Rs 697	11.6% (.000)	Rs 788
stayers	704	11.1% (.000)	782
% difference	11.0% (.029)		5.8% (.204)
leavers/newcomers	634	16.6% (.064)	739
stayers	699	13.0% (.000)	785
owners % difference	3.2% (.300)		4.7% (.301)
leavers/newcomers	677	10.8% (.187)	750
stayers	728	2.9% (.402)	749
tenants % difference	20.1% (.106)		9.0% (2.66)
leavers/newcomers	606 (.201)	13.4%	687

$^{+}$inflation corrected.

The anticipated change from rented houses to owned houses (the original or a new owner establishes himself in the house) seemed to come true: 25% of the rented houses in 1977 had been occupied by the owner in 1979 (while only 1.5% of the owner-residents in 1977 let their house in 1979). Besides, the percentage of tenants was considerably higher among the leavers (57%) than among the newcomers (45%). Consequently the percentage rented houses decreased from 13.6% in 1977 to 11.1% in 1979.

The fact that about half of the leavers found another dwelling in Baldia, does not imply that these residents have not been dispelled by the announcement of regularization and improvement. In Baldia the cost of housing varies considerably between the various parts of the area. Low-income residents might have gone to muhallahs (i.e. quarters) where housing is cheaper. In Rashidabad, a muhallah near the hills, some tenants started squatting at the fringe of Baldia. They immediately built permanent houses, expressing their raised level of perceived security of tenure.

Thus, the residents who left their dwellings since 1977 belonged to low-income groups. They were replaced by households with mainly low and middle incomes (Rs 301-900), who earn on an average more than their predecessors but less than the residents who have stayed since 1977. However, the second part of the hypothesis had to be rejected because the results are not significant.

The relatively low migration rate (annually 8.5%) included a majority of tenants. It cannot be traced whether this is a rather normal phenomenon in a katchi abadi or an expression of dispelling mechanisms.

4. CONCLUSIONS

Katchi abadi improvement knows various problems: the acquisition of the land, the choosing of standards and the changing security of tenure. Next to this, katchi abadi improvement can have negative consequences. The widening of the real estate market and internal differences in the katchi abadi necessitate evaluation to ascertain whether or not the aim (liveable housing for the low-income groups) has been achieved. In Baldia Township the announcement of regularization and improvement were evaluated. The hypothesis on dispelling mechanisms could not be confirmed. This may partly be due to the short period of time between the two surveys and to the fact that the implementation of the plans had not yet started. Besides, the percentage of tenants is low in Baldia, while they seem to be more sensitive to dispelling.

REFERENCES

1. C. Ward, in the preface of *J. F. C. Turner*, Housing by people, London, 1976.
2. J. C. Turner with R. Goetze: Environmental security and housing input; *Ekistics*, vol. 23, no. 135, February 1967.
3. J. J. van der Linden, *The bastis of Karachi, Types and Dynamics*, Amsterdam, 1977, p. 116.
4. J. van der Harst, Low-income housing, Karachi, 1975.
5. *Joint Research Project-IV*: Usmania Muhajir Colony; Karachi, 1975.
6. R. Burgess, Petty commodity housing or dweller control? A critique of John Turner's views on housing policy, *World Development*, 1978, vol. 6, no. 9/10.
7. R. Janssen: "Wij hebben zelfs geen recht op de stad", vogelvrij wonen in Santa Rosa de Lima: een stadssociologisch onderzoek naar de woon- en levensomstandigheden in een volksbuurt van Bogotá, Colombia, Amsterdam, 1978.
8. E. A. Wegelin, Money for slum-upgrading, *Pakistan Economist*, vol. 19, no. 2, 13 January, 1979.
9. In Baldia, Karachi, 15% of the residents have bought their house at an average price of 14.5 times a median monthly income in 1979, while 39% have built their house on land they paid for - on an average 1.3 times

a median monthly income in 1979 (32% built their house on free land; 11% were tenants, the remaining respondents got their house in another way). M. Schuringa, S. A. Khan, E. Meijer and K. S. Yap (ed.); Baldia Evaluation Survey Report, a study on improvement of living conditions in a katchi abadi, Karachi, 1979.

10. In Karachi blockmakers (small-scale producers of dried sand-cement blocks) and cement dealers play an important role in the "illegal" real estate market. One can really speak of a market: for instance, one week after the sale of a house (with option for a lease) for Rs 30,000, it has been resold for Rs 35,000, a profit comparable to that of speculators in Amsterdam.
11. R. Janssen, *op.cit.*, p. 133.
12. J. J. van der Linden, *op.cit.*, p. 62.
13. A. A. Laquian, Slums are for people, Honolulu, 1971.
14. Schuringa *et al.*, *op.cit.*
15. On the basis of criteria with regard to security of tenure, the quality of the house, the income distribution and ethnicity.
16. Joint Research Project IV: Socio-economic survey Baldia Township; Karachi, 1978.
17. Calculation of the inflation:

	1	2	3	4	5
food, beverages and tobacco	269.19	290.00	7.73	0.5843	4.5166
apparel, textile and footwear	267.64	283.37	5.88	0.0960	0.5645
housing and household operation	237.90	266.21	11.90	0.1674	1.9921
miscellaneous	243.11	292.27	20.22	0.1522	3.0775
					10.1507

1. Consumer price index figures November 1977.
2. Consumer price index figures March 1979.
3. Percentage difference between 1 and 2.
4. Consumption weights of the income group "up to Rs 300".
5. 3 multiplied with 4.

July 1969 = 100

Source: *Central Statistical Office*, Karachi.

18. In a Lorentz curve the percentage of the households arranged from the poorest to the richest are represented on the horizontal axis and the percentages of income enjoyed by the bottom x% of the households is shown on the vertical axis. The Gini coefficient is the ratio of the difference between the line of absolute equality (the diagonal) and the Lorentz curve to the triangular region underneath the diagonal. The coefficient of variation is the square root of the variance divided by the mean income level. Kuznets index D is the absolute mean deviation of the income share of each 5 percentile group from 5%, divided by 9.5. In the calculation of "H" the deviation is taken from the arithmetic mean.

    S. Jain, Size distribution of income, a compilation of data, Washington DC, 1975.

    A. Sen, On economic inequality, Oxford, 1973.
19. Joint Research Project-IV, *op.cit.*, 1975.

Actors in Squatter Settlement Upgrading: Their Interests and Roles

J. J. van der Linden*

1. INTRODUCTION

In 1975/1976 the Karachi Metropolitan Corporation formulated its "Improvement Policy for Substandard Urban Areas",[1] which embodied an approach to the housing problems of low-income groups that was completely new to Karachi. The adoption of this approach can be understood in the light of the ever-increasing numbers of low-income people who could not be sheltered through traditional means. Secondly, previously attempted ways to cope with this problem had either completely failed or met with only limited success.[2] Finally, extensive research had shown that the application of a different approach was imperative if problems were to be tackled on the scale required.[3]

Basically, the "New Policy" seeks to recognize a number of rights to the to date illegal squatters and to institutionalize systematic efforts for the improvement of the squatter settlements. Main points in the "New Policy" are:

(a) The policy stresses improvement of existing "bastis".[4] By improvement is meant:
   1. Legalization of the existing situation as far as possible, and
   2. Improvement of the physical and social infrastructure (environmental sanitation, roads, schools, playgrounds, etc.) - housebuilding will be left to the inhabitants themselves.

(b) Improvement programmes have to be financially sound, in order to be replicable. In fact, this implies a substantial share in the expenses on the part of the residents.

(c) In view of the above points, the residents' participation in the whole process is vital. To give one example: the first consideration (a) implies that standards have to be flexible. Costs will much depend on the standards applied. Thus, an optimal balance has to be found between an ideal situation and one that can be afforded. For this and similar points to be decided, the people's participation is indispensable.

---

*An abridged version of this article appeared in Open House, Quarterly publication of the Stichting Architecten Research, Vol. VI, 1981, pp. 36-43.

2. PITFALLS IN THE IMPLEMENTATION; THE BACKGROUND

In the implementation of the new policy, there are many problems of a financial, technical or legal nature. However, implementation is chiefly hindered by communication gaps and clashes of interests between the different actors involved. In this section I will describe features of the main actors: basti dwellers, the government and the politicians. From this description it can subsequently be seen where communications are poor and where interests clash.

2.1. The Bastis, Types and Types of Organization

Although, from a formal point of view, practically all the bastis are illegal settlements, this does not imply that they arise in a disorganized manner. Precisely because they are illegal, often much organization is needed to resist the government's attempts to demolish a basti. But the degree of organization tends to diminish when the basti - for whatever reasons - gets a certain recognition from the side of the government. I will come back to this point later.

Broadly speaking, there are two types of bastis with their own special kinds of organization, that are relevant in this context.[5]

2.1.1. The First Type; Bastis with Smooth Development

There are, firstly, bastis that have come about more or less spontaneously, because (often quite small) groups of people erected their huts on some spots (often marginal lands alongside riverbeds or railway tracks; but sometimes less marginal open spaces). Right from the beginning, these people have to defend themselves against the government's attempts to evict them. Often, they invite as many people as possible to join them, seeking greater safety in numbers.[6]

Once they turn out to be somewhat successful in their efforts to be allowed to go on dwelling where they are, the next step is to lobby and try to obtain some basic facilities (firstly: water) in their basti. Both types of activities call for strong organization and much participation on the part of individual dwellers. This participation is already given with the risk the individual runs when erecting his hut in such a basti. There are cases known, where, at crucial times, a plenary meeting of the basti dwellers was held daily, to discuss the current problems.

Once the threat of being evicted diminishes and the basic facilities have been obtained, the degree of organization also diminishes; quite often organization for the survival, legalization or betterment of a basti completely disappears. In some cases, it re-appears when the government decides to legalize a basti: again some organization is needed to bargain with the government about prices and fees to be paid for land and facilities.[7]

2.1.2. The Second Type: Bastis with Initial Partial Development

The second type of bastis mostly comes about in the periphery of the city, where "middlemen" or "brokers" have obtained indications from the side of the government that they will not be disturbed if they sub-divide government's land for residential purposes under certain conditions (recompensation of the informant and other parties concerned; conditions of standards).

Here, it is the middleman who gets unofficial protection from the authorities, and this protection makes a strong organization or, even, much cohesion amongst the dwellers redundant. It is the middleman who has laid out the basti, who sells plots to individuals, who organizes the provision of water and transport. The middleman's protection appears to be a sufficient guarantee to the basti dwellers, who do not get any documentary evidence of a title to their plots.

As a result, participation on the part of the residents in the organization for betterment of the basti is often very weak, or non-existent. The middlemen and a rather small group of influential people around them are the "natural leaders" of the basti, namely the ones who have easy access to governmental institutions - per definition - ever since the inception of the basti. When in the basti - e.g. political - organizations come about, these are also mainly centred around the middlemen.

2.2. Aims of the Basti Dwellers

Whatever the differences between types of bastis, or their inhabitants, to the "common" basti dwellers the main aims are:

(a) to have secure tenure,
(b) to have some basic facilities,
(c) to pay a minimum for (a) and (b).

These three requirements are interdependent and a kind of market-mechanism fixes the balance between them in every stage of the life of a basti. When security and facilities in a certain place are at a low level ("scarce"), the inhabitants are willing to pay much to obtain them.[8] When facilities are brought to a basti, this fact is perceived as a sign of recognition from the government; the perceived security increases, and - with it - the willingness to pay for it diminishes.

In this context, the above-described difference between bastis with smooth development and those with partial initial development is relevant.[9] Generally speaking, in bastis with smooth development, the population's eagerness to obtain a lease is greater than in the other type of bastis. With it, the willingness to pay is likely to be greater in bastis with smooth development. Besides, in these bastis land speculation takes a much less prominent place and the degree of residents' organization tends to be higher than in bastis with partial initial development. All of these circumstances point to a greater likelihood of success of a legalization- and improvement programme in bastis with smooth development.

However, for reasons which will become clear later in this article, on the government's part, there is a tendency to give priority to bastis with partial initial development.[9]

In the development process of bastis, there is increasing involvement on the government's part, illustrated by the stage-wise provision of facilities. Legalization is the final stage of government's involvement in a basti's life, as after legalization the basti stops to be a basti and becomes a regular residential area in which, at least theoretically, the government's involvement is at its normal or official 100% level. By the time legalization is decided upon by the authorities, often the basti has reached a stage, where the dwellers are absolutely sure that they will never be evicted and where they enjoy a reasonable facility level, and where - consequently - the willingness to pay for codified security is minimal.

In such a case, legalization means nothing but an official sanction to an already existing situation; a sanction that is not very meaningful, but - at the same time - costly to the common basti dweller.[10] Probably, in such cases, the common basti dweller can be convinced to pay only if - either - legalization is combined with visible and meaningful improvements in the infrastructure - or - if lease-charges are very nominal and procedures extremely simple. If this last option is chosen, the - now legal - basti dwellers can legally pressurize the local government for obtaining facilities practically free of cost: under the law, it is the Municipality's duty to provide and maintain physical infrastructure.[11]

There is one more factor of influence in the basti dweller's motivation to want - or not to want - legalization. As long as a basti is an illegal settlement, land prices are relatively low, because the illegal land market operates mainly for low-income people. Once legal titles to land - in whatever shape - are issued, also middle- and high-income people start competing in the market. As a result, prices tend to rise. This rise, although quite substantial, is not very sharp, as legalization is always anticipated well in advance.

Of course, it is in the basti dweller's interest to see the value of his plot rise, but in most cases, he is not interested in immediately cashing this profit; he will feel happy and proud of being the owner of his plot, and he knows that he has to pay an equal amount of money, should he sell his property and move to another, equivalent, place. His immediate profit lies in an increased socio-economic security, being the legal owner of an inflation-free asset. However, as this profit normally is not immediately tangible, the basti dweller is only interested in it, if it is not too expensive. Once he has no more fear of being evicted, his priority demand will be for facilities. Still, when in financial problems, the poor basti dweller will feel tempted to cash the - to him - incredible bid he can get for his plot from richer persons. Thus, in the long run, the legalized and improved basti could be slowly taken over by middle-class people.[12]

Different is the case of the middlemen who organize the settlement of the "second type bastis", described above. Initially, these brokers mostly sell plots quite cheaply, but see to it that a number of plots - especially the potentially commercial plots along prospective main roads - are kept in reserve, as these plots can fetch very high prices once a major part of the basti is inhabited. This, of course, is plain speculation. Because of this speculation, the middlemen are very interested in legalization of bastis, as it increases their speculative profits enormously. For reasons which we will describe below, they are much less interested in obtaining facilities along with legalization.

2.3. Institutions of the Basti Dwellers

The "common" basti dweller, whom we have referred to, is a poor man. It can be estimated that about three quarters of the heads of households in bastis are semi- or unskilled labourers, salesworkers (mostly hawkers or small shopkeepers in the basti) or servants.[13] Clearly, they are low-income people, having little bargaining power. How then do they face the government to obtain security and facilities at costs which they can afford?

In 2.1 we have described two types of bastis with their different forms of organization. Whatever the differences, however, the leaders, the spokesmen of the basti dwellers, have to be people who have access to the government machinery, i.e. per definition they have to be more educated, rich and/or more powerful than the common basti dweller and they are not very representative of the average basti dweller.[14] This, of course, is not unusual for leaders as these tend to be recruited from elites, and the fact that leaders are not representative of their followers does not necessarily imply that they can not represent their followers' interests. Theoretically, and in fact, these interests may coincide.

In the Karachi bastis, leadership is part of an all-pervading system of "patron-client relationship".

> "Patronage is an institutionalized, albeit often informal, transaction between two persons who differ regarding the degree to which they can influence the allocation of goods and services. The transaction implies that the one who has more influence will use it for the benefit of the other party, the client, who, in turn, will render all kinds of services in the interest of the patron."[15]

A basti leader, then, qualifies as such because he can exert influence or power, and because he has got entrance into the hierarchy where decisions are taken. This is the leader's role; what his personal aims and motivations are is only of secondary importance.[16]

What are the aims of the leaders? Obviously, to the broker-leadership in the "second-type bastis", speculation is a main aim. But to a lesser extent, this often holds true for leaders in the "first-type basti" as well, as the leaders - being the richest and most powerful people - often hold large, or several, plots in such bastis.[17] For this reason, the leaders' aims partly coincide with those of the common basti dwellers: they will bargain for cheap leases and so fulfil a part of their share in the transaction between patrons and clients.

However, as already indicated, the basti dwellers attach more value to obtaining facilities, by which an increased security of tenure is automatically implied. The leaders, in their turn, prefer to separate legalization and improvement: separation of the two keeps the lease-rates low and especially the leaders can pressurize and slowly obtain the required facilities. To them, this not only is a cheaper procedure, but it probably also sustains their power, which would become weaker once the main aims of the basti dwellers have been fulfilled. Namely:

> "The brokers must serve some of the interests operating on both the community and the national (in our case: mainly the local, JL) level, and they must cope with the conflicts raised by the collision of these interests. They can not settle them, since by doing so, they would abolish their own usefulness to others. Thus they often act as buffers between groups, maintaining the tensions which provide the dynamic of their action."[18]

There is, finally, one more aspect of leadership in the bastis which also makes for an institutional constraint. There is a strong tendency towards competition amongst the leaders. Often, within a single basti, several leaders operate, each with his own cluster of followers, who oppose each other whenever possible. This fact raises even more doubts about the representativeness of such leaders.

2.4. The Government : Compartmentization and Systematic Chaos, a Case of Bureaucratic Involution

Just as is the case of basti leadership, the (local) government is strongly compartmentized. In Karachi, at the local level, there are over 60 government and semi-government organizations involved in planning and execution in the fields of public works, house building, services and economic development.[19] The coordination between these agencies is poor; rather they all tend to create their own kingdoms than to share or delegate (parts of) their powers or at least coordinate efforts. Often jurisdictions and responsibilities of the agencies are shady and fights between these agencies are common.[20] Within the agencies often the same kind of poor coordination prevails between and even within departments.

To an outsider, it looks as though all decisions are random.[21] However, the chaos thus created is highly systematic, even to the extent that it can be predicted where, for example, files get misplaced.

To explain this situation, let me use a somewhat fictitious, but quite imaginable example.

Suppose there are, in a certain department, 10 officers who have to share 4 cars for their fieldtrips and other official transport requirements. Suppose they have agreed to use the vehicles on a "first-come-first-serve"-basis. The obvious system would be to have a simple chart hanging in some central place in the office, on which the different vehicles and the (parts of) days of the month are shown, so that any of the officers can book any of the cars at any moment and also it can, at every moment, immediately be seen who is using which car and which car would be available.

All the clerk in charge would have to do in this case, would be to check whether claims were correct, hand over keys and logbook and receive these two again when the officer returns. This, however, is not a very exciting job to the transport clerk. So this clerk has forms cyclostyled on which the claims are to be made. The forms require much rather irrelevant information (duplication of the logbook) and are poorly laid out and cyclostyled. These forms are piled up on the transport clerk's desk and only a fan is needed to completely disorganize the pile at least once daily.

Now, instead of a smoothly-running, completely transparent system plus an uninteresting job for the one in charge, the system will, opaquely, work all the same, but the clerk has gained a monopoly on information. Instead of handing over keys according to the rules, he is now in a position where he can use his discretion to give or refuse favours. It makes him more important in terms of prestige. When the need arises, he can claim counter-favours from the officers, who will think twice before they refuse.

Finally, many of the officers will not really mind the system working this way, because it also provides them with the opportunities for less official uses of the vehicles, which, in turn, enhance the power, prestige and/or income of the clerk even further.

In fact, the clerk of our example has managed to grasp some "influence in the allocation of goods and services" and has established a relationship with the officers that again strongly resembles the patron-client relationship.

"Particularistic use of public means is at least expected."[22]

Although the above example is not devoid of a certain logic - and it is by no means unknown in the West - some points may further clarify how this systematic chaos became an "organized way of doing", an institution.

(a) "The colonial era has also bequeathed to the new states a peculiar tradition of "public service". The salient features of this tradition are that it is authoritarian in spirit and negative in purpose."[23]

(b) "The system of government in Pakistan is founded on the principle that policy-making in administration can be sharply differentiated and separated from the execution of policy. Pakistan has also inherited a very strong tradition that the former function can be performed better by the public servants whose dominant professional value is classical generalism or guardianship ...
The direct result of this policy is that administratively the technical specialist is bound to remain under the control and discipline of the generalist."[24]

(c) "... a habit pattern seems to have been built up under which there is such constant and frequent movement in and out of key government posts ... that it can not fail to affect the efficiency of individual agencies and officers."[25]

Regarding this third point, one may wonder whether it is the cause or the effect of what I have called "systematic chaos". It certainly is a result of the tradition of an authoritarian divide-and-rule system, while its operation is eased by a system in which generalists take such an important role. Because of patron-client-like relations between public servants and the (leaders of the) public, the consequences of frequent movements are even more serious than one might - at first sight - expect: it is not only a matter of continuous re-adjustment of new persons to new situations. The particularistic use of public means implies that the policy of individual key-persons is often directed towards the granting of favours to their clients. These favours make for the power and popularity of a high officer. But a successor,

"can not gain credit with what his predecessor has made ready; this fact is the cause of the discontinuity in every policy."[26]

(d) Frequent political changes and prolonged political insecurity reinforce the power of the administration but at the same time result in a tendency to be over-careful in taking important policy decisions.[27]

(e) The logistic machinery is weak.

(f) The officers are often insufficiently remunerated.

From these points (I do not claim completeness; I only point to a number of influential tendencies), two important effects on implementation of a policy for sub-standard urban areas follow.

(a) As explained in 1.1, main features on this policy are:
  1. The recognition of certain rights of the basti dwellers (the right to dwell; the right to have a say in the process of improvement).
  2. A systematic approach by which procedures are fixed - and preferably streamlined - (e.g. residents' participation, a revolving fund, simple lease procedures, linking of leasing and physical improvement, etc.).

  Neither of these two points is in the interest of those who love chaos, be it an individual public servant or one of the many agencies involved. By leaving the rights of the basti dwellers vague and undefined and by using a (systematic) random-approach, much more discretion - i.e. power - is left for the agency or the individuals in it.

(b) Chaos everywhere frustrates the efforts of many competent officers, who deserve support both from the hierarchy and the logistic machinery. In this way, many well-qualified and devoted people in the government agencies are led to give up. The dilemma to them is that they cannot achieve much when they stick to their proper, official roles. If - on the other hand - they are eager to achieve something, participation in the unofficial system is forced upon them, which very much destroys the long term effects of any achievement. Thus, the system reinforces and perpetuates itself .

Drawing comparisons between the bureaucratic system described here, and what Geertz has called "agricultural involution"[28] may enhance our understanding of the system. McGee has borrowed the term "involution" from Geertz and applied it in the urban context when describing the "bazaar-economy".[29] He also indicates "that the patterns of bureaucracy tend towards labour-intensive practices which are essentially a reflection of the bazaar-economy principles."[30] Involution can be described as a process of continuous further internal refining and complication of a system that fails to adapt itself through transformation. A basic concept of involution is intensification without change, or, in Geertz' words: "working old plots harder rather than establishing new ones", a "changeless change", an "indeterminateness which did not so much transform traditional patterns as elasticize them", "static expansion".[31]

As the 4 characteristics of the process in involution, Geertz mentions:
1. Tenacity of the basic pattern.
2. Internal ornateness and elaboration.
3. Technical hairsplitting, and
4. Unending virtuosity.[32]

These characteristics apply to the government machinery in Karachi to an amazing extent, so that it is justified to speak of bureaucratic involution.

In his article "The case of Bhutta Village"[33] Yap describes in detail how - in themselves completely sound - bureaucratic procedures result in no result, except for much routine work for government servants and employees from high to low, and back again. The case regards a possibility for the local administration to save in terms of money and time to obtain much better results in surveying urban areas. By strictly sticking to established - and partly out-dated - procedures with all the built-in safety-valves against corruption or misuse of power, with all the stipulations about who is competent under what conditions and so on, and also by an enormous inventiveness to use and misuse these rules (sending a file back down the chain because one page was upside down!), even discussion on the issue was avoided. The whole process resulted in nothing but kept the hierarchy working.

Another illustration regards the leasing procedure in Karachi, which could perhaps fit the situation of a moderate-sized township but which is completely unworkable in Karachi. In this case, the tenacity of the basic pattern finds its expression in, for example, the fact for each lease-document to be issued, a corporation resolution has to be passed and the signature of the Administrator is required. The "internal ornateness" may be exemplified by the fact that the applicant for a lease has to obtain his application form from one office, but it is of no use as long as he does not obtain official stamps from another office: applications can be only submitted along with the stamps. "Technical hairsplitting" in this case is illustrated by the fact that the applicant has to make at least 8 visits to different and partly the same offices, if the whole procedure is executed neatly (which for obvious reasons rarely will be the case). Finally, the fact that a fossilized procedure has been adapted so that - at least theoretically - it can work and is - again: theoretically - foolproof, proves the enormous virtuosity of the system.

Calling this process "bureaucratic involution" points to some features worth mentioning.

(a) The basic function of the involution process is to allow the system to absorb ever more individuals who can have their small share in a condition of shared poverty,[34] and with it, a politically-stabilizing function.[35]

(b) The system as it is, is so established and refined, and so many have interests in its maintenance, that it can be changed only with great difficulty.[36]

(c) Just as there are relations of interdependence between the agricultural peasant system of production and the urban bazaar-economy,[37] it is probable that relations between an involuted bureaucracy and the equally involuted non-public networks (e.g. commercial and political) are essential for the survival of each of these networks and those who partake in them. It could be hypothesized that this all-encompassing interdependence makes almost everybody participate in the system which makes for its tenacity. At the same time, the bureaucracy, with its relationship to the capital-intensive sector, can serve to let some of the profits made in this sector trickle down into its own organization and related networks.[38]

2.5. The Politicians

In this section, we will only deal with the (mostly local) politicians who are directly involved in slum upgrading programmes. Their role is very much comparable to that of the basti-brokers. Often, local politicians do have personal interests in bastis and the basti-brokers are their clients. Sometimes the basti-brokers and the politician are the same person.

Within the pattern of a patron-client relationship, the politician will rather bargain for a favour to be bestowed upon his clients than fight for recognition and/or application of the rights of those whom he represents. As a result, the politician's interest too lies in the (systematic) random-approach: if today he can achieve a community tap for basti X and next month a paved street for basti Y, this means much more to the politician than having once and for all the rights of his clients recognized. Because with these rights, they would become much less dependent upon the politician.

Besides the politicians' activities directed at obtaining *ad-hoc* improvements for their clients - which activities, under circumstances, may be considered somewhat beneficial - the politicians also sometimes interfere when the government is in the process of execution of certain works.

A recent and rather notorious example is the case of Lyari, a central city slum area with a population of 600,000. The feasibility, and in fact the execution of an improvement programme for this area were completely upset when, during the election campaigns, a politician announced to the cheering crowds that the lease rates would be no more than the ridiculous Rs 4.-- per square yard. As a result, to the Municipality, it was no longer possible to either charge more, or to carry out a financially feasible improvement programme. So the whole programme was discontinued.

3. PITFALLS IN THE IMPLEMENTATION: RELATIONS BETWEEN THE ACTORS

In the above paragraphs, we have analysed some aims and methods of each group playing a role in the process of basti improvement. In the present paragraph, we will describe some of the relations between groups. The channels of communication between these groups can - simplifiedly - be represented as follows:

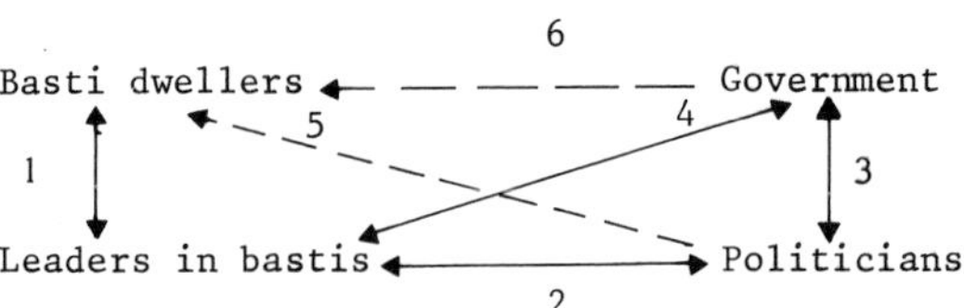

In connection with this chart of communication flows, we can make the following observations:

(a) Whatever the problems between (both "high" and "low"-level) leaders and the government, a basic point is that interests of those leaders and of individuals in the government greatly coincide. On the one hand, this makes for much competition between and amongst them, on the other hand, the result is that deals are often reached between these groups, irrespective of the basti dwellers' interests.
The existence of bastis with partial initial development is an example of such deals and it is logical that these bastis enjoy relatively much benevolence on the government's part.[39] The following point also can be viewed as one aspect of this coincidence of interests.

(b) There is no direct communication between the government and the basti dwellers, although (arrow 6) occasionally the government may reach the basti dwellers with official announcements, as do the politicians (arrow 5). In both cases, it concerns a one-way communication. Besides the technical difficulty for the government to reach large numbers of people who are poorly represented by their leaders, there is also a class difference between the higher public servants who, in general, represent the middle class, and the lower class basti dwellers.[40] This difference does not facilitate mutual understanding.

> "...regularization and improvement of squatter settlements generally takes place in an atmosphere of confrontation between the residents and authorities and is dominated by mutual mistrust. The residents cannot but see the authorities as an adversary who at the worst always wanted to demolish their houses and shift the occupants to some far-off place, and at the best promised improvement of their living conditions but never kept that promise. The authorities see residents of squatter settlements above all as trespassers who occupied private or public land and constructed their dwelling without prior formal approval from the authorities."[41]

(c) The basti dwellers and the government communicate with each other through the leaders of the bastis, the "low-level brokers" (arrow 1 and 4) either directly, or via the politicians, the "high-level brokers" (arrow 1,2 and 3). Indeed, to KMC, it is impossible to approach each individual resident and there seems to be no alternative to working through local organizations and notables to reach the mass of the population.[42] However, as we have explained above, often the interests of leaders and basti dwellers do not coincide in all respects. Sometimes leaders only inform their own supporters and represent only their interests. Quite often, leaders are supported only by a fraction of the population of an area.[42] More serious even, a recent survey indicated that basti dwellers who had been informed about an improvement programme by their leaders were the poorest informed (as compared to those who had got the information via KMC, newspapers or neighbours).[43] No doubt, in these cases the leaders had given biased information on purpose. No wonder,

> "the authorities may get the feeling they work in a vacuum, never reaching the mass of the population and mainly dealing with notables who do not represent anything but their own personal interests".[44]

(d) This last quotation already touches on the communication between the government and the politicians, either "low" of "high-level brokers" (arrow 3 and 4). Although, technically, there is hardly an alternative to communication between authorities and mass than through their leaders, and although several of the aims of leaders and the bureaucracy coincide, communications between the two groups are often difficult. The basic reason for this probably lies in the competition for power, as for example, illustrated in the above example of Lyari. Ahmad, when elaborating on the difficult communications between officers and politicians, mentions three causes:
  (a) a tradition (from the colonial period) of a paramount position of the bureaucracy and hostility on the part of the (nationalist) politician towards the civil servant,
  (b) the relative superiority in personal ability and experience of the average public servant over the average politician,
  (c) the instability of the political governments in Pakistan.[45] As far as the above points suggest a certain advantage on the part of the bureaucracy, we may add that the politician, bearing much less responsibility, has much more freedom than the bureaucracy to manipulate.

A main problem appears to be that the common basti dwellers do not have the means to communicate with the government. An intermediate organization, (such as proposed by Yap)[46] would be of use to bridge the communication gap. Communication certainly is a key-word if the basic aim of basti-improvement: the recognition of the rights of basti dwellers, is to be attained. For this, in its turn, a weakening of - or at least a check on - the patronage system is required. This weakening is implicity-given by defining the rights and duties of the participants,

> "Not only in politics and policy-making, but also in the economic conditions, clarification of rights and duties will weaken patronage".[47]

Thus, the recognition of the rights of the basti dwellers has a far greater bearing than a mere means to improve living conditions in bastis, and probably, this is the main reason why basti-improvement is so difficult.[48] Much more and better use could be made of communication channels (arrow 6) - e.g. with the help of notice boards, hand bills, press, radio - to tell the basti dwellers what their rights and duties are. But this, of course, presupposes that these rights and duties be defined and applied as far as possible. It presupposes policy-makers and a bureaucracy that really wants to solve problems. As, evidently, in Karachi these conditions are not being met,[49] involving an intermediate organization to carry out these tasks may be a viable way-out for the time being.

4. A CONCLUDING REMARK

The tone of this article is not very optimistic. Neither am I. To conclude slightly more optimistically, let me emphasize one point which I have dealt with in the above somewhat implicitly. The whole structure in which slum upgrading is to be executed has more of the characteristics of a jungle than of a conspiracy of the devil. No doubt, the laws of the jungle are not very conducive to the execution of human rights. I have tried, however, to discover that there is some system in the jungle. Once we know under what circumstances the jungle flourishes, and how it grows, it might also be possible to stop its growth or attack it - for those who want to.

REFERENCES

1. KMC, An improvement policy for substandard urban areas, Karachi, 1976 (revised 1977).
2. See K. S. Yap, Introduction to Chapter III of this reader and J. J. van der Linden, *The bastis of Karachi, Types and Dynamics*, Amsterdam, 1977, pp. 10-14.
3. Mainly by the Joint Research Project of the Karachi University and the Free University of Amsterdam, 1970-1975.
4. "Basti" is one of the local terms for illegal low-income settlements.
5. These types are described more elaborately in J. J. van der Linden, The bastis of Karachi, the functioning of an informal housing system. Elsewhere in this book.
6. See W. Mangin, Squatter settlements, *Scientific American*, 1967, Vol. CCXVII, pp. 21-29.
7. See J. J. van der Linden, 1977, p. 257, and different cases described in Ch. X. See A. Portes, Rationality in the slum. In Comparative studies in society and history, 14 (1972), pp. 268-286, and A. Portes, the politics of urban poverty, in A. Portes and J. Walton, *Urban Latin America*, Austin & London, 1976, pp. 71-110.
8. An interesting example is the case where basti dwellers bribed officers to be allowed to pay Municipal taxes, the receipts of which provided them with some documentary evidence of recognition on the part of the Municipal government.
9. See 5.
10. See K. S. Yap, Residents' participation in katchi abadi improvement, *Pakistan Economist*, 13 January 1979, pp. 21-24, and J. J. van der Linden, 1977, pp. 311-312.
11. See E. A. Wegelin, Money for slum upgrading, *Pakistan Economist*, 13 January 1979, pp. 13-21.
12. See E. N. Meyer, Dispelling mechanism at Katchi Abadi Improvement. Elsewhere in this book.
13. See J. J. van der Linden, 1977, p. 4 of Appendix V.
14. Even when asked what a "leader" *should* be like, from 142 replies of basti dwellers, almost 50% refer to education, influence and wealth; only 16 replies indicate that a leader should be from the community proper. R. A. Chughtai, H. Kiestra, T. E. L. van Pinxteren and M.H. Weijs, Miran Naka, Karachi 1975, p. 94.
15. B. F. Galjart, Patronage als integratie mechanisme in Latijns Amerika. *Sociologische Gids*, 1969-VI, p. 402.
16. Typically, in Panjabi, there is one single expression meaning both "a good man" and "a rich man". Clearly, here "good" is not measured in for example, moral terms, but in terms of the man's capacity to do, or to get done something for one's good. (It is also of interest to note that the expression ("mota-pet-wala") literally translated, means "man with a fat belly".) Again, in Karachi, one interviewee, when talking about leaders stated: "All of them are friends of money, but only through them we can achieve something".
17. T. J. Segaar, *Karachi en de basti*, Amsterdam, 1975, p. 85.
18. E. R. Wolf, Aspects of group relations in a complex society, Mexico, *American Anthropologist*, Vol. 58, 1956, pp. 1056-1078.
19. T. J. Segaar, 1975, p. 27.
20. See J. J. van der Linden, 1977, pp. 265 ff.
21. As an example may serve a redevelopment scheme in a slum area, where (officially) the slum dwellers are to be resettled in flats on the spot. Both the Master Plan Department of the Karachi Development Authority and a Federal Ministry have disapproved of this scheme. Yet it was initiated without there being decisions on the rents to be paid, or

about the allocation system to be adhered to. See Weijs' article on Jacob lines. Elsewhere in this book.

22. B. F. Galjart, 1969, p. 404.
23. M. Ahmad, The civil servant in Pakistan, Karachi, Lahore, Dacca, 1964, p. vii.
24. *Ibid.*, pp. 183, 184.
25. *Ibid.*, p. 226.
26. B. F. Galjart, 1969, pp. 404-405.
27. An interesting example is the slip of the tongue of one officer, who stated: "Some of our Federal Ministers try to pressurize the government ...but we..."
28. C. Geertz, *Agricultural involution*, Berkeley & Los Angeles, 1970.
29. T. G. McGee, The urbanization process in the third world, London, 1971. Chapter III, Revolutionary change and the third world city: a theory of urban involution.
30. *Ibid.*, p. 69.
31. C. Geertz, 1970, resp. pp. 32, 96, 103, 137.
32. *Ibid.*, p. 81.
33. K. S. Yap, The case of Bhutta Village, in K. S. Yap, Leases, land and local leaders (forthcoming).
34. T. G. McGee, 1971, (quoting Wertheim), p. 69.
35. *Ibid.*, p. 78.
36. C. Geertz, 1970, p. 82.
37. T. G. McGee, 1971, p. 78.
38. See T. G. McGee, 1971, pp. 74-75.
39. See J. J. van der Linden, The bastis of Karachi, the functioning of an informal housing system. Elsewhere in this book.
40. See M. Ahmad, 1964, p. 240 and p. 176, where the author comments: "It is revealing that only eight officials (out of the 432 interviewed, JL) thought that people looked upon a public servant as a friend and guide".
41. K. S. Yap, 1979, p. 21.
42. *Ibid.*, p. 27.
43. M. Schuringa, S. A. Khan, E. Meyer and K. S. Yap, *Baldia Evaluation Survey Report*, Karachi, 1979, pp. 66, 67.
44. K. S. Yap, 1979, p. 28.
45. M. Ahmad, 1964, pp. 125-128.
46. K. S. Yap, 1979, p. 24. See also K. S. Yap: On possibilities left. Elsewhere in this book.
47. J. E. Ellemers, Patronage in sociologisch perspectief, *Sociologische Gids*, 1969-VI, p. 440.
48. Contrary to the allegations of several authors that basti improvement along the lines described in 1, only reinforces existing power structures and hinders the emancipation of the poor classes, the authorities' resistance against active adoption of this strategy suggests that in fact it is threatening their positions. See R. Burgess, Informal sector housing?, a critique of the Turner school, London, 1977; R. Burgess, Petty commodity housing or dwellers control?, a critique of John Turner's views on housing policy, *World Development*, Vol. VI, 1978, pp. 1105-1133. R. Janssen, Wij hebben zelfs geen recht op de stad, Amsterdam, 1978. P. Van Lindert, Intra-urbane mobiliteit en het ontstaan van spontane volksbuurten in de steden van Latijns Amerika: zelf voorzienende wongingbouw als oplossing voor het woningvraagstuk?, Utrecht, 1979.
49. See E. A. Wegelin, Slum improvement in Karachi: look back in despair, *Pakistan Economist*, 30 June 1979, p. 9.

On Possibilities Left

K. S. Yap[1]

"Housing needs of low-income people in Karachi are catered for by an informal system that in the circumstances works reasonably well. It works better than any alternative thus far tried, and whatever attempts are made, it could not be stopped. Given these facts, the authorities would do well, if they were to accept the system and the situation and to try to accompany and guide the process rather than first oppose it and later "run behind the facts". (..). The acceptance of the system gives a basic guideline not only for the upgrading of existing settlements, but also for the planning of the future settlement of low-income people. The role of the Government does not appear to be "competing with the Pathans (i.e. the middlemen in the settlement process, YKS)", nor leaving them completely on their own, but rather cooperating with them even more than is presently being done in an informal way."[2]

KATCHI ABADIS AND POLITICS

Although most people agree that housing conditions of low-income families in Third World cities are generally miserable and that the urban poor are also entitled to decent housing, self-help housing and slum upgrading projects are being criticized for serving the interests of the ruling classes rather than of the urban poor.

These types of projects would give the government an opportunity to rid itself of the responsibility to provide houses to low-income groups at payable rates. They would pass the burden of solving the housing crisis on to the weakest group: the urban poor. They would appease the discontent of large portions of society by solving one of their immediate problems, housing, without tackling the real cause of the crisis: the capitalist mode of production.[3]

But is it fair to assume that advocates of the so-called self-help school are so naive to think that governments adopt self-help housing and slum-upgrading policies merely out of concern for the living conditions of the urban poor? And if they have been so naive initially, some practical experiences with this type of project have definitely made them face up to reality. Take the example of Karachi.

The major motives for the repeated announcement by Prime Minister Bhutto about regularization and improvement of unauthorized settlements (katchi abadis), for the adoption of the Improvement Policy for Sub-standard Urban Areas by the Karachi Metropolitan Corporation (KMC) for the proclamation by Chief Martial Law Administrator General Zia-ul-Haq of the *de facto* regularization of katchi abadis created before 1 January 1978, and for issuing of the Martial Law Orders 67 and 110 (Regularization and Development of Katchi Abadis Orders) were probably two-fold.

In Karachi alone, the katchi abadi population counts more than 1.5 million people and thereby forms an important political force. Some electoral constituencies consist almost entirely of katchi abadis, and since regularization and improvement are among the first priorities of the population of these settlements, politicians and election candidates for these constituencies simply have to urge the government to give attention to these areas.

Secondly, some of the katchi abadis are politically very sensitive areas and their population is easily mobilized in times of political crisis. Post-election riots in Spring 1977, which eventually lead to the overthrow of the Bhutto Government started in some of these katchi abadis.

The announcements of katchi abadi regularization and improvement are indeed attempts by the government to win the katchi abadi population over to its side. But the government has only reluctantly yielded to the demands of the people and converted the announcements into a general policy. It is therefore not improper to say that the people have gained the policy through direct action and political pressure on government and politicians.

The political pressure the katchi abadi can exert is considerable, but at the same time rather diffuse. It is strong enough to press the government into making announcements of regularization and improvement and into formulating a general policy, but it is not sufficiently concentrated to force the government into executing the policy, i.e. approving and implementing regularization and improvement plans for specific areas.

So, contrary to what critics of the self-help school assume, the government does not seem to be all that eager to execute the policy it has adopted, probably because it runs counter to interests of other powerful groups in society.

CONFLICTING INTERESTS

For politicians, katchi abadis are interesting mainly in times of elections and political crisis, and at those moments promises, plans and proposals usually seem to suffice.

In intervening periods, a politician's power is based on personal contacts with other politicians and government officials. These contacts enable him to grant favours and provide services to clients and client groups in return for political support. Regularization and improvement of katchi abadis in a systematic way, like the Improvement Policy advocates, may well undermine this power base of politicians in katchi abadis.

The individual resident of an illegal settlement is an outlaw at the mercy of the municipality and its representatives, unless he is protected by local leaders and politicians. The local leaders have often founded the settlement after having obtained support from powerful politicians and protection from government officials.

They have allocated and sold the plots in the new settlement and they have arranged the first amenities provided by KMC by using the influence of some politicians with government officials in favour of their settlement.

Piecemeal improvement of living conditions in still illegal katchi abadis by KMC allows for discretion on the part of the official concerned about when and where to provide the amenities. The decision is negotiable and therefore becomes the outcome of an exchange of information, support, influence and money in a transaction between government officials, politicians, local leaders and katchi abadi residents.

So, piecemeal improvement of illegal settlements is much more lucrative for politicians, government officials and local leaders than a systematic and planned improvement of regularized settlements according to a fixed policy.

Furthermore, the interests of the local leaders in katchi abadis do not necessarily run parallel to the interests of the common katchi abadi residents

Besides the fact that local leaders are generally linked to politicians and political parties, they often earn an income as landlord and property broker. Being among the founders of the settlement, they usually own more than one plot and they rent out houses and shops. They sometimes make money by speculating with open plots and live as rack-renters.

Common people use their plot as a permanent residence. Since the government announcements about regularization they have an almost maximum feeling of security of tenure. Now they demand first of all improvement of their living conditions.

Local leaders, on the contrary, may give priority to regularization of their plot(s) to capitalize on their property, for regularization increases the value of plots and houses. They may even urge for regularization at such low rates that financing improvement of settlements out of lease proceeds becomes impossible. This will not bother them too much, as they can arrange improvement of the then regularized katchi abadis along other, informal lines.

To certain politicians and government officials, regularization of katchi abadis without immediate improvement looks rather attractive. It would content local leaders and residents and simultaneously preserve the opportunity "to sell piecemeal improvement" in katchi abadis.

However, other government officials worry about the financial implications of such a policy. The government will have to provide amenities to regularized katchi abadis anyway, but under these conditions residents will be ready to pay for regularization only and improvement will have to be financed out of general revenues.

There are also groups opposing any form of regularization and/or improvement of illegal katchi abadis. We may, first of all, think of private building promoters, who would like to utilize the katchi abadi land for other, more profitable purposes.

Probably more important in this respect than the private building promoters are the government bodies. More than 80% of the land in the Karachi Metropolitan Area is publicly owned. As a result, government interests in land rather than private interests are affected by squatting and most katchi abadis have in fact been constructed on public land.

Moreover, the early (informal) involvement of certain government officials in the creation of katchi abadi is to some extent a guarantee that land meant for high-cost development by private building promoters is not occupied by squatters.

The interests of the various government bodies faced with the problem of spontaneous settlements on their land are not identical, however.

Specialized agencies like Pakistan Railways, Karachi Port Trust and Sind Industrial Trading Estate reject any regularization or improvement of katchi abadis on their land. They argue that this land is necessary for future development of their activities, which are of national interest and that the katchi abadis have to be demolished.

Government bodies like Board of Revenue, Karachi Cantonment Board and to some extent Karachi Development Authority own vast areas of land with a high development potential. They fear that regularization and improvement of existing katchi abadis will merely encourage further squatting on still vacant land.

KMC as a government body without much vacant land but faced with the practical consequences of spontaneous settlements would, on the contrary, prefer to see katchi abadis regularized and improved. This would facilitate the provision of municipal services it has to supply anyway and it would increase tax revenues of the Corporation.

In brief, after the government had adopted the Improvement Policy for Substandard Urban Areas under pressure of the katchi abadi population, the decision to execute the policy came under the pressure of groups mainly within or directly linked to the government: politicians, government officials, government bodies.

By not executing the policy, the government did not have to fear a reaction from groups opposing regularization of katchi abadis, while the announcement of regularization as such was good enough for the katchi abadi population to maximize its feeling of security of tenure.

This was probably the situation the Dutch Advisory Mission (DAM) had to face during the second year of its project.

A NATIONAL POLITICAL CRISIS

There were obviously more reasons why DAM's efforts to regularize and improve katchi abadis in Karachi remained largely unsuccessful. They were mainly linked with political events during the project period which created unfavourable circumstances for a prompt execution of the policy and led to a shift of power in the country and thereby to a shift in priorities.

DAM had been constituted after a request by the Government of Pakistan and the World Bank in 1975. By the time DAM finally arrived in Karachi in June 1977, the World Bank had withdrawn from the project because of the breakdown of the Lyari project in the heat of the 1977 election campaign.

Four weeks after DAM's arrival, the Government of Zulfiqar Ali Bhutto was overthrown by the armed forces in a *coup-d'état* and Martial Law was imposed throughout the country. Political activities were banned and centre of political power as well as political channels were thereby obscured.

In the aftermath of the fall of Bhutto and the Pakistan People's Party, numerous government officials were dismissed, arrested or transferred. Among them were KMC officers who had been the motive force behind the Karachi Slum Improvement Project and had played an important role in the formulation of the policy and the establishment of the Central Planning Team (CPT).

The almost half-yearly repeated promise of national elections within six months and the trial of former Prime Minister Bhutto (which lasted almost the entire project period and ended with his execution) increased the political instability of the country. It was not surprising that under these circumstances, without a ministerial government to take the political responsibility, many government officials were reluctant to take major decisions.

Nevertheless, as a result of the political instability and the irresolution of the national political centre, the Provinces (i.e. the bureaucrats of the provincial government) seized the opportunity to define their policies independently of the national centre.

The Government of Sind gradually shifted its priorities from the development of Karachi to the development of the interior of Sind. Since Independence, Karachi has always been a "fremdkörper" to Sind and the Sindis; a city inhabited by Muhajirs (i.e. refugees from India), Punjabis and Pathans but not by Sindis. Although it could not neglect Karachi completely, the Government of Sind concentrated its attention more and more on the development of rural areas and smaller towns of Sind, to the detriment of Karachi.

These circumstances definitely contributed to the creation of a situation, in which no decisions were taken, all options remained open and all concerned could protect their immediate interests. However, the situation would not solve the housing crisis of low-income groups in Karachi.

POSSIBILITIES LEFT

The main lesson to be learned from these experiences is probably that the katchi abadi population is an important political force the government has to take into account when defining its policy. But the adoption of a policy by a government as such does not guarantee its execution, as opposition from other groups in society may obstruct its coming into operation. But where do we go from here?

One may draw the conclusion that it is obviously impossible to give credit to a government which adopts a policy, sets up a separate department for the execution of the policy and invites foreign assistance for the department, but when it comes to implementation of plans, backs out.

In this view, the critics of the self-help school may be right when they say that governments announce regularization and improvement policies merely in their own interest and do not want to tackle the real problem.

But if these critics expect radical changes in society and the dissolution of the capitalist system in a foreseeable future, partly as a result of the non-improvement or deterioration of living conditions of the urban poor, they will certainly be disappointed.

The rejection of the regularization and improvement policy may save the katchi abadis from some of the negative developments these critics anticipate for regularized areas, but it will definitely not improve the living conditions of the urban poor in the short or long run.

Another conclusion could be that since the government does not seem to be really interested in katchi abadi residents and improvement of their living conditions, the katchi abadi should better look after itself.

Residents could finance and carry out the improvement of their area on their own or with assistance from local non-government organizations. They could even defend their self-improved settlement against government intervention or reprisal, if necessary by force.

But by stimulating this course of action, one would walk straight into the trap so well described by the critics of the self-help school. Adequate shelter and basic services are recognized as a human right and it is a government responsibility to guarantee that all people and in particular low-income groups have access to houses and basic services.

Moreover, only the government can provide complete security of tenure to residents by leasing plots, and only the government can arrange the provision of major infrastructural works to katchi abadis. So, if one wants to improve living conditions in urban poor communities, involvement of government bodies is essential.

Hence, instead of abandoning the Improvement Policy, the only proper conclusion appears to be to further promote the regularization and improvement policy for katchi abadis, involving both KMC as most concerned government body and the katchi abadi residents.

As we have seen, the main obstacles for a prompt execution of the Improvement Policy for Substandard Urban Areas are located within the government and the political system: government officials, politicians and local leaders consider their interests better served by the present system of piecemeal improvements than by a planned regularization and improvement of katchi abadis according to a fixed policy.

By nature, government and political groups are susceptible to public pressure and if katchi abadi residents could exert more pressure on government officials, politicians and local leaders, they might be able to force the government into executing its policy, like they forced the government into adopting it.

In Bombay, people from squatter settlements established the Bombay Slum Dwellers United Front (BSDUF) to oppose the enforcement of two laws which would facilitate the eviction of squatters from government land and to demand security of tenure and the provision of basic services.[4]

In Karachi, such an organization would definitely help the cause of the katchi abadi residents, but its establishment seems quite unfeasible. The Bombay squatters are threatened with eviction and this has certainly facilitated the formation of the organization. In Karachi the interests of the groups vary considerably and the basic problem is the multitude of community organizations, rather than their absence.

The establishment of one more organization would probably only provoke the antagonism of existing organizations. It may, therefore, be more advisable to work through existing channels and to see to it that these are put under public pressure. This would better be achieved by a community assisting organization than by a community organizer.

Such an independent and non-profit community assisting organization should obviously have good contacts with and easy access to government institutions as well as community organizations and local leaders. It will have to work very carefully, since information and access to information are valuable goods in katchi abadis usually marketed by local leaders.

The role of the organization should not be to compete with local leaders, but rather to cooperate with them as much as possible. It should reinforce and motivate existing community organizations and at best try to coordinate the activities of community organizations and local leaders.

ASSISTANCE TO KATCHI ABADI COMMUNITIES

Non-accessibility to information and public institutions is one of the main problems katchi abadi residents (and other underprivileged groups) face when they try to gain their rights to basic services. Katchi abadi residents very often even lack information where to obtain information and where to apply for basic services.

And if they know where to go to, they usually have to wait for hours before they are admitted. Many katchi abadi residents are day-labourers and petty shopkeepers, who cannot afford to spend a day in an office waiting for admission. Sometimes, they are even put off with useless or incorrect information or they have to pay for information they need.

Therefore, the tasks of a community assisting organization could be manifold and cover numerous fields of katchi abadi regularization and improvement.

As soon as the selection of an area for regularization and improvement by KMC is announced in the newspapers, residents should be informed and instructed about the approach KMC will follow in the planning process.

In particular the rights and duties of KMC as well as the katchi abadi residents have to be emphasized, and local leaders and residents have to be prepared for their roles in the planning work.

When KMC officers approach local leaders and residents to present and discuss proposals for their area and neighbourhood, the population will need technical assistance to be able to form their opinion about the proposals and plans.

Although it is surprising to see how much (often illiterate) katchi abadi residents understand about plans for their neighbourhood (muhallah) some technical details will have to be translated into commonly understandable language. May be, even technical alternatives could be developed, which better suit the needs and priorities of the residents.

The "Public Objections Period" is the only official opportunity for residents of a katchi abadi under planning to come forward with objections to proposals of KMC, but the initiative to raise objections is left to the individual resident.

So, there is an obvious need for an organization which can point out this opportunity to the residents and which can help them to formulate the objections in the right wordings and to send them to the right department.

It is also almost impossible for residents to know if and when the Public Objections Hearing Committee meets to discuss the objections and subsequently to find out what has been the outcome of the meeting. It is sometimes even difficult to get information how and when to apply for a lease, pay the lease charges and collect the lease document.

There is a whole range of activities a community assisting organization could undertake to help katchi abadi residents, but the objective of these activities should not be limited to help to residents, when KMC involves them in the planning work. They should also make the residents aware of the next steps KMC is supposed to take in the planning and implementation process, so that residents and local leaders can urge KMC to speed up the work, when it is delayed.

Moreover, the assistance activities should not be restricted to the katchi abadi regularization and improvement programme of KMC. Katchi abadi residents definitely need information and assistance in other related fields, too.

Access to services of public and private institutions as the Gas Company, Electricity Supply Corporation, health and educational institutions, banks, etc. is as much important as access to the municipal services of KMC.

There is an obvious need to collect all information likely to be relevant to katchi abadi residents, to extend this information to people concerned and to help them to gain access to these services.

The Improvement Policy assumes that regularization and the provision of infrastructure will encourage katchi abadi residents to improve their house and its direct surroundings. People in regularized katchi abadis may need advice how to improve their house in the most inexpensive way.

Besides, the Improvement Policy will only be successful, if the population is instructed how to make proper use of the infrastructure provided. Consequently, the regularization and improvement programme in a certain settlement has to be followed by a public education campaign and in this campaign, other relevant subjects such as health care could simultaneously be introduced.

Assistance to katchi abadi communities in the planning process, efforts to gain access to public and private institutions for katchi abadi residents, education and information campaigns and even self-help activities to improve living conditions in the settlement will, however, remain futile, unless KMC executes its Improvement Policy.

One of the continuous and perhaps main tasks of a community assisting organization will therefore probably be to help residents and local leaders to exert pressure on KMC and other government bodies to not only announce but also promptly execute its Improvement Policy for Substandard Urban Areas.

EPILOGUE

Since the end of the Karachi Slum Improvement Project two developments have occurred, which have some relevance to the above-formulated ideas about political pressure and community assisting organizations in katchi abadis.

First of all, in the course of 1979, local elections were held in Pakistan and for the first time in more than 10 years the Karachi Metropolitan Corporation now has an elected house and an elected mayor. From Baldia Township, four persons have been elected in the council, while a fifth person has been nominated as representative from "labour". Through these councillors, who seem to be considered as real representatives by the Baldia population, pressure may be exerted on KMC to speed up the work on Baldia Township. The same can and will of course be done for other katchi abadis.

Secondly, when DAM left Karachi, it handed one part of its project, the construction of soak-pits in Baldia, over to the United Nations International Children's Emergency Fund (UNICEF) Pakistan. For the execution of this soak-pit project, UNICEF provided funds to the Pakistan Jaycees and the Social Work Department of Karachi University, which would be responsible for the actual implementation of the project.

In about one year's time the Pakistan Jaycees have constructed about 65 soak-pits in Muslim Mujahid Colony, while the Social Work Department of the Karachi University has constructed 30 pits in Niazi Para and 30 pits in Turk Colony, all in Baldia Township.

The Pakistan Jaycees meet many of the requirements of the community assisting organization DAM had in mind for the katchi abadis. They have good contacts with and access to influential people and relevant institutions; they can find their way through the government bureaucracy; they have a good reputation and are too well-do-do and upright to be corrupt or become involved in local politics. Their main deficiency however is their social remoteness from the population of the katchi abadis.

The Social Work Department has, on the other hand, established good contacts with the population, especially in Turk Colony, where it works in collaboration with a local community organization. In this muhallah. UNICEF booklets on mother-and-child health care have been distributed, water supply has been improved by construction of four additional water taps on a self-help basis and plans are being made to start a health clinic in the area. Main deficiencies with the Department are the shortage of technical know-how and the lack of contacts with political and governmental institutions.

However, if well-guided and assisted, the soak-pit project in Turk Colony could well become the start of a movement which goes far beyond the mere construction of soak-pits and turns into a community assisting programme as proposed in the previous sections of this article.

REFERENCES

1. The writing of this article was made possible by a grant from the Netherlands Foundation for the Advancement of Tropical Research (WOTRO), The Hague. It forms part of K. S. Yap, *Leases, land and local leaders,* An analysis of a squatter settlement upgrading programme, Amsterdam, 1982.
2. J. J. van der Linden, *The bastis of Karachi, Types and Dynamics,* Amsterdam, 1977, p. 301.
3. R. Burgess, Petty Commodity Housing or Dweller Control? A Critique of John Turner's Views on Housing Policy, in, *World Development,* 1978, Vol. 6, No. 9/10, pp. 1105-1133.
4. R. Singh, Bombay Slum-Dwellers Organise, *How,* November, 1979.

Part VI

The Role of the University in Application-oriented Research

J. W. Schoorl

1. INTRODUCTION

The Karachi project, which was conducted under the auspices of the Free University in Amsterdam, consisted of a number of different stages characterized by different types of co-operation with various official bodies in Pakistan. This is clear from the historical survey given in the introduction. During the lengthy history of the project, a great deal of experience was gained in application-oriented research. The university can pose the question as to whether it is advisable for a university to conduct research which is so strongly oriented toward application. Shouldn't university research be more fundamental? This question is of all the more importance if, in addition to research, a university also becomes involved in the process of drawing up policies, and even in the process of carrying them out, as was the case in the last 2 years of the project.

The question of the university's role in this type of situation is not solely a question for the university itself. For all the parties involved, the question of the university's role in the problems of policy-making is an important one. The question must even be posed as to whether the university should play any role at all in this process.

From the university's point of view, for example, this kind of involvement in policy-making might be thought of as a jeopardy to objectiveness. One comes to share responsibility for situations which, from certain angles, might be totally unacceptable. These practical activities can also be thought to cause the real work of the university, the theoretical work, to be neglected. Some people even speak of academic prostitution if the university accepts government funds and then goes on to betray its own calling and ideals.

From the government's point of view, one might wonder whether the theoreticians behind this university involvement in policy-making are sufficiently aware of the specific problems and limitations of the government. There is always the fear that the researchers might give the local population "irresponsible" ideas, only making the problems worse.

From the population's point of view, the "outsiders" from the university might be viewed as intruders, who can only ask questions and don't have anything to offer in return. Their ideas and plans, which might conflict with those of the government, could very well get the local people into trouble. These outsiders can always leave at the first sign of trouble. They have no power to help the local population with the problems they leave behind. This is all the more true if the university people are foreigners to boot.

In the following article, we shall try to clarify the role of the university in this type of case from the points of view of the three parties involved. Experiences in the course of the Karachi project will serve as illustrations.

2. FROM THE GOVERNMENT'S POINT OF VIEW

A university specialized in the urban problems of the Third World has access to a wide range of literature in this field, including literature about the problems of the squatter settlements. On the one hand, the problems of a city like Karachi are unique, but on the other hand they fit into a general pattern which can be seen throughout the Third World. This makes it possible for the university to make an important contribution to the policy-making process, simply by viewing the problems of a city like Karachi within a broader framework. In a certain sense, this can have the effect of "exonerating" the people responsible for policy-making. It makes them aware that it is not a problem peculiar to Pakistan or to Karachi. It is part of the pattern of a developing country. This also means that it is possible to learn from the policies that are made and carried out in other countries. For instance, in other Third World countries, slum clearance policies were also unable to solve the enormous problem of housing squatters. It is no mere coincidence that the idea of slum improvement became prevalent in various countries at more or less the same time. Universities can help transform local discussions of the problem into an international discussion. Universities can also fulfil the important task of "translating" ideas and theories back into the local or national context. Research into national processes of urbanization and the specific problems in specific cities can show how the theories and ideas in the literature are or are not applicable to a country like Pakistan and a city like Karachi. It is clear that there are differences between the processes in Latin America and those in Asia, as well as between those in Indonesia and those in Pakistan.

Time and again, research results prove to actively stimulate the recognition of phenomena and processes in the local or national context. But each national and local situation has its own specific qualities, its own conditions, its own social aspects. These factors all play an important role in shaping policies. This is why on-the-spot research is indispensable. This is where universities can be a great help to the government and to international (aid) organizations. For example, the study by van der Linden (*The bastis of Karachi, Types and Dynamics, 1977*) shows what building one's own house meant to the people who lived in the squatter neighbourhoods of Karachi: it was a source of security when faced with a future of insecurity, a source of money in times of need due to unemployment and illness. This was why the low-cost housing schemes were not successful, since these houses could not offer this kind of security (see van der Linden's article *The Squatter's House As a Source of Security* in this book).

This example also shows that the government bases its policies on certain theories or ideas without knowing whether they coincide with social reality.

An additional factor is that in Third World settings, particularly in the cities, a great deal of clever ingenuity is called for in order to gather the necessary data. It is impossible to simply utilize the methods and techniques developed in western countries. Universities can be helpful in developing methods and techniques especially suited to the local situations (see Van Pinxteren's article *Methods and Techniques of Research* in this book).

Universities can provide assistance or even supervision when research projects are assigned to commercial research agencies. It is difficult for the government to know whether a certain research project is advisable or necessary. Commercial research agencies sometimes propose a research plan with insufficient "scientific" justification. And sometimes a research plan is proposed which is much too extensive for the aim in mind and consequently too time-consuming and expensive. It is also essential that a research project be supervised to see that it is carried out properly and according to schedule. Government agencies are not equipped to deal with these tasks. This is where universities with experience in urban studies can play an important role.

From the government's point of view, research can also serve as a means of discovering and formulating the ideas and wishes of the population. Relations between the government and the citizens, particularly the squatters, are not always optimally conducive to an exchange of ideas. In so far as there is any representative body or any more or less regular contact with representatives, it is still not likely that these representatives will have a clear picture of the problems and wishes of all the segments of the population. Research can reach the groups most apt to be overlooked and oppressed, the ones most in need.

Moreover, contact with the researchers can give people an opportunity to express their frustrations. For it is inevitable in contacts with a bureaucracy that there should be frustrations. And this is certainly true in cases where the bureaucracy is weak, as in the developing countries. If a government has the good of the people in mind, it can make good use of this kind of pipe-line of frustrations and complaints in the course of its policy-making processes. Particularly if it is willing to listen to suggestions for improvement.

An advantage of university research is that the government is not at the mercy of commercial research agencies. A dangerous thing about commercial projects is that they might be subjected to unwarranted limitations just to keep expenses down.

Research projects might also lead to certain specific recommendations requiring the services of their own firm or another commercial firm that they have good relations with. Moreover, research results might be drawn up in such a way as to please the government, in the hope of being assigned new projects in the future. University research is an academic process rather than a profit-making one. The chance of more responsible and more objective research is greater. And it is not the aim of the universities to play a profitable role in the carrying out of whatever policies they might recommend. At most, they might play a role in supervisory or evaluation studies.

Of course the question can be posed as to whether the government itself should not be the one to conduct the research. The ideal situation is a department for research (and planning) within the governmental body. Even so, I think co-operation with universities remains desirable. Due to fluctuations in the number and size of research projects needed, a governmental research department can't have a sufficient number of researchers permanently in its employ to always be able to conduct any desired research project. In my opinion, it is always best to involve outside bodies in research projects. The government research department can help to draw up the aims and to check the results and translate them into actual policy. At any rate, universities can undertake more comprehensive research, which might not affect policies directly, but does so indirectly. Contact between researchers with a practical orientation and those with a more theoretical one can be stimulating and inspiring for both groups. If a government is unable to set up its own research department, it will have to rely on universities or commercial agencies, even for the tasks most obviously calling for a government agency.

All the comments made here about the advantage of research for the making of policies equally hold true for the carrying out of policies.

Of course, from the government's point of view, a number of disadvantages and dangers of research can be noted as well. One of the possible dangers of university research is that it might become too extensive or too time-consuming, because the researchers deem it irresponsible to leave anything out, and insist on including all kinds of purely theoretical aspects. Compared with commercial research, university projects and recommendations can also be less practical. The university is not adequately equipped to play a role in the actual carrying out of policies. Moreover, university researchers are rarely familiar with the day-to-day functioning of officialdom. Thus they often lack insight into the legal regulations and administrative rules and traditions which officials have to adhere to. Their ideas, proposals and criticism can then fail to take them into consideration. Then research creates more problems than it solves.

From the government's point of view, researchers can arouse expectations in the population which will never be fulfilled. A certain manner of introducing oneself, of asking questions or of presenting ideas can magnify existing frustrations or create new ones. In the final instance, researchers bear no responsibility for the way the country is run. It is also relatively easy for them to deny responsibility for the consequences of their research.

Moreover, university researchers rarely have the time or the patience to follow each step of the laborious process by which policies are made and carried out. They have their own schedules and their own research aims. If the research results fail to contain new information, the university will soon lose interest.

Although there are disadvantages from the government's point of view, I think the advantages still tip the scale in favour of university research.

3. FROM THE POPULATION'S POINT OF VIEW

The local population can view the researchers and the research project as a sign of growing interest in them on the part of the government. This can arouse squatters' hopes for more certainty about whether they can stay where they are, or for future improvement of the basic facilities. It is even feasible that a research project in itself might be enough to make a squatter decide to invest more in his home, even without any "other" government activities. This was illustrated by the study conducted in 1973 in Usmania Muhajir Colony. Although the authorities did not make the slightest move to carry out the proposed legalization and improvements - for the land itself was "pure gold" (van der Linden, 1977, p. 306), residents began to improve their homes, simply on the grounds of the activities concerned with the study.

The population might very well view the researchers as a (new) way of getting their voice heard on a wide range of levels. They might view them as a new communication channel with a government that is usually difficult to reach and to persuade. The role of the researcher as a voice-giver to those who have no voice (Oscar Lewis, *The Children of Sánchez: Autobiography of a Mexican Family*, Random House, New York, 1961) is easily perceived as such by the local population. (Political) leaders will have no illusions about the effectiveness of this channel.

Another factor is that the research projects and the researchers can focus attention on certain groups or categories which are otherwise never seen or heard. (Examples in Karachi are noted in: Van Pinxteren, *The Dera, A Housing Facility for the Male Migrant*; id., *Mini-slum in A Posh Locality*, both Karachi, 1974). They often take advantage of this opportunity to have their leaders promote their interests.

For the population, research can be instrumental in correcting the ideas held by the authorities about the residents of the squatter neighbourhoods. Research projects can make it clear that "normal" or "healthy" people live in these areas, where the percentage of criminals is no higher than elsewhere, and that they are citizens of the city, playing an indispensable role in its everyday functioning. It can also become evident that the large majority of these people are not temporary migrants who will soon move on. So they have the same needs as anyone else for urban facilities, and the same right to them. Research studies can show how much squatters have already invested in their homes. And that they would be willing to invest more, if the government were to provide more certainty about their right to stay, and were to furnish the indispensable basic urban facilities (van der Linden, 1977). In short, for these people research can be instrumental in turning the government into an ally instead of an opponent and a perpetual threat.

If it is a university that is conducting the research, there is the advantage that the researchers are likely to have a more independent attitude toward the government, and consequently be better equipped to intercede as mediators.

In addition to advantages, however, research can also have disadvantages and dangers for the population. Research can be one of the many activites on the part of the government that arouse hopes which are never to be fulfilled. So it is no wonder the population can also be distrustful of researchers. Though they might be sympathetic to the researchers, they fail to share the optimistic view that research will lead to improvements. (This was the reaction in Baldia.) In their view, the government is perhaps using research as an excuse for not really doing anything.

The researchers themselves might also be to blame for the "misuse" of research. They might be more interested in the theoretical results than in the social consequences for the population.

Another peril that both the researchers and the population should be aware of is that the government might use research to the detriment of the population. It is understandable and, unfortunately, also necessary that the population view research with a certain degree of distrust. The researcher/

the university should be capable of understanding this, and should be wary of misuse itself. It is necessary to keep in constant communication with the population. The researcher also has a responsibility to the population. It seems to me that the advantages outweigh the disadvantages for the population as well.

4. FROM THE UNIVERSITY'S POINT OF VIEW

For the university, it is important to be involved in an issue of social relevance. Though it was a bit late, in 1975 the World Bank drew attention to this point and made large sums of money available. Of course the question of rural development, particularly with respect to poor peasants and landless labourers, deserves extensive attention and efforts. But all the analyses show that urban questions, particularly those related to housing, play an increasingly important role in the problems of the developing countries. By conducting research, universities can play an important social role in this respect.

The closer university research is to policy-making and the actual carrying out of policies, the closer the link will have to be between complicated theories and concrete social reality. Research in relation to policies, and participation in their execution, means putting ideas to a test. Recommendations are a kind of hypotheses based on theories. The tenability of the hypotheses can be proved or disproved when the policies are actually put into practice. It might then be necessary to improve upon, to supplement, or to reject the hypotheses and theories. This was the case in the Karachi study with Turner's theories which, though they did serve to stimulate the study by van der Linden and Yap, had to be altered on the basis of day-to-day experience in Karachi.

In the course of the study, the question of just exactly how the data should be gathered came up repeatedly. The very size of the squatter issue, the large number of neighbourhoods and the large number of residents in some of the neighbourhoods (Baldia 175,000, Lyari 600,000) on the one hand, and the Karachi bureaucracy's lack of reliable data on the other, made it necessary that the study be planned and carried out with a great deal of inventiveness (see the article by Van Pinxteren, *Methods and Techniques of Research*, in this book).

Another problem which researchers are inevitably faced with is bureaucratic uncooperativeness. Every bureaucracy has its own system of who is in charge of what, its own interests and its own traditions. The private interests of individual officials, which can play a role on any and every level, only make matters more complex. Sometimes there is also a hierarchy of corruption, with profits coming from all the various levels. Sometimes corruption is a private enterprise of one individual official. The efficiency of the bureaucratic machinery can depend on how flexible or how strictly the existing rules and regulations are applied, on whether or not bribes are involved, and on whether bureaucratic and political interests coincide. Just about the same holds true for the political structure and the political leaders involved in it. (See the article by Emiel Wegelin and K. S. Yap in *VU-Magazine*, Vol. 8, No. 8, 1979).

The researcher who lacks insight into the functioning of the bureaucracy and the political system can hardly make adequate policy recommendations. But the researcher who has this kind of insight can play a useful role. He can tell people how to make the best use of the existing relations with the bureaucracy or the political leaders.

In short, if one is to conduct research or make policy recommendations, one should know how the bureaucracy and the political system work. This kind of involvement also means a good opportunity to study the way they work from the inside, and thus acquire new information. This information can also serve as a basis for the "policy" of the researcher himself, also influencing the recommendations he makes to the population, as is evident in the possibilities cited by Yap in his article *On Possibilities Left* in this book.

University research also has certain disadvantages and dangers. If research only consisted of the routine collection of data, without there being any theoretical, methodological or technical problems involved, it would not in any way be in the interest of a university to become involved at all. Research has to present some "scientific" challenge. This is especially true in cases where the stage of preparing policy makes way for the stage of carrying it out. But for the university, in the sense of social relevance as well as that of scientific relevance, it can still be important to play a role at this stage. In the first place, new thorough studies can be made of certain subjects which were hitherto difficult to approach. In the second place, the continuous evaluation and monitoring of how policies are carried out can also be a university task. In university circles, the view is voiced that in the stage of preparatory research and the related planning stage, the university can play a role by conducting research and basing recommendations on the results. But in the stage where policies are carried out, there is no longer thought to be a task for the university. I do not agree with this view. Continuous evaluation can make it clear whether or not the recommendations based on the research results can hold their ground. This can be viewed as the testing of the hypotheses. In this manner, continuous evaluation can lead to a confirmation or a rejection of these hypotheses, and thus to an adjustment of the theory. This continuous evaluation can also lead to new recommendations. Moreover, in the theories of planning, the assumption no longer need be made that a plan that has been drawn up necessarily has to be carried out in its entirety. There has to be a permanent interaction between the planning process and the carrying out process. The planning process gets feedback from the carrying out process. It is not realistic to suppose that research and recommendations can lead to a plan that can simply be carried out without further ado. The social sciences are not capable of looking into the future like this. In the first place, social reality is too complicated. And in the second place, individuals can choose to behave in a manner that deviates from earlier behaviour patterns. Thus research remains equally important in the carrying out stage. From the point of view of the government, of the population and of the university.

I mainly have in mind here projects that are new, where experience has yet to be acquired. Once government bodies have had (greater) experience with the carrying out of certain types of projects among certain types of target groups, there will no longer be any need for research to go with it in the form of continuous evaluation or monitoring. Moreover, the university will not get much information from the evaluation, so that its usefulness will diminish. The same can also be said of the preparatory research. And the interests of the target groups in question can also be assumed to be adequately seen to.

There is a danger that research conducted by the government might be used in an effort to obtain development aid funds from the World Bank or from some foreign agency, or for political or prestige purposes. In the case of the study that was conducted for 5 years in Karachi by the Karachi University in conjunction with the Free University of Amsterdam, partially on the request of the government of Pakistan (Joint Research Project-IV, 1970-1975), there turned out to be little or no chance that the recommendations made on the basis of the study would lead to policies that would actually be carried out. In 1975, the Free University decided not to continue the research under these conditions. It will only be continued if and when there is a clear alteration in the attitude of the Pakistani authorities.

One problem for the university researcher is the following question: to what degree does his research benefit a regime which he himself can not support for various reasons, for example because of the sharp contrast between rich and poor, or because of the widespread corruption and/or political oppression? Of course what is involved here is a political decision on the part of the researcher and the university. Some researchers and universities are of the opinion that in certain cases their research can make a contribution toward the improvement of the position of the target groups in question, whereas other researchers and universities, on the grounds of their theories and/or idealogy, do not have favourable expectations. In the case of Karachi, we were of the opinion that the research did play a role in altering the attitude of the authorities toward the squatter issue. Slum clearance was viewed less and less as being feasible. The construction of flats and even the "sites and services" projects (metrovilles) were also viewed less and less as being the solution to the housing problem of the lower-income groups. A policy of giving the squatters more security about where they were living and of making simple improvements in the area, a policy we had long been advocating, was increasingly accepted as being the only feasible one. This does not necessarily imply that the authorities actually carry out this policy in a systematic manner. But university research can help to overcome the obstacles.

In short, application-oriented research such as the Karachi project is also of great importance for the university. The usefulness diminishes, however, when it is routine research into the preparation and application of policies.

5. CONCLUSIONS

For all the parties involved, it is important that university research play a role in the making and carrying out of government policies regarding the main issues of urban development, particularly the housing issue. The government then gets a clearer picture of the needs and the wishes of all the segments of the population.

For the government, this means a greater guarantee of reliable research that takes into account experience obtained elsewhere. The policy recommendations that are made are not influenced by commercial interests. The recommendations are more "independent" with respect to the government, and in the long run the government also benefits from this.

This does not necessarily mean that certain research projects should not be done by commercial agencies, but that it would then be very advisable to have university researchers check the results and/or make the ensuing recommendations.

For the population, an independent researcher is very valuable as a mouthpiece for their ideas and wishes and as an intermediary with the authorities. Research can also serve to correct the negative picture that often exists, and to make it clear to the government which measures are and which are not suited to the lives of these citizens.

For the university itself, this kind of research means an involvement in an important social issue, and an opportunity to thus promote the interests of large segments of the population. By means of policy recommendations, presuppositions can be tested. The involvement in policy also means an opportunity to gain insight into the bureaucratic and political processes which shape policies and their execution.

If new projects are involved, it is advisable that the university remain involved during the actual carrying out of the policies in question, particularly the carrying out of the continuous evaluation or monitoring. On the grounds of this research, conclusions can be drawn as to whether the recommendations were or still are correct, and whether anything needs to be added or altered. It is then possible to recommend additions or alterations to the policy in question. The more experience the government has with a certain type of project, the less need it will have for the university, first in carrying out policies and then in conducting preparatory research. For the university, the usefulness of this research will then diminish.

Methods and Techniques of Research, Some Experiences from Karachi*

T. E. L. Van Pinxteren

1. INTRODUCTION

Social research in developing countries is often confronted with problems of a methodological or technical nature, for which no ready solutions are available. Especially when studying areas that were planned informally and for which no maps or population data exist, the researcher has to find his way out of innumerable problems for the solution of which hardly any prescription can be found amongst the literature.

The present paper describes some of these problems and the different ways in which solutions were attempted in the Karachi situation. By the very nature of the problems, the solutions found cannot be copied blindly. Often the problems are specific to the place and to the nature of the research. Similarly, solutions are often geared to the specific aims and requirements of the particular research. The aim of this paper is merely to illustrate how particular problems in urban research in Karachi were dealt with.

2. PROBLEMS OF DEFINITION

Often, concepts of crucial importance to a study are ill-defined in colloquial speech. It is, for instance, not always clear what is meant by the term "slum", or "basti" (settlement). Again, within the bastis, what should be considered a dwelling unit? As long as dwelling units define themselves by their surrounding compound walls, there is not much of a problem. However, when a number of families have grouped their huts around a communal space and when there are no clear cut boundaries between individual dwellings - or when some of the dwellings are shared by different households - problems of definition arise. Also, how does one precisely define different structures: does, for example, a cooking place without a roof qualify as a "kitchen"? And what, if it has got only three walls, or two, or only one? Similar problems crop up regarding the inhabitants. Which unit should be considered "a family" or "a household"? Who is the head of the household in

*This paper is a somewhat revised version of T. E. L. Van Pinxteren, Samples designed by JRP-IV, Karachi, 1975.

the case of a group of single-living men who dwell together in one house and share meals from one kitchen, and who, accordingly, can be considered as "a household" in some definitions?

Under, we give some examples of definitions applied in different researches undertaken by the Joint Research Project-IV (JRP-IV). The definitions are of course, arbitrary. What is important, however, is that concepts are accurately described for the purpose of the particular study. There should be no possibilities left for misunderstanding by interviewers, data-processors, and those who use the results of the study.

Mostly some pretesting of proposed definitions is required to see whether all the cases are clearly included or excluded by the definition and whether definitions are mutually exclusive. Provided this is the case, any arbitrarily chosen definition will do as a principle, since it enables the researcher to account for his data.

In several cases, an additional requirement of a definition is that it can be used also by the authorities planning on the basis of research reports. If, for instance, "plots" are planned to be leased to "heads of households", care is to be taken that definitions chosen can be applied by the administration.

Especially when use is made of the services of several interviewers, another requirement of a definition is that it must be simple and not prone to misinterpretation. Of course, wherever established definitions exist - e.g. such as used by the Statistical Office or by the administration - these should preferably be used so as to enhance the potential for comparison of the data obtained. However, when they existed, these definitions were sometimes found to be not applicable in some specific studies.

2.1. Some Examples

Basti: the largest residential area which the residents understand to be one unit, but which is more or less uniform as far as the elements of the research are concerned (viz. the house conditions and the public facilities).[1]

Dwelling unit: the place in which a household lives.[2]

Household: a group of people living together and taking at least one meal per day from the same kitchen.[3]

Room: an enclosed space surrounded by more than three walls and covered by a roof.[4]

Latrine: a space surrounded by one or more walls, used exclusively for defecation.[4]

Wall: any structure separating one space from another having a height of at least three feet.[4]

Having defined the different concepts relevant to the research, it is also of importance to pinpoint what is the unit of research, for example, the household, the dwelling unit or the plot. Again, there is to be clarity about who are the informants, for example, the heads of households (or their representatives), any member of the household, the occupier of the plot, the owner of the structure, etc.

3. PROBLEMS OF PHRASING

Example 1: the "anne-hope question".

In one illegal settlement, it was considered important to find out how much hope the inhabitants had that their settlement would eventually be legalized. During free interviewing, we found that the amount of hope could be expressed in terms of anne in a rupee (one rupee is divided into 16 anne) as an approximation of the percentage chance of legalization as perceived by the inhabitants.

Although the concept of "anne in a rupee" worked as a measuring instrument, it often turned out to be difficult to make the interviewee express his opinion. Although, no doubt, the residents did have outspoken ideas on the subject, they certainly were not used to expressing these ideas in measurable terms. Also, they probably were reluctant to be outspoken on a touchy subject which after all is beyond their control.

After much probing, the question was phrased as follows: "Different happenings are such that their occurring or not occurring is not in our power. But nevertheless they can be estimated by reckoning with time and circumstances. For instance, if many clouds spread, then only God knows whether there will be rain or not. But even so, when looking at the clouds, it can be estimated how much hope there is that it will rain. Exactly in the same way, could you tell us how many anne in a rupee do you have hope that people will be allowed to stay here?" In this way, the question was generally well understood and resulted in 234 replies against 6 "no-replies".[3]

Example 2: eliciting imagination.

When information was sought on how a family would deal with an emergency situation, the clearest example would be the death of the breadwinner. During free interviewing, however, it soon appeared that this was not a good thing to use to evoke the interviewee's imagination. When a milder example was introduced, namely the breadwinner falling seriously ill, even so the words "God forbid!" had to be added, to make clear that the example was only mentioned for the sake of the question.

Again, when in the same study a question was asked regarding the behaviour of a poor man who suddenly received a lot of money, many informants immediately thought that this man could not have been honest. When we had rephrased the introduction to the question: "imagine a poor man receives a very great sum *from a lottery or as a present......*", these connotations no more came up.[1]

Both above examples show the importance of much free interviewing and probing in order to ensure that the wording of the questions used in, for example, surveys really convey what is intended.

4. PROBLEMS OF SAMPLING

4.1. Introduction

Problems of sampling arose in many studies, since maps of the areas to be studied were rarely available, let alone census data. A number of factors influence the decision on how to go about sampling problems. Amongst these factors, we mention: (a) aim of the study, (b) basic material available, (c) size of the area to be studied, (d) homogeneity of the area (regarding items relevant to the study). Besides, pragmatic considerations, such as, for example, the time available to carry out the study, also play their roles.

Underneath, we give some examples of how particular situations have been dealt with.

4.2. The Chanesar Goth Studies[4]

Chanesar Goth is the first area where JRP-IV carried out an in-depth study. The aim was to obtain a detailed profile of the socio-economic circumstances of the population, and of the environment.

A very detailed map of the area was drawn and a 100% census of the population was taken. On this basis, for further study, a stratified sample could be drawn according to ethnic affiliation and dwelling type.

For a number of additional studies on specific topics, several sampling methods were again used with the sample of the socio-economic survey as a starting point. Namely, the socio-economic survey provided important basic data which could be used in subsequent studies elaborating certain topics in detail. Thus, for an attitude study, every third household from within the socio-economic survey was included in the sample. For a study on household income and expenditure, a stratified sample was taken, on the basis of ethnic affiliation and household income.

As a principle, the sampling methods used in Chanesar Goth are the best way of coping with the lack of basic data. For want of a map and census data, a map was drawn and data collected. No doubt, this is a very time-consuming exercise, feasible only on a limited scale.

4.3. The Usmania Muhajir Colony Studies[3]

The Usmania Muhajir Colony study had the same aim as the Chanesar Goth's. The area being much smaller than Chanesar Goth, it would have been possible to adopt the same strategy for sampling. However, there was not much time, and it was considered a waste of time to let the researchers wait for the detailed map.

Instead, a sketch map was drawn, on which all doors that give on to streets and lanes were indicated. The doors then formed the basis for the sample: 25% of the doors indicated were selected randomly and included in the sample. The population, however, consisted of households and the informants were the heads of the households or their representatives. In most cases, the sample unit - the door - coincided with one household. In a number of cases, however, one household coincided with more than one door, and again, sometimes one door was the entrance to the abode of more than one household. On the basis of the 25% (doors) sample, the actual number of households could easily be calculated.

The method is fair and reliable. The map, although sketchy, enabled the interviewers to locate the sample doors without difficulty. Although drawing of a sketch map took less than one tenth of the time needed for a detailed map, even this method would not be practical in large areas.

4.4. The Lyari Studies[5]

Again, from Lyari, the same kind of information was sought as from Chanesar Goth and Usmania Muhajir Colony. However, Lyari is a very large area (1600 acres as against Usmania Muhajir Coloney: 9 acres!) with some 600,000 inhabitants. On the other hand, for Lyari, aerial photographs were available. Obviously, in the case of Lyari, the sample fraction had to be much smaller than in Usmania Muhajir Colony, especially since the results of the survey were required within the shortest period possible.

From the aerial photographs, a map was drawn indicating as many streets and lanes as could be distinguished from the photographs. Non-residential areas were indicated and the residential areas were subdivided into sectors according to the street pattern and predominant house types. These criteria could be partly observed from the aerial photographs and partly by checking on the spot to achieve the required subdivision into residential sectors. For each sector, then, a middle point was fixed through two diagonals in the sector. This centre point of each sector was made the centre of a circle, like a clock. From each sector two "pies" (the hours of the clock) opposite each other, were selected. Within those "pies", all the street crossings were indicated on the map. Interviews were taken around these street crossings.

The sample size was decided at 5%. From the aerial map, numbers of houses were counted for each sector. These numbers were divided by 20 and again by the number of street crossings found within the "pies" that demarcated the sample. Thus, it could be calculated how many interviews around each street-crossing had to be taken.

Locating the - of course imaginary - "pies" in the field was complicated at times, but proved feasible. Obviously, this method can be only used when a map or aerial photograph is available.

4.5. The Jacob Lines Studies[6]

Circumstances around the Jacob Lines study were somewhat similar to those of Lyari: a large area (some 700 acres) which is in parts rather densely populated. Again here, there was a serious time constraint. Also, much less personnel were available for the Jacob Lines study than were available for the Lyari study. For the Jacob Lines area, a base map was available.

The aim of the study was somewhat different from that of the previously mentioned studies. Originally, when plans were framed to rehouse the population of the Jacob Lines Area into flats to be built on the spot, a request had been made that JRP-IV evaluate the results of this rehousing exercise in an early stage. However, when the time scheduled for this evaluation had come, no rehousing had taken place. The first flats were still under construction. In view, however, of the importance of the evaluation, it was decided that even so a study has to be undertaken amongst the intended flat dwellers. Main questions to which answers were sought regarded the inhabitant's attitudes towards living in flats and their financial capacity to do so.

First of all, the area to be studied was limited to the parts where unauthorized settlement is a common phenomenon. This area, covering some 200 acres, is very heterogeneous in many respects. Because of the limitations mentioned above, the sample fraction had to be small. Therefore, it was imperative to stratify the sample as much as possible according to the heterogeneous components of the area. On the basis of the map, and especially on the basis of very close and detailed observation, the area was subdivided into 54 sectors, more or less uniform regarding:

- land use (fully residential; mixed with non-residential),
- presence of "quarters" (i.e. dwellings owned by some government department and let out for residential purposes),
- quality of dwellings and materials used,
- residential density,
- presence of public facilities and neighbourhood cleanliness,
- location with reference to roads or other separating landmarks.

In all sectors, the number of doors in one or two building blocks were counted with exclusion of the "quarters". These numbers were then extrapolated to sectors. Thus, a total of 13,500 doors - i.e. approximately an equal number of squatters' dwellings - was found in the whole area. The number of interviews per sector was calculated according to the total number of doors per sector. The sample fraction was fixed at 1.5%, or 200 interviews in all.

The interviewers found their informants by entering into a sector from the north-east corner. Proceeding towards the sector's centre, they had to obtain the first interview from the first door on the right, the second interview from the sixth door on the right, and so on at intervals of five doors. The interviewers were permitted - when necessary - to take the second or third, resp. 7th or 8th door, etc., in the case of non-response or refusal from the intended interviewees. The speed of the survey was thus greatly increased. Any bias possibly incurred in this way was made more explicit by asking the neighbours about the originally intended informant's job, which was noted and compared with the jobs of the respondents.

Locating the sectors did not pose any serious problem, nor did locating the (intended) informants. The collection of data could in this way be accomplished in a very short time indeed and the data appear to give a fairly reliable picture of the population's attitudes and financial capacity. Application of this method would have been hardly possible without a map as a guide for further observation on which the refined subdivision rests.

4.6. The Miran Naka Study[2]

In Miran Naka, which actually is a part of Lyari, information was needed on improvements which were felt to be required and on possibilities of people's participation in improving the area. A map of the basti was available, on which doors could be easily indicated, together with the probable ethnic affiliation of the inhabitants. Namely, in Miran Naka, ethnic groups live in easily-observable clusters.

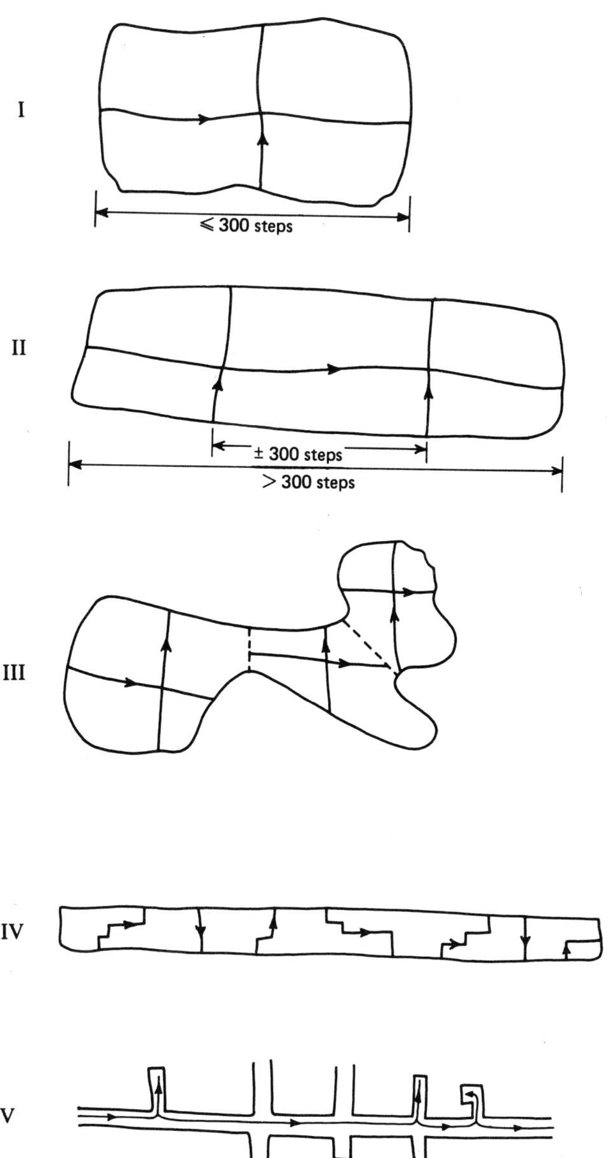

Fig. 49.

The number of interviews was fixed at 100 which implies a sample fraction of about 15%. On the basis of the numbers of doors "belonging" to different ethnic groups, the number of interviews to be taken from each group could be easily calculated as a proportion of the total sample. Within the building blocks, dominated by a particular ethnic group, again attempts were made to stratify according to a number of factors, so that from every ethnic group informants were included who:

- live on corner plots,
- live at the edge of the area,
- live in the centre of the area,
- live next to people belonging to a different ethnic group.

4.7. The General Inventory of Bastis[1]

For a general inventory of some 250 bastis of Karachi, samples of the dwellings in each of these basti had to be taken. Obviously, no maps were available for a great majority of the bastis. Besides, the large number of bastis from which samples were to be taken, necessitated the use of very simple methods with universal applicability.

Broadly speaking, the method applied consisted of crossing the bastis at regular intervals and in two directions. The interval distances, fixed at 300 yards, were to be approximated by counting steps. All the houses found on one side of the thus-described way through the basti were included in the sample.

The instructions to the field assistants read:

1. Walk around the basti and be secure of its boundaries. Make a rough sketch. Count your steps when walking around and keep record of the thus found distances.
2. (a) If the basti has a more or less rectangular or square shape, the two streets will be taken that run approximately through the centre of the area, connecting the middle of one bordering street with the middle of the bordering street on the opposite side.
   (b) If the length and/or width of the basti exceeds 300 steps (to be counted in your first tour around), then cross the area more than once, approximately after every 300 steps of length in a bordering street.
   (c) If the shape is very irregular, subdivide the area into more or less rectangular parts and treat these as above indicated. (Always keep record of how you do it, e.g. in the rough sketch.)
   (d) If the basti is very much long-stretched (e.g. some bastis alongside river beds) and has little width, then zig-zag from the first crossing street, and go left, right, left, etc., until reaching the other end, from where you start anew.
3. Take information on all houses on your left and include the left side of all dead-end streets you find on your left. Skip open end streets.

Disadvantages of this method are:

- the sample fraction is not constant,
- relatively more attention is paid to the inner parts of a basti than to the outskirts, especially the border streets.

In a number of bastis 100% samples were taken along with the samples taken according to the above instructions. It turned out that in 14 of the 17 cases the reliability of the sample is decidedly high.

REFERENCES

1. J. J. van der Linden, *The bastis of Karachi, Types and Dynamics*, Amsterdam, 1977.
2. R. A. Chughtai, H. Kiestra, T. E. L. Van Pinxteren and M. H. Weijs, *Miran Naka*, Karachi, 1975.
3. JRP-IV, *Usmania Muhajir Colony*, Karachi, 1975.
4. JRP-IV, *Chanesar Goth*, Karachi, 1977.
5. JRP-IV, *Socio-economic survey of Lyari*, Karachi, 1975.
6. M. H. Weijs, *Report in-depth study of Jacob Lines Area*, Karachi, 1975.

Literature Quoted in this Book

*AERC, *Cost-benefit analysis of regularization and improvement of katchi abadis in Karachi,* First round report, Karachi, 1980.

Ahmad, M., *The civil servant in Pakistan,* Karachi/Lahore/Dacca, 1964.

*Ahsan, A., *Historical developments of Chanesar Goth* (mimeo.), Karachi, 1972.

Alcock, A. E., K. N. Misra, J. L. McGairl and G. B. Patel, Self-help housing, methods and practices, *Ekistics,* Vol. XVI, 1962, pp. 81-87.

Ali, A., A. Mahmood, A. K. Barwa and Z. A. Nezami, *Operation Rehasp.* (mimeo.), Karachi, 1969.

Alonso, W., The form of cities in developing countries, *Regional Science Association Papers,* 1964, Vol. XII, pp. 165-173.

Angel, S. and S. Benjamin, Seventeen reasons why the squatter problem can't be solved, *Ekistics,* Vol. 41, 1976, pp. 20-26.

Angel, S., Land tenure for the urban poor, *Working Paper no. 1, Human Settlements Division, Asian Institute of Technology,* Bangkok, 1980.

Anzorena, J. (S.J.), *Report to SELAVIP-Members* (mimeo.), Santiago de Chile, 1980.

Baillie, A. F., *Kurrachee, past, present and future,* Calcutta, 1980 (reprinted Karachi 1975).

Beier, G., A. Churchill, M. Cohen and B. Renaud, The task ahead for the cities of the developing countries, *World Development,* 1976, IV-5, pp. 363-404.

Bell, M. and J. Pickford, *People and pit latrines in Africa,* Proc. 6th WEDC Conference, Water and Waste Engineering in Africa, Loughborough, 1980.

*Bos, A., *Structure of social welfare services* (mimeo.), Karachi, 1970.

*Bos-Kunst, E., *Women of Azam Basti,* Karachi, 1970.

Bose, S. R., East-West contrast in Pakistans agriculture development. In Keith Griffin and Azizur Rahman Khan (eds.), *Growth and Inequality in Pakistan,* London, 1972.

Burgess, R., *Informal sector housing? A critique of the Turner School,* London, 1977.

Petty commodity housing or dweller control? A critique on John Turner's views on housing policy, *World Development,* Vol. VI, 1978, pp. 1105-1133.

† Publications marked with * came about in relation with Free University's activities in Karachi.

Caminos, H., J. F. C. Turner and I. A. Steffian, *Urban dwelling environments*, Cambridge (Mass.), 1969.

Castells, M., *La luche de clases en Chile*, Buenos Aires, 1974.

*Chughtai, R. A., T. E. L. Van Pinxteren, H. Kiestra and M. H. Weijs, *Miran Naka* (mimeo.), Karachi, 1975.

CSO, *A survey of the shelterless people in Pakistan*, Karachi, 1969.

*De Goede, J. H. and T. J. Segaar, *Report Azam Basti*, Amsterdam, 1969.

Ellemers, J. E., Patronage in sociologisch perspectief, *Sociologische Gids*, 1969-1976, pp. 432-440.

Eyre, L. A., The shantytowns of Montego Bay, Jamaica, *Ekistics*, Vol. XXXVI, 1973, pp. 132-138.

Fathy, H., *Architecture for the poor*, Chicago, 1973.

Feachem, R. and S. Cairneross, *Small excreta disposal systems*, London, 1978.

Frank, E., *Illegale wijken in Karachi; een onderzoek naar de mogelijkheden ven de doe-het-zelfbenadering* (mimeo.), Rotterdam, 1978.

Galjart, B. F., Patronage als integratie mechanisme in Latijns Amerika, *Sociologische Gids*, 1969-1976, pp. 402-411.

Geertz, C., *Agricultural Involution*, Berkeley & Los Angeles, 1970.

Government of Pakistan,
The municipal administration ordinance 1960, Karachi, 1960.
Census of Pakistan 1961, Vol. I, Karachi.
Provisional figures released for the 1972 census, Karachi.
National Pilot Project 3, Final report on low-income settlements in Karachi, Karachi, 1977.

Government of Sind
Sind Peoples Local Councils (land) Rules, Karachi, 1975,
Martial Law Order no. 67, Regularization and Development of Katchi Abadis, Karachi, May 1978,
The Sind Local Government Ordinance 1979, Karachi, 1979,
Martial Law Order no. 110, *Regularization and development of Katchi Abadis order*, Karachi, 1979.

Griffin, K., Financing development plans in Pakistan, In K. Griffin and A. R. Khan (eds.), *Growth and Inequality in Pakistan*, London, 1972.

Griffin, K. and A. R. Khan (eds.), *Growth and Inequality in Pakistan*, London, 1972.

*Hashmi, S. H., *The slums of Karachi; a conspectus* (mimeo.), Karachi, 1973.
Karachi Metropolis, Challenges of a Growing Population and the Government Response, *Journal of Administration Overseas*, Vol. XIV, no. 3, July 1975.

HBFC
A house for every household, Karachi, 1978,
Loaning during 1977-1978 (mimeo.), Karachi, 1978.

Hollnsteiner, M. R., People power: community participation in the planning of human settlements, *Assignment Children*, no. 40, 1977.

Hussain, N., *Problem of urban growth in Pakistan and a two-pronged remedy* (internal paper ISS), The Hague, 1974.

Institute of Economic Research, Osaka, *Rural-urban migration and pattern of employment in Pakistan*, Osaka, 1978.

Interdisciplinaire Studiegroep Planologie, *Huisvesting in Karachi, situatie en strategie* (mimeo.), Delft, 1977.

*Islamuddin Siddiqi, *Goths at a glance* (mimeo.), Karachi, 1971.

Jain, S., *Size distribution of income, a compilation of data*, Washington DC, 1975.

Janssen, R., *Wij hebben zelfs geen recht op de stad*, Amsterdam, 1978.

Jones, G. N., Municipal administration in Pakistan: elements contributing towards a modernization complex, *NIPA Journal*, Vol. VI, no. 4, 1967, pp. 190-199.

*JRP-IV
* *Usmania Muhajir Colony*, Karachi, 1975,
* *Socio-economic survey of Lyari* (mimeo.), Karachi, 1975.
* *Chanesar Goth* (mimeo.), Karachi, 1977,
* *Socio-economic survey Baldia Township* (mimeo.), Karachi, 1978.

Karachi Local Authorities Reorganization Committee, *Final report*, Karachi, 1968.

KDA
A report on the unauthorized settlements and squatters in Karachi (mimeo.), Karachi, 1959.

*KDA, JRP-IV, *An inventory of building materials used in slums of Karachi*, Karachi, 1974.

KDA
Metroville, an experiment in human settlement at Karachi, Pakistan (Karachi undated).
Brochure "Metroville", Karachi (undated).

Khan, M. A., *Friends not masters*, London, 1967.

*Kiestra, H., *How to improve a slum?* (mimeo), Karachi, 1975.

*Kiestra, H. and F. Quint, *Water in Karachi*, Karachi, 1975.

KMC, *An improvement policy for substandard urban areas*, Karachi, 1976 (revised 1977).
*PC-I, *Baldia Township Regularization and Improvement Project*, Karachi, 1979.
Facts in Figures, Vol. V, 1979-1980, Karachi, 1980.

Laquian, A. A., *Slums are for people*, Honolulu, 1971.

Lari, J., *Pre-planning report on Jacob Lines*, Karachi, 1974.

Lewis, O., *The children of Sánchez: Autobiography of a Mexican Family*, New York, 1961.

Mangin, W.,
Squatter settlements, *Scientific American*, Vol. CCXVII, 1967, pp. 21-29,
Latin American squatter settlements, a problem and a solution, *Latin American Research Review*, Vol. II, 1967, pp. 65-98.

Martin, R., Comments in Architectural Design, no. 4, 1976, pp. 232-237.

McGee, T. G., *The urbanization process in the third world*, London, 1971.

McNamara, R. S., *Annual speech of the President of the World Bank*, Washington, 1975.

Meyerink, H. and R. Vekemans, Huisvesting in Karachi, *Zone*, 11, 1979, pp.31-59.

MPD
Redevelopment of Jacob Lines (2 volumes), Karachi, 1972.
Karachi Development Plan 1974-1985, Karachi, 1974.
Regularization of unauthorized colonies (mimeo.), Karachi, 1972.
Master Plan for the Karachi Metropolitan Region, First Cycle Report, Vols. I, II and III, Karachi, 1972.
Master Plan for the Karachi Metropolitan Region, Second Cycle Report, Part I, II, III-a and III-b, Karachi, 1973.

Mujahid, M., Migration and earning differentials in Pakistan, *Review of World Economics*, Vol. III, 1975.

Nierstrasz, F. H. J. and H. M. J. van Gogh, *Housing finance for Pakistan*, Rotterdam, 1979.

Nooyens, A., *Immigration and intra-urban migration in Karachi, Pakistan*, Tilburg, 1981.

Pacey, Arnold (ed.), *Sanitation in developing countries*, Chichester, 1978.

Pasha, H. A., *Is the local tax base adequate? A casestudy of the Karachi Metropolitan Corporation* (mimeo.), Karachi, 1978.

Peattie, L. R., Social issues in housing, In B. J. Frieden and W. W. Nash (eds.), *Shaping an urban future*, Cambridge (Mass.), 1969.

Pickford, J. Sanitation for building in hot climates, *Public Health Engineer*, Vol. 7, 1979, pp. 158-161.

*Pickford, J. and R. Reed, *Sanitation for Baldia Township, Karachi* (mimeo.) Loughborough, 1979.

Pickford, J., Control of pollution and disease in developing countries, *Water pollution control*, Vol. 78, 1979, pp. 239-249.

Portes, A.,

Rationality in the slum, *Comparative studies in society and history*, 14, 1972, pp. 268-286,

The politics of urban poverty, In A. Portes and J. Walton (eds.), *Urban Latin America*, Austin & London 1976, pp. 71-110.

Sarin, M., *Progress and problems related to slums and squatter settlements in the ESCAP region* (mimeo.), Bangkok, 1978.

*Schuringa, M., S. A. Khan, E. Meyer and K. S. Yap, *Baldia Evaluation Survey Report* (mimeo.), Karachi, 1979.

*Segaar, T. J., *Karachi en de basti* (dissertation), Amsterdam, 1975.

Sen, Amartua, *On economic inequality*, Oxford, 1973.

Shah, A. A., *Housing in Pakistan*, Islamabad, 1977.

Sharique, T. R., National Gas supply for Karachi, In S. H. Hashmi and G. N. Jones (eds.), *Problems or urbanization in Pakistan*, Karachi, 1967.

Shibli, K., Low-income housing policy for urban areas. In: KDA, The problem of shelterless people and squatters in Pakistan, Karachi, 1966.

Singh, R., Bombay slum dwellers organise, *How*, November, 1979, pp. 3-6.

*Streefland, P. H., *The sweepers of slaughterhouse, Conflict and survival in a Karachi neighbourhood*, Assen, 1979.

Subcommittee on Housing, Ministry of Production and Presidential Affairs, Islamabad, 1973.

Sudra, T. L., *Low-income housing system in Mexico City*, Cambridge (Mass.), 1976.

Sultan, N. M. A., Regularization and improvement of Katchi abadis in Karachi. *BIE-Bulletin* no. 9, Rotterdam, 1980.

Turner, J. F. C. and R. Goetze, Environmental security and housing input, *Ekistics*, Vol. XXIII, 1967, pp. 123-128.

Turner, J. F. C.,

Housing priorities, settlement patterns and urban development in modernizing countries, *AIP-Journal*, Vol. XXXIV, 1968, pp. 354-363,

Uncontrolled urban settlement, problems and policies, In G. Breese (ed.), *The city in newly developing countries*, Prentice Hall, 1969,

Housing by people, London, 1976,

Housing as a support system, *Architectural Design*, no. 4, 1976, pp. 222-226.

*Van der Harst, J.,

Low income housing (mimeo.), Karachi, 1974.

* *Cost of residing of low-income groups* (mimeo.), Karachi, 1974.

* *Land policy for spontaneous settlements* (mimeo.), Karachi, 1974.

* Factors affecting housing improvement in low-income communities, Karachi, Pakistan, *Ekistics*, 1975, Vol. 39, no. 235, pp. 394-397.

*Van der Linden, J. J.,

Lyari, an inventory (mimeo.), Karachi, 1975.

* *The bastis of Karachi, Types and Dynamics* (dissertation), Amsterdam, 1977.

Slum upgrading in karachi, necessities, possibilities and constraints, Paper read at the Congress of the International Federation for Housing and Planning, Göteborg, 1979.

Van Huyck, A. P., Towards a housing policy for Karachi, *Morning News*, Karachi, 18 March 1972.

Van Lindert, P., *Intra-urbane mobiliteit en het ontstaan van spontane volksbuurten in de steden van Latijns Amerika, zelf voorzienende woningbouw als oplossing voor het woningvraagstuk?* (mimeo.), Utrecht, 1979.

*Van Pinxteren, T. E. L., *Minislum in a posh locality* (mimeo.), Karachi, 1974,

* *The dera, a housing facility for the male migrant* (mimeo.), Karachi, 1974,
* *Samples designed by JRP-IV* (mimeo.), Karachi, 1975.
*Van Pinxteren, T. E. L. and F. Quint, *Low-cost housing in Karachi,* Karachi, 1975.
Vernez, G., *A housing services policy for low-income urban families in under-developed countries,* New York, 1976.
*Wegelin, E. A., Money for slum-upgrading, *Pakistan Economist,* Vol. XIX, 13 January 1979, pp. 13-21.
* Slum improvement in Karachi, look back in despair, *Pakistan Economist,* Vol. XIX, 30 June 1979, pp. 7-9.
*Wegelin, E. and K. S. Yap, Krotbewoners van Karachi moeten nog even wachten, *VU-Magazine,* 1979, VIII, 8, pp. 3-8.
*Weijs, M. H.
* *Jacob Lines Survey, an outline* (mimeo.), Karachi, 1975.
* *Report in-depth study of Jacob Lines Area* (mimeo.), Karachi, 1975.
White, L. J.,
Industrial concentration and economic power in Pakistan, Princeton, 1974.
Wolf, E. R.,
Aspects of group relations in a complex society: Mexico, *American Anthropologist,* Vol. 58, 1956, pp. 1065-1078.
*Yap, K. S.,
Residents' participation in Katchi Abadis improvement, *Pakistan Economist,* Vol. XIX, 13 January 1979, pp. 21-24.
* *Leases, Land and Local Leaders, an analysis of a squatter settlement upgrading programme in Karachi,* Amsterdam, 1982.

List of Abbreviations

AERC — Applied Economics Research Centre (University of Karachi).

AFU — Amsterdam Free University.

BEST — Baldia Evaluation Survey Team.

BSDUF — Bombay Slum Dwellers United Front.

CPT — Central Planning Team of KMC (A cell within KMC, especially created for the planning and execution of KMC's policy for substandard urban areas).

CSO — Central Statistical Office.

DAM — Dutch Advisory Mission (from Amsterdam Free University to KMC, 1977-1979, under a bilateral agreement between the Governments of Pakistan and the Netherlands).

GARV — Gross Annual Rental Value.

GOS — Government of Sind.

HBFC — House Building Finance Corporation.

HSD — High standard development.

IRP — Improvement and regularization of unauthorized areas.

JRP-IV — Joint Research Project-IV for urban development and slum improvement (a joint project of the Pakistan and the Netherlands Governments, in which the Karachi University and Amsterdam Free University were charged with the execution).

KDA	Karachi Development Authority.
KESC	Karachi Electric Supply Corporation.
KGC	Karachi Gas Company.
KMC	Karachi Metropolitan Corporation.
KSIP	Karachi Slum Improvement Project.
LIPT	Lyari Improvement Planning Team.
MLO	Martial Law Order.
MPD	Master Plan Department (of the Karachi Development Authority).
MPP	Master Plan Project.
MPECD	Metroville cell of the Master Plan and Environmental Control Department.
MWC	Metroville Welfare Centre.
NARV	Net Annual Rental Value.
NCC	National Construction Company.
OPD	Open Plot Development.
PADCO	Planning and Development Collaborative International.
PICRP	Pakistan Institute of City and Regional Planning.
PNA	Pakistan National Alliance.
PPP	Pakistan People's Party.
SITE	Sind Industrial Trading Estate.
SUA	Substandard Urban Area.
UNDP	United Nations Development Programme.
UNICEF	United Nations Children's Fund.
UWD	Utility Wall Development.
WEDC	Water and waste engineering for developing countries, Group at Loughborough University of Technology, England.

Glossary*

Anna: 1/16 part of a rupee.

Baraderi: brotherhood, small community, patrilinear group of relatives.

Basti: settlement, mostly: low-income settlement.

Bisi (-committee): informal saving organization.

Chatai: (reed) matting.

Chauki dar: watchman.

Dal: pulse.

Goth: village.

Jhuggi: hut.

Kachcha: unbaked, clay-built, below a fixed standard, half-done.

Karor: 10,000,000.

Katchi Abadi: unauthorized settlement.

Mistari: artisan, mason, carpenter, etc.

Muhajir: refugee, evacuee, emigrant.

Muhallah: district, division, quarter (of a city or town), ward.

---

*Transcriptions of Urdu words into Roman script have been taken from Ferozsons' *Urdu-English Dictionary*, except in the case of generally-used expressions which are normally transcribed otherwise, such as 'katchi-abadi' (Ferozsons' *Urdu-English Dictionary*, 2nd Edition, Lahore, 1962).

Nala: watercourse.

Pakka: baked, strong, solid, firm, lasting, permanent.

Pardah: veil, curtain, cover, privacy. The word is also used to indicate the system by which women are secluded from the outside world.

Qaum: tribe.

Roti: bread.

Sabzi: vegetables.

Sahib: sir.

Tandur: oven.

Thala-wala: blockmaker.

About the Contributors

(Only association with squatter settlement upgrading studies and other activities in Karachi are mentioned, besides the authors' present occupation.)

Professor Dr S. H. Hashmi, Senior Project Officer JRP-IV, 1970-1973, presently Dean Faculty of Social Sciences, Qaid-e-Azam University, Islamabad.

Islamuddin Siddiqi (M.A. Karachi, M.Sc., Bangkok), worked in JRP-IV in different capacities, 1970-present, presently Senior Officer MPD-KDA, Karachi.

Ir H. Meyerink, Physical Planning Advisor, DAM, 1978-1979, presently on an NGO assignment in Indonesia.

J. Pickford, guided and partly executed the study on sanitation for Baldia, 1978-1979, presently Leader of the "Water and Waste Engineering for Developing Countries Group", Loughborough University of Technology, Loughborough.

Professor Dr J. W. Schoorl, was responsible for all Free University's activities in Karachi, 1967-present, presently Head of the Department of Development Sociology, Free University, Amsterdam.

Drs M. H. A. Schuringa, took part in Baldia Evaluation Study, 1979.

Dr T. J. Segaar, carried out the Azam Basti study (together with Drs J. H. de Goede), 1968-1969, and was posted (by UNDP) to the Karachi Master Plan Department KDA, 1970-1973, presently Inspector at Operations Review Unit, Directorate General International Cooperation, Ministry of Foreign Affairs, The Hague.

Drs J. van der Harst, Member of Dutch Team JRP-IV, 1971-1974, presently Head Department of Social Housing, Ministry of Housing and Physical Planning, The Hague.

Dr J. J. van der Linden, Member of Dutch Team JRP-IV, 1971-1975, Coordinator DAM, 1977-1979, presently lecturer Department of Development Sociology, Free University, Amsterdam.

Drs T. E. L. Van Pinxteren, Member Dutch Team JRP-IV, 1971-1975. presently Sociologist and Urban Planner, DHV-Consultants, Amersfoort.

Ir R. Vekemans, wrote his thesis on housing problems in Karachi.

Dr E. A. Wegelin, Economic Planning Advisor, DAM, 1977-1979, presently working with Asian Development Bank, Manila.

Drs M. H. Weijs, Member of Dutch Team JRP-IV, 1974-1975, presently Urban Planner, Department of Regional Planning, Amsterdam Municipality, Amsterdam.

Dr K. S. Yap, Community Relations Advisor, DAM, 1977-1979, presently working with U.N. Habitat Centre, Nairobi.